THE MODERN
HISTORY OF IRAQ

THE MODERN
HISTORY OF IRAQ

Second Edition

PHEBE MARR

A Member of the Perseus Books Group

Maps of Iraq are from the US Central Intelligence Agency, *Iraq: A Map Folio* (CPAS 92-10004, August 1992).

Copyright © 2004 by Westview Press, a member of the Perseus Books Group.

Published in the United States of America by Westview Press, A Member of the Perseus Books Group, 5500 Central Avenue, Boulder, Colorado 80301–2877, and in the United Kingdom by Westview Press, 12 Hid's Copse Road, Cumnor Hill, Oxford OX2 9JJ.

Find us on the World Wide Web at www.westviewpress.com

Westview Press books are available at special discounts for bulk purchases in the United States by corporations, institutions, and other organizations. For more information, please contact the Special Markets Department at the Perseus Books Group, 11 Cambridge Center, Cambridge, MA 02142, or call (617) 252-5298, (800) 255-1514 or email special.markets@perseusbooks.com.

Library of Congress Cataloging-in-Publication Data

Marr, Phebe.
　The modern history of Iraq / Phebe Marr.—2nd ed.
　　p.　cm.
　Includes bibliographical references and index.
　ISBN-13 978-0-8133-8214-2—ISBN-13 978-0-8133-3615-2 (pbk.)
　ISBN-10 0-8133-8214-9—ISBN-10 0-8133-3615-5 (pbk.)
　1. Iraq—History—1921-　I. Title.
DS79.65.M33　2003
956.704—dc21

2003009967

Designed by Reginald R. Thompson
Set in 11-point AGaramond by Perseus Books Group

BRIEF CONTENTS

CONTENTS

PREFACE

Although Iraq is a comparatively new state and a country of modest size, it has had a remarkably rich and varied history, much of which has been obscured by the crisis-driven headlines of recent years. Even before three Gulf wars made Iraq a household word in the West, it was difficult to do justice to the complexity of Iraq's modern history and to explain the impact of rapid change and modernization on a society going back six millennia. Updating and revising this historical narrative is now complicated by Iraq's sudden prominence on the world scene, by the enormous, but often distorted, media attention focused on it, and by the controversy repeated crises have generated. Although much more is now known (but possibly misunderstood) about contemporary Iraq, much remains opaque because, until the fall of the Saddam Husain regime, its closed political system made access to source material very difficult. This will now change. The coalition occupation of the country will open archives and documents to scholars, allowing a fuller picture to emerge.

This book is not meant to be an exhaustive and detailed history of modern Iraq; rather my aim has been to present a clear, readable one-volume account of the emergence of modern Iraq and the forces that shaped it. To understand how and why Iraq has reached this point in the context of a longer historical perspective, I have drawn extensively on many perceptive monographs and studies that have appeared on modern Iraq. I hope the book will be of use both to the lay reader and to students of the Middle East. I have tried to include enough general interpretation of events to make the country and its people understandable and enough detail to give color to the events described. Above all I have tried to be evenhanded in depicting the course of events and to avoid oversimplifying complex situations. Although the book is directed at the general reader, I hope that scholars of the Middle East will also find it useful.

The material has been grouped around several themes that, in my view, have dominated Iraq's history from 1920 to the present. The first is the creation and construction of a modern state within the boundaries bequeathed to Iraq by the British in 1920 and the search by Iraq's leaders for a cultural and national identity capable of knitting together its various ethnic and religious groups within the broader Arab and Middle Eastern world. This project is far from complete; hence the history must take account of differing subidentities and the rich tapestry of cultural expression they have created. A second theme is the process of economic and social development, a process that began at the end of the nineteenth century but greatly accelerated in the 1970s, although it has since declined. Third and most essential, the history deals with the development of political institutions and ideologies and their interrelationship with domestic society and the world outside Iraq. It seeks to show both changes and continuities in Iraq's political dynamics and to explain how and why a brutal totalitarian system—that of Saddam Husain—managed to gain—and maintain—power through multiple crises and upheavals, ultimately leading to war and occupation of the country by the United States and its allies. At the beginning of the millennium, Iraq's future is clouded, but it is better understood through historical perspective.

In recent years a growing and valuable body of literature on Iraq written by Iraqis themselves has appeared, including memoirs, firsthand accounts, and studies; I have drawn on these whenever possible. Quantitative data and statistical reports from the United Nations (UN) and other international agencies and from the Iraqi and US governments have also been voluminous. The reader is warned that statistics are not only difficult to gather but often subject to controversy. The reader should treat all figures with caution, concentrating on the broad trends and not on specific numbers.

Traveling in Iraq, accessing government records and archives, and talking to people openly and freely has been increasingly difficult since the 1960s and virtually impossible in recent years. Hence the closer we came to the millennium, the more tentative must be our conclusions. To supplement the published record, I have made extensive use of interviews with Iraqi educators, writers, political figures, and ordinary men and women, many of whom must remain anonymous. I would like to acknowledge the help of these Iraqis, who gave so generously of their time in answering my questions, analyzing their experiences, and gathering material for me. The book could not have been written without their help.

I would also like to thank a few of the individuals who have helped me during preparation of the original manuscript and this updated, second edition: Khaldun al-Husri, whose knowledge of old-regime politics was invaluable; Amatzia Baram, for many hours of fascinating details on the Saddam Husain regime; Falih Abd al-Jabbar, for his sharp insights on social and political structure and in providing much invaluable data; Walid Tamimi, Tariq Salih, and Raki'ah al-Kaisi for their expert knowledge on elites; and Muwaffiq al-Ruba'i, Ghassan Atiyyah, Sa'd Jabr, and Hazim al-Mushtaq, for their insights on Iraqi history over the past three decades; and Gareth Stansfield, for his help on the Kurds. I also owe a great debt of gratitude to Mas'ud al-Barzani, Kurdistan Democratic Party (KDP) chairman, and Jalal al-Talabani, Patriotic Union of Kurdistan (PUK) chairman, for their support and hospitality in making trips to Iraqi Kurdistan possible, and to their staff in providing unfailing assistance and much valuable information.

I am also greatly indebted to the Woodrow Wilson Center for International Scholars for providing funds for a year of research and writing to revise this book. I would also like to thank a number of interns who provided help in assembling data and charts and sifting through much of the recent literature in Arabic: particularly Nahlah Hilmi, Nagmah Sorabi, and Abd al-Qadir Rashid.

The greatest gratitude goes to my husband, Louay Bahry, first, for the invaluable insights on Iraqi history of a former professor of political science at Baghdad University, and second, for his patience in putting up with my long hours in the library and at the computer.

Naturally the interpretations, as well as any historical errors in the manuscript, are my own.

NOTE ON TRANSLITERATION

Arabic words in this text have been transliterated according to the accepted system for written standard Arabic, with some modifications. The spellings reflect neither pronunciation, which may vary from place to place, nor accepted English spellings, which often reflect the way a word "sounds" in English rather than how it is spelled in Arabic. (It may be helpful to the English-speaking reader to note that Arabic uses only three vowels—*a, i,* and *u;* there is no *e* or *o* in Arabic spellings.) Hence, to the average reader the spellings of some words may be unfamiliar. For example, *sheik* appears as *shaikh;* the surname *Hussein,* as *Husain.*

However, I have simplified the standard transliteration to make Arabic spellings more accessible to ordinary readers and easier and less costly to print. These modifications need to be clarified:

• The subscript dots used to distinguish some Arabic consonants from others and the superscript lines used to indicate long vowels have been eliminated.

• The *ta marbuta,* which frequently appears at the end of words as an *h,* has been dropped except when used in a construct, where it appears as a *t.*

• The diphthongs "aw" and "ay" are represented as *au* and *ai* in the middle of words but not at the end.

• The letters *ain* and *hamza,* usually represented by an apostrophe, are omitted at the beginnings of words but are used to indicate either letter in the middle of a word; the *ain* is represented if it is the last letter in a word.

• The definite article *al* has also been omitted when a word stands alone but is used if the word is in a construct phrase. Hence *al-'Iraq* is simply *Iraq.*

These changes, though not satisfying purists, should make the text easier to read.

Words of Persian, Turkish, or Kurdish origin that have become Arabized through usage in Iraq have been given their Arabic spelling. Exceptions have been made for a few names for which Kurdish or Persian spelling differs from Arabic. A few proper names have been spelled according to their common English usage, such as *Gamal Abdul Nasser* and *Ahmad Chalabi.* On occasion, well-known political figures, such as Nuri al-Sa'id and Saddam Husain, are referred to by their first names (*Nuri* and *Saddam*), since this is common Iraqi practice.

It may also be useful to explain the distinction between *shi'a* and *shi'i*, words referring to the same religious community in Islam. *Shi'a* is a noun, denoting the entire group, as for example, the *shi'a* in Iraq; *shi'i* is an adjective, the form used to modify a noun, as for example, *shi'i* rituals.

This transliteration system has not been applied to the maps because of technical difficulties in changing the names on maps secured from outside sources. Hence, spellings on maps may differ from those in the text and from other maps. However, the map spellings are close enough to the transliteration system used in the text to make the place names easily identifiable.

THE MODERN
HISTORY OF IRAQ

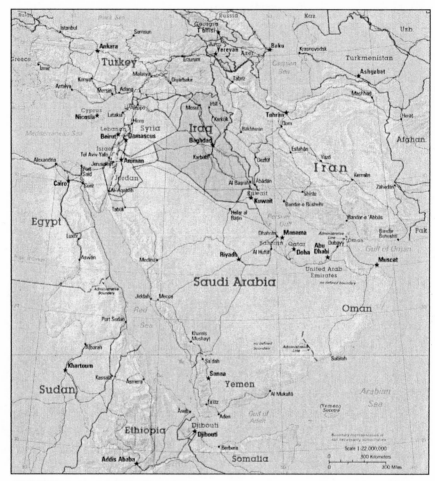

FIGURE 1.1   Middle East: Iraq

1

THE LAND AND PEOPLE
OF MODERN IRAQ

The state of Iraq is a new, twentieth-century creation, brought into being by politicians and statesmen, but the area included within its borders is home to several of humankind's oldest and most creative civilizations. All have shaped Iraq's current identity. In the past, as today, diversity—of terrain, of resources and, above all, of people—has been the chief characteristic of the territory and inhabitants that constitute contemporary Iraq. This diversity has been both a strength and a challenge. Harnessing Iraq's rich resources, whether its fertile river systems or the black gold under its surface, and absorbing and managing the medley of peoples who either lived in the river valleys or migrated to their shores has been the major preoccupation of Iraq's leaders, past and present. When its human and material resources have been well managed, Iraq has been a center of civilization and creativity whose benefits have spread to the rest of the world; when its leaders have failed, the result has been chaos, civil war, and economic stagnation. This phenomenon is just as true today, in the twenty-first century, as it was at the dawn of history in the fourth millennium B.C.

Legacy of the Past

Iraq has a rich and variegated historical legacy on which to draw in shaping its national identity and its institutions. In fact three elements of this past have been most important in forming the collective memory and consciousness of

3

twenty-first-century Iraqis and shaping their institutions and practices: the civilization of ancient Mesopotamia, the Arab-Islamic heritage, and the legacy of the Ottoman Empire.

Ancient Mesopotamia

Although the oldest and possibly the most creative, ancient Mesopotamian civilization has only recently come to play a role in shaping Iraqi consciousness, as a distinctive Iraqi identity gradually took shape in the twentieth century. Ancient Mesopotamia's contributions to humankind's progress were many and varied, including the development of writing, the wheel, metalworking, literature, and science. Sumerians and their successors wrote poetry and created a mythology and the world's first epic, the story of Gilgamesh. They built the first cities on the flood plains of the Tigris and Euphrates. Sumerian mathematicians used square roots and quadratic equations and created the first accurate calendars.[1]

But knowledge of this ancient civilization and its contributions was scant until the nineteenth century, when its remains were unearthed by archeologists. Until the midtwentieth century, ancient Mesopotamian civilization was taught in Iraq—if at all—mainly as a distant phenomenon almost unrelated to the modern country. This gradually changed in the second half of the twentieth century, however, when Iraqi artists and poets began to draw on this heritage in paintings and literature, while the government turned its attention to propagating the notion of a Mesopotamian heritage as an integral part of Iraqi tradition. Mesopotamian civilization is now firmly rooted in Iraqi consciousness, but in the early decades of the modern state it played a very small role.

The Arab-Islamic Civilization

The same cannot be said for the Islamic era. The Arab-Islamic conquest of the seventh century was the decisive event in shaping current Iraqi identity. Arabic eventually became the predominant language of Mesopotamia, while Islam became the religion of almost all the country's inhabitants. It is mainly to the Islamic conquest of the seventh century that most Iraqis look for the source of their identity and the roots of their culture.

The decisive battle of Qadisiyya in 637 opened the rich territory of Mesopotamia, then under Persian control, to the invading Muslim army. However, the territory was only gradually absorbed and Islamized. During much of the first Islamic century, Iraq remained in turmoil. Many early Islamic political struggles were fought in Iraq. Husain, the Prophet's grandson, was killed near Karbala in 680, giving *shi'i* Islam a martyr. Iraq acquired a reputation that it retains today of a country difficult to govern.

This changed for a time, beginning in 650 with the establishment of the Abbasid Caliphate. The Abbasid Caliphate marks one of the greatest periods in Islamic history. Iraq came into its own as the center of a prosperous and expanding empire and an increasingly brilliant civilization that drew on the traditions of its immediate predecessors, the Greeks and Persians, in forming the emerging Arab-Islamic culture. The river valleys were now given the centralized control they needed; irrigation channels were extended and agriculture flourished. So, too, did trade and urban life. By the tenth century, Baghdad, founded by the caliph Mansur in 762 as his capital, had a population estimated at 1.5 million and a luxury trade reaching from the Baltic Sea to China.[2] Baghdad also had a vigorous scientific and intellectual life, with centers for translations of Greek works and scientific experiments.

This period is remembered today with pride, but it did not last. By the middle of the ninth century, decline had set in that would last for almost a millennium. The empire broke up. There were incursions from nomadic groups. A succession of dynasties governed parts of Iraqi territory with increasing indifference. The once great irrigation system deteriorated and economic hardship followed. The Mongol attack on Baghdad in 1258 by Hulagu and another, even more devastating attack by Timur the Lame in 1401 delivered the final blows. Baghdad never recuperated.

It is this decline and its heritage of poverty, backwardness, and intellectual stagnation that is the central fact of Iraq's modern history. Although the Abbasid Empire is remembered as part of a glorious past, it is the centuries of stagnation that followed that shaped the environment and character of the early period of the Iraqi state.

The Ottoman Empire

The third legacy is that left by the Ottoman Empire, which governed Iraq for four centuries. Its institutions, political culture, and even the people it trained were what the British found when they occupied the country during the First World War. In patterns of government, in law, and in the outlook and values of the urban classes, the Ottomans played a role in shaping modern Iraq second only to that of the Arab tribe and family.

The Ottoman conquest of Iraq began in 1514 as an outgrowth of a religious war between the *sunni* Ottoman sultan and the *shi'i* Safavid (Persian) shah. As the wars continued, the territory making up most of contemporary Iraq came under permanent Ottoman rule. When it first conquered Iraq, the Ottoman Empire was at the peak of its power and was able to give Iraq stable government and a uniform administration. While the Ottoman establishment was *sunni,* it tolerated the *shi'a*—at first. Unfortunately, these benefits were not to last, for two essential reasons. The first was the Ottoman-Persian conflict, which continued off and on until 1818. The wars created in the minds of the Ottomans a suspicion and fear of the *shi'a* of Iraq as prone to side with the Persians. Soon the Ottomans came to rely on the only element in the region they believed would support them—the urban *sunnis.* During these long wars the seeds of *sunni* dominance in government were sown.

As the *sunnis* tightened their grip on the reins of power, the *shi'a* became alienated and naturally developed a counterfocus of their own. They strengthened their ties to Persia, especially in the holy cities of Najaf and Karbala. These cities played a significant role in the conversion to *shi'ism* of the Arab tribes migrating into the Tigris and Euphrates Valleys south of Baghdad. By the end of the nineteenth century, Persian influence in the holy cities and in much of southern Iraq was strong.[3]

The second and more important reason for Ottoman failure in Iraq was the weakness of the empire's own central government and its deteriorating control over its provinces. As the seventeenth century began, direct administration in the river valleys ceased, and Iraq faced another long period of stagnation and neglect. In the north, new Kurdish dynasties were established in the mountains and valleys. In the center and south, there were great tribal migrations from the Arabian peninsula that reinforced tribalism.

This decline did not end until early in the nineteenth century, when direct Ottoman rule was gradually reimposed on the Iraqi provinces. In the south the *shi'i* cities of Karbala and Najaf were brought under the authority of the Baghdad government. In the Kurdish countryside the local dynasties were broken up one by one and made to accept Turkish rule. Even more important were the reforms brought into Iraq by Ottoman administrators. These began when Midhat Pasha was appointed to the governorship of Baghdad in 1869. His short tenure (1869–1872) marks the first concerted effort to build for the future.

Midhat's reforms fell into three general areas: administrative reorganization, settlement of the tribes, and establishment of secular education. Midhat introduced a new, centralized administrative system into the Iraqi provinces and extended it into the countryside, thus establishing the administrative framework of contemporary Iraq. Second, Midhat attempted to provide a regular system of land tenure with legally confirmed rights of ownership. Although urban speculators and merchants frequently bought up land at the expense of the peasants, the policy did enjoy some success. About one-fifth of the cultivable land of Iraq was given to those possessing new deeds of ownership.

The third area of reform, education, was the most important. Midhat laid the groundwork for a secular education system in Iraq by founding a technical school, a middle-level school *(rushdiyya)*, and two secondary schools *(i'dadi)*, one for the military and one for the civil service. Midhat's new schools brought striking innovations in two directions. First, they were public and free and hence offered a channel of mobility to children of all classes and religious backgrounds. Second, they introduced a variety of new subjects, such as Western languages, math, and science, hitherto unavailable in religious schools. The education movement started by Midhat continued far beyond his tenure; by 1915 there were 160 schools.[4] The three-year Law College was founded in 1908, providing the only higher education in the country. These schools represented the first and most important beachhead of modernization in the country.

These reforms, together with the growth of regional security, helped create the conditions for economic revival. The telegraph was introduced into Iraq in the 1860s, a steamship line on the Tigris in 1841. Cash cropping was introduced for the first time, as Iraq slowly began to move away from subsistence farming. Iraq's trade grew rapidly.

By 1905 the population had risen from 1.2 million in 1867 to 2.2 million. There was a striking change in the balance between the nomadic and settled populace. In the midnineteenth century, 35 percent of the population had been nomadic and only 40 percent rural. By 1905 the nomads had declined to 17 percent, while the rural population had risen to 60 percent.[5]

Contacts with the outside world also produced a revival of local learning and letters, as well as new ideas. The development of a press helped spread all of these among the literate public. These intellectual and educational developments produced a new urban, literate class, a native Iraqi elite. Most members of this elite were the products of the secular schools established in the last quarter of the nineteenth century and the higher schooling in Istanbul, now available to Iraqis. Many went through the military academies, which were the chief vehicles of mobility for Iraq's lower-middle- and middle-class families.

By 1914 graduates of these schools were already staffing posts in the administration, army, new secular courts, and government schools. Although tiny in number, the influence of this group was immense. From its ranks came almost every Iraqi leader of any significance in the post–First World War period, and a number continued to dominate Iraqi politics until the revolution of 1958.

Nevertheless, the successes of the Ottoman reformers should not disguise the weaknesses of the Ottoman legacy. The Ottomans were foreign, and their reforms were aimed at recasting the population into an Ottoman mold. A native elite was being trained, but it was trained in an Ottoman pattern.

Moreover, this native elite was drawn from only one segment of the population, the urban *sunnis*. It was primarily the *sunnis,* whether Arab or Kurd, who attended public schools and were given posts in the army and the bureaucracy. Not surprisingly, the *sunnis* came to think of themselves as the country's natural elite and its only trustworthy leaders. Two important segments of the population, the rural tribal groups outside the reach of urban advantages and the *shi'a,* were consequently excluded from participation in government. Little wonder that they should form the nucleus of opposition to the government in the early decades of the twentieth century.

The ideas behind Ottoman government were duly passed on to the Iraqi officials trained in the Ottoman tradition, which was founded, above all, on the bedrock of authoritarian paternalism. This encouraged elitism, the attitude that the rulers know best and need not consult the ruled. Although these ideas were modified in time, they persisted with remarkable tenacity among Iraq's ruling group right through the first half of the twentieth century.

The Land

The state of Iraq has existed only since 1920, when it was carved from three former provinces of the Ottoman Empire and created under British aegis as a mandate.[6] With a land area of 168,000 square miles (436,800 square kilometers) and a population of over 23 million in 2003, Iraq is the largest of the Fertile Crescent countries rimming the northern edge of the Arabian peninsula.[7] Lying between the plateau of northern Arabia and the mountain ridge of southwest Iran and eastern Turkey, Iraq forms a lowland corridor between Syria and the Persian/Arabian Gulf.[8] From its earliest history Iraq has been a passageway between East and West. Its borders are for the most part artificial, reflecting the interests of the great powers during the First World War rather than the wishes of the local population. As a result, Iraq's present borders have been continuously challenged by peoples living inside and outside the country. The southern section of the border with Iran, a contributory cause of the Iran-Iraq war of the 1980s, has not been finally settled, while a new, UN-demarcated border with Kuwait, agreed to by Iraq in 1993, under pressure, is still contentious.

The southeastern portion of the country lies at the head of the Gulf. Iraq controls a thirty-six-mile (fifty-eight-kilometer) strip of Gulf territory barely sufficient to provide it with an outlet to the sea. From the Gulf, Iraq's border with Iran follows the Shatt al-Arab north, then skirts the Persian foothills as far north as the valley of the Diyala River, the first major tributary of the Tigris north of Baghdad. From here the frontier thrusts deep into the high Kurdish mountain ranges, following the Diyala River valley. Near Halabja it turns northward along the high mountain watersheds—incorporating within Iraq most of the headwaters of the major Tigris tributaries—until it reaches the Turkish border west of Lake Urmiyya. The mountainous boundary with Turkey ends at the Syrian border just west of Zakhu, Iraq's northernmost town. This northeastern region includes difficult and unmanageable mountain terrain and a substantial Kurdish population. The loss of control by the central government over substantial portions of this region in the 1990s made Iraq's northern borders with Turkey and Iran porous.

In the northwest the frontier separating Iraq from Syria meanders south across the Syrian desert from the Turkish border until it reaches the Euphrates near Qa'im. Here the borders make little pretense of following geography, jutting out into the adjacent desert and incorporating large areas of steppe. At the Euphrates the border turns west until it reaches Jordan, also a former British mandate, and then south a short distance to the Saudi frontier. From this point the border follows a line of water wells separating Iraq from Saudi Arabia until it reaches the Kuwaiti border at Wadi al-Batin, at which point it turns north again, forming a common frontier with Kuwait, until it reaches Umm Qasr on the Khaur Abd Allah channel leading to the Gulf.

The terrain included within these boundaries is remarkably diverse, making Iraq a country of extreme contrasts. The Shatt al-Arab is a broad waterway with villages on its banks, lined with date groves. To the north of the Shatt lies swampland, traditionally inhabited along the Tigris by marsh

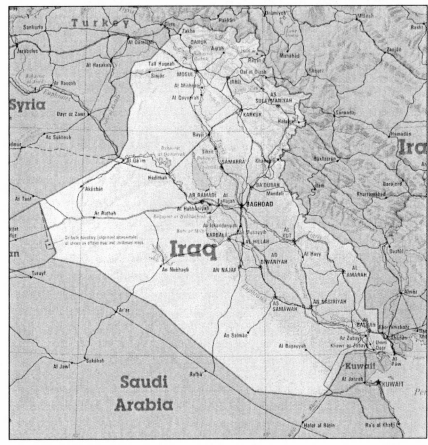

FIGURE 1.2   Iraq

dwellers living in reed houses built on stilts and raising water buffalo, and along the Euphrates by rice-growing villagers. This natural wetland area, with high reeds and hidden waterways, has often functioned as a refuge for dissidents. A massive drainage system, constructed by the central government in the 1990s, has progressively dried up much of this terrain and is ending a traditional way of life. Between the marshlands and Baghdad is the delta, the most densely populated area of Iraq, once inhabited by the Sumerians and Babylonians of ancient Mesopotamia. It is a dry, flat area consisting almost entirely of irrigated farmland, with large mud-hut villages and regional market towns hugging the river banks. North of Baghdad the two rivers diverge widely to form the Jazira (Island), the territory between the two. Although some irrigation farming is practiced here, it is mainly rain-fed territory—a land of gentle uplands sprinkled with smaller villages and provincial towns. Mosul, near the site of Nineveh, is the Jazira's major city and the center of its commercial life. To the north and east of the Jazira, the plains give way to foothills filled with settled villages and prosperous towns (mainly inhabited by a mixture of Turkish- and Kurdish-speaking people) and then to the high mountains, the home of the Kurds. Iraqi Kurdistan, as this territory has frequently been called, is a remote and inaccessible area of deep gorges and rugged, snow-capped mountains rising to 12,000 feet (over 3,600 meters), broken only by the fertile valleys of the Tigris tributaries.

Within this diversity of territory the unifying feature of Iraq's geography is its twin river system. From the dawn of civilization the rivers have provided the irrigation that made life possible for those inhabiting the flat, dry plains through which they flow, uniting the populations of the north and south and giving them a common interest in controlling the rivers and their tributaries. The rivers have also provided the arteries for trade and communication without which the cities that have made Mesopotamia famous could not have flourished.

The rivers are not an unmixed blessing, however. The Tigris has often delivered torrential floods in the spring, too late for the winter crop and too early for the summer. The south of the country has a poor natural drainage system, causing progressive salinization of the soil if irrigation is not controlled or the soil flushed. Without dams, barrages, and artificial drainage systems, the rivers cannot support continuous agriculture. Whenever such an organized system has existed, the country between the two rivers has flourished; when it has not, decline, unrest, and turmoil have often resulted.

Iraq today is a country rich in resources. With proper management, the river system can provide agricultural production to feed a good portion of the population. Its agricultural potential, declining through overuse and, in recent years, neglect and abuse, is now dwarfed by petroleum. Iraq's proven oil reserves in 2000 were over 112 billion barrels, with another 200 billion of probable or possible reserves in areas not yet extensively explored. These reserves are the world's second largest, exceeded only by Saudi Arabia.[9] With a national income of ID 15.3 ($51 billion) in 1980, before revenues declined owing to wars and sanctions, Iraq has ample sources of capital for development, if properly used and husbanded.[10] After three quarters of a century of modern education, Iraq's population has acquired much of the technical capacity to manage a complex economy. Yet Iraq's problems as it faces the twenty-first century resemble those of its past. The challenge is to organize the political and social environment in a way that will bring Iraq's considerable potential to fruition, give peace and prosperity to its people, and put an end to the repression and mismanagement that have often led to conflict, disunity, and decay.

The People

If one can speak of an Iraqi state, it is not yet possible to speak of an Iraqi nation. Iraq's present borders incorporate a diverse medley of peoples who have not yet been welded into a single political community with a common sense of identity. The search for this identity has been a shared, if elusive, project of all Iraqi governments. Considerable integration and assimilation has taken place since the inception of the mandate, but there have also been setbacks—especially in recent years—to the process of nation building, revealing the fragility of the demographic mosaic and even of the state itself.

The first and most serious demographic division is ethnic, or more properly speaking, linguistic. Arabic speakers constitute 75 to 80 percent of the population; Kurdish speakers, 15 to 20 percent. The Arabs dominate the western steppe and the Tigris and Euphrates Valleys from Basra to the Mosul plain; the Kurds have their stronghold in the rugged mountain terrain of the north and east. However, the Iraqi Kurds are only a portion of a larger Kurdish population with whom they identify on linguistic, cultural, and nationalistic grounds. In 2003 there were a little over 4 million Kurds in Iraq; about 13 million in Turkey (about 23 percent of the population); 5 million to 6

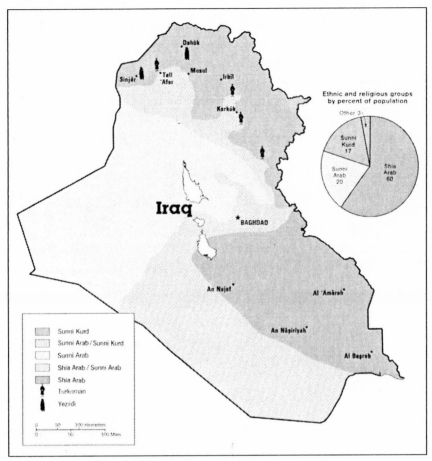

FIGURE 1.3   Ethnoreligious Groups in Iraq

million in Iran (10 to 12 percent of the population), and fewer than 1 million in Syria. There are smaller numbers in Armenia, Azerbaijan, and Europe.[11]

A second major division splits the population along religious lines between the two great sects of Islam, the *shi'a* and the *sunni*. Since the overwhelming majority of the Kurds are *sunni,* this division affects mainly the Arabs, but the outcome has been to segment Iraqi society into three distinct communities: the Arab *shi'a,* the Arab *sunnis,* and the Kurds.

Arab Shi'a

The division of the Muslim community originated shortly after the Prophet's death in a political dispute over who should be selected caliph, or successor. The *sunnis,* the majority, have accepted all caliphs who have held office regardless of the method of selection, so long as they were able to make their claims effective. The *shi'a*, the minority, took the side of the fourth caliph, Ali, cousin and son-in-law of the Prophet, claiming that the leadership of the community should have been his from the first and that only his heirs were legitimate successors. Eventually the leadership of the *shi'i* community devolved on religious scholars, called *mujtahids.* The fact that each individual *shi'a* is expected to follow a leading *mujtahid* gives the *shi'i* community stronger leadership and a greater sense of cohesion than its *sunni* counterpart. The *shi'a* began as a political party, gradually became an underground opposition movement, and finally evolved into a distinct religious sect.

From the first, southern Iraq has been a stronghold of *shi'i* Islam. Various *shi'i* movements either originated or found a firm reception in southern Iraqi cities, where *shi'i* Islam eventually established a foothold so firm it could not be dislodged by the *sunnis.* As Arab tribes migrated from the Arabian peninsula in the eighteenth and nineteenth centuries and settled in the river valleys, they were converted to *shi'i* Islam by religious scholars and their emissaries. Today the *shi'a* are the largest single religious community in Iraq, outnumbering the Arab *sunnis* three to one and constituting a solid majority of the total population.

Under the *sunni* Ottoman administration of Iraq, which began in the sixteenth century, Iraqi *shi'a* were largely excluded from administrative positions, from the military, and from government-sponsored education institutions that trained for them. Instead, *shi'i mujtahids* in the holy cities, often Persian in origin, were influenced by events in Persia. Not surprisingly, the *shi'a*, so long excluded from government, came to be deeply alienated from it.

Arab Sunnis

In contrast to the *shi'a*, the Arab *sunnis* in Iraq tend to be more secular and, with the exception of some recently settled tribes, more urban in composition. As a result, their communal identity has been less developed. Unlike the *shi'a*, the *sunnis* do not accord special religious authority to their leaders—the scholars, jurists, and judges collectively known as *ulama* who define and uphold the rules that guide the community. Rather they follow the *sunna*, or customs of the Prophet (from which they take their name), and the *shari'a*, the body of Islamic doctrine, law, and ritual derived from the Quran and the *sunna*. It is to the *shari'a*, rather than to any particular leader, that the *sunni* community owes adherence, a factor that has made it far more loosely structured than the *shi'i* community.

Despite their minority status, the Arab *sunnis* have traditionally dominated the political and social life of Iraq, originally due to Ottoman support but later due to the ability of *sunnis* to maintain the command posts of power. Although no census has been taken that distinguishes among various Muslim groups, the Arab *sunnis* probably represent about 15 to 20 percent of the population.[12] Geographically they are concentrated in the northern part of the country, including the Arab tribal groups of the western steppe and the Arab villages of the northern Tigris and Euphrates areas. The remainder of the Arab *sunni* community is almost wholly urban, situated in the cities and towns of the central and northern provinces. Substantial numbers of *sunnis* also live in some cities of the south, especially Basra.

Although the collapse of the Ottoman Empire in the First World War removed Ottoman support for *sunni* supremacy, it did not end *sunni* dominance. Although that dominance has waxed and waned over time, especially socially and intellectually, *sunni* political control was more pronounced at the end of the twentieth century than at any time since the mandate. This political dominance and the resulting enjoyment of most of society's benefits have given the *sunni* community a closer association with—and vested interest in—the emerging Iraqi state. Arab *sunnis* have also had considerable affinity for the secular philosophies of Arab nationalism originating in neighboring (and largely *sunni*) Arab countries.

The Kurds

The third major group, the Kurds, has proved the most difficult to assimilate. Language has been a major stumbling block. The Kurds speak an Indo-European language closely akin to Persian, while Arabic remains the official language of the central government and of the higher educational institutions in Iraq. Even more important has been the sense of ethnic—even national—identity that the Kurds have developed, especially in the twentieth century.

The origin of the Kurds is still a matter of some historical dispute, with most Kurdish scholars claiming descent from the ancient Medes. However, because there was no written Kurdish literature until the tenth century, it is difficult to substantiate this identification.[13] Whatever their origins, the Kurds were almost completely converted to Islam. They became orthodox *sunnis,* part of a vast Muslim empire and often its staunchest defenders. From time to time, particularly in the seventeenth and eighteenth centuries,

Kurdish dynasties arose but lacked cohesion and were unable to maintain their autonomy. In the twentieth century, a sense of Kurdish identity based on language, close tribal ties, customs, and a shared history inspired Kurdish nationalist movements. Like their predecessors, however, these political groups lacked sufficient cohesion and coordination to achieve lasting results.

The majority of Iraq's Kurdish population today is to be found in the mountains of the northeast, with Sulaimaniyya as its intellectual center and stronghold and Arbil its political capital. Until recently most Kurds were rural. However, the destruction of much of the Kurdish countryside, especially adjacent to Iran, and the forced migration of much of this population due to local wars and Iraqi government actions, has resulted in resettlement of large numbers of Kurds in cities and towns.

Of all Iraqi minority groups, the Kurds have been the most difficult to assimilate because of their numbers, geographic concentration, mountain inaccessibility, and cultural and linguistic identity. However, many bilingual Kurds have assimilated into Iraqi society sufficiently to enable them to play an active role in state and society.

Other Minorities

Aside from these three major demographic groups, there are several smaller ethnic and religious communities in Iraq. In northern towns and cities along the old trade route that led from Anatolia along the foothills of the Zagros to Baghdad live members of a Turkish-speaking group known locally as the Turkman. Comprising between 2 and 3 percent of the population[14] and most numerous in the cities of Kirkuk and Arbil, they are probably remnants of migrations of Turkish tribes dating from the Seljuk era of the twelfth century and of the Turkman tribal dynasties of the fourteenth and fifteenth centuries. The Turkman, mainly *sunni* and middle class, have for decades produced a disproportionate number of bureaucrats and have integrated rather well into modern Iraq.

In the south is a group of *shi'i* Persian speakers with strong ties to Persia that have never been severed. Until the 1980s, they constituted 1.5 to 2 percent of the population, but in the wake of the Iran-Iraq war, this community was largely expelled from Iraq.[15] The Iraqi Persian speakers have frequently looked to Persian rulers to support their interests, causing them to be regarded with suspicion by the Ottoman Turks and more recently by Arab nationalist governments. Another Persian-speaking group distinct from these town dwellers is the Lurs, less than 1 percent of all Iraqis. Often called *faili* or *shi'i* Kurds, they are almost all tribally organized villagers concentrated near the eastern frontiers of Iraq.[16]

Iraq also has a number of non-Muslim minorities—Christians, Jews, and a few other communities that predate Islam. Until 1951 non-Muslims comprised about 6 percent of the Iraqi people,[17] and the Jews were the oldest and largest of these communities, tracing their origin to the Babylonian captivity of the sixth century BCE. Overwhelmingly urban, the bulk of the Jewish community lived in Baghdad, where Jews were often prosperous and influential merchants. The position of the community was radically changed by the impact of Zionism. With the establishment of Israel in 1948, the situation of Iraqi Jews became untenable, and their exodus in 1951 left only a handful, whose position today is unenviable.

Various Christian sects comprise a little less than 3 percent of the population. The largest denomination is the Chaldean Church, founded in the fifth century by the followers of the theologian Nestorius. In the sixteenth century they unified with Rome. Centered in Mosul and the surrounding plains, most Chaldeans speak Arabic, although some use a modified version of Syriac as a vernacular.[18]

Second in importance are the Assyrians, those Nestorians who did not unite with Rome. The British settled about 20,000 of them in the northern areas of Iraq around Zakhu and Dahuk following the First World War. The Assyrians, so called because they claim descent from the ancient Assyrians, proved to be one of the most unsettling elements in Iraq's modern history prior to the Second World War. Their uninvited intrusion into the country through the intervention of a foreign power was deeply resented by the Muslims and especially by the Kurds in whose areas they were settled. In recent years, they have become more integrated.

Other Christian groups include the Armenian, Jacobite, Greek Orthodox, Greek Catholic, and Latin Catholic communities, but their numbers are small in comparison to other Christians. A small number of Protestants, almost wholly the result of the nineteenth-century Baptist and Congregational missions, live mainly in Baghdad and Basra.

Two other religious communities of obscure origin deserve mention. One is the Yazidis. Racially and linguistically Kurdish,[19] they are village dwellers located near Mosul. Their religion is a compound of several ancient and living religions, and its most notable element is a dualism most likely derived from Zoroastrianism. They have resisted attempts to integrate them into the larger society. The second group, the Sabians, is a sect of ancient origin and diverse elements inhabiting portions of the southern delta. Their faith stresses baptism and contains elements of Manicheanism, but not Islam.

Town and Tribe

To these ethnic and sectarian divisions, somewhat blurred since mandate days, must be added a third social dichotomy that has played a profound role in Iraq's modern history—the division between town and tribe. Though greatly softened in recent years by the growth of cities and the spread of education to the countryside, the legacy of tribalism is subtle but pervasive in Iraq.

The historical importance of the tribes in Iraq can scarcely be exaggerated. Nomadic, seminomadic, or settled, at the time of the mandate they surrounded the handful of cities and larger towns, controlled the country's communications system, and held nine-tenths of its land.[20] In 1933, a year after Iraqi independence, it was estimated that there were 100,000 rifles in tribal hands and 15,000 in the possession of the government.[21] Although only a few of these tribes were nomadic, the bulk of the settled population of the country, whether Arab or Kurd, was tribally organized and retained tribal mores and customs.

The extension of tribal organization and institutions to rural Iraq has meant that much of the rural population failed to put down deep roots in the soil. The settled village community with its attachment to the land—the backbone of the social structure throughout most of the Middle East—has been a missing link in Iraq's social fabric. Settled agricultural communities completely divorced from tribal structure have emerged in only two areas, the carefully tended date gardens of the Shatt al-Arab and the rain-fed, grain-producing plains of Mosul.[22] Instead of love of the land, loyalty to family and tribe has dominated Iraq's social and political life. Among the legacies of tribalism in Iraq are intense concern with family, clan, and tribe; devotion to personal honor; factionalism; and above all, difficulty in cooperating across kinship lines—the underlying basis of modern civic society.

The only significant counterbalance to tribalism has been the economic and political power of the cities, but until modern times these were few in number and economically and culturally unintegrated with the rural hinterland. Aside from Basra, Baghdad, and Mosul, there were few cities worthy of the name at the end of the Ottoman era. Most were simply caravan stops like Zubair; fueling stations like Kut; or religious shrines like Karbala and Najaf, in which the benefits of law and order, trade and manufacture, were noticeable only against the background of poverty in the countryside. At the beginning of the nineteenth century, about a quarter of a population of a little over 2 million were urban; a quarter of these were concentrated in Baghdad.[23]

Rapid urbanization, the spread of education, and the extension of government into the countryside in the last half of the twentieth century have greatly eroded tribalism and decisively shifted the balance of power to the cities. Nevertheless, although tribal organization is rapidly disappearing in the countryside, tribal customs and attitudes have left tangible influences. In political life, family, clan, and local ties often take precedence over national loyalties and broader ideologies.

For centuries this diverse medley of people has lived together in symbiotic proximity within the territory comprising Iraq. Although the population was often difficult to subdue by central governments, real civil conflicts, based on ethnic and sectarian animosities, were rare. But traditional society was a true mosaic, with considerable religious and social autonomy for its various components. The twentieth century, especially its fast-paced second half, with the emergence of new nationalist and religious ideologies and the need for greater interaction and cooperation—even integration—among communities has brought greater social tensions and challenges of organization and leadership not always met by the state.

2

THE BRITISH MANDATE,
1920–1932

The impact of British rule in shaping Modern Iraq has been second only to that of Ottoman rule. In some respects the British left remarkably little behind; in others they made a more lasting impression. Before the British mandate, there was no Iraq; after it, a new state with the beginnings of a modern government had come into being. Along with the creation of the state, the British bequeathed Iraq its present boundaries and, as a result, potential minority problems and border problems with its neighbors.

As state builders the British created or developed an impressive array of institutions—a monarchy, a parliament, a Western-style constitution, a bureaucracy, and an army. The bureaucracy and the army—both of which predated the British—remained after they departed, but the monarchy and the Western-style democratic institutions were swept away after 1958. This is perhaps not surprising. Britain's stay in Iraq was one of the shortest in its imperial career. Moreover, for much of Britain's tenure in Iraq, its policy was vacillating and indecisive.

In three respects, however, the British made a lasting, if unintended, impact. The first effect was to hasten, broaden, and deepen the drive for modernization already under way and, through development of oil resources, to provide the country with the revenues to finance this drive and accelerate Iraq's economic development. The second was the Arabization of the administration, and the third was the creation of a nationalist movement whose leaders, placed in power largely by the British themselves, would do more to shape modern Iraq than the British had.

The British Occupation
and the Institutions of the Indian School

The occupation that was to change the future of Mesopotamia came about less by design than by accident. Despite Britain's long-standing interests in the Gulf, the British had no intention of occupying the Tigris and Euphrates Valleys at the outbreak of the First World War. However, when it became apparent late in 1914 that Turkey, Britain's traditional ally, would enter the war on the side of the Central Powers and was mobilizing at the head of the Gulf, Britain decided to occupy Faw and Basra to protect its strategic interests and communications and its oil fields at the head of the Gulf. On 6 November 1914 the troops landed at Faw, and by 22 November they had moved up to Basra. In March 1917 they took Baghdad and in 1918 they occupied Mosul.[1]

The British wartime conquest of most of the Iraqi provinces was complete, but several key areas had not as yet been pacified. These included all of the Kurdish highlands bordering Turkey and Iran, the Euphrates from Baghdad south to Nasiriyya, and the two *shi'i* cities of Karbala and Najaf. It is no accident that these were to be the most unstable areas of Iraq throughout the mandate and beyond.

While the conquest and occupation of the Iraqi provinces was taking place, the first rudiments of a British administration were introduced. The administration imposed on Iraq was overwhelmingly the work of men seconded from the India Office and was modeled largely on Britain's imperial structure in India. The philosophy guiding the group was largely based on nineteenth-century ideas of the "white man's burden," a predilection for direct rule, and a distrust of local Arabs' capacity for self-government. These attitudes deterred the appointment of local Arabs to positions of responsibility. Meanwhile, the British dismantled and supplanted the Ottoman administration as rapidly as possible. Mesopotamia was divided into political districts, each under the charge of a British officer, and administration at the highest levels was kept in British hands. A new civil and criminal code based on Anglo-Indian laws replaced the old Turkish laws, the Indian rupee became the medium of exchange, and the army and police force were increasingly staffed with Indians.

Much of this Anglo-Indian structure was later swept away, but there was one area—tribal policy—in which the India Office legacy remained intact. Reversing Turkish tribal policy, which had aimed at weakening tribal leaders and bringing the tribes under the control of the central government, the British now attempted to restore tribal cohesion, to make the paramount *shaikhs* responsible for law and order and the collection of revenue in their districts and to tie them to the nascent British administration through grants and privileges. This policy was not only applied in the Arab areas but also rapidly extended to the Kurdish provinces as they were taken. This policy was efficient and economical, reducing the need for highly paid British staff in the countryside, but ultimately it strengthened the hold of the *shaikhs* over their tribesmen and their land. Entrenchment of a class of landlord-*shaikhs,* though not wholly a British invention, was certainly one of the most lasting and problematic legacies of the Indian school.[2]

It was not long before the policies of the Indian school generated opposition both in Britain and Iraq. In March 1917 the British government issued a memo making it clear that an indigenous Arab government under British guidance was to be substituted for direct administration. As a response to the memo, the Anglo-Indian civil code was replaced by a return to Turkish courts and laws. However, little else was changed. Local British bureaucrats continued to strengthen their hold on the country, appointing few Arabs to senior positions. The result was not long in coming.

The 1920 Revolt and Its Results

The 1920 revolt, directed above all at evidence of continued foreign control, was sparked by the announcement in April 1920 that the conference at San Remo had assigned a mandate for Iraq to Britain. Opposition to the British had been growing for some time among Iraqi communities inside and outside the country.

Inside Iraq, rising anti-British sentiment had been fanned by the nationalists in Baghdad, the *shi'i* religious leaders of the holy cities, and disaffected mid-Euphrates tribal leaders.[3] Though the motives of these groups were mixed, all were united by a desire to be free of British rule. A chief feature of the movement was the unprecedented cooperation between the *sunni* and *shi'i* communities; in Baghdad both used the mosque for anti-British gatherings and speeches, clearly mixing religion and politics.

It was not in Baghdad or Mosul but in the mid-Euphrates that the revolt began on 2 June 1920, when a *shaikh* who had refused to repay an agricultural debt was placed in prison at Rumaitha. His incensed tribesmen rose up against the British, and they were soon joined by others. Anti-British sentiments were aroused and the revolt spread. All in all, the insurgency lasted for about three months and affected about one-third of the countryside; none of the major cities and few of the urban nationalists were affected.[4] As in later revolts, notably in 1991, the movement was disorganized, diverse and localized, making it vulnerable to suppression by a determined central government.[5]

Although the British have often claimed that the revolt did not change British policy, the claim is not entirely borne out by the evidence. The uprising cost the British over four hundred lives and up to 40 million pounds sterling.[6] Even more important, the upheavals undid much of the work accomplished by the administrators in the previous five years and very nearly wrecked the British position entirely. Although the revolt did not achieve Iraqi independence or turn real authority over to the Iraqis, it did succeed in discrediting the India Office policy thoroughly, and it assured a much larger measure of participation by the Iraqis in their first national government.

On 1 October 1920 Sir Percy Cox landed in Basra to assume his responsibilities as high commissioner in Iraq. His new guidelines provided for the termination of military administration, the formulation of a constitution in consultation with the populace, and the establishment of a provisional government with an Arab president and council of state. It was clear from the first, however, that this government was temporary. What was to take its place emerged gradually, as British policy shifted. The first decisive step in creating the institutions and structure of the new Iraqi state and the British role in it took place at the Cairo Conference of 1921. It was here that the three pillars of the Iraqi state were conceived: the monarchy—in the person of Faisal, the third son of the sharif of Mecca; the treaty—the legal basis for Britain's rule; and the constitution, designed to integrate elements of the population under a democratic formula. All three were intertwined.

The Monarchy

The man who was to found the Hashimite dynasty in Iraq was born in Mecca in 1883 to a family tracing its lineage back to the Prophet. In traditional fashion, he spent some of his early years among the bedouin, although he was educated by tutors at home. He was thus a man who felt equally at ease among townsmen and tribesmen.

Faisal was firmly rooted by practice and conscience to the Arab nationalist cause. He did not initially favor the Arab alliance with the British and became a supporter only by necessity. Faisal's subsequent career as head of the short-lived Syrian kingdom between 1918 and 1920, his fruitless efforts at the European peace conference on behalf of the Arabs, and his humiliating removal from power in Syria by the French served to sharpen his sense of realism and his ability to deal with a variety of people and groups.

While some of his associates saw Faisal as weak, others saw him as a subtle politician, one of the few capable of manipulating and balancing various Iraqi forces. Whatever his style, it is clear that Faisal's position was weak. As a monarch imposed on Iraq by an alien, dominant power, Faisal was always conscious of the need to put down roots in Iraq and to appeal to its different ethnic and sectarian communities if the monarchy was to remain.

Once Faisal had been nominated, he needed to be elected. There followed a well-managed plebiscite which indicated that 96 percent of the populace favored Faisal. In fact, his real support was nowhere near that figure. The Kurdish portion of the population and the pro-Turkish groups in the north wanted no part of Faisal, while many of the local Iraqi notables were jealous and resentful of his position. The *shi'i* religious leaders wanted a theocratic government. Yet there is little doubt that no other candidate had his stature or could have received anywhere near the acclamation he did. On 27 August 1921, Faisal was installed as Iraq's first king.

With Faisal's accession the Iraqi nationalists who had served with him in the war and who had formed the backbone of his short-lived government in Syria returned to Iraq. Staunchly loyal to Faisal, Arab nationalist in outlook, yet willing to work within the limits of the British mandate, these repatriated Iraqis rapidly filled the high offices of state, giving Faisal the support he lacked elsewhere in the country. This handful of young, Ottoman-educated Arab lawyers, officers, and civil servants soon achieved a position in Iraqi politics second only to that of the British and Faisal, displacing the older notables originally installed by the British.

The intrusion of these Iraqis into the administration at all levels marked a first step in establishing Arab *sunni* dominance in government. At the same time, it also had the effect of Arabizing the regime, a process intensified by the shift from Turkish to Arabic in the administration and the school system. English became the second language. Although the Ottoman civil code was retained and made the basis of its curriculum, the Law College, the institution responsible for training most bureaucrats, was also put under Arab administration. This Arabization process and the Arab nationalist orientation which underlay it can best be seen in the education system established under the mandate.

The Ministry of Education, though it had a British adviser, was greatly influenced in these early years by Sati'-l-Husri, its chief administrator. Husri emphasized injecting a sense of Arab nationalism and patriotism into the curriculum and ridding it, where possible, of the effects of past and present imperialism. His nationalism, while progressive, was distinctly secular and pan-Arab, and he was opposed to sectarianism and ethnic separatism. Eventually, clashes with the British and the *shi'a* led to Husri's resignation as director-general of education, but not before he had installed a centralized education system with a uniform curriculum that emphasized the Arabic language and Arab history and with an underlying thrust toward secularism. However positive these contributions, they had two negative consequences for the future. The strong pan-Arab orientation thwarted—perhaps permanently—the development of a more inward-looking, Iraq-centered patriotism, while it excluded and alienated large elements of the Arab-speaking *shi'i* population and the Kurds, who might have been more attracted to a distinctly Iraqi identity.[7]

What was true of the bureaucracy and the educational system was also true of the army. An important decision the Cairo Conference made was to establish a native Iraqi army. By 1921 the recruitment of officers and men was in full swing. The lower ranks were drawn from tribal elements, often *shi'i*, but the officer corps came almost solely from the ranks of former Ottoman army officers. Inevitably, these officers were *sunni*, perpetuating *sunni* dominance of the officers corps. Officers with pro-Turkish sentiments were soon weeded out, making the army officer corps primarily Arab in composition and orientation. Some Kurdish officers were eventually brought in, as well.

The Treaty

The second major decision made at the Cairo Conference concerned the treaty between Britain and Iraq. The mandate awarded to Britain by the League of Nations had specified that Iraq should be prepared for self-government under British tutelage but left the means and mode to the mandatory power. The British decided to express the mandatory relationship by a treaty, deemed the most imaginative way to neutralize Iraqi opposition. Treaty negotiations with the Iraqis were begun shortly after Faisal was installed as king, and in October 1922 the Council of Ministers ratified the treaty.

The treaty was the backbone of Britain's indirect rule. It provided that the king would heed Britain's advice on all matters affecting British interests and on fiscal policy as long as Iraq was in debt to Britain. A subsequent fi-

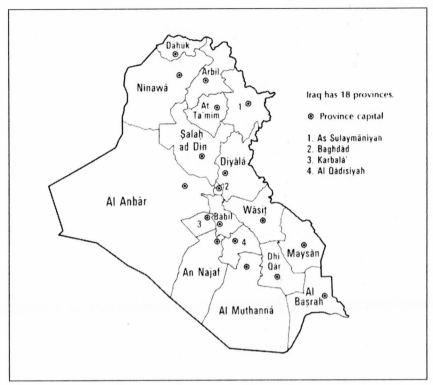

FIGURE 2.1   Administrative Divisions of Iraq, 2003

nancial agreement required Iraq to pay half the costs of the British residency and other costs, which not only placed Iraq in a state of economic dependence on Britain but helped retard its development. The treaty also required Iraq to appoint British officials to specified posts in eighteen departments to act as advisers and inspectors.[8] It was with this network of intelligence and influence, supported by the provisions of the treaty and the option of military sanctions, that the British governed during the mandate. In return Britain promised to provide Iraq with various kinds of aid, including military aid, and to propose Iraq for membership in the League of Nations at the earliest possible moment. The duration of the treaty was to be twenty years.

The Constitution

Closely intertwined with the treaty was the third pillar of the regime, the constitution. The constitution was meant to give the king and the high commissioner sufficient executive power to govern effectively and to uphold the necessary provisions of the treaty and also to provide for the political representation of various elements of the population. The first critical issue between the British and the Iraqis revolved around the powers of the king, whom the British hoped to make their instrument, and of parliament, which the Iraqi nationalists hoped to dominate. Parliament was given sufficient power to bring down a cabinet, but this was counterbalanced by granting the king the right to confirm all laws, to call for general elections, and to prorogue parliament.

Passed in all its essentials by the Constituent Assembly in 1924, this constitution became the law of the land, and with a few modifications it provided the country's political and legal structure under the monarchy until the revolution of 1958. It was an instrument well designed to foster Britain's indirect control. The monarch functioned partly as a symbol of unity but mainly as a means by which the high commissioner could bring his influence to bear in cases of conflict. Parliament soon became a stronghold of the tribal leaders whom the British had done so much to protect and strengthen. The British insisted upon these leaders' representation in the legislature, and all attempts by the urban nationalists to put obstacles in the way of the tribal leaders were systematically and successfully resisted.

The constitution did integrate various social and political communities into state institutions for the first time, creating a means of resolving conflicts peacefully and, more important, of learning how to cooperate across ethnic and communal lines. The constitution failed to take root, however— partly because Iraqis were never given real responsibility in the government and partly because they came to regard it as an instrument of foreign manipulation and control. As a result, Iraqi elites focused their energies not on developing these institutions as a foothold of eventual control but rather on removing unwanted British influence.

The Kurdish Problem

It had originally been expected by the European policymakers that the Kurds, like the Armenians, would be given national autonomy or independence under a mandate. In fact, the abortive Treaty of Sevres, concluded in August 1920 with the Ottoman sultan, had provided for an autonomous Kurdish state and had stipulated that the Kurds of Turkey and Iraq could apply for admission to the League of Nations within a year. The Treaty of Sevres was made obsolete by the emergence in Turkey of a successful nationalist movement, led by Mustafa Kamal, that established effective control over Kurdish areas in eastern Turkey. This situation made the position of the Kurds in the Mosul *wilaya,* or province, problematic. The British considered establishing autonomous provinces in the Kurdish areas of the Mosul *wilaya* that could be loosely attached to their Arab administration in the plains. The problem lay in finding suitable Kurdish leaders to assume responsibility for such an administration.

The one experiment the British had attempted in this direction had failed. In 1922 they had appointed Shaikh Mahmud al-Barzinja, a descendant of a famous family of Kurdish religious leaders from the village of Barzinja, as governor of Sulaimaniyya for a second time. (A similar attempt in 1918 had failed.) It was a decision based on expediency. Shaikh Mahmud was expected to establish a viable Kurdish entity there, yet remain compliant toward British influence. In short, Mahmud was to become a Kurdish Faisal. To aid him in the task, the British allowed a number of Ottoman-trained Kurdish army officers and administrators to join him. In many ways, these were the Kurdish counterparts of the young Arab nationalists attaching themselves to Faisal in the south. The hope was that they could infuse a sense of nationalism—and realism—into an essentially tribal environment.

But Mahmud attempted to carve out an independent principality, sacrificed the loyalty of his Kurdish officers in appointing his relatives to high positions, and was also in touch with the Turks. These actions alienated any British support Mahmud might otherwise have acquired, and in February 1923 the British forced him out of power for the second time. By the summer of 1923, when the elections for the Constituent Assembly were finally held, the Kurds were no longer offered a choice of joining the new Iraqi state or holding aloof. The government issued an announcement guaranteeing that Kurds would be appointed in Kurdish areas and that the Kurdish language would be employed in Kurdish territory, and it instructed its officials to proceed with the elections in all Kurdish areas under their control. The Kurds were thus brought under the sovereignty of the new Iraqi state by fiat.

The Kurdish failure to achieve even rudimentary self-government and the inclusion of the Kurdish minority into the Iraqi state—albeit with special considerations for language—was a fateful decision both for the Kurds and for the future stability and direction of the Iraqi state.[9] The border with Turkey remained to be fixed. In March 1925 an international commission recommended that the boundaries of the old Mosul *wilaya* be accepted and that the province be incorporated into Iraq, provided Kurdish rights were protected.

The Modest Impact of Oil

Although the oil concession and the revenue it eventually brought Iraq are among the most important legacies of the British mandate, the benefits from oil were slow to materialize. Negotiations between the British and the Iraqis for an oil concession began late in 1923 and generated a protracted and acrimonious debate. Although a number of issues were at stake, the main sticking point was Iraq's demand for 20 percent ownership in the company, which would have given Iraq a voice in company management and some control over oil production. The company negotiators refused and, fearing loss of the Mosul *wilaya* to Turkey if they did not give in, the cabinet signed the concession in March 1925.

It was not until October 1927 that the new Iraq Petroleum Company (IPC) brought in its first well north of Kirkuk. In 1934 it completed a twelve-inch pipeline going to Haifa and Tripoli with the capacity to deliver 4 million tons a year to the Mediterranean. By the end of the year, Iraq was exporting 1 million tons a year, and payments to the government totaled ID 1.5 million.[10] This was still a modest sum for development, however. It was not until the 1950s that substantial revenues from oil began to accrue to Iraq.

During the entire mandate period, Iraq lacked the funds for development, and penury was widespread. Continuing budget deficits were exacerbated by Iraq's obligation to pay its share of the Ottoman debt and to pay for the public facilities constructed by Britain. As a result, little was accomplished under the mandate in the way of economic or social development. Although there was some increase in agriculture, Iraq's resources were underdeveloped and a large proportion of its population remained illiterate.[11] The educational situation under the mandate was poor, owing partly to lack of funds and partly to the small numbers trained by the British, who were afraid of producing more graduates than the bureaucracy could absorb. In 1930 only 159 secondary students passed the public examination.[12] At the end of the mandate, much of Iraq's countryside—where 70 percent of the population lived—was still virtually untouched by modernization, and modern industry had scarcely begun.

In the cities a small middle class of civil servants, retail merchants, and professionals had begun to emerge, but the bulk of the population—urban and rural—remained at or near the poverty level. Urban migration, although not as severe as in the 1930s, produced a group of uprooted people inhabiting urban slums. A small number of workers benefited from the start of the oil industry and the development of the port and the railroad system, but the lack of funds slowed the growth of industry and infrastructure. Meanwhile, local artisans and craftsmen were gradually undermined by foreign imports.

The Nationalist Movement: Composition and Outlook

The early 1920s, which brought the creation of the state and its instrumentalities, also marked the beginnings of strident opposition to foreign control. Nationalist opposition was to dominate the political scene right up to the revolution of 1958. The treaty conflict distracted the leadership from pressing internal problems and stood in the way of cooperation with the West that might have been beneficial to Iraq. Moreover, the opposition's dislike of the foreign connection came to include the parliamentary institutions established by the British and the groups they placed in power, contributing to the removal of both in 1958.

The period of opposition, despite its spasmodic and spontaneous nature, can be divided into three overlapping waves. The first wave was the 1920 revolt already discussed. Based mainly on tribal insurgents, urged on by *shi'i* religious leaders and various urban elements, it was the first and only armed confrontation with the mandatory regime. In addition to its effects on British policy, the revolt's impact on Iraqis was profound. The decisiveness with which the tribes were defeated convinced many of the urban leaders that recourse to armed revolt would be futile while British troops remained on Iraqi soil and were not counterbalanced by an Iraqi force. They promptly turned their attention to the development of a regular army, which would replace the tribes as a military force and could ultimately be used as an instrument against the British. As for the tribal leaders, their power to influence events was greatly diminished after 1920, although not entirely eliminated.

The second wave of opposition accompanied the cabinet's treaty discussions in 1922 and the subsequent election of the Constituent Assembly that was to ratify the treaty. This opposition, led primarily by urban nationalists and expressed through political parties and the press, had a much stronger *shi'i* component. In the early stages, *shi'a,* such as Ja'far Abu-l-Timman, a businessman and politician, had been willing to cooperate with moderate *sunnis*; they refused to collaborate when foreign rule appeared irrevocable. In June 1923 a series of *fatwas* (religious decrees) against the election were issued at the instigation of *shi'i* religious leaders. When the king and the government, backed by the British, decided shortly thereafter to arrest the offenders, including a leading *shi'i* cleric, a number of *shi'i mujtahids* withdrew in protest to Persia, expecting this act to generate pressure on the cabinet from disaffected *shi'a* and from the Persian government. It did not. In fact, the appeal of the *mujtahids* to a foreign power—Persia—alienated not only the British but the *sunni* politicians as well. When the *mujtahids* were allowed to return much later, it was only on the condition that they formally renounce their political activities. The failure of this move dealt a decisive blow to *shi'i* clerical participation in politics.[13]

The Arab *sunni* opposition, though it shared the antiforeign sentiments of the *shi'a,* disliked the prospects of *shi'i* dominance even more. Many feared that *shi'i* leadership of government would open the door to sectarianism and even to theocratic rule. To many *sunnis* the creation of a secular state based on Arabism, even under temporary British control, seemed preferable. In any event, the suppression of the *shi'i* militants left the leadership of the nationalist movement in the hands of Arab *sunni* nationalists willing to cooperate with the British.

Arab *sunni* nationalists led the third wave of opposition to the treaty, which began at the Constituent Assembly in 1924 and continued until the end of the mandate. The opposition attempted to strengthen the Chamber of Deputies at the expense of the cabinet and the king and to tighten the election law to reduce government interference in the election process.[14] The nationalists also introduced an amendment requiring literacy as a prerequisite for parliamentary delegates, a provision that would have drastically reduced tribal representation in the chamber in favor of the urbanites.[15] It did not pass. This struggle for control of parliament would continue to the end of the monarchy.

Despite its antipathy to tribal representation in parliament, however, the opposition was not averse to working with tribal leaders to achieve its political goals. In general, tribal groups joined the opposition in return for compensation in two areas: confirmation of their rights to land and a guarantee that their disputes would be settled according to tribal custom embodied in a separate code. On both counts they were successful. These compromises ultimately helped to bolster the position of the emerging tribal landlord class and to forge an alliance between the urban *sunni* politicians and the *shi'i* tribal leaders of the south, an alliance subsequently supported by legislation granting the *shaikhs* tax immunities and benefits.

Political and social dynamics soon took on a character that persisted right up to the revolution of 1958. Political life came to revolve around a tripartite balance of power. One element consisted of the king, a foreign monarch dependent on the British for his position but anxious to develop a more permanent power base among the local politicians. Another comprised the British, anxious to neutralize the opposition and to see their supporters in the offices of prime minister and minister of interior. The third component consisted of a shifting group of Arab *sunni* politicians, some more anti-British than others but all willing to assume office. Some were strong and capable personalities. Some came from wealthy and prestigious families, such as Abd al-Muhsin al-Sa'dun, a *sunni* notable from a landholding family from the Muntafiq.[16] Others, like the Sharifian officers, came from undistinguished families but supported Faisal. Nuri al-Sa'id, born of a modest Baghdad family but a staunch supporter of the Arab revolt and of Faisal and the monarchy, was a leading exponent of this group.[17] A few Kurds and *shi'a* joined this contingent. Indeed, one feature of the period was political pluralism and sometimes intense competition for power at the top. Unused to political parties, the politicians formed parliamentary blocs, based mainly on personal ties and shifting political alliances.

Few of these politicians had roots in any large constituencies outside the halls of parliament, except for their links with tribal leaders. The failure to build broadly based political institutions or to reach out to groups beyond their personal or familial circles was a critical weakness of the nationalist movement. It allowed for manipulation by the British and the monarchy and prevented any one group from establishing sufficient power to move the country along in a particular direction.

The establishment of these urban Arab *sunnis* in the political sphere was accompanied by developments in the economic sphere that gradually gave them an economic and social base as well: the growth of a new landed class, due largely to the acquisition by private individuals of prescriptive rights over large tracts of land. Many of these investors were resident tribal *shaikhs* anxious to gain legal title to the land inhabited by their tribes, but most were urban investors and speculators who, profiting from the security introduced by the mandate, borrowed capital and bought up land. By 1930 the growth of a new oligarchy of landlords, urban entrepreneurs, and politicians was well under way.

Meanwhile, a second development was under way—the buildup of the army and the security system under British aegis. These institutions soon became the real support base for the urban Arab *sunnis*. The majority of army recruits came from the *shi'i* south—the area the nationalists most desired to penetrate; the officer corps continued to be mainly *sunni*. Pinning their hopes on the army, nationalists attempted several times to introduce a conscription bill, but this was opposed by the British and the tribes, and the bill was withdrawn. Meanwhile, the reach of the central government was extended, slowly but surely, into the countryside. One indication of this expansion was the increased effectiveness of tax collecting, which now reached groups and individuals who previously were only marginally involved. By the end of the mandate virtually all citizens of every class were liable for taxes.

The 1930 Treaty and the End of the Mandate

In June 1929 a newly elected labor government in Britain announced its intention to support Iraq's admission to the League of Nations in 1932 and negotiate a new treaty recognizing Iraq's independence. Nuri al-Sa'id was the new Iraqi prime minister. Although the British had some doubts about Nuri's ability to handle the situation, they were soon disabused of this idea. Nuri's firm hand was needed, for the government was faced with an opposition movement more broadly based and vocal than ever before. For the first time, Nuri was to use the tactics for which he later became famous. The opposition was silenced, the press muzzled, and parliament prorogued. Nuri's successful handling of the treaty issue and the internal opposition raised him to the position of Iraq's first politician in the eyes of the British, a position he was to hold thereafter.

In April 1930 treaty negotiations were resumed. They culminated in June 1930 in the long-awaited treaty that would take Iraq into the League of Nations. In the autumn, Nuri held a strictly controlled election, and on 16 November 1930 the parliament ratified the treaty sixty-nine to twelve. The treaty ended the mandate but retained British influence. Britain leased two bases and retained a right to all Iraqi facilities; British "advisers and experts" remained. In return, Iraq was to receive military training, equipment, and assistance from Britain.[18]

Although suppressed by Nuri and tempered by subsequent events, opposition to the treaty and the foreign tie continued to surface in subsequent years, and even during periods of calm, suspicions of Britain's hidden hand remained. It is only in the light of this continued opposition to the treaty that the revolution of 1958 and the anti-Western sentiment since that date can be understood. Though unsuccessful in eliminating British influence, the nationalist agenda and the anti-imperialist orientation it projected came to exercise profound sway over successive generations of educated Iraqis.

Although the nationalists opposed the treaty because it did not sever the British tie, Iraqi minorities—in particular the Christians and the Kurds—opposed the treaty because it weakened the tie. Fearful for their status, they began the agitation that was to plague the new state in the decade after independence. Through all of this, however, the king and Nuri stood firm, and in October 1932 Iraq was admitted to the League of Nations, the first mandated state to receive its independence.

The period between the signing of the treaty and the annulment of the mandate signaled a delicate shift in the balance of power inside Iraq. Some power remained in British hands, but much was transferred to Iraqis. By 1930 Faisal and his supporters, especially the Ottoman-trained army officers such as Nuri al-Sa'id, were moving to fill the power vacuum. They were firmly backed by the British, but the tightening grip of Faisal and his pro-British cohorts spawned a new opposition, far more broadly based and ably led than the opposition movements of the 1920s. This opposition was also led by Arab *sunni* officers and lawyers but included new elements, such as the *shi'a* Ja'far Abu-l-Timman and a liberal, left-wing reformer, Kamil al-Chadirchi, who joined a new party, the Ikha-l-Watani (National Brotherhood).

As British advisers departed from Baghdad, their place was taken by just the constellation of forces the British had envisaged. The throne inherited most of their power, and cabinets continued to be controlled by pro-British former army officers and lawyers, led by Nuri al-Sa'id. The new opposition party was briefly allowed into the citadels of power, but it soon split over the willingness of some members to collaborate with the British and accept the treaty. In the countryside, tribal leaders, well contented with the privileges they had received for their support, remained for the moment quiescent.

Although the *shi'a* and the Kurds were mainly excluded from the emerging structure of power, their opposition had been neutralized by a few seats in the cabinet and by representation of their more moderate elements in parliament. The main weakness of the mandate and mandatory institutions was their narrow scope. They reached only the upper urban strata, scarcely affecting the rural areas and the lower urban classes.

Such a result in 1932 is not surprising. In retrospect, British tutelage had been short—a mere decade or so. While "liberal" institutions had been created in Iraq—a parliament, elections, an open press, and political parties—their effective operation was hampered not only by British limits but by the absence of Iraqi "liberals" and a home-grown liberal ideology. Indirect rule generated, instead, strong antiforeign sentiments and a national movement that, because of its leaders' Ottoman background and training, had deeper roots in the army and the bureaucratic structures of state than in the parliament or political parties. This would color much of Iraq's subsequent political history.

3

THE EROSION
OF THE BRITISH LEGACY,
1932–1945

The end of the mandate ushered in a period of transition and of troubles for the new state and its leaders. The gradual withdrawal of the British advisers brought Iraqi politicians face-to-face with a variety of internal problems they had thus far avoided. One was the breakdown of Iraq's fragile unity. A number of religious and ethnic groups reasserted their claims to autonomy or a greater share of power in the central government. These problems were compounded by a resurgence of tribalism in the south, now mixed with *shi'i* disaffection.

The withdrawal of the British and the diminution of their influence also led to a noticeable disillusion with the constitutional system and a search for new principles of social and political organization. The search was impelled by pressures for faster economic development and greater social justice in the distribution of wealth and privilege. Reinforcing these trends were new currents of thought from abroad that crystallized into two schools of thought that tended to divide the Iraqi intelligentsia between them.

On one hand were the Arab nationalists, interested in building up the institutions of state and expanding Iraq's influence in the Arab world; hence they were drawn into Arab politics. On the other were the social reformers, moved by growing awareness of social discontent and discrepancies in wealth and opportunities. They were more focused on Iraq and had more appeal to minorities and the *shi'a*.

Continued social disturbances and their manipulation by politicians gave the new army its first opportunity. In 1936 Iraq underwent its first military coup, which very nearly brought about the collapse of the constitutional regime. However, the new government established by the coup was willing to work for social reform and to concentrate more on Iraq than on the Arab world. The attempt did not succeed. Instead, the military—and more specifically, the sector of the military with strong Arab nationalist sentiments—came increasingly to dominate the political system.

British pressures to involve Iraq more deeply in the Second World War increased anti-British sentiments and polarized Iraq's politicians, who were unprepared to deal with such weighty matters. These events led in 1941 to a temporary unseating of the pro-British politicians, a counterinvasion of British forces, and the second British occupation of Iraq. This occupation was a decisive turning point in Iraq's history. The British restored the former pillars of the regime to a position from which they could not be dislodged except by revolution. Their intervention created considerable resentment not only of the occupation but also of the ruling group and its association with a foreign power. These sentiments were suppressed during the war, but they did not disappear.

An Era of Communal and Tribal Rebellion, 1932–1936

With the end of the mandate and the withdrawal of the British, Iraq attempted to create a strong government of national unity. King Faisal moved to propitiate the nationalist opposition by bringing some of its members into the government, but a series of problems threatening the national unity of the new state soon challenged this cabinet. It began in the summer of 1933, when tensions with the newly settled Assyrian community exploded in a serious crisis.

The Assyrian Affair
To many outsiders the Assyrian affair was symptomatic of how Iraq would deal with a dissident minority. Iraqi nationalists saw the Assyrians as a military and ideological challenge to Iraq's national unity. The crisis began when the Assyrian community made a claim to autonomy based on its previous status as a separate religious community under the Ottomans. The settlement of

the Assyrians in Iraq after the First World War and continued British protection of the group had long been resented by the Muslim population. On one hand, British reliance on the Levies, a British-trained force wholly recruited from Assyrians, was feared and resented by the fledgling Iraqi army, sensitive to its own weakness.[1] On the other hand, Iraqi independence and the shift in responsibility for internal defense to the Iraqi army worried the Assyrian community. The Levies threatened to resign en bloc and to regroup in the north with a view to forming an Assyrian enclave there.

The situation came to a head in August, when fighting began between the Assyrians and the Iraqi army. Who fired the first shot has not been clearly established, but at the end of the battle, thirty Iraqi soldiers were dead and about half as many Assyrians. A few of these Assyrians managed to reach their villages, about five hundred crossed the border to Syria, and the rest were rounded up and shot by the army.

Worse was yet to follow. Anti-Assyrian and anti-British sentiment among the Iraqi population had reached an unprecedented pitch. By the beginning of August something close to panic had gripped the government. Soon after the first affray, armed Kurdish irregulars massacred about a hundred Assyrian villagers at Dahuk and Zakhu. The worst act, however, occurred on 11 August in Sumayyil, when unarmed Assyrian villagers, clustered at the police station for protection, were killed by an army company, possibly under orders from Bakr Sidqi, the general in charge of the forces in the Mosul area. Whether or not Sidqi was responsible, 315 Assyrians perished at Sumayyil and at least forty villages were looted and partially destroyed.[2]

Apart from the human tragedy, the consequences of these acts were far-reaching. Iraq's capacity for self-government, and particularly its treatment of minorities, was challenged by many in the international community and the reputation of its newly independent government harmed. Inside Iraq distrust between minorities and the government would poison the political atmosphere for some time to come. At the same time, a torrent of anti-British nationalism was unleashed, foreshadowing the events of 1941 and discrediting Faisal and his policy of moderation.

A less spectacular but more significant outcome was that the Assyrian affair brought the army into national prominence for the first time and showed its future political potential. The affair elevated Bakr Sidqi to the position of a national hero. Offers to serve in the army now poured in from tribesmen and Kurds, making possible the passage of a conscription bill. This legislation strengthened the military and the nationalists.

The Death of Faisal

In September 1933 Faisal left for Europe in ill health and ill spirits. He died suddenly on the 7th of a heart attack, partly induced by the strain of the previous weeks. Faisal's death removed one of the few men capable of moderating the differences among Iraq's diverse elements. It destroyed the promising start he had made in incorporating opposition elements into a coalition government. His sense of realism and his experience in knowing how far he could go against British rule was soon missed.

His son Ghazi assumed the throne. At twenty-one Ghazi was as yet too young and inexperienced to fill his father's role of political balancer. Educated partly in England and partly at the Military College, he identified with the young army officers who were becoming increasingly nationalist in ideology and outlook. His father had been at home among the townsmen and tribesmen and had taken to the interpersonal style of politics in Baghdad with zest, but Ghazi cared little for the intricacies of Baghdad politics and often neglected his royal duties. On the positive side, however, his youth, his genuine nationalist feelings, and his proclivity for the army put him in tune with the emerging educated classes.[3] Had he tempered his personal life with some moderation, Ghazi might have matured to fill the widening gap between the throne and the middle class. The change in monarch also meant a decline in British influence, for much of Britain's control had been exercised through Faisal. As events were to show, Ghazi would prove much less amenable to British suggestions.

Meanwhile, politicians in Baghdad continued to jockey for position, ignoring real problems. The resignation of Faisal's coalition cabinet led to a struggle for power within governing circles. As cabinets succeeded one another with little rhyme or reason—four within a year and a half—the fabric of state and the constitutional structure began to erode. The machinations of politicians would have been less serious had they not come on top of tribal dissatisfactions that had been smoldering for some time. These now provided the raw material for disruptions that politicians could—and did— manipulate.

Tribal Revolts

The complex causes of tribal unrest in the mid-Euphrates area must be understood in order to grasp the significance of the tribal revolts that dominated the political scene for the next two years. At the root of this tribal unrest was the transition from a society based on tribal organization and val-

ues to one based on settled agriculture. A striking manifestation of this transition was the erosion of the power and authority of the *shaikh* within the
tribe as the new state extended its authority into the countryside.

The conscription law was a prime example. Passed in January 1934, it
deprived the *shaikh* of able-bodied tribesmen at the same time that it built
up the force ultimately capable of subduing him. The *shaikh's* administrative
position was also increasingly eroded by the inexorable growth and spread of
bureaucracy. This was evident in a host of measures, passed in the 1930s, designed to place local authority in the hands of educated townsmen and reduce tribal autonomy. With an election in 1934 that further reduced tribal
influence in parliament, it is perhaps not surprising that tribal leaders decided the time was ripe to reclaim their old privileges.

More important in generating tribal feuding, however, was the struggle
for land and water, particularly on the part of the *shaikhs*. This struggle was
a result of the complex agricultural difficulties involved in the shift from
raising livestock to settled agriculture and from subsistence agriculture to
cash cropping. Throughout the 1930s attention was focused on fixing
rights of land ownership and tenure to encourage investment in agriculture
and expansion of cultivated land. The practice of modern agriculture and
the need to encourage investment required fixed titles over specified territorial plots.[4] The welter of claims and counterclaims finally gave rise to the
Land Settlement Law of 1932. Under this law a new form of tenure—
lazma—could be granted by the settlement authorities to anyone who had
enjoyed usufruct of the land for at least fifteen years, but land so granted
could not be sold outside the tribe without the approval of the government.[5] The intent of the law had been to safeguard the tribesman against
alienation of the land, but except in a few areas, it was in fact used by urban
investors and tribal *shaikhs* to secure legal title and to reduce the tribesmen
to the status of sharecropping tenants. Far from ameliorating the problem,
the law spurred intense competition for land titles, which played a major
role in stirring up tribal insurgence.

The scramble for the land was accompanied by the gradual dispossess-
sion of the peasant. In 1923 only an estimated one-tenth of the peasants
could claim traditional personal rights in the land. The remainder were at
the mercy of the newly established landlord-*shaikhs*. By 1930 the reduction
in tribesmen's status had resulted in widespread migration to the cities. It
was this state of affairs that gave rise to the notorious Law for the Rights
and Duties of Cultivators, passed in 1933. The law contained a provision

stipulating that no peasant could be employed unless he were free from debt. Since almost all peasants were indebted to their landlords, their legal mobility was virtually eliminated. Despite the law, however, the tide of migration continued.

Bad as they were, these difficulties were further compounded by *shi'i* grievances. The main *shi'i* grievances, of course, were the paucity of *shi'i* representation in the central government and an inadequate share of the national resources. A number of religious *shi'a* further believed that the government in Baghdad was illegitimate because it was secular, *sunni,* and foreign dominated and that participation in the government was both unlawful and sinful. However, this attitude was being challenged by a number of Arab *shi'a* who, by the late 1920s, preferred to participate in politics and were willing to protest their underrepresentation.[6]

Attempts by Arab *sunni* politicians to dissolve *shi'i* particularism in a philosophy of secular Arab nationalism also created some animosity. Such an orientation expressed aspirations for eventual integration of Iraq into a greater Arab state that would, inevitably, be mainly *sunni.* The alternative, focusing on an Iraqi state with its *shi'i* majority, might require adjustments in the power structure and even a modified stance toward Persia, a prospect causing fear and anxiety among many Arab *sunni* elites.[7] These *sunni* sentiments were expressed in a book, *al-Uruba fi-l-Mizan* (Arabism in the Balance), published in June 1933, which was critical of *shi'a's* unwillingness to give their loyalty to the state and to pan-Arabism. The author was brought to trial and briefly imprisoned, but *shi'i* hostility had already been aroused and turned against the government.[8]

These underlying factors would not in themselves have been sufficient to cause a tribal revolt. The final ingredient was provided by personal rivalries among Baghdad politicians. Perceiving the road to power as blocked by constitutional means, one group, the National Brotherhood Party, organized a conspiracy aimed at overthrowing the cabinet by threat of tribal rebellion. After an outbreak of tribal rebellion in Daghghara on 15 March 1935, the king decided to install the opposition in a new cabinet. This cabinet, headed by Yasin al-Hashimi, a former Ottoman-educated general and leader of the National Brotherhood Party, was drawn almost exclusively from the strongest and most experienced of the inner circle of Arab sunni nationalists. But in forming his cabinet, Hashimi made a critical tactical error by excluding Hikmat Sulaiman, who had taken much of the initiative in organizing the conspiracy. Sulaiman had recently become a marginal member of the Ahali group, a left-wing reformist association, and Hashimi feared that his appointment would ease the way to power of left-wing intellectuals and radical reformers. Instead, he preferred to rely on supporters of the pan-Arab orientation. Sulaiman and the Ahali group were not the only ones disturbed by the new cabinet. Members of the previous government and their tribal supporters were furious. Worse, the *shi'a* took the opportunity to set forth even more stringent demands in a fascinating document, Mithaq al-Sha'b (the People's Pact). It was the clearest statement yet of *shi'i* alternatives to the current government, demanding equal representation in the central government and more local rule in the south.[9] An election to the assembly, enlarged to make room for more *shi'i shaikhs,* failed to satisfy the *shi'a* or to prevent a resurgence of tribal rebellions.

There is little need to chronicle the various revolts here, which, with one exception, took place in the south. Disturbances began in May 1935, in Rumaitha. Local politics and a land dispute were involved. From Rumaitha rebellion spread to Suq al-Shuyukh, prompted by land tenure problems and an attempt to apply the conscription law. This was followed by the Yazidis in Sinjar, who rose up against conscription. A second rash of outbreaks began in Nasiriyya in 1936, followed by others in Rumaitha and Daghghara. Greed, tangled land claims, religious sentiment, and the weakening of tribal authority—especially symbolized by conscription—contributed in differing degrees.[10]

Dominance of the State and the Army

This time the cabinet acted with unexpected firmness in upholding the authority of the state and the central government, essentially ending tribal insurgence as a tool for political change. The initial rebellions were put down by Bakr Sidqi, who was lenient at first. When the rash of revolts continued in 1936, however, Sidqi became more ruthless. Military forces were sent to rebellious areas, and air force bombing took a heavy toll in lives. Summary executions were carried out under martial law. These measures were sufficient to bring peace to the tribal areas of the south, but they also helped bring Sidqi and the army to the fore and gave rise to the notion in military circles that the army was being used as a tool of civilian politicians and that politics might be better served by direct military intervention.

At the same time, the cabinet fortified and expanded the army and the bureaucracy. By 1936 the number of men in the armed services had risen to about 23,000, double the figure for 1933, and the Royal Iraqi Air Force

grew from a few planes to three squadrons.[11] A paramilitary training program with a nationalist orientation, known as *futuwwa* (named after a medieval brotherhood devoted to chivalry), was introduced into the school
system. These policies were accompanied by a strong Arab nationalist campaign in the press.

What proved to be the government's undoing, however, was not the
problem of the tribes but the increasingly authoritarian posture of the prime
minister, Yasin al-Hashimi. Feeding opposition fears of a dictatorship, he began clamping down on open political activity and concentrating power in
his own hands. He dissolved his own party, the National Brotherhood, and
then the opposition party, Wahda (Unity). Hashimi's repression of the press
made Nuri's previous treatment seem mild. Hashimi was referred to as the
Bismarck of the Arabs, intimating his possible leadership of a greater Arab
unity scheme.[12]

By 1936 Hashimi began to hint at a prolonged tenure, claiming he
hoped to be given the next ten years of his life to realize the aims desired by
the country. The pronouncement caused immediate controversy. Whatever
Hashimi's motives, his wish was soon dispelled. A carefully planned conspiracy had been afoot for some time, involving not unruly tribes but the
instrument on which nationalist politicians had lavished so much attention—the army.

The Bakr Sidqi Coup, 1936

The coup revealed the mix of forces at work in Iraq, as well as the different
directions the state might have taken. While personal ambition surely played
a role, so, too, did the impetus for reform. Although the coup was known by
Bakr Sidqi's name, it was not initially the work of the general but of Hikmat
Sulaiman. A member of a well-known Ottoman family, Sulaiman was interested not only in power but also in more rapid economic and social development. His model, however, was not Fabian socialism but the paternalistic
authoritarianism of Mustafa Kamal. He advocated a thoroughgoing secularism and modernization on Turkish lines. This attitude brought him into
close communion with Sidqi and the army.

Sidqi's motives, like Sulaiman's, were mixed. He had reached the highest
position open to him in the army and now found the way to advancement
blocked by the prime minister's brother, who was chief of staff. But Sidqi

also wanted the army expanded and modernized, which could not be achieved without removing the prime minister and his cabinet. Thus, when Sulaiman first broached the idea of a coup to Sidqi in the autumn of 1936, the suggestion fell on fertile ground.

The Political and Intellectual Climate

To understand the coup, however, one must also grasp the political and intellectual climate that enabled Sidqi and Sulaiman to mobilize enough support to carry out their conspiracy. New ideas were permeating Iraq during the 1930s, influencing Iraq's intelligentsia. Substantial elements of two schools of thought, in particular, have continued to influence Iraqi political life to the present day.

The first school was drawn from the rising dictatorships of Europe. As educated Iraqis traveled through Germany and Italy or read of these countries' spectacular economic and social advances, they began to identify progress and efficiency with authoritarian governments and social mobilization. A monolithic form of government seemed to offer a more effective means of unifying fragmented countries and modernizing backward societies than did constitutional democracy and the free enterprise system. More rapid development, political unity, and greater social discipline were the desiderata of this school of thought. Fascist Italy and Germany in the early days of Hitler were the models. The *futuwwa* system, for example, was partly modeled on Germany's youth movement.[13]

The authoritarian regime that exerted the most powerful influence on Iraqis, however—especially on the older generation of nationalists—was that of Mustafa Kamal. As an Islamic country with a background of traditions and problems similar to Iraq's, Turkey offered a more attainable example than European regimes. The use of the state to encourage the development of industry, agriculture, and education had wide appeal. Above all, Kamal's masterful handling of parliament and its fractious politicians seemed—particularly to the military—to set an example worth following.

The second school of thought to stir the Iraqi imagination was democratic socialism. Iraqis were inspired less by the example of the Soviet Union than by the British Labor movement. The need for social rather than mere political reform, an appreciation of the economic basis of power, and dissatisfaction with the policy of the ruling oligarchy of politicians and landowners were keenly felt by the younger generation of Iraqis, the first to receive a Western-style education. This school of thought emphasized social justice, a more equitable distribution of political power and wealth, and genuine economic reform.[14] In the early 1930s, young reformers began to coalesce in a loosely knit organization known as the Ahali group.

By 1935 Ahali had attracted several older and respected politicians, including Ja'far Abu-l-Timman and Hikmat Sulaiman. With the addition of these politicians, the emphasis of the group shifted from intellectual matters to achieving political power. But the Ahali group did not become a political party; it was still new and lacking structure and organization, and with no grassroots support as yet, it was prone to exploitation.

The Coup Unfolds

The actual steps leading up to the Bakr Sidqi coup were kept secret. About a week before the coup, Sidqi approached the commander of the first division and secured his cooperation. When all appeared ready in the army, Sulaiman appealed to the Ahali group for support. Although some hesitated before committing themselves to a breach with the constitution, most joined the conspiracy, convinced that the group would have an unprecedented opportunity to put their ideas in practice.[15]

Events then marched to a swift conclusion that took all but a few by surprise.[16] On 29 October 1936 planes dropped leaflets over Baghdad demanding Hashimi's resignation and the appointment of Sulaiman as prime minister. Meanwhile, the army began a march on Baghdad under Sidqi's leadership. The king was anxious about his own future, but once it was clear that the coup was designed to replace the cabinet and not the king, Ghazi was willing to acquiesce. Meanwhile bombs were dropped near the Council of Ministers' building killing one person and wounding six. Shortly thereafter, Hashimi resigned and Sulaiman was appointed prime minister. The following day Yasin al-Hashimi, Nuri al-Sa'id, and Rashid Ali al-Kailani left the country—Nuri for Egypt and Kailani and Hashimi for Beirut, followed by a number of supporters. Hashimi died of a heart attack in 1937, but Nuri and Rashid Ali returned later to play a pivotal role in their country's political life.

The coup was a major turning point in Iraqi history.[17] It made a critical breach in the constitution, already weakened by government politicians and their willingness to stir tribal rebellion, and opened the door to military involvement in politics. The coup also made a clean, if temporary, sweep of the old ruling group that had governed the country since its founding. Only one veteran politician, Sulaiman, found his way into the new government.

The change seemed to spell the gradual demise of the establishment. It also raised the possibility of a new direction in domestic politics. Much depended, however, on whether the new government could keep the army out of politics, restore constitutional procedure, and move ahead on some basic reforms.

Attempts to Liberalize and Their Failure

The cabinet Sulaiman appointed after the coup represented a mixture of coup participants. Sulaiman became prime minister, Sidqi became chief of staff and the Ahali group received the lion's share of economic and social ministries. The new government represented a striking contrast with its predecessors in several ways. It brought new people to power for the first time in more than a decade, many of whom had been educated under the British rather than the Ottomans. Liberal, leftist reformers acquired power for the first time. They meant to bypass the established alliance of urban *sunni* politicians and rural landlords, redistributing power and privilege and developing a broader-based constituency among the middle and lower classes. Had their program succeeded, Iraq's subsequent history might have been very different.

A less noticeable but more significant change was that the new government contained few Arab *sunnis* and not a single advocate of the pan-Arab cause on which all previous governments had been founded. This configuration resulted in a more Iraq-centered foreign policy oriented toward better relations with Turkey and Iran instead of the Arab countries. In 1937 the Sa'dabad Pact was concluded between Turkey, Iran, Iraq, and Afghanistan, a group that prefigured the later Baghdad Pact. Iraq also reached an agreement with Iran (mediated by Britain) attempting to settle the boundary between Iran and Iraq on the Shatt al-Arab. It gave freedom of navigation on the Shatt to Iran and increased the territory under Iran's jurisdiction, concessions which aroused some public opinion against the government.[18] Hikmat's cabinet gave birth to the "Iraq First" policy of Iraq for the Iraqis and took cognizance of the need for good relations with Iraq's non-Arab neighbors. However, its neglect of the Arab nationalist cause was soon to cause it considerable trouble.

The new government began its work amidst considerable popular support, but popular support could not for long mask the ultimate incompatibility of its two major components. Authoritarian by training and outlook,

Sidqi was determined to make the army the main vehicle of power in the state; the liberal democratic reformers were bent on changing the social structure of the country. These differences, papered over in the common desire to overthrow the previous regime, soon generated conflict.

Initially the reformers appeared to be strong. The new government promised an end to the suppression of liberty and advocated reforms in the educational system and the distribution of state lands. Its program called for the annulment of laws against the peasants, the encouragement of trade unions, and the spread of culture among the masses—a call for broad-based rather than elite education. It was, in short, a bold attack on privilege.[19]

However, it was not long before opposition began to surface from a number of sources. Chief among these were the landlord-*shaikhs,* who felt their authority to be threatened, and the Arab nationalists, who were unhappy over the Turkish orientation of the cabinet and over the agreement with Iran. Most important was opposition from Bakr and his supporters in the army.

A conflict between Sidqi and the Ahali group was probably inevitable. It came when tribal supporters of the previous cabinet rebelled and Sidqi and Sulaiman decided to crush them by force. Sulaiman's decision was made without consulting the cabinet. When the three reform ministers heard of it, they resigned. The episode signaled a clear victory for Sidqi and his contingent. Sulaiman promised the dissolution of the newly elected parliament, and a second election was in fact held to remove leftist influence. Thus ended any attempt to tamper with Iraq's social structure until after the revolution of 1958.

These moves came too late to save the regime. Opposition to Sidqi had been growing, chiefly among the Arab nationalist politicians, who were in contact with a group of Arab nationalist army officers.[20] The Arab nationalist officers resented Sidqi as a Kurd who had encouraged Kurds in the army, and they felt the policy of Sulaiman's government had been too pro-Turkish. The *shi'a* detested Sidqi for his brutal suppression of the tribes. Above all, the opposition was aided and abetted by members of the previous cabinet. Nuri al-Sa'id, motivated partly by revenge and partly by opposition to the cabinet's policy, waged an incessant campaign from Egypt against the cabinet.[21] Once again the army, or a portion of it, intervened. On 11 August 1937, as Bakr Sidqi and the commander of the air force were resting at the Mosul airport on their way to Turkey, both were shot point-blank by a soldier under orders from the Arab nationalist officers.

Sidqi's assassination put Sulaiman and his regime in a critical position. It soon became clear that the bulk of the officer corps in Mosul sided with the plotters. When units in Baghdad also sided with these officers, civil war seemed possible. To avoid this contingency, the government resigned on 17 August 1937. The new regime, which had come to power with such great expectations of reform, had fallen within ten months.

The Bakr Sidqi coup and the collapse of the coalition government had far-reaching results. One was to remove the left from power. The reformers were unprepared for their task in terms of organization, ideological cohesion, and political experience and were no match for the army. Moreover, Sulaiman and the left grossly underestimated the strength of two other political forces in the country—the Arab nationalists and the conservative landowners. Had they succeeded, Iraq might have shifted its foreign policy to a more Iraq-based orientation.

With the weakening of the left, power gravitated into the hands of the conservative and nationalist elements at a critical time. Opening the door to the misuse of power by the military, the coup of 1936 was followed by a series of less overt but continuous military interventions behind the scenes, which became the most marked feature of political life in the years between 1936 and 1941.

The Army in Politics, 1937–1941

In the years immediately following the assassination of Bakr Sidqi, three distinct strands developed in Iraqi politics. One was the return of the establishment politicians and their pursuit of business as usual. These politicians—especially Nuri—continued to wage their own power struggles and personal vendettas, neglecting pressing social issues and the threatening international situation brought about by the onset of the Second World War. Second was the reemergence of the Palestine problem and the resulting intensification of anti-British and Arab nationalist sentiment, especially among key groups such as the students, intelligentsia, and officer corps. Third was the increased intrusion of the army in politics and the continued erosion of the constitutional system established by the British. Previously, parliament had unquestionably been manipulated by the politicians and the British, but military dominance in politics was to prove even more damaging. The intertwining of these three strands gradually drew the young officers further into politics, intensified their pan-Arab feelings, isolated the pro-British politicians, and eventually precipitated the crisis of 1941.

The Return of the Establishment

In the wake of Sulaiman's resignation, Jamil al-Midfa'i was appointed prime minister; his conciliatory policies were well known. To heal old wounds, he adopted a policy of "dropping the curtain" on the past. This policy, backed by the moderates and the king, did not satisfy Nuri, who began to agitate for the removal of his cabinet and for punishment of Sulaiman and his supporters. On this issue, Nuri found common ground with the Arab nationalist officers who opposed Midfa'i's policy and who feared retribution for Sidqi's assassination should Sulaiman return to power. When Midfa'i refused to take action, Nuri secretly collaborated with the Arab nationalist officers to end Midfa'i's cabinet and seize power.

Matters came to a head in December 1938, when Midfa'i took steps to retire or transfer the Arab nationalist officers and thus end their influence in politics. On 24 December the officers insisted on the resignation of the cabinet on the grounds that the army no longer had confidence in it. Nuri made clear that he fully supported the officers, and Midfa'i's resignation followed the same day. Nuri al-Sa'id became prime minister for the first time since 1932. The episode illustrates Nuri's willingness to drag the officers into politics when it suited his purpose.

He then attempted to deal with Hikmat Sulaiman and his collaborators in the coup. Since he was unable to bring them to trial for the coup because of an amnesty law previously passed by the Sulaiman government, a new charge had to be found. An alleged plot against the life of the king was "discovered" in March 1939, and Sulaiman and a number of his group were implicated, brought to trial, and convicted. The evidence convinced no one. Only the intervention of the British ambassador got the sentences reduced and saved Sulaiman's life. This indicates the extent to which Nuri was willing to go to achieve retribution and the degree to which personal feelings were allowed to dominate politics.

The Death of Ghazi

No sooner had the trial been settled than the government was faced with a serious—and unexpected—crisis at the palace. On 4 April 1939 the king, under the influence of alcohol, drove his car at high speed into a power pole. He died of a fractured skull shortly thereafter. This official version of the king's death has always been suspected by Iraqis and particularly by the nationalists, who have claimed that Nuri and the British had a hand in it.[22] There is no hard evidence to support this conclusion, but there is little doubt that Ghazi's death came as a relief to Nuri and the British. Always in tune with the younger army officers, the young king had become an outspoken advocate of anti-British and nationalist sentiment. In 1937 he had begun broadcasting from a private radio station in his palace, denouncing French rule in Syria and Zionist claims in Palestine and attacking British influence in the Gulf. He even advocated the absorption of Kuwait by Iraq (the first time this claim was publicly made).

Ghazi's death created a serious political vacuum at the center of power. The young king left an infant son, Faisal II, but no clear-cut provisions had been made for the regency. This was a delicate matter since the regent would exercise the power of the throne for the next fourteen years. Among the contenders was Abd al-Ilah, Ghazi's cousin. At the time of Ghazi's death, he was something of a cipher. He was known to be pro-British and had good relations with Nuri and the officers who supported him. He was also young— twenty-six—and for that reason, the politicians probably felt that they could control him. On 6 April 1939 Abd al-Ilah was appointed regent.[23]

Abd al-Ilah was born in Mecca, the son of Ali and grandson of the Sharif Husain. He was raised in the insulated environment of Mecca and came to Iraq only in 1926. He later attended the British-run Victoria College in Alexandria. Partly because of his background and training, partly because of his shy nature, he always seemed to feel an outsider in Iraq, more at home among the English than Iraqis, a factor that later put him at a disadvantage. Nonetheless, Abd al-Ilah used his position to draw the establishment closer to the British than to the nationalists. As a result the year following the king's death was one of relative stability. The calm was deceptive. Beneath the surface, nationalist sentiment continued to mount, creating a climate of opinion that would eventually isolated the pro-British politicians and create irresistible pressures within the establishment.

The Rising Tide of Nationalism

These pressures were exacerbated by events outside Iraq that inexorably drew the country and its politicians deeper into regional and international affairs. By the end of the decade, two issues had come to a head. Both worked against the British connection. The first was the partition of Palestine and Britain's role in furthering that outcome. The second was the onset of the Second World War in Europe, in which Britain and its allies were challenged by the forces of Fascism. The two issues were intertwined. The Palestine issue helped fuel indigenous anti-British feeling, while the divisions in Europe appeared to some to provide alternative sources of support.

Despite residual anti-British feelings, it is doubtful whether the Palestine struggle would have inflamed public opinion to the extent it did, had it not been for the influence of Amin al-Husaini, the *mufti* (religious jurist) of Palestine. The resistance movement, led by the *mufti* in Palestine, had reached a peak between 1936 and 1939 with riots and armed resistance to the British. After the British crushed the resistance movement, the *mufti* took refuge in Baghdad, adding his voice to the mounting anti-British sentiment.

Meanwhile, the onset of the Second World War exacerbated social and economic problems in Iraq, leading to commercial disruptions, inflation, and a shortage of funds. The mass of the population in rural and urban areas continued to live in poverty that was soon to be intensified by the shortages of the war. The slow pace of development and the disruption of a war thrust on Iraq by foreign powers increased the rancor of Iraqi politicians and fed the intense anti-British feeling that was shortly to engulf Iraq.

These sentiments were stoked by the growth of Arab nationalist ideology in the school system, particularly at the secondary and college levels, where the Arab nationalist seeds planted earlier by Sati'-l-Husri had taken root. By the 1930s the introduction of new texts, heavily oriented toward pan-Arabism, in history and the social sciences were having an impact. Pan-Arab sentiments were strongly influenced by German ideas of nationalism and were encouraged by Fritz Grobba, German minister in Baghdad until 1939.

Intrusion of the Officers into Politics

A commitment to Arab nationalism was clearly shared by the younger generation of army officers; indeed, it was the main motive force behind their increased forays into the political arena. Politicization of the army officer corps had begun at least as early as 1930, when Taufiq Husain, a fiery lecturer at the Military College, advocated military intervention in politics on the model of Turkey and Iran. By 1934, there were at least seventy officers in his circle. It was not long, however, before a number of these broke away from Husain and formed their own group, oriented toward a more pan-Arab policy. Alienated by Bakr Sidqi's lack of interest in Arab affairs, this group had been behind Sidqi's assassination and the subsequent military action that had put Nuri back in power in 1938.[24] By 1940 the core of this group, which had originally included at least half a dozen officers, had narrowed down to four: Salah al-Din Sabbagh, Muhammad Fahmi Sa'id, Mahmud Salman, and Kamil Shabib. All were to be key participants in the events of 1941. One more individual, Yunis al-Sab'awi, a journalist, also played a key role in sharpening the Arab nationalist sentiments of the officers and encouraging their political activism.[25]

By 1940 all three strands of politics—personal fear, the pan-Arab issue, and the intrusion of the military in politics—came to a head once again. In February Nuri tried to resign. Personal dissension in the cabinet over his treatment of adversaries, as well as the general tensions brought about by the Palestine issue, had made his position untenable. The young officers, however, fearful of losing their positions, organized yet another quiet coup to keep him in power. Nuri stayed temporarily but used his time to retire several senior officers who favored ending the intrusion of the young officers in politics. This act secured their position and eased the situation temporarily. On 31 March 1940 Nuri was finally able to step down as prime minister. On his advice, former prime minister Rashid Ali al-Kailani formed the new cabinet. However, the damage had been done. The third coup had put the young nationalist officers in complete control of the country's armed forces. It would not be long before they would precipitate another crisis, one the civilian politicians were unable to handle.

The 1941 Coup

Much ink has been spilled on interpreting the events of 1940 and 1941 and the brief war that resulted in the second British occupation of Iraq.[26] The Anglophile party in Iraq has always regarded the movement labeled with Rashid Ali's name as illegal and a breach in the constitutional system. This view prevailed for a time in Iraq with the victory of the regent and the pro-British forces. The nationalists, more closely tied to opinion inside Iraq and less attuned to foreign concerns, viewed the movement as a genuine assertion of Iraq's national rights, a further step in achieving Iraqi independence, and a blow struck for the Arab cause and the Palestinian struggle. In the long run, with the eventual domination of nationalist governments after 1958, this interpretation prevailed.

The difficulty began when Italy declared war on the Allies on 10 June 1940. The British asked Iraq to break off diplomatic relations with Italy, fearing that the Italian embassy would be used as a center of espionage and propaganda for the Axis powers. Meanwhile, Britain's war situation worsened. In May the fall of France put the Vichy government in control of neighboring Syria, threatening British communications in the Middle East.

When Nuri, as foreign minister, asked the cabinet to comply, a rift in the government opened. One group, led by Nuri and supported by the regent, favored the British and estimated that, despite early reverses, the Allies would eventually win the war. They wished to support the British. The other faction, represented by Rashid Ali but led by the *mufti* and the officers, wished to remain neutral or to bargain support for reducing British influence in internal affairs. This group won out. In the summer of 1940 they tentatively explored the possibility of German support in case of an open conflict with Britain. The results of the negotiations were disappointing. The Germans clearly warned against precipitating armed conflict with Britain. Despite these warnings, the anti-British party persisted.[27]

In the meantime, British patience had run out. In November 1940 the British forced the issue by delivering a virtual ultimatum to the government, giving Iraq two choices: It could keep Rashid Ali or retain the friendship of Britain. By interfering so directly in internal politics, the British themselves helped undermine the constitutional system. A rapid succession of events followed. Rashid Ali, the prime minister, refused to step down and submitted a request to the regent for the dissolution of parliament and the calling of a new election, designed to bring in a chamber that would back his position. The regent refused to sign the order. To force a cabinet resignation, he left Baghdad and took refuge with units of the armed forces in Diwaniyya. Still unwilling to make an open breach in the constitution, Rashid Ali resigned on 31 January 1941.

A new cabinet came in, led by Taha-l-Hashimi, brother of the former prime minister and an army officer, presumed able to deal with the officers. He secured the return of Abd al-Ilah to the capital on the assurance that the army would be put back in the barracks. He then tried to live up to his promise, but it was too late. By this time the officers were determined to rid themselves of Hashimi in favor of Rashid Ali, who was supporting them. Once again, they threatened force, and Hashimi resigned. Meanwhile, they mobilized their forces and surrounded the royal palace. Once again, however, the regent managed to give them the slip, thanks to the US minister in Baghdad, who smuggled him out of the capital in the back of his car. Nuri, and several other pro-British politicians, managed to escape at the same time. The regent's departure made it necessary for the four officers and Rashid Ali to act outside the constitutional system. This came to be known as the Rashid Ali coup.

Rashid Ali and the officers now formed a new government, composed wholly of the nationalist party, an act accomplished in the midst of a high tide of nationalist sentiment. On 10 April they deposed Abd al-Ilah, appointing a distant relative in his place. The new regent accepted Hashimi's resignation, and Rashid Ali was deputized to form his third and last cabinet. Even with the crisis completely out of hand, Rashid Ali desperately tried to find a compromise. However, the British had already decided it was too late. They demanded that British troops be allowed to land in Iraq, presumably to be transported through the country in accordance with the treaty. Rashid Ali agreed, and on 17 and 18 April British troops landed at Basra.

From here on, Rashid Ali lost whatever measure of control he once held over the officers. Apparently blind to the probable consequences, the officers informed Rashid Ali that the British troops would have to leave the country in a few days. The British, who were attempting to evacuate women and children by plane from Habbaniyya, were told that if the plane left the ground it would be fired upon. The British regarded this as an act of war, and on 2 May the local British commander decided to attack the Iraqi forces surrounding the base without warning.

The rest of the story is soon told. Within hours, the Royal Air Force (RAF) had destroyed twenty-five of Iraq's forty planes. The Iraqi army withdrew to Falluja, destroying the Euphrates dams and flooding the area as they retreated. This delayed the British advance but hardly stopped it. In the meantime, British reinforcements began to stream in from Jordan, including contingents from Glubb Pasha's Arab Legion. Falluja was captured on 19 May and the way lay open to Baghdad.

In Baghdad the government proved as ineffective as the army. No plans had been made prior to precipitating the crisis for help from the Axis powers, nor in retrospect, was any likely to have been forthcoming. At this point, Hitler was mobilizing for an attack on the Soviet Union and was not prepared to help Iraq in any substantial way.

The government that had precipitated the war collapsed shortly. On 29 May, as British columns approached Baghdad, the four officers escaped to Iran, where they were soon joined by Rashid Ali, Amin al-Husaini, and their followers. On 30 May a new mayor of Baghdad and a committee he formed signed an armistice with Britain. On 1 June Abd al-Ilah arrived in Baghdad with Nuri and others. They were entrusted with the formation of a government made up of the pro-British party alone. Thus ended the most serious attempt since the 1920 revolt to sever the British tie and to unseat the regime Britain had established. Once again, it ended with a British victory.

On the positive side, the victory bought the British and the regime they had established additional time—almost two decades—to put down roots and work on a better foundation. It restored a constitutional system to Iraq and buttressed Iraq's relations with the winning side and the dominant European powers. However, the crisis also had profound negative repercussions for the future; all the participants paid a price sooner or later.[28] Many supporters of Rashid Ali were executed or imprisoned; suspected sympathizers were dismissed or confined in camps. Rashid Ali began a long exile. Retribution to the regent and Nuri came later, in 1958. The British also paid at this later date with the fall of the regime they had done so much to foster. Most important, the events of these years generated a deep rift in Iraqi society. Opposition to the regime could henceforth be contained but not compromised. Those who were executed for precipitating the events of 1941 were regarded as martyrs by much of the army and the Iraqi population. The young officers who overthrew the regime in 1958 believed they were but completing the task left unfinished in 1941. As for the British influence and the constitutional system Britain established, events showed how thin they were. Without the second British occupation, it is doubtful how much longer Britain's work would have remained. As it was, thanks to the urgent wartime situation and the presence of British troops on Iraqi soil, the regime was given another lease on life.

The Second British Occupation and Its Legacy, 1941–1945

In June 1941 the first contingent of forces reached Baghdad and began to requisition houses and buildings; the second British occupation of Iraq had begun. Like the first, twenty-five years earlier, it was carried out under the exigencies of war and maintained for the benefit of the Allied war effort. It was clearly recognized, however, that the situation was temporary and would lapse at the conclusion of the war with the withdrawal of British troops.

The real significance of the British occupation lay in its reinstatement of the pro-British ruling group. The second occupation indissolubly linked the ruling circles of Iraq, especially the regent and Nuri, to the British. The willingness of these politicians to act as mediators between the British and their own people and their pursuit to the death of the followers of Rashid Ali gradually cut the regime off from much of the articulate middle class, making them ever more dependent upon the British.

The occupation began, however, with a policy of moderation under Jamil al-Midfa'i, the perennial compromiser. A number of army officers and civil servants who had participated in the events of May 1941 were retired. Key figures in education, such as Sati'-l-Husri, were deprived of citizenship and deported. The *futuwwa* movement was abolished. But this did not go far enough to satisfy the British. On 9 October, to no one's surprise, Nuri was asked to form a new cabinet.

Internment, Trials, and Reorganization of the Government

Shortly thereafter preparations were made for the internment of those the regime considered dangerous. Although this category was supposed to include only Rashid Ali supporters and those with open Axis sympathies, personal motives were also at work in the arrests. The total of those interned during the war may have reached 700 to 1,000.[29]

Of far more significance than these internments were the trials and executions of the movement's leaders. Late in 1941 an Iraqi court-martial was established; on 6 January 1942 it handed down the severest possible sentences. Rashid Ali, three of the four colonels, Yunis al-Sab'awi, and one or two others were all sentenced to death in absentia; others received long sentences of imprisonment. Demands were made for extradition of prisoners who were in British hands in Rhodesia. British compliance with the Iraqi request and the subsequent executions of the main participants raised questions over the responsibility for the trials and executions. Nationalist historians have put the blame equally on the British and on the regent and Nuri. It is more likely that responsibility rests with the Iraqis, particularly the regent, anxious to eliminate their opposition.

During a second trial, many of the original sentences were reduced. This did not hold true for the four officers involved in Rashid Ali's government. All four of the officers and Yunis al-Sab'awi were eventually captured and hanged. Of the leaders who had participated in the movement, only Rashid Ali and the *mufti* managed to escape, the former ultimately to Saudi Arabia and the latter to Germany and later to Egypt. These proceedings bit deeply into the public consciousness. Many army officers in particular were bitter over the treatment accorded their colleagues. The exile and internment of the regime's enemies might have been forgotten, but the executions created a vendetta and marked a point of no return in the attitude of many Iraqis toward the regime.

The regime turned next to the army and the education system. Throughout the remainder of the war, Nuri reduced both the size and influence of the army. In the spring of 1944 a British officer, Major General Renton, was sent to Iraq to reorganize the military. He put the army in the shape it was to assume right up to the revolution of 1958. Ottoman-trained officers were replaced by younger men, mainly trained by the British.

The regime turned next to the Ministry of Education. The British rightly attributed much of the pro-Axis sentiment in the country to the spread of extreme nationalism in the curriculum and textbooks and among the teachers. Offending teachers were dismissed and some of the most offensive texts removed.[30] Finally, the regime took steps to protect itself from a repetition of the events of 1941 through a constitutional amendment designed to buttress the throne. The king was given the right to dismiss the prime minister if necessary, a prerogative that would be exercised by Abd al-Ilah until the young king's maturity. The regent could thus legally remove an obstructive cabinet such as Rashid Ali's should it come to power.

The removal of so many nationalists had thinned the ranks of the Arab *sunnis* from which the regime had usually drawn support. One of the little-noticed, but important, consequences was a shift in the composition of the ruling group. The remaining wartime cabinets drew far more heavily on the *shi'a* and the Kurds, who for the first time equally balanced or together sometimes outnumbered the Arab *sunnis* in the cabinet.[31] This circumstance provided an opportunity for the emergence of new political figures and a younger generation among the shi'a and the Kurds.

This was accompanied by a political shift of far more significance for the future—encouragement of the left. The departure of the strong Arab nationalists opened the door to the liberal-leftist elements that had supported the Ahali group. At the same time, the regime itself began to take a more benign view of the leftists. Underground Communist newspapers were distributed freely without police interference. A number of leftists—even some Marxists—received high positions in education. The liberal attitude toward the left during and shortly after the war gave the Communist Party and other left-wing movements an opportunity to organize and to establish roots in the schools and among the workers. The Communist Party achieved a position of first rank among the intelligentsia and the working class that it retained in spite of the persecution of the late 1940s and the 1950s.

The Wartime Economy

The war years marked a turning point in social and economic life as well. Spiraling wartime prices (especially for grains) and the shortage of goods created unprecedented opportunities for exploitation. The resulting scramble for wealth created some affluence but more often built breathtaking fortunes for a very few. Gradually the gap between the rich and the poor, and even between the wealthy and the merely well-to-do, widened, creating new social tensions and breaking down the old ties of family and community and the values that sustained them. What made the situation even more intolerable was the close tie between political power and wealth and the obvious corruption in high places. As a close-knit oligarchy of wealth and power evolved, the legitimacy of the regime was further eroded. Meanwhile the middle class of civil servants, army officers, and teachers, caught on a treadmill of fixed salaries, saw their economic and social position worsen daily. The situation of the poor often became extreme, and bitterness against the government broke out in riots and strikes.

The first and most important factor in the postwar economy was inflation, produced partly by the descent of British troops on Iraq and partly by war shortages. The price index leaped from 100 in 1939 to 650 in 1942. Grain prices rose from an index of 100 in 1939 to 773 in the peak year of 1943; textiles, to 1,287.[32] Even these figures probably understate the level of inflation. Among those who profited most from these circumstances were the grain producers and dealers, who suddenly found an expanded market for their produce at higher prices.

But the grain trade, though the most lucrative, was not the only means of gaining wealth. Another profitable business was importing. All sorts of items were in short supply, and those who could corner the market on some item turned a nice profit. In fact, the government was forced to institute an import licensing policy, but import licenses then became a scarce commodity themselves. The profits made in the purchase and sale of valuable import licenses often exceeded the profitability of the import trade itself. So valuable were these licenses that ministers, senators, and almost all deputies registered as licensed importers, even though they did not engage in business themselves; they then sold the licenses to merchants.

Meanwhile, salaried employees working for the government suffered. While the cost of living rose five-, six-, and sevenfold,[33] employee salaries rose only 25 percent.[34] As for workers, their wages in 1939 were estimated at ID 3.38 a month or ID 40 ($95) a year.[35] The war years were punctuated by bread strikes, especially in the year 1943, when shortages were greatest and prices reached a peak. The strikes were put down by the police, although police action was accompanied by attempts to supply bread to the masses.

The closing years of the war hastened the polarization of society and helped set the stage for the revolution of 1958. Economically, the war created an ever more visible oligarchy. Politically, it brought back a regime tied almost wholly to the British, the landlords, and the wealthy. The removal of the nationalists gave opportunity to other groups. The introduction of more *shi'a* and Kurds into leadership posts alleviated ethnic and social tensions. But the regime, in the hands of old-school politicians like Nuri and a pro-British regent, failed to provide a new matching vision of Iraqi identity that would appeal to moderate nationalists. The demise of the nationalists also opened the door to the left. Some of these leftists were genuine liberals, interested in reforms and constitutional processes, but others were committed Marxists, who now worked to widen the gap between the regime and the people and to pave the way for the new social conditions of the postwar era.

4

THE END OF THE OLD REGIME,
1946–1958

The last decade of the old regime was a study in contrast. On the surface, political life appeared stable. The establishment politicians, supported by the landlord-*shaikhs,* the new urban wealthy, and the upper reaches of the army, seemed firmly entrenched in power. Beneath the surface, however, new social groups, motivated by different ideals and aspirations, emerged to challenge establishment values and policy. In country and city alike, poverty was widespread, even as new oil wealth was creating visible pockets of urban affluence and modernity. The regime recognized the need for change and attempted some modest reforms, but it tried to circumvent the established classes with a development program that avoided problems rather than addressing them.

Perhaps the most significant change occurred in the intellectual and cultural realm. Along with the spread of education and the press, increased contact with the West introduced new ideas and values that posed a sharp contrast with the past. The left demanded rapid social change, a more egalitarian society, and greater personal freedoms; the younger generation of Arab nationalists wanted faster movement on Arab unity and greater independence from the West. The old regime did little to counteract these ideas or to put forth a social vision of its own.

Nowhere were these contradictions more apparent than in the area of foreign policy. While the regime clung to the British tie, bitterness over the events of 1941 and the wartime arrests and executions spread. These feelings were exacerbated by the Arab defeat in Palestine and the establishment of the Israeli state. In the 1950s the eruption of revolutionary movements in other Middle

Eastern states—Mussadiq in Iran, Nasser in Egypt—caused strong reverbera-
tions inside Iraq. Regional changes occurred against the backdrop of the Cold
War and its intrusion into the Middle East. The Soviet Union's support for local Communist parties, aimed at disrupting or unseating pro-Western governments, was matched by the West's attempts to shore up its supporters; both
efforts helped polarize political forces in the region and inside Iraq.

Foreign policy problems were matched by and intertwined with domestic
difficulties. Aided by the spread of the press and radio and by an expanded
educational system, new political parties proceeded to politicize the new so-
cioeconomic groups, especially the educated middle class and the new working class. Their influence was increasingly evident in strikes, demonstrations,
and riots that further undermined and weakened the establishment.

In the face of these difficulties, the regime failed to shift the locus of its
support or to develop the political institutions bequeathed to it by the British.
Instead it continued to rely on the police to put down disturbances and on
the manipulation of elections to assure compliant parliaments. Neither was
the opposition up to the challenge: The only common ground on which the
opposition could unite was anti-imperialism and a severing of the regime's
foreign tie. In the end, domestic discontent and foreign policy issues coalesced
to overwhelm the regime and remove most vestiges of the British legacy.

Further Attempts at Liberalization

In the aftermath of the war and the Rashid Ali coup, the regent recognized
the need for change and devised a formula to gain public support—more
political freedom at home and a modification of the treaty with Britain. The
first step, a liberalization policy, was set forth in a speech on 27 December
1945 in which the regent promised permission for political parties, a new
electoral law, measures to improve social security and unemployment, and
some redistribution of wealth. The most important step taken, however, was
the decision to license five new political parties, the first such attempt in ten
years. Although three of the five proved to be short-lived, the remaining
two, the Istiqlal (Independence) and the National Democratic Party, survived to play a critical role in the postwar period and in the early part of the
revolutionary era. Both helped to shape the mentality of the emerging middle class, and between them they captured the minds and hearts of the
younger generation of educated Iraqis.

The Istiqlal Party was anti-British and pan-Arab. It called for the elimination of remaining British influence in Iraq, espoused independence for Muhammara (now Khuzistan, a province with a majority of Arabic speakers) in Iran, and championed the Palestinian cause. In the search for national identity, the Istiqlal came down heavily on the side of secular pan-Arabism and against the development of a separate Iraqi identity. Its greatest ideological weakness was its lack of a social program. It drew its support mainly from the *sunni* Arab population, although it was headed by a *shi'a*, Muhammad Mahdi Kubba, and some *shi'a* joined. There were no Kurds in Istiqlal.[1]

The National Democratic Party, led by Kamil al-Chadirchi, was an outgrowth of the older Ahali movement. It stood for political freedoms, land reform, the abolition of monopolies, and a more equitable distribution of wealth to be achieved mainly through tax measures. Because of its emphasis on domestic policy and reform and its lack of interest in pan-Arab schemes, the National Democratic Party appealed to minorities and the *shi'a* as well as to the liberal and left-leaning elements of the educated middle class.[2]

Both parties were opposed to the Western alliance. Both the Istiqlal and the National Democratic Party appealed almost wholly to the urban literate classes. Their impact on the lower classes was minimal. Neither had a widespread or tightly knit organization. Whatever their faults, however, the two parties dominated the legal opposition and helped to create and spread a climate of hostility to the establishment and its foreign tie.

Although the Iraq Communist Party was not among the licensed parties, it had roots going back to the 1930s. Its real impetus came in 1941 when Yusuf Salman, a Chaldean and a self-educated worker known as Comrade Fahd, took over the party leadership. He put together a central committee whose membership consisted primarily of journalists, teachers, and lawyers.[3] Almost half of the members were Jews, Christians, or *shi'a*, indicating the appeal of the party to the minorities and to *shi'a* still resentful of their small share of power and privilege. By 1946 the Communist Party was the best-organized political group in the country. The party's support was drawn partly from the literate intelligentsia—especially students, bureaucrats, and teachers—at the lower end of the middle-class pay scale, and partly from workers, particularly those in the vital oil, port, and railway sectors. The Communists had little influence in rural areas among the peasants. Another weakness was their lack of concern for Arab nationalism, including the Palestine issue.

Despite the flowering of new political parties, the liberalization program was short-lived. Its failure clearly demonstrated the insecurity of the regime,

its fears of instability, and the contradictions inherent in the regime's attempts to open up the political system. The activities of the newly licensed
parties, especially the intemperate attacks on the regime by the two Marxist
parties, soon confirmed the opponents of reform in their belief that an open
political system would lead only to an overthrow of the regime itself. A
strike by oil workers in Kirkuk proved so serious that even the British became worried. On 12 July workers clashed with police; eight workers were
killed and scores were wounded when police fired into the crowd. There is
little doubt that the Communist Party had a hand in fomenting the strike.

The incident, dubbed the Kirkuk Massacre by the opposition, caused an
uproar in the press, but the offending papers were suppressed. The incident
clearly worried the regime. On 16 November the cabinet resigned. The
main casualty of the affair, however, was not the cabinet but the reform program. With matters out of hand, the regent turned to Nuri to conduct an
election. To no one's surprise, the new parliament was mainly conservative
and predominantly rural. No liberalization program could be expected from
it. Interestingly, a new cabinet was formed under Salih Jabr, the first *shi'i*
prime minister in Iraq's history. A member of the younger generation educated under the mandate, he represented a step forward in the integration of
the *shi'a* into the upper echelons of power. But despite progressive views on
some issues, Jabr proved even less liberal than his predecessors. Within six
months of taking office he had banned the two left-wing parties.

The Portsmouth Treaty and the *Wathba*

The regent now turned to the second half of his reform program—revision
of the 1930 treaty with Britain, which he hoped would meet the objections
of the opposition. In this he was misguided. The treaty had always been a divisive issue in Iraqi politics, and the opposition wanted it eliminated, not
modified. The British were also skeptical of revision, fearing negotiations
would open a Pandora's box.

Nevertheless, in May 1947, negotiations with the British began in Baghdad. The major issue was who would have control over the air bases. By December a preliminary agreement had been reached on Iraqi control. A
meeting of senior politicians was then called at the palace to discuss the
treaty, but no opposition members were included.[4] The opposition parties
protested both the meeting and the fact that the treaty was not being

brought before the public for discussion. Ignoring or misinterpreting these warning signals, an Iraqi delegation left for London to complete the negotiations. There the two sides quickly reached agreement and signed the treaty at the Portsmouth naval base on 15 January 1948.

The Portsmouth Treaty was undoubtedly an improvement over the 1930 treaty. It provided for the removal of British troops from Iraqi soil and gave Iraq sovereignty over the bases, but it was hardly a treaty of equals, as the regime claimed. Iraq was still tied to Britain in terms of supplies and military training, and the agreement to surrender the bases to Britain in time of war negated any possibility of future neutrality. The life of the treaty was extended until 1973, whereas the old one had been due to expire in 1957. However, the treaty's actual provisions were not at stake; what was at stake was the continuation of a treaty at all and the whole issue of the British tie.

While the British and Iraqi delegations were exchanging congratulatory speeches in Portsmouth, events in Iraq were reaching the crisis that has come to be known as the *wathba* (rising).[5] On 16 January 1948, during a student demonstration against the treaty, police fired on the crowd, killing four people and wounding more. An uproar ensued. By the end of January, virtually every articulate element in the country—the parliament, students, professors, and the lower classes—had come out against the treaty. For a time, a real atmosphere of civil war prevailed in Baghdad.

Demonstrations and uprisings were nothing new in Iraq. What was new and startling in the current situation was the extent of the disorders, the size of the demonstrations, and the bitterness of the protest. The *wathba* showed that by 1948 the urban population at least had been thoroughly won over by the opposition, which was able to mobilize large crowds. The *wathba* inaugurated a period in which "the street" played an increasing role in political dynamics.

On 27 January, there was another clash between demonstrators and police, this one worse than any in Iraq's recent history. According to official sources, at least seventy-seven were killed and several hundred wounded; the actual numbers were undoubtedly higher. The regent was clearly frightened, and on 21 January he partially yielded to the opposition by proclaiming that the Anglo-Iraqi treaty signed at Portsmouth did not realize the country's aspirations. On 27 January, the day after Jabr returned, there was another clash between demonstrators and police, and Jabr resigned. Although it remained for the succeeding cabinet to repudiate the Portsmouth Treaty, the opposition had clearly achieved its main aims: cancellation of the treaty and the fall of Jabr's cabinet.

The *wathba* illustrated the depth and breadth of resentment, from both left and right, against the regime and its foreign connection. Though the British were silently outraged, the rejection of the Portsmouth Treaty made little real difference to them: They merely fell back on the old 1930 treaty. Inside Iraq the *wathba* gave the opposition more confidence and encouraged them to challenge the establishment more aggressively. The *wathba* made a lasting impression on Nuri, influencing his suppression of the opposition six years later when he wished to conclude the Baghdad Pact.

The Portsmouth Treaty and the *wathba* illustrated the strong tie between domestic and foreign affairs, as well as the difficulties in opening the system and managing social change. A new cycle of politics ensued. When faced with a crisis, the regent would attempt to arrange the return of Nuri and his colleagues as the only one strong enough to protect the throne. The appointment of these politicians, especially Nuri, would trigger the eruption of opposition. This would be followed by attempts to appease the opposition by bringing in new men or known moderates and temporarily removing Nuri. The opposition would seize this opportunity to push for more drastic changes in domestic and foreign policy; the situation would deteriorate; and Nuri and his cohorts would be brought back to deal with it. At each turn of the wheel the same methods were tried—street violence by the opposition and police action by the regime. In the process, no strong center group emerged within the establishment or between moderate members of the establishment and the opposition.

War in Palestine

The British treaty was not the only foreign policy problem facing Iraq. All through the Portsmouth crisis, the Palestine problem had been a gathering storm. It finally broke with the start of the first Arab-Israeli war in May 1948. The Palestine problem was the one issue that could unite the Iraqi population, *sunni* and *shi'i*, religious and secular, rich and poor. Strikes and demonstrations protesting the division of Palestine and the establishment of a Jewish state had taken place in November 1946, September 1947, and again in November 1947. By the outbreak of the war in Palestine in May 1948, Iraqi passions were thoroughly aroused.

In May 1948 Iraqi troops were dispatched to Palestine, where they fought with Jordan's Arab Legion on the central front, north and west of Jerusalem, and a swift victory was expected back home. In fact, the troops expected orders to advance, but none came, which later gave rise to accusations of betrayal on the part of Arab regimes. These circumstances came amidst a cease-fire, concluded under pressure from the UN at the end of May that worked to the advantage of the Jewish forces. When fighting resumed, the tide turned in their favor, an advantage they retained until their final victory.[6]

Although the British and the Americans received most of the blame for the debacle, the poor Arab showing in the war focused attention on the economic, social, and political conditions at home that had caused the Arab failure. It also strengthened the position of those who had been calling for greater Arab unity. These sentiments were particularly acute among the younger members of the officer corps who had fought on the front and who felt cheated out of victory.

Meanwhile, the large and well-established Jewish community in Iraq had come under attack, and its position became increasingly untenable. In 1951 the Iraqi government decided that Jews should be allowed to leave if they wished, thinking that only a few thousand would do so. To their surprise, the number exceeded 100,000, almost the entire community.[7] The withdrawal of the Jewish community left a large gap in the economy and the professions, in which Jewish expertise and foreign contacts had contributed much to Iraqi society.

Though a loss in one sense, the vacuum left—particularly in the business world—by the Jewish exodus was soon filled by enterprising *shi'a* and Christians, providing both communities with a new channel of mobility. The younger generation of *shi'a,* educated in technical and professional subjects, moved into positions in medicine, law, and finance. Some used the capital acquired by an older generation of *shi'i* landlords and merchants to become entrepreneurs, creating the backbone of a new *shi'i* middle class.

Oil and Economic Development

Despite these roiling political events, the 1950s were a decade of economic and social change, beginning in the oil sphere but spreading to other areas as well. These developments began to change Iraq in some fundamental ways. The first step in this direction was increasing Iraq's oil revenue and then turning toward long-term development. New oil agreements with IPC increased oil royalties. As a result, by the early 1950s, oil production began to

TABLE 4.1 Iraqi Oil Fields, 1960

Field and Discovery Date	Daily Average in Barrels
Naft Khana, 1923	3,300
Kirkuk, 1927	643,087
Ain Zala, 1939	18,425
Zubair, 1949	72,936
Butma, 1952	8,516
Bay Hasan, 1953	33,387
Rumaila, 1953	172,648
Jambur, 1954	11,033
Total	963,332

SOURCE: Reprinted by permission from Charles Issawi and Mohammed Yeganeh, *The Economics of Middle Eastern Oil* (New York: Praeger, 1962), p. 93.

be a major factor in Iraq's economy. Between 1952 and 1958, output and revenues doubled, raising Iraq's oil income to ID 84.6 million ($237.7 million) in 1958.[8] Large new fields were developed—in Zubair in 1949 and Rumaila in 1953; both were in the south near Basra. (See Table 4.1.) Iraq now took the first steps toward a phenomenon that would become more pronounced in later decades—increased dependence on the export of a single resource controlled by a foreign-owned company and subject to international market conditions beyond Iraq's control. In short, Iraq became a "rentier" state, dependent for its livelihood not on its productive sectors but on "rents" from oil. By 1959 oil revenues contributed some 60 percent of the government budget.[9]

Oil revenues enabled Iraq to make a sustained effort at long-term development for the first time. Seventy percent of oil revenue was now set aside for development and a Development Board, independent of the government, established to spend the funds. The Iraqi budget showed its first surplus in years. The development program was Nuri's answer to social and political unrest. Emphasis was put on long-term investment in the country's natural resources and development of infrastructure.

First priority went to agriculture, which received 33 to 45 percent of total allocations. The bulk of this went toward large-scale flood control and irrigation schemes. By 1958 a number of these projects had been completed or were near completion, including the Tharthar Dam (opened in 1956), which prevented the flooding of Baghdad; the Habbaniyya scheme, which provided a water storage facility and a dam on the Euphrates north of Ramadi; and two dams in Kurdish territory—the Dukan Dam on the Lesser Zab and the Darbandikhan Dam on the upper reaches of the Diyala.

The second priority was transportation and communications. Here too, large scale projects—roads, railroads, ports, and airports—were stressed. By 1958, 2,000 kilometers (1,243 miles) of main roads, 1,500 kilometers (932 miles) of local roads, and twenty bridges had been built, while the Basra port was enlarged and a new airport was constructed in Baghdad.[10] Allocations for industry were low. However, the Development Board did construct five electric power plants, the Daura refinery, and light industries such as cement and textile plants. No allocations were included for health and education, although funding for these areas was included in the regular budget.

The achievements of this program, particularly in harnessing the country's agricultural potential, were considerable. The area under cultivation increased and so did production. One study concluded that the area used for grain production increased 50 percent over pre–Second World War levels, while grain production increased 56 percent.[11] Despite population growth, by 1958 Iraq was self-sufficient in wheat and rice and produced enough barley to export 25 percent of its crop.[12] Most of the growth in this period, however, took place in the private sector and was due to individual investments in pumps and tractors, not the development program. By 1955 no less than 20 percent of all cultivated land was being irrigated by pumps.[13]

Though these advances were considerable, too little was done to modernize existing agricultural practices and to improve the productivity of land already under cultivation. Most agriculture was still practiced by primitive methods. Rectifying this situation would have required a substantial investment in agricultural education and help for farmers. Development along these lines was neglected mainly because of opposition from the landlords. By 1958, 70 percent of the population still earned a living in agriculture, but they produced only 30 percent of Iraq's income.[14] The government attempted to skirt the problem of land reform by appropriating development funds for the distribution of uncultivated state lands to peasants. However, these projects were too small in scope to relax the grip of the large landholders on the rural economy. In 1958 some 3 percent of large and very large landholders controlled almost 70 percent of the land (see Table A.5).

TABLE 4.2 Size of Industrial Establishments, 1954

Number of Workers in Establishment	Number of Establishments	Percentage of Total	Total Number of Workers	Percentage of Total
1	10,157	45.2	10,157	11.2
2	5,651	25.2	11.302	12.5
3	2,805	12.5	8,415	9.3
4	1,383	6.1	5,532	6.1
5	804	3.6	4,020	4.5
6–9	933	4.2	6,455	7.2
10–19	433	1.9	5,718	6.3
20–99	199	0.9	8,185	9.1
Over 100	95	0.4	30,507	33.8
Total	22,460	100.0	90,291	100.0

SOURCE: Adapted from Kathleen Langley, *The Industrialization of Iraq* (Cambridge, Mass.: Harvard University Press, 1961), p. 90. Taken from the Industrial Census of Iraq, 1954.

Meanwhile there was little industrial development to employ the rural population flowing into the cities. In 1950 it was estimated that of the 60,000 people engaged in industry other than oil, almost all were working in small undertakings where work was done mainly by hand. It was falsely assumed that industrial investment would be undertaken by private entrepreneurs. (See Table 4.2.)

While these shortcomings were structural, more serious politically was underspending in the social sphere, the origin of the regime's main problems. Little was spent on short-term projects that would have raised living standards, particularly among the volatile urban population, whose expectations increased as more oil funds were generated. These expenditures were urgently needed. In 1950 only 23 percent of the school-age population was in school; illiteracy was estimated at nearly 90 percent. By 1958 Iraq's institutions of higher education were turning out only a little over a thousand graduates a year (see Tables 4.3 and A.4.) Despite progress in health services, which had reduced epidemics, endemic diseases such as malaria and trachoma were still widespread. Only 40 percent of municipalities had safe water supplies; most had no electricity; and sewage was almost totally neglected, even in Baghdad.[15]

TABLE 4.3 College Graduates, 1958

College	Graduates
Law	164
Education	213
Engineering	82
Tahrir (women)	102
Commerce	104
Arts and Sciences	148
Medical	75
Pharmacy	29
Police	20
Divinity	58
Agriculture	44
Nonacademic Institutions	88
Total	1,127

SOURCE: Iraq, Ministry of Planning, *Report on Education in Iraq for 1957–1958* (Baghdad: Government Press, 1959), pp. 16, 26.

The Uprising of 1952

These economic and social shortcomings help explain the periodic out-breaks of violence and the emergence of "the street" as a factor in Iraq's polit-ical life. Demonstrations by students, workers, and others, often organized by the left and the ICP, would get out of control, leading to violence. This was the case with the so-called *intifada* (uprising) of 1952, the most serious outbreak of violence since the *wathba*. The unrest was sparked by events in neighboring Middle Eastern countries that created a new political climate in the area, hostile to established regimes and their collaboration with the West. The rise of Musaddiq in Iran and the Iranian nationalization of the oil company in 1951 inspired demands from the opposition in Iraq for nation-alization of IPC. In Egypt a new group of young officers successfully over-threw the monarchy on 23 July 1952 and installed themselves as rulers.

More important for Iraq, however, was a strike of port workers on 23 Au-gust 1952. Generated by a dispute between workers and the government over pay, the strike soon escalated under the leadership of the Communists. They even managed to take over Basra's generator, temporarily cutting off water and electricity in the city. Police moved in, the inevitable clash took place, and once again injury and death were the result.[16]

Things calmed down in the fall in preparation for an election, but before the election could be held, a riot erupted over an unrelated issue. On 26 October students at the College of Pharmacy struck over an amendment to the rules governing their examinations. By this time strikes had become a way of life among the student population. Before long, the localized strike turned into riots, spreading throughout other cities as well. By mid-November most of the urban centers of Iraq were in disorder. Included in the attacks was the American Information Office, indicating that the United States was associated in the public mind with the British as an unwanted power.

On 23 November Iraq's first military government was appointed under the chief of staff of the army. Martial law was announced, all political parties were banned, a number of newspapers were suspended, and a curfew was declared. Wholesale arrests of rioters and politicians—including some former ministers and deputies—ensued. This ended the *intifada,* but it marked another turning point for the regime. Although the opposition was insufficiently organized to unseat the regime, the widespread alienation of critical sectors of the population was clear. The establishment had been forced to rely on the army as well as the police to maintain order. The *intifada* also convinced many of the younger generation that more ruthless, clandestine activities would be necessary to accomplish their aims.

The Accession of Faisal II

On 24 May 1953 Faisal II reached his majority and became king of Iraq. His enthronement should have initiated a new era. He was young (eighteen), Western-educated, and had democratic ideas. As a member of the younger generation he might well have been able to identify more readily with the newly emerging Western-educated class in the cities. However, Faisal was inexperienced and shy. Educated mostly by British tutors, he was out of touch with Iraqi popular opinion. Of far more importance, Abd al-Ilah had no intention of relinquishing real power to the young king, even after 1953. For the remainder of the old regime the crown prince continued to dominate palace politics, although he no longer had the legal authority to do so. One aspect of that domination was seeking ways to isolate Nuri and to pursue his own policy. After consulting with a number of politicians, Abd al-Ilah decided on the dissolution of parliament and a new election.

The Elections of 1954

Whatever the motivation for it, the election of June 1954 has rightly been regarded as the freest in Iraq's history, although some of the usual controls were retained. It produced the country's most representative chamber. All licensed parties participated, and the campaign was intense, with some 425 candidates standing for 135 seats. When it was over, Nuri's party, though obtaining the largest single bloc of seats—51—fell below a controlling majority. The National Democratic Party returned 6 members, including Kamil al-Chadirchi; Istiqlal returned 2. Even a known Communist sympathizer was elected. To all appearances the stage was set for the revival of legal opposition and possibly some reform. This was not to be. And once again, the culprit was foreign affairs.

The Anglo-Iraqi Treaty of 1930 was due to expire in 1957, and the old treaty provided that a new one be negotiated between 1952 and 1957. For any new treaty to be negotiated and a repetition of the *wathba* avoided, most establishment politicians believed that Nuri was essential. However, Nuri laid down several conditions for his return to power—among them the dismissal of parliament and a new election.[17] This sealed the fate of the newly elected chamber and, as it would turn out, any chances for political reform.

On 27 June 1954 parliament was adjourned, and on 3 August Nuri began a systematic suppression of all political activity that surpassed any previously undertaken and began a new era in Iraq. In particular, Nuri turned against the left. A series of decrees designed to uproot the left permitted the Council of Ministers to deport persons convicted of advocating communism or anarchism or working for a foreign government, and to strip them of Iraqi citizenship. The cabinet broke off diplomatic relations with the Soviet Union. As a fitting climax to these activities, in September 1954 a new election produced what has been called "the unopposed parliament." So tightly was it controlled that before the election was held over one hundred delegates were returned unopposed, with only twenty-two seats contested.[18]

The election and the decrees effectively put an end to any open political activity for the next four years, and Iraq settled down to rule maintained by the police and the army. There is little doubt that this suppression produced sufficient stability to shepherd the soon-to-be-concluded Baghdad Pact through parliament and later to ride out the Suez crisis. But it ultimately had fateful consequences. It put almost complete power in the hands of a man increasingly unable to come to terms with the new forces about to shake the Arab world. It eliminated any challenge to Nuri from within the establishment that might have caused him to moderate his policies. The opposition, deprived of any hope of change, was driven from the halls of parliament underground, where it inevitably became more revolutionary.

The Baghdad Pact

At the time that the renegotiation of the Anglo-Iraqi Treaty began, the defense posture of the Middle East and its relations with the West were still in a fluid stage. A younger generation of Arabs wanted complete independence from the West. The older politicians, still in control in Iraq, understood the inherent weaknesses of the regime and the state and the need for some kind of support from outside.

One possibility was to join with the states of Turkey, Iran, and Pakistan in the collective defense arrangement then beginning to take shape under the guidance of US Secretary of State John Foster Dulles. This arrangement was based on loose bilateral agreements that could later be joined by other countries, including Arab states. Nuri liked the shape of this arrangement, but an alliance of Iraq, Turkey, and Iran was a connection that the Arab nationalists in Iraq had always opposed because both states were non-Arab and firmly allied with the West. The most serious problem was posed by Egypt. Due to strong anti-British forces in Egypt, Nasser felt the need to distance himself from Western alliances. Aware of the need to consult with Nasser, Nuri went to Cairo to discuss matters with him. There is no published record of the discussion, but according to those present, there may have been some misunderstanding on both sides. Nasser asked Nuri to wait but told Nuri he was free to do what he thought was best. Nuri seems to have left with the dangerously erroneous impression that he had secured Nasser's agreement to pursue a treaty of alliance with Britain and the other non-Arab countries.

On 2 April 1954 Turkey signed a treaty with Pakistan. The Turkish prime minister, urged on by the Americans, was anxious to include Baghdad. Nasser issued a warning against Arabs joining the new pro-Western bloc. Nonetheless, Nuri went forward, and on 24 February 1955 the Iraqi-Turkish agreement was signed. England joined the agreement, placing the two bases at Habbaniyya and Shu'aiba under Iraqi management in return for the right of air passage in Iraq and the use of the bases for refueling. In case of attack on Iraq, Britain would come to Iraq's aid, and the British would continue to equip, supply, and help train Iraq's military forces. In fact, a main Iraqi motive behind joining the pact was to revise the Anglo-Iraqi Treaty in a way that would neutralize domestic opposition; adhering to a regional security agreement seemed to accomplish that purpose. On 23 September Iran joined the agreement; on 3 November Pakistan followed suit. Baghdad became the headquarters of this new alliance system—known as the Baghdad Pact. The United States, which had originated the idea, did not officially join the pact, but it became a member of the pact's various committees and cooperated fully with it.

Egypt's rejection of the pact was immediate. There was no secret made of Iraq's intention to induce the other Arab countries to follow its lead. If this had been achieved, Iraq would have led the way into a new security arrangement, forming the cornerstone of a new alliance system tying the Arab countries to the West. This prospect threw down a challenge to Nasser that he could not fail to take up. Arab unity, independence from the West, and the struggle for leadership of the Arab world were at stake.

The consequences of the pact for Iraq's subsequent history cannot be exaggerated. On the positive side, the pact unquestionably strengthened Iraq's internal defenses and helped build up the state's infrastructure. Good relations with Turkey and Iran also paid internal dividends in continued peace with the Kurds and the *shi'a,* an important factor neglected in subsequent regimes. But its disadvantages were overwhelming. The Baghdad Pact split the Arab world into two camps—those favoring a Western alliance and those favoring neutrality or even joining the USSR (Union of Soviet Socialist Republics). It brought the Cold War to the Middle East and embroiled Iraq in a constant succession of foreign policy problems at a time when it needed to concentrate on the home front. It revived a heated anti-Western campaign in the area that Iraq, with its anti-Western opposition, did not need. The challenge to Nasser's leadership initiated a cold war between Egypt and Iraq, aimed at the elimination of either Nasser or Nuri. The intensity of this struggle swept all other issues aside for the next four years.

The first and ultimately most damaging manifestation of this cold war was the propaganda campaign broadcast by the Voice of the Arabs in Cairo. From the moment the first Iraqi-Turkish communiqué was issued in Baghdad, the Voice of the Arabs proceeded to vilify the entire regime that had signed the pact. Nuri's regime was unable to control this new technological weapon, the transistor radio. Heretofore, opposition had surfaced through demonstrations, strikes, and newspaper articles, which could be dealt with by arrests, police actions, and suspensions. But the Voice of the Arabs penetrated the village, the field, the barracks, and the dormitory. Gradually its message spread hostility—previously limited mainly to the urban groups—among rural areas as well, swelling the numbers of those opposed to the regime.

The Suez Crisis

In the midst of this situation, Nasser precipitated the Suez crisis. His successful nationalization of the Suez Canal in 1956 and the resulting tripartite attack on Egypt by Britain, France, and Israel, had profound repercussions throughout the Middle East. In Iraq the actions of the British in Suez undercut the regime's entire position. The Suez disaster confronted Nuri with a crisis almost as severe as the *wathba*. Throughout the remainder of 1956 the country was in an uproar. Strikes spread to Najaf and the four northern provinces, threatening to destabilize *shi'a* and Kurdish areas. In November 1956 the IPC pipeline through Syria was blown up by hostile forces drastically cutting back Iraq's oil revenues and its development program. While the disturbances tended to subside by 1957, many saw Nuri and the regime in a race against time that he appeared to be losing.

The UAR and the Federation

Before long, Iraq was faced with another foreign policy crisis. On 1 February 1958 Egypt and Syria announced the formation of the United Arab Republic (UAR). This relatively short-lived experiment was launched largely to avoid further Communist penetration in Syria, but it created immediate fears in Jordan and Iraq that the next step would be the overthrow of their own regimes by forces favorable to the union. King Husain of Jordan now took the initiative. He invited the Iraqis to Jordan and proposed, as a joint reply to the new UAR, an Iraqi-Jordanian federation. Very little discussion appears to have taken place on the merits and demerits of the federation. Like the UAR, it was formed in haste and as a reaction to external events.

The federation was negotiated in Amman between 11 and 14 February 1958. Nuri was the only one to voice skepticism from within the Iraqi establishment. He felt the federation was unnecessary and would be a burden on Iraq's finances, and events proved him correct. The constitution of the federation provided that each country was to retain its political system and gave

Jordan an escape clause that absolved it from joining the Baghdad Pact. Significantly, Iraq was to supply 80 percent of the federation's budget.[19]

The tale of the federation is soon told. One of Nuri's first acts as the federation prime minister was to invite Kuwait to join the federation, a move that would have made the federation more palatable to Iraqis. Kuwait could have shared the expenses, and many Iraqis regarded Kuwait as a part of Iraq, detached from the Ottoman Empire by the British. However, for Kuwait to join the federation, Britain would first have to recognize Kuwait's independence. The federation idea was unenthusiastically received in Kuwait, which did not want its territory or its oil resources swallowed up by Iraq and Jordan, and by Britain, which was not ready to relinquish control over Kuwait. In the early summer Nuri had an angry session over the issue with Selwyn Lloyd, Britain's foreign minister, in London. He gained few concessions.[20]

Opposition and the Establishment

While the regime was involved in federation affairs, the opposition, now underground, was coalescing into a united front. This process had begun as early as September 1953, when the Istiqlal began to cooperate with the National Democratic Party. In 1957 the Istiqlal and the National Democratic Party turned to the more radical elements in the political spectrum, forming the United National Front, which included the Communist Party and a relative newcomer to the Iraqi scene, the Ba'th (Renaissance) Party. The Arab Ba'th Socialist Party, as it was officially known, had originated in Syria in the early postwar years. Its program combined the two strands of political thought that had dominated the intelligentsia since the 1930s—pan-Arabism and radical social change. Early on, the Ba'thists had adopted the Communist tactic of cell organization, which soon made them one of the best-organized and -disciplined parties in the Middle East. Led by Fu'ad al-Rikabi, a *shi'a* from the south, the Ba'th, in this period, was nonsectarian and appealed to both *shi'a* and *sunni* Arabs.

Far more serious for the regime was disaffection in the army. Troubles in the officer corps had come to light as early as 1956, when a plot to overthrow the regime had been discovered. Though the leaders had been dispersed, intelligence sources in 1958 revealed new conspiracies.[21] Lulled into a false sense of security by his repressive tactics, Nuri evidently dismissed these signs. In May 1958 civil war broke out in Lebanon. Fearing that it might spread, King Husain asked that Iraqi troops be sent to Jordan to protect its frontiers, and this event sealed the fate of the monarchy in Iraq. Ordered to march to Jordan, the troops marched instead on Baghdad. A swiftly executed coup ended the Hashimite monarchy and Nuri's regime in the early morning hours of 14 July. At the time, few mourned their passing.

The Old Regime in Retrospect

The old regime has been much maligned by successor regimes, which have often conveniently forgotten its real accomplishments. The old regime achieved a relaxation of communal tensions, especially in the postwar period; created a professional army and bureaucracy of impressive proportions; and initiated an economic development program that would sustain revolutionary regimes for some time to come. Consciously or otherwise, it did much to create the modern Iraqi state and the beginnings of an Iraqi national identity. Despite considerable progress, however, the regime's economic achievements were not sufficient to stem the tide of opposition or to prevent the regime's overthrow.

One of the most serious of the regime's weaknesses was its continual involvement in foreign affairs at the expense of domestic problems. Nuri's declining years were spent with the Baghdad Pact, the Suez crisis, and finally the federation, while lesser men were left to deal with domestic issues. By 1956 the foreign pillar on which the regime largely rested—its alliance with Britain—had also become more of a liability than an asset in the aftermath of Britain's inept handling of the Suez crisis.

The regime's greatest weakness was its failure to build viable political institutions to support its rule. Leaders relied on the army and bureaucracy as the mainstay of the state and on martial law rather than political bargaining. The old regime refused to shift its basis of support from the rural class of tribal leaders and landlords (now augmented by the urban wealthy) to the new urban middle class. Tribal *shaikhs* and Kurdish *aghas* and landlords continued to form about 45 percent of all postwar parliaments, even though they represented few besides themselves. Urbanites, particularly from the middle and lower-middle classes, remained underrepresented in the political structure, and they rapidly came under the influence of the opposition.

The old regime allowed the opposition to dominate cultural and ideological discourse in Iraq, failing to articulate an ideology of its own that might have appealed to a broader spectrum of Iraqis. It vacillated between a policy of Iraq for the Iraqis and pan-Arab nationalism. An "Iraq first" policy could have brought social benefits to a country still attempting to integrate diverse sects and ethnic groups into a national entity, yet no such policy was articulated. While there was some integration of *shi'a* and Kurds into the organs of state, little was done to foster a distinct Iraqi identity that would encourage this trend. Rather, most politicians continued to hanker after pan-Arab policies. Perhaps the greatest disservice to the country was the regime's refusal to deal with the opposition in parliament, where opposition leaders could have achieved a measure of responsibility and experience. Instead their steady exclusion from power reinforced their isolation and their radicalism.

Failures in domestic affairs were matched by foreign policy failures. The increasingly visible British tie, the renewed treaty negotiations, and the new alliance with the West—achieved through relentless domestic suppression—only served to intensify, rather than to ease, the desire for independence and the nationalist sentiments that had been the main motive force behind Iraqi politics since 1920. The opposition had failed in 1920, 1941, and 1948 to bring the regime down; it succeeded in 1958.

5

THE QASIM ERA,
1958–1963

The "revolution" of 1958, designed to reform and modernize Iraq, instead brought a decade of instability and military dictatorship. The Western style political institutions that, fragile as they were, had begun to take root, were gutted. Progress in knitting ethnic and sectarian communities together in the new state was also unraveled, though more slowly.

Revolutionary regimes did make substantial changes in a number of directions—some badly needed. They ended the grip of the landed class and the urban wealthy over the political system and placed the new middle class firmly in power. Initially, civilian opposition politicians, particularly reformers and leftists, played a role in government. They introduced policies of egalitarianism, the spread of economic development to poorer areas and greater social mobility for the dispossessed. But it was not long before these civilians were displaced by their military colleagues and Iraq settled into a pattern of military dictatorship.

The main problem for new regimes was the absence of political structures for governance and an inability to mobilize wide enough constituencies to rule. The result was a constant attempt to overthrow the government in power—from within and from without. Between 1958 and 1968, there were four changes of regime and countless failed coups. Qasim's regime, which made a genuine attempt at reform, was too left leaning for the Arab nationalists and was overthrown by the conspiratorial Ba'th party in 1963. Their authoritarian rule, far more oppressive than Qasim's, ended in a short nine months. A "palace coup" brought Abd al-Salam Arif and then his brother, Abd al-Rahman, to government until 1968. While they were more moderate, they also relied mainly on the military to govern. The Arif regime was finally overthrown in 1968 by another combination of disgruntled military and the Ba'th, anxious for their turn at power.

With this level of instability, little could be accomplished in the realm of economic and social development. Ruling elites were badly split ideologically and in their political orientations. The left wanted concentration on Iraq and radical social change; the Arab nationalists wanted union with other Arab states. The Kurds, whose movement was now revitalized, demanded autonomy and more separation. The absence of a common agenda helped unravel the consensus underlying the state.

New regimes also realigned Iraq in foreign policy. Ties with Britain and the West were loosened and, indeed, often became acrimonious. A bitter struggle ensued with Britain over oil, with detrimental effects on Iraq's oil revenues. Closer ties, and an arms import relationship, with the Soviet Union gradually drew Iraq into the orbit of the Soviet bloc.

The Qasim era began this revolutionary process. It was most notable for its "Iraq First" orientation and its attempt at social reform. But like its historical predecessor, the Bakr Sidqi regime of 1936, which had tried to marry the military with leftist reformers, the experiment ended with the dominance of the military. The Qasim regime ushered in an era of change. But it also opened the door for a domestic struggle for dominance of the state that ended by destroying more than it could create.

The Military Revolt of 1958

The military coup that finally overthrew the monarchy and inaugurated a new era in Iraqi history succeeded more because of luck and audacity than of good planning or organization. Although the coup unquestionably reflected deep-seated discontent in the military, the Free Officers, as their movement came to be called, gave far more thought to the overthrow of the existing regime than to what would replace it. As a result, they were unprepared for the responsibilities thrust upon them. Like their civilian counterparts in the opposition, they were riddled with internal disagreements and jealousies, as well as profound differences on the direction and orientation the country should take. These very diversities would soon cause problems and open fissures in society difficult to control without increased coercion.

The Free Officers' Movement

The military had remained aloof from politics in the early postwar years, but trouble in the officer corps began again in 1952. That year's riots against the regime played a role in crystallizing discontent among the officers, but what really set them thinking about a coup was the successful military revolt on the Nile. Officers and civilians alike had been increasingly impressed with Nasser's social reforms in Egypt and his nonalignment movement.

The first revolutionary cell in the officer corps was apparently organized as early as September 1952, and by the summer of 1956, enough cells had spread to attract the attention of the chief of staff, who transferred some of the officers and demoted others. His action did break up the movement and disperse its leaders, but only temporarily.[1]

The movement revived in the autumn of 1956 under the impetus of the Suez crisis. Several new groups were formed, some apparently influenced by the liberal democratic program of the National Democratic Party (NDP) and others by the communists. Most, however, were pan-Arab in orientation. The cells were dispersed and loosely organized, but a number of these groups gradually coalesced and by 1957 had formed the Baghdad Organization, the nucleus of the Free Officers' executive committee. Brigadier General Abd al-Karim Qasim became head of the group because of his seniority in rank. The Baghdad Organization had contacts with junior officers and with other cells in various places, but in 1957 the Free Officers still numbered only between 170 and 200.[2]

The fourteen members of the central committee may be taken as fairly representative of the movement.[3] The overwhelming majority were Arab *sunni*. There were only two *shi'a*, reflecting the weakness of *shi'a* in the officer corps, and no Kurds, although a few joined the movement to represent Kurdish views. Most came from the middle or lower-middle class, although three—Qasim and the two Arif brothers, Abd al-Salam and Abd al-Rahman—came from poor families. Five had studied in England, but they were a distinct minority.

This committee functioned as the executive and planning arm of the Free Officers, but there was apparently little cohesion of aims and policy among its members. According to one member of the group, a general program was drawn up. The program called, among other things, for (1) a struggle against imperialism and an end to pacts and foreign bases; (2) the removal of feudalism and the freedom of the peasants from exploitation; (3) an end to the monarchy, together with the announcement of a republic; (4) a constitution and the establishment of a democratic regime; (5) complete recognition of the national rights of the Kurds and other minorities within the framework of national unity; (6) cooperation with all Arab countries; (7) Arab unity; and (8) the return of Palestine to its people.[4] The program was primarily concerned with foreign policy. Some kind of land reform was contemplated, but beyond the call for social justice, economic and social goals were vague in the extreme. An eventual return to civilian democratic rule was expected, but little thought was given to constitutional processes or procedures.

The 14 July Coup

When the coup finally came on 14 July, it was not the work of the Baghdad Organization, but rather of two men, Abd al-Karim Qasim and Abd al-Salam Arif, who found themselves in a position to carry it out and seized the opportunity. A close working relationship between the two men apparently developed in Jordan in 1956, when Arif was head of a battalion under Qasim's command. Upon their return to Baghdad, Qasim brought Arif into the central committee. However, the actual planning of the July coup did not take place in Baghdad, but in Jalaula, northeast of Baghdad, where both men were stationed in 1958.

The coup was triggered by the unexpected revolt in Lebanon against the pro-Western regime of President Kamil Sham'un, and the resulting fear in Baghdad and Amman that the revolt might spread to Jordan. The Twentieth Brigade, in which Arif headed a battalion, received orders to proceed to Jordan to strengthen King Husain's forces. Arif and Qasim, the latter in charge of the Nineteenth Brigade, decided to act. Arif, with his orders, was to move on Baghdad. Qasim was to remain with his brigade at Jalaula as a backup force in case resistance was encountered and then move slowly to the city later on.

Arif took charge of his brigade himself and began the march on Baghdad. In the early hours of 14 July, he occupied the broadcasting station that became his headquarters. Arif personally made the first announcement of the revolution on the radio, on behalf of the commander of the armed forces. He denounced imperialism and the clique in office; proclaimed a new republic and the end of the old regime, identified as the Rihab Palace (the monarchy) and Nuri al-Sa'id; announced a temporary sovereignty council of three members to assume the duties of the presidency; and promised a future election for a new president.

Meanwhile, two detachments of his own battalion were dispatched, one to the Rihab Palace to deal with the king and the crown prince and the other to Nuri al-Sa'id's residence. The crown prince did not resist. Had the crack royal brigade resisted, the revolt might have been put down then and there. But the crown prince, partly because of a failure of will and partly to save his life and that of the king, ordered no resistance. This sealed his fate and that of the royal family. At about 8:00 A.M., the king, the crown prince, and the rest of the family left the palace and assembled in the courtyard. There a young captain opened fire. Others joined in, and they were killed.[5] This ended any hope of restoring the Hashimite dynasty in Iraq.

The force that went to Nuri's house was less successful. Nuri had managed to escape, but on 15 July he was recognized in a street in a local quarter in Baghdad as he was trying to escape from the house of a friend disguised in a woman's black cloak. He was shot dead on the spot. His body was taken to the Ministry of Defense and quietly buried in a cemetery that night.

About noon on 14 July Qasim arrived in Baghdad with his forces and set up his headquarters in the Ministry of Defense. His late arrival gave color to suspicions that the revolution itself was carried out by Arif, not Qasim, and it was not long before Arif was to take full advantage of this. Even with his arrival, the officers were still in a precarious situation. The attitude of the remainder of the army and of the regime's allies abroad was unknown. Internal resistance in the army did not, in fact, materialize. Key officers who could offer resistance decided to wait and see what would happen. Iraq's allies were in the same quandary. King Husain, who had tried to warn the chief of staff of the Free Officers' movement some two weeks earlier, wanted to intervene, but he too hesitated, because of his own internal situation and because of lack of support from Western allies.[6] Thus a coup, organized by a small group of officers acting on an ad hoc basis, succeeded.

For most of the early hours of the revolution, Arif, an impetuous man, was in control. The first pronouncements of the revolution, promising freedom and an election, had inspired confidence, but Arif soon urged the liquidation of traitors. Uncontrollable mobs surged through Baghdad. The body of Abd al-Ilah was taken from the palace, mutilated, and dragged through the streets and was finally hung at the gate of the Ministry of Defense. Several Jordanian ministers and US businessmen staying at the Baghdad Hotel fell into the hands of the mob and were also killed. Finally, Qasim imposed a curfew, which brought some order out of chaos but did not entirely end the barbarities. The day after Nuri's burial, his body was disinterred by the mob and also dragged through the streets. The overwhelming majority of Iraqis regarded these deeds with horror and disgust. They caused irreparable damage to Iraq's international reputation and marred the revolution's image in the minds of many of its own people.

The Coup Government

The new government, agreed on by Qasim and Arif himself, had at its head a three-man sovereignty council designed to appease Iraq's three major communities, the *shi'a,* the Kurds, and the Arab *sunnis.* Muhammad Mahdi Kubba, the *shi'i,* was the former head of the Istiqlal party; Khalid al-Naqshabandi, the Kurd, was a former officer. Najib al-Rubai'i, the Arab *sunni,* was an officer and a tacit supporter of the Free Officers' movement.

A cabinet, remarkable for the spectrum of opposition it included, was also announced. It comprised two National Democratic party representatives, one member of the Istiqlal, one Ba'th representative, and one Marxist. It also included a strong representative of the Kurds and a liberal Arab nationalist.[7] Aside from Qasim and Arif, only one Free Officer, Naji Talib, was given a cabinet post (social affairs). The cabinet was a master stroke that showed considerable consultation with the politicians. It propitiated the entire opposition movement and lent the regime a legitimacy and respect that would have been difficult to achieve as a mere army movement. However, as a sign of future problems, the lion's share of power went to Qasim, who became prime minister and minister of defense while retaining his position as commander in chief of the armed forces, and Arif, who became deputy prime minister and minister of interior, as well as deputy commander in chief.

Though less evident, the cabinet and the sovereignty council were also fairly representative of Iraq's ethnic and sectarian communities. Together they comprised six Arab *sunnis,* five Arab *shi'a,* four Kurds, and one person (Qasim) of mixed *sunni-shi'i* parentage. In particular, the Kurds were propitiated by recognition as equal partners in the state. More important, the new government symbolized empowerment of the new, educated middle class which saw itself replacing an upper class of landlords and urban wealthy. There were five army officers, four professional politicians, three lawyers or judges, one civil servant, and one doctor.[8] Above all, the group signified the transition of power to the old regime's opposition.

However, this group also reflected a wide range of views that were soon to surface. First was the military-civilian dichotomy. Control by Qasim and Arif of key military and security functions left little doubt of where real power lay. Second was the range of policy orientations incorporated in the government. Included in the cabinet were liberals, Marxists, Arab nationalists, and Kurds committed to greater Kurdish autonomy. All, however, agreed on ending Western political and, if possible, economic control over the country (the Baghdad Pact, foreign bases, the Iraq Petroleum Company [IPC]), together with a reorientation in foreign policy toward the Soviet Union.

The Temporary Constitution

Thirteen days after the revolution, a temporary constitution was announced, pending a permanent organic law to be promulgated after a free referendum.[9] According to this document the state was a republic, Iraq was part of the Arab nation, and Islam was the religion of state. The Council of Sovereignty was to carry out the powers of the presidency, and the powers of legislation were vested in the Council of Ministers, with the approval of the Sovereignty Council. The executive function was vested in the Council of Ministers. Clearly there was no separation made between executive and legislative powers.

The constitution was most important for what it left unsaid. There was no mention of a new representative assembly or an election. Nothing was said, for example, about how the Council of Ministers was to be appointed and dismissed. Nor did it disentangle the army from politics. The constitution merely masked the real power structure that was emerging—joint rule by two military men behind a cabinet of respected political leaders who did not yet suspect what was in store for them.

One potential source of problems was that many Free Officers who had expected to participate in the new government through a Revolutionary Command Council (RCC) or a similar mechanism were excluded or put in subordinate positions. The disaffection of the Free Officers sowed the seeds of much future discord, but this was not the cause of the first rift in the revolutionary front. A struggle for power between the two main protagonists of the coup began no less than five days after the stunning revolt that put the country in their hands. This conflict, partly over policy directions, partly over leadership, set the parameters for the struggle of the next decade.

The Struggle for Power

The struggle must be seen in the context of the ideological conflict that now emerged in Baghdad. On one hand were opposition forces whose main thrust had been Arab nationalist and who saw the revolution as the first step toward greater Arab union. On the other were those less interested in unity than Iraqi independence from the West and thorough political and social reform at home. In this struggle the "moderate middle," lacking organization or a vision, was soon left weak and disabled. Whatever the ideological issues, they were soon subordinated to a struggle for power between two men desirous of controlling the state.

Qasim Versus Arif

The struggle between Qasim and Arif was initiated over a key policy question—union with Egypt. Arif, encouraged by the Ba'th and the Arab nationalists, favored prompt union; Qasim was more cautious in his approach to this issue. While policy issues were at stake, so, too, were personal aspirations. Despite the fact that the revolt had been a joint effort made in Qasim's name, Arif soon began to put himself in the limelight. In a widely publicized tour of the provinces, Arif made ill-considered speeches strongly advocating union with the United Arab Republic (UAR). He referred frequently to Nasser, while scarcely mentioning Qasim. There is no evidence that Qasim was opposed to better relations with other Arab countries, but Arif's challenge to his leadership and the precipitous and untimely drive for unity, particularly under Nasser's leadership rather than Qasim's, forced Qasim into action.

Qasim's patient and clever manipulation of affairs behind the scenes assured his success in the ensuing power struggle. He found opponents of unity among the Communists, who organized demonstrations in favor of Qasim and against immediate union. In September, after Arif had made another bid for leadership by reviving the idea of the RCC in a public speech (an appeal to other Free Officers), Qasim moved to retire Arif from his posts. On 30 September he was retired as deputy prime minister and minister of interior and relieved of his position in the military.

Qasim now attempted to remove Arif from the country by offering him an appointment as ambassador to Bonn. At first Arif refused, and the clash between the two men continued. Finally, Arif agreed to leave for Bonn temporarily.[10] But the agreement did not last. On 4 November, amidst rumors of an attempted coup against the regime, Arif returned to Baghdad. This time Qasim lost his patience. On 5 November Arif was arrested on charges of attempting to assassinate Qasim and of trying to overthrow the government. A month later he was sentenced to death. The sentence was commuted to life imprisonment on the recommendation of the court.

Ideological Issues

The personal aspects of the struggle for power must not obscure the genuine policy issues that were involved. In one respect, the struggle was over Iraq's new identity. Would the revolution focus on an Iraqi state in which various communities had a greater share of power, or on merging Iraq into a larger Arab entity with greater collective power to challenge the West? In another respect, it was also a struggle over how far to go in restructuring society. How much emphasis should be put on social justice, perhaps creating a state on the socialist model, and how much on liberal democratic ideals more on Western lines of parliamentary democracy? In this struggle, all elements of the opposition under the old regime played a role. In the course of the decade, one and another of these elements came to the fore, in different combinations, but the very intensity of the struggle, right from the beginning, eroded the unity of the new regime and its prospects for eventual political stability.

The chief participants can easily be identified. On the nationalist side were two main groups. A loose coalition of Arab nationalists who favored the ideal of pan-Arabism continued the tradition of the older Istiqlal Party but drew their inspiration primarily from the Egyptian revolution and often looked to Nasser for leadership. Closely allied with the Arab nationalists and drawing on much of the same support was the Ba'th Party. The major impetus for the Ba'th Party's growth came after the 1958 coup, when it utilized a surge of pan-Arab sentiment to organize and gain adherents. Nasser was not their hero, however. The Ba'th Party looked instead toward Syria, where the party had originated and where its firmest base lay. Its leadership, though unknown to the general public, was youthful and zealously committed. Its strong organization and its ideology made it a much more effective competitor in the struggle for power than the amorphous Arab nationalist group.

The leading group on the left was clearly the Communist Party. The communists continued to make inroads among the dispossessed, the *shi'a*, the Kurds, and the intelligentsia. The other main contender on the left was the National Democratic Party, the main group standing both for socialist reform and liberal democratic institutions and procedures. Qasim appeared to be leaning in their direction. Unfortunately, that party was no better organized than it had been in Nuri's day, and it soon split between those supporting and those opposing Qasim.

These four groups vied with each other for the dominant position in the state. The struggle perpetuated the old polarization of the intelligentsia between the Arab nationalists and the leftists, but this time with a difference. The older opposition groups had been rooted in liberal traditions favoring elections and an open political system; the Ba'th and the Communists were both clandestine, highly organized groups committed to a total monopoly of power, by ruthless means if necessary.

With Arif gone, the situation of the Arab nationalists and the Ba'thists deteriorated, and both groups soon attempted to recoup their losses. The fierce struggle of the next year and a half was precipitated by nationalist efforts to dominate the power struggle by removing Qasim and, in part, by a growing fear of Communist ascendancy. Qasim's increased reliance on the left was a response to this challenge. The struggle left scars that remain today. It generated a fear of chaos on the part of successive governments that soon ended any hope of returning to a democratic system. It polarized the ruling elite between nationalists and leftists, and it left a legacy of escalating violence and ruthlessness that worsened as time went on.

The Challenge of the Nationalists

The nationalist forces soon put forth a succession of challenges to Qasim. The first, and most easily deflected, came from an unlikely candidate, Rashid Ali al-Kailani, who had returned to Baghdad after seventeen years of exile. He was accused of planning a coup and on 9 December Kailani and a few of his supporters were arrested and tried. On testimony that he had been working for a union with Nasser, Kailani was sentenced to death but never executed.[11] This sentence persuaded the Arab nationalist politicians in the cabinet to resign in February 1959. Their place was quickly filled by leftists supported by Qasim.

Outside the government, the communists moved into the breach. They sent cables to Qasim urging death for Arif and other traitors and addressing him as Qasim, the "Sole Leader." They infiltrated key organizations, including the broadcasting station, the press, and the proliferating professional associations. The officer corps remained a nationalist stronghold, although the Communists made inroads there as well. To compensate for their weakness in the military, the Communists attempted to capture the Popular Resistance Force, a civil militia.

The Mosul Revolt

This rising tide of Communist influence and the Communists' radical rhetoric, which Qasim appeared to support, provoked the next—and the most
serious—nationalist challenge, the Mosul revolt. Led by Arab nationalists,
the revolt was actually inspired by a mixture of motives. It was as much anti-
Communist as it was pro-nationalist. The main leader of the revolt, was Abd
al-Wahhab al-Shawwaf, commander of the Mosul garrison. He and other officers who supported him came from conservative, well-known Arab *sunni*
families with little to gain from communism.[12] As members of the Free Officers' movement, they resented the fact that they had been shunted aside to
less important posts.

Although tentative plans for a coup had been laid by these officers, their
hand was forced prematurely by the leftists and Qasim. The Peace Partisans,
a leftist organization, announced that they would commemorate their
founding in Mosul on 6 March 1959 with a huge rally. Peace Partisans and
their Communist supporters poured into Mosul from all over Iraq, and by 6
March they numbered about 250,000. The nationalist officers decided to
act. Plans had already been made for the cooperation of two other groups
outside the army: the Shammar tribe surrounding Mosul and the UAR, now
openly hostile to Qasim. Although the Peace Partisans' rally passed without
a major outbreak, on the following day demonstrations, attacks, and coun-
terattacks escalated between the Communists and the nationalists, now reinforced by Shammar tribesmen. On 8 March the revolt was proclaimed and
fighting broke out in earnest.

From the start, the revolt suffered from haste and poor planning. Only
two units from outside Mosul joined Shawwaf. The radio transmitter from
the UAR did not arrive in time. An attempt to bomb the broadcasting station in Baghdad on 8 March failed. On 9 March Qasim sent airplanes to
bomb Shawwaf's headquarters. Shawwaf was wounded in the attack and
killed in the hospital where he went for treatment. Shortly thereafter, the
movement collapsed.[13]

For Mosul the aftermath of the revolt was far worse than the rebellion itself. As the Shammar tribes faded into the desert, Kurds looted the city and
attacked the populace. The Communists and the Peace Partisans massacred
the nationalists and some of the well-to-do Mosul families, looting their
houses. Hundreds of people were killed, the overwhelming majority of them
Arab nationalists. An informal court was established by some Communists,
and at least seventeen people, including some with no connection to the

revolt, were summarily executed. All kinds of animosities festering beneath the surface erupted. Christians killed Muslims, Kurds attacked Arabs, and the poor looted the rich. The chaos that ensued provided a stark glimpse of what might be in store for a "new" Iraq if order were not restored with a firm hand. Leaders of the revolt were swiftly taken into custody by Qasim and brought to trial. They were sentenced to death, and on 20 September 1959, under pressure from the Communists, they were executed. Others had met the same fate earlier.

The Ba'th Attempt

The failure of the Mosul rebellion, the execution of its perpetrators, and the engulfing tide of communism had convinced the Ba'th Party that the only way out was to eliminate Qasim himself. In the spring of 1959, a group of young Ba'thists, including Saddam Husain, were selected to train for the assignment. The plot was to shoot Qasim as he passed through Rashid Street in his car on 7 October. In fact, the attempt was botched and failed in its objective.[14]

The group did succeed in wounding Qasim, but he was soon discovered by a passerby, who rushed him to the hospital. Within weeks, Qasim had recovered, although the attempt undoubtedly had a substantial impact on him—and his regime—psychologically and politically. Some of the Ba'thists managed to escape to Syria, including Husain, but seventy-eight others were rounded up and taken to court where they courageously defended their acts.[15] Indeed, it was the trial and the testimony of the participants that first brought the Ba'th national attention. Some of the conspirators were acquitted; others were given the death sentence and imprisoned. None of the death sentences were carried out.

The assassination attempt was later used to glorify Saddam Husain. The way he was wounded, his removal of the bullet from his thigh, and his escape to Syria have been exaggerated, distorted, and memorialized in print and film, conveniently glossing over his mistakes.

The Challenge of the Communists

The collapse of the nationalist attempts against the Qasim regime[16] left the Communist Party as the most powerful and influential political force in the country. Well before the Ba'th attempt on Qasim, the Communists had moved to consolidate their already impressive position. Leftist officers had replaced the commanders responsible for the revolt in the north. In April 1959 the Communists began a campaign for the licensing of political parties and for representation within the cabinet. On 13 July several Communists or Communist supporters were appointed as ministers, thereby shifting the cabinet toward the radical left. Not surprisingly, the domination of the left was reflected in the regime's foreign policy and its domestic social agenda, aimed at ameliorating conditions for the poor.

Foreign policy was decisively reoriented. On 24 March 1959, two weeks after the Mosul revolt, Qasim announced Iraq's withdrawal from the Baghdad Pact, a move that had long been expected. Ties were formed with the Soviet Union, which had been permitted to reopen its embassy in Baghdad immediately following the overthrow of the old regime. These steps were followed by extensive economic, military, and cultural agreements with the USSR. The regime also took its first steps toward social reform. Among the first of several measures were those designed to help the urban lower classes. Rent ceilings were lowered and eviction by a landlord was made more difficult.[17] Price controls on foodstuffs were instituted, and merchants making excessive profits were threatened with stiff punishment, but both measures proved difficult to enforce and had to be dropped. More lasting were improvements in workers' conditions. Trade unions were now permitted, although they later came under government control. Income taxes were reduced for lower income groups. Most important of all, the regime attempted to address the festering slum problem in Baghdad. New housing allocations were immediately appropriated, and construction and slum clearance proceeded simultaneously. Many of the former slum dwellers were eventually settled in simple, sanitary brick houses, which partially replaced the Bund (Dike), the festering ghetto area that had surrounded the east side of Baghdad. The area was named Madinat al-Thaura, "City of the Revolution."

The Kirkuk Eruption
Despite these early victories, the Iraq Communist Party (ICP) recognized how precarious their position was. The hostility of the nationalists, though temporarily sidelined, was clear. Even within the reform movement, they faced some opposition. The Communists were interested in moving toward the Soviet model of state control over the economy and society and the development of mass organizations that they could control. The NDP wanted redistribution of income to the middle and lower classes, political liberties and elections, and the reinstitution of a more responsive and representative

parliament. The issue of communist control of the state was stirring even greater animosity from conservative elements in society. Some in the party reckoned that they would need to move fast to consolidate their gains or the regime might turn on them as had happened in the past. They determined to eliminate their enemies first.

Kirkuk, the Communists reckoned, would be an ideal location for the intimidation of their adversaries. The leading families in the city were Turkman. They formed a well-educated, relatively conservative group of upper and middle-class bureaucrats, merchants, landowners, and businessmen. The town was also inhabited by a substantial number of Kurds, many of whom had migrated there to work for the oil company as laborers. A number of Kurds had joined the Communist Party; others belonged to the Kurdistan Democratic Party (KDP), which was allied with the Communist Party. Kirkuk also had a large concentration of oil workers, who could be mobilized by the Communists. Flushed by the earlier success they had achieved in Mosul, the Communists attempted to achieve a similar victory in Kirkuk.

The Communists announced that on 14 July 1959, the first anniversary of the revolution, they would hold a rally in Kirkuk, designed to show mass support for the party. Unfortunately, matters got out of hand. A bloody battle followed in which at least thirty were killed and over a hundred injured.[18] As in the Mosul revolt, traditional animosities between the Kurds and the Turkman erupted. The Kurds were responsible for most of the deaths.

The Decline of the Communists

The Kirkuk affair sealed the fate of the Communists. On 20 July Qasim condemned the episode as barbaric. A number of Communists responsible for the event were rounded up and sent to a special martial law court, where they were tried in secret. Some were sentenced to death. In Baghdad, Communist Party leaders denounced the criminal acts committed, but the damage had been done. In retrospect, this episode represented the high tide of Communist influence. Qasim now moved to clip the wings of the extreme left. The Communist press was gradually extinguished, and the Communist newspaper was banned for nine months and soon disappeared. Many communists in high posts were gradually removed. Communists and their supporters were dismissed from the cabinet. Despite these setbacks, the Communists still supported Qasim. They remained his main support until the end of his regime, and a number of Communists retained their high posts.

The wave of Communist activity has raised questions as to whether the party actually could have captured the government. In retrospect this seems unlikely. Although there was a groundswell of new Communist members in 1959 (20,000 to 25,000), the hard core of the ICP was much smaller. In the mid–1950s, it had only about 500 registered members.[19] They were largely helped into power by Qasim to counteract the nationalist threat; to the end, they remained dependent upon him, and he had no intention of relinquishing power. Nor did the party hold sufficiently strong appointments in the bureaucracy and the army to take power. Qasim's supporters were preponderant in these crucial areas. Realizing the inherent weakness of their new membership and fearing a bloody civil war if they pushed the issue too far, the majority backed away from confrontation with Qasim and contented themselves with a supportive, rather than a dominant, role.

Even if the party had wished to take over the government, it would not have been able to accomplish this without the backing of its ally the Soviet Union, and the Soviet Union was opposed to a takeover. The Soviets did not wish to risk retaliation from the West nor to assume economic responsibility for Iraq if the Western powers should use oil as a weapon against the regime. Above all, they were unwilling to risk their newly won position in Egypt for an as yet unknown regime in Iraq.[20]

Attempts to Liberalize and Their Failure

The negative effect of Kirkuk did not prevent an attempt at some liberalization. Partly in response to pressure from the Communists and partly to generate popular support for himself, Qasim announced on the anniversary of the revolution in 1959 that a permanent constitution would be drawn up and political parties licensed by January 1960. The constitution never materialized, but the political parties did. On 1 January 1960 a new law of associations was proclaimed. The action was widely hailed as a return to much-needed normalcy and as a step toward the promised freedom long sidetracked in the grisly power struggle. This hope proved ephemeral. Qasim soon showed that he was not, in fact, interested in the creation of any parties that could possibly challenge his leadership.

Formation of Political Parties

Among the first to apply for licenses were two parties, both calling themselves Communist. One represented the Iraq Communist Party and its central committee; the other, unquestionably instigated by Qasim, was headed by a dissident Communist Party member. The latter party was quickly granted a license, while the real Communist Party, despite its willingness to make concessions on its programs, was refused. The National Democratic Party was also divided over the issue of whether to support Qasim. The party head, Kamil al-Chadirchi, disillusioned by the military dictatorship, refused to do so. Nonetheless, the NDP was awarded a license. This caused Muhammad Hadid, a leading member and a finance minister in Qasim's cabinet, to resign both from the party and the government. He organized a party of his own, the National Progressive Party, but it had no real support.

Several other parties applied for licenses, with mixed results. The Kurdistan Democratic Party (KDP) received a license because of its favorable attitude toward Qasim, but it was soon harassed when it took a position of opposition. Two Muslim-oriented parties came into the field: the Islamic Party and the Tahrir (Liberation) Party. Both were refused licenses, but the former, which had the backing of the powerful *shi'i mujtahid* Muhsin al-Hakim, appealed to the Court of Cassation and won its case. The Islamic Party took a decidedly anti-Communist line and was increasingly hostile to Qasim. Its license was withdrawn in 1961 and some of its leaders jailed. For obvious reasons, no Arab nationalist parties applied for licenses.

The parties initially issued programs and engaged in political activities. With the Communists and the Arab nationalists sidelined, most parties were essentially "Iraq First" in orientation and relatively moderate in their demands. In time they should have been able to take root, but it soon became clear that there was no hope of achieving power under Qasim. As time went on, the projected constitution, with its presumed legislature, elections, and public legal system, did not appear, and the political parties gradually disappeared. In the spring of 1961 the KDP ceased to function (many of its central committee members were in jail); the rump Communist Party had never really functioned. In October 1961 Chadirchi closed the NDP and ceased publishing its newspaper, *Ahali,* claiming that parties could not work under military government. By the end of 1961 the short-lived multiparty experiment had come to an end, although Hadid continued his activities until July 1962, when he too finally gave up.

The Mahdawi Court and the Rule of Law

The revolution also failed to establish a rule of law. Indeed, official violence practiced by the state increased substantially. Ad hoc trials, random imprisonment, and the use of torture became a regular part of the state apparatus. Iraq's human rights record, never flawless under the old regime, began a steady downward cycle. The most visible mechanism in eroding the rule of law and entrenching Qasim's position was the notorious Mahdawi Court.

The function of the Mahdawi Court, established in August 1958, was to try Old Regime leaders. Under the nominal direction of Fadil Abbas al-Mahdawi, a cousin of Qasim's, the court was in fact controlled by Qasim. The first proceedings of the court were conducted in a relatively quiet and dignified manner. Gradually, Communist influence increased in the courtroom, as elsewhere, and the tone and proceedings of the trials altered radically. The court became a platform to attack the British and Americans and to praise Nasser. Once relations between Iraq and Egypt soured, of course, Nasser was attacked just as savagely.

The court rapidly became a "show," or as some said, a circus. It featured speeches against the accused, poetry recitations, and homilies by the court's president on a wide variety of subjects. Standards of justice deteriorated rapidly. By the end of 1959 the court trials were discontinued, but by then they had eliminated Qasim's enemies, thoroughly cowed the opposition, and created sufficient fear in Iraqi political circles to allow Qasim to govern alone.

Qasim, the "Sole Leader"

With the failure of political parties, the collapse of a rule of law, and no constitution on the horizon, Iraq settled down for the first time to a period of genuine military dictatorship from which it would not easily escape. By 1961 all civilian politicians of any note had withdrawn from the cabinet. Thereafter, Qasim appointed either officers obedient to himself or the usual array, prevalent in all military regimes throughout the Middle East, of technocrats and civil servants with no political affiliations.

Qasim had begun his political career with good intentions and democratic leanings, and he succeeded in bringing respected opposition politicians to power. His was the first real attempt at a redistribution of domestic power. But the parties were too fractious and their bases of power too weak to build on. In the end, the institutions of the military and the bureaucracy proved far stronger.

Qasim's own background and personality proved an obstacle, as well. Born into a relatively poor family from Baghdad, he had not distinguished himself academically. From the first, his teachers and colleagues noted his withdrawn and aloof nature, a trait that seemed to become more accentuated after the assassination attempt. This was an event that marked a turning point both in Qasim's attitude and capacity. His grip on affairs slipped markedly. He became more withdrawn and isolated, virtually barricading himself in the Ministry of Defense, where he now lived, spending fourteen hours a day working, most of them in the small hours of the morning.[21] The remainder of Qasim's rule (after 1961) was marked by his increasing inability to acquire real control over the political situation.

The Social and Economic Revolution

The political struggles of the first two years should not obscure the social and economic revolution that was begun under Qasim, although the measures taken did more to destroy the edifice of the old regime than to construct the foundations of the new. Political instability slowed progress to a halt, yet the reforms initiated by Qasim at the beginning of his rule are still important, for as the decade wore on, the revolutionary impetus was renewed. Much of the reform effort had an ad hoc quality. Nonetheless, the general thrust was designed to benefit and empower the middle—and sometimes the lower—classes and to use the state apparatus to develop Iraq's resources, especially its oil and industry, as freely as possible from Western control.

Land Reform

The most significant and far-reaching revolutionary program undertaken by the regime was land reform. First, reformers began to dismantle the old feudal structure of the countryside. The 1933 Law of Rights and Duties of Cultivators, which had virtually placed the peasant in servitude to the landlord, was replaced, as was the Tribal Disputes Code, which had provided a separate system of justice for tribesmen. Henceforth, all Iraqis would be judged according to common civil and criminal codes. This was a long overdue step in bureaucratic modernization and national unity.

The Agrarian Reform Law, promulgated on 30 September 1958, attempted a large-scale redistribution of landholdings and placed ceilings on ground rents. Holdings were henceforth to be restricted to 1,000 dunams of irrigated land; 2,000 of rain fed. Compensation was to be paid to the landowners for their lands in 3 percent government bonds over a period of twenty years. The land was to be distributed among the peasants in lots of 30 to 60 dunams in irrigated areas; 60 to 120 in rain-fed lands. The farmers were expected to pay for the land, with an additional charge of 20 percent of the value for the expenses of distribution, together with 3 percent interest over a period of twenty years. Expropriations and distribution, to be completed over a five-year period, would be overseen by a ministerial committee under the prime minister. The law also provided for the establishment of cooperative societies to replace the services the landlords had provided. The law set a scale of rents and fees to be paid the landlord. The fixed rents gave the peasant between 55 and 70 percent of the total crop.[22]

The reform law was ambitious in conception but relatively conservative in the amount of land it left to the landlords. It left midlevel landowners in possession of their land, although it raised the peasants' share. In spite of this, the reform ran into difficulties from the first. Even before the legislation was drafted, peasants in the south took matters into their hands. In the late summer and fall of 1958, peasants swept through Kut and Amara, looting and sacking landlords' property, burning residences, and destroying accounts and rent registers. The spontaneous movement was quickly joined by the Communists, who urged the peasants on and moved rapidly into the countryside to organize them. The Communists established peasant societies and infiltrated their leadership. The societies were then amalgamated into a National Federation of Peasants, which the Communists then demanded be recognized as the legal authority for land distribution.[23]

These events shocked the landlords, who were frightened by the drift to the left and the specter of incipient anarchy. Many refused to cooperate with the government. They locked up their pumps and machinery and moved to the city, thus putting large areas out of production. In July 1959 Qasim was forced to conciliate the landlords by raising their share of the crop. He also postponed the expropriation of land belonging to some landlords and leased tracts to others in order to keep production going. In the meantime, disputes over land policy arose in the cabinet between the Communists, who wanted the state to retain as much land as possible and eventually to establish state farms, and the moderates, led by the NDP, who envisioned widespread distribution and the evolution of a class of small landowners.

Eventually the latter won, but not without a slowdown in the application of the law and increased uncertainty about its direction.

Even without political problems, the economic and social difficulties of applying the Agrarian Reform Law were enormous. Most important was the problem of distribution, which required extensive state machinery not yet in existence. As a result, some 4.5 million dunams of land had been expropriated by 1963, but only about 1.5 million had been distributed.[24] Even for those who received some land, inadequate facilities were available for cultivation and marketing. Without supervision, and especially without management of water distribution in the south, the peasant was lost. Moreover, the landlord had frequently been a tribal leader as well, responsible for many social and quasi-governmental functions. These could not be immediately replaced by the government. As a result, throughout much of the countryside the populace lapsed into old ways. The landlord leased his land from the government but continued to function as a patriarch, or his place was often taken by his *sirkal,* or agent. Production declined drastically. By 1961 Iraq had ceased exporting barley and was importing rice and wheat to cover 40 percent of its consumption.[25]

The Personal Status Law

The agrarian sector was not the only area in which Qasim attempted to bring about greater equality. He also helped raise the status of women. In December 1959 he promulgated a significant revision of the personal status code regulating family relations, traditionally governed by Islamic law. One of its provisions (article 3) severely limited the right of polygamy. Men were forbidden to take a second wife without the authorization of a judge, and then only for legitimate reasons. Articles 8 and 9 stipulated the minimum age for marriage as eighteen, which could be lowered in special cases to sixteen, thus eliminating child marriage. Article 35 protected women against arbitrary divorce by invalidating divorces pronounced by a man under certain circumstances. Most interesting and most revolutionary was a provision (article 74) that, through an indirect legal mechanism, gave women equal rights with men in matters of inheritance. The new code applied to both *sunnis* and *shi'a,* thus bringing all Iraqis under one law.[26] Although not as radical as laws promulgated earlier in Turkey or Tunisia, the revised code clearly showed a liberal intent. Unfortunately, it aroused considerable opposition among religious leaders and conservative elements and did not survive intact after Qasim's regime.

Economic Development

In other fields as well, the revolutionary regime showed a sharp change of direction from its predecessor. Education was greatly expanded. The education budget was raised from nearly ID 13 million ($36 million) in 1958 to ID 24 million ($67 million) in 1960, almost doubling the budget of the old regime.[27] Enrollment increased at every level. Unfortunately, the advance in quantity was often made at the expense of quality.

The new regime also displayed a new attitude toward economic planning and the priorities of investment. It adopted the concept of a planned economy, partly influenced by the Soviet model and partly by a desire for more rapid economic development. The Development Board was dismantled, and in 1959 a Ministry of Planning was created. In December 1959 a provisional revolutionary plan was published, to be succeeded in 1961 by a more detailed five-year plan. These plans indicated a new set of priorities. Social welfare and investment in housing, health, and education received considerable attention, whereas the share devoted to agriculture and irrigation was greatly reduced. The largest share of investment—30 percent—went to industry. Interestingly, the 1961 plan almost exactly reversed the priorities of the old regime. Industry was placed at the top and agriculture at the bottom. Little of the plan was implemented before Qasim fell.[28]

Qasim's Oil Policy

Perhaps the most far-reaching of Qasim's economic moves was in the field of oil policy. It set the stage for the more radical measures to follow. If there was any rationale behind Qasim's policy, it was to reduce the influence of the oil companies over Iraq's economy and to gain control over the country's major resource. In this the Iraqis were ultimately successful.

In 1961 oil revenue provided 27 percent of total national income and 90 percent of all foreign exchange.[29] Iraq's dependence upon oil was clearly recognized by Iraqi leaders, and in the early months of the revolution, the regime made no move to disturb existing conditions. But the new regime had inherited a number of oil problems, and in the spring of 1959 negotiations were begun with IPC. They continued off and on until October 1961.

There were at least a dozen points of difference with IPC. The two most important from the Iraqi point of view were the demand for 20 percent Iraqi ownership of IPC and relinquishment by IPC of the unused portion of its concession area. Iraqis insisted that the company relinquish 75 percent of the concession immediately and more later, until it held only 10 percent.

Qasim proved to be an intransigent and somewhat erratic negotiator, but the parent companies in IPC were also clearly insensitive to the Iraqis' real grievances.[30] Although willing to concede minor points, they were not yet ready to compromise on the fundamental changes demanded by the Iraqis, as they would then have to institute these changes in other countries as well—in fact, undoing much of the concessionary system in the area.

On 11 October 1961, after a number of stormy sessions and delays for consultations with the parent companies, Qasim delivered an ultimatum to IPC. Iraq would give up the demand for 20 percent ownership if IPC would relinquish 90 percent of its territory, increase the government's share of the profits, and grant Iraq partnership with IPC in developing the remaining 10 percent. IPC could not agree to this sudden proposal, and negotiations broke off. On 11 December Qasim replied by announcing Public Law 80, which dispossessed IPC of 99.5 percent of its concession territory, leaving it to operate only those areas currently in production. He announced the establishment of an Iraq National Oil Company (INOC) to exploit the new territory. IPC protested and demanded arbitration, which the Iraqis did not accept. Recognition and acceptance of PL 80 by IPC then became a prime Iraqi aim, indeed a sine qua non of future negotiations.

The effects of PL 80 were far-reaching. The law began the battle to remove foreign control over the economy and to isolate the foreign oil interests that had been a key support of the Old Regime. It put much oil territory into the hands of the government, including the rich Rumaila field in the south, which had previously belonged to the Basra Petroleum Company (BPC). At the same time, it did not touch the current flow of oil, since IPC continued to produce from the Kirkuk field. Although other points of disagreement were not yet settled, the government could now develop its own oil resources in competition with the foreign-owned IPC. This would not happen for some time, however.

PL 80 also had negative effects. Iraq was ahead of its time with its demands. Market conditions in the early 1960s and the interests at stake in the parent companies' concessions elsewhere did not incline them to begin the whole process of change in the concessionary structure in Iraq, one of their least important producers. As a result, the law initiated a long, protracted, and costly struggle with IPC, which resulted in reduced income for Iraq and a slipping production position with respect to other Gulf producers.

Erosion of National Unity

Whatever the benefits of social and economic reforms initiated by Qasim, they could not compensate for the other flaws in his administration: the gradual concentration of power in his own hands, his increasingly erratic and unsophisticated leadership, and the lack of a coherent vision for the future. Qasim's regime should have been favorable to ethnic and sectarian integration and the development of an Iraqi identity. Qasim himself came from mixed *sunni-shi'i* parentage—and focused on domestic reform. The regime was more generous in recognizing Kurdish rights. But in fact, the regime failed to prevent serious erosion of Iraq's national unity. The revolution itself had unleashed forces, including ethnic and religious aspirations, long repressed or dormant. These now reemerged. After the struggles of the first two years and the attempted assassination, the drive for order overtook the impetus for reform. By 1960 Qasim came to think of himself as the embodiment of the nation. As the drive for uniformity and control intensified, Iraq's fragile national unity began to unravel.

The Shi'i Revival

One unintended consequence of the Qasim era, and especially its left-leaning social and economic reforms, was a revival of *shi'i* activism, long dormant during the Old Regime. The intense secularism of the regime and its support for leftist policies soon provoked a reaction from conservative *shi'i* elements and a religious revival among *shi'i* youth. The same reforms that garnered support among the poor, generated fear and alienation on the part of *shi'i* landlords and merchants and, more important, opposition from the *shi'i* clerics, many of whom had derived income from a religious tax (*khums*) on tribal leaders and wealthy *shi'a*. The clergy also disapproved of the Personal Status Law and the appeal of Marxism to *shi'i* youth and took steps to counteract them. In 1960 the chief *marji'* (religious source), Muhsin al-Hakim, issued a *fatwa* (religious decree) against communism and was instrumental in the formation of the Islamic Party, reversing a long period of *shi'i* political passivity in Iraq.[31] At the same time, the removal of Old Regime constraints and the current regime's loosening political control provided space for the emergence of new groups.

Among the *shi'a* two important Islamic groups emerged. While both were dedicated to the revival of Islamic ideals, they were different in orientation

and support. The Society of Ulama was a group of senior and some junior
clerics from Najaf, formed in 1960.[32] Propelled by the rising tide of communism and by the enactment of the personal status law in 1959, the group was
committed to reasserting religious values. The society helped spread mosques,
schools, and services to other cities and encouraged a wide variety of *shi'i*
activities and organizations.

Even more important over the long run was the Da'wa (Islamic "call"),
which began among a younger generation of laymen and junior members of
the clerical establishment.[33] The Da'wa was interested in reshaping Islam
and its teachings to meet the needs of the modern world and in organizing
to protect and spread these ideas. It is not entirely clear when the group was
first formed. Some have put it just before 1958; others just after.[34] A rising
young cleric, Muhammad Baqir al-Sadr became its chief intellectual guide.[35]
A slight majority of its members were clerical, but the group also included
members with degrees in modern subjects like engineering. Sadr also gave
the movement the intellectual vision needed to reshape traditional *shi'i* ideas
through two seminal studies he published, one on Islamic philosophy
(1959) and the other on Islamic economics (1961). His works had widespread appeal. The Da'wa became a political party—with a cell-based structure like that of the Communist Party, functioning underground, in secret,
for some time. It aimed at the eventual establishment of an Islamic state. In
its early phase the Da'wa was universalist, willing to cooperate with *sunni*
groups. However, such cooperation was minimal. In fact, the Da'wa came to
be an expression of *shi'i* religiopolitical aspirations.

While these activities did not yet challenge the Iraqi state or its unity,
they revitalized *shi'i* consciousness and created new organizations and networks able to mobilize large numbers of *shi'a* for change within the state.
The result was the beginnings of a more modern, but distinct, *shi'i* identity,
imbedded in a framework of opposition to the regime and the state as it was
presently structured.

The Reemergence of the Kurdish Question

Even more serious in eroding national unity was the reemergence, in virulent form, of the Kurdish question. This is somewhat surprising, since the
Qasim regime moved, at least initially, to accommodate the Kurds and some
of their nationalist aspirations. Most Kurds had supported the revolution of
1958 enthusiastically. One reason was the temporary constitution promulgated by Qasim and Arif, which stipulated that Kurds and Arabs would be

partners in the new state. Another was the return of Mustafa-l-Barzani and his followers from exile. Barzani was given a triumphal entry into Baghdad, put up in the palace of Nuri's son, and given a cash allowance for himself and his retinue. A Kurdish paper, *Khabat* (the struggle), was published openly.

However, the honeymoon between Qasim and Barzani did not last long. Qasim, who had brought Barzani back to Baghdad partly as a counterforce to the Arab nationalists, soon began to fear that demands for Kurdish autonomy within the Iraqi state, if truly granted, would lead to Kurdish independence. For his part, the Kurdish leader increasingly came to distrust the "Sole Leader's" all-embracing concept of himself as leader of a united state. He rightly suspected Qasim of giving only lip service to Kurdish demands for autonomy.

The return of Barzani was critical to the revival of the Kurdish insurgency. Qasim had a formidable opponent in Barzani. At fifty-five Barzani had been fighting the central government and rival tribal groups off and on since 1931 and had demonstrated his military capacity time and again. His strength came from the guerrilla forces he could muster and from the Barzanis, a group of tribal followers from the village of Barzan, his birthplace and headquarters. It was not long before Barzani began mobilizing tribal support. In this effort he was assisted by Qasim's land reform program, bitterly opposed by Kurdish landlords in the north. Barzani's fighting force grew from about six hundred armed men in 1961[36] to about 5,000 a year later. In addition, he had another 20,000 from other Kurdish tribes.[37]

Barzani was not the only factor in the revival of the Kurdish movement. Qasim also had to contend with the Kurdistan Democratic Party—the urban, professional wing of the Kurdish movement. By 1958 the KDP had come under the influence of left-wing intellectuals. At its first party congress in 1947, the KDP had modeled its party structure on that of the ICP and adopted a very progressive, anti-imperialist platform.[38] The party was now led by Ibrahim Ahmad, its secretary general, and Jalal al-Talabani, his younger son-in-law, a member of the KDP politburo since 1953. Both were leftist middle-class lawyers. In January 1960, when Qasim licensed parties, the KDP received a license, and in May 1960, at its fifth party congress, Barzani was elected its head.

However, relations between the two wings of the Kurdish movement were tense and fractious. Although the splits were papered over, the differences remained profound. Barzani represented the landed establishment and the wealth and power of the *aghas;* the party leadership under Ahmad and Talabani, the town-bred intellectuals interested in reform as well as Kurdish rights. Both, however, aimed at recognition of Kurdish autonomy.

In 1960 and early 1961 the situation was still fluid. Barzani had gradually become dissatisfied with the lack of progress in meeting Kurdish demands. In October 1960 he went to Moscow to complain to the Soviet leaders of Qasim's treatment of the Kurds and to seek Soviet pressure on Qasim to meet Kurdish demands. In this he was unsuccessful. In his absence, however, Qasim began to clip his wings. He took back Barzani's house, his car, and his subsidy. Qasim also began to encourage Barzani's tribal enemies to move against him. When Barzani returned from the Soviet Union in January 1961, he moved from Baghdad to Barzan, where he could mobilize his tribal support and move against his opponents. From these tribal skirmishes Barzani emerged victorious. At the end of August, much strengthened, he sent an ultimatum to Qasim, demanding an end to authoritarian rule, recognition of Kurdish autonomy, and restoration of democratic liberties.

The Kurdish War

Earlier in September, tribes loyal to Barzani attacked an army column, and Qasim responded by bombarding Barzan village and other surrounding hamlets. This event was pivotal. Barzani now decided on an all-out revolt. Events moved swiftly, and both parties were soon involved in what would prove to be a long, drawn–out conflict. What had started as a tribal clash had now escalated to a full-fledged war for Kurdish autonomy. Before long, it enlisted the support of not only the tribal contingents, always ready to fight, but the sophisticated urban intellectuals as well.

Although the KDP had played virtually no role in these tribal events, on 23 September the party was banned in Baghdad and several of the leaders were arrested. In December 1961 the leadership met in the north and agreed to support the revolt. Although far weaker than Barzani, by 1962 they had about 650 *peshmergas* (party militia).

As the fighting began in earnest, Barzani's tribal forces were boosted by Kurdish army officers who deserted the regular army to go over to his side, strengthening the rebels and also providing much-needed arms. At the same time, their defection weakened the regular army. By 1963 many Kurdish tribes had also joined the rebels, and it was estimated at the end of that year that for every three Kurds fighting for the government, there were four fighting for Barzani. Adopting guerrilla tactics, the rebels held their strongholds in the mountains and ambushed army garrisons in the cities, cutting off their supply lines. They never attempted to hold sizable cities (where they often went to buy grain), but gradually the cities became isolated and surrounded, while the more remote outposts were in danger. In these encounters the Kurds came out ahead, consistently growing stronger in morale and in weapons.

By the spring of 1962, the war was costing Qasim considerable money and prestige. In the summer of that year, the headquarters of the first army division, usually stationed in Diwaniyya, had to be moved to Mosul. Meanwhile, the regular army, now essential to Qasim if he was to remain in power, was considerably demoralized because of its inability to defeat a much smaller group of Kurdish irregulars.[39]

Although the war was by no means entirely Qasim's fault, it badly sapped his strength at home and distracted his attention from other problems. Development slowed, and the opposition began to regroup. In order to garner some needed support, especially among the Arab nationalists and the Ba'thists, Qasim released their members from prison, whereupon they reorganized and began to plot the overthrow of the regime. During the early days of 1963, contact was made between the Ba'thists and the KDP, and a tentative agreement appears to have been reached that if Qasim could be overthrown, Kurdish autonomy would be granted. This unlikely alliance is remarkable mainly in revealing the extent of Qasim's internal isolation.

Foreign Policy Failures

Qasim's domestic isolation was more than matched in foreign affairs. The revolution of 1958 had made a fundamental change in Iraq's foreign policy orientation. Formerly dependent on the West, primarily Great Britain but also the United States, for arms and economic support, Iraq now turned to the Soviet Union as a substitute, swayed mainly by the Qasim regime's anti-imperialist outlook as well as the rising influence of the left. The shift was to prove permanent, putting Iraq in the Soviet orbit for decades and distancing it from the West and its regional allies. On 16 March 1959 Iraq signed an extensive economic agreement with Moscow, the first of several. It provided Iraq with a substantial loan. The funds were to be used for industrial equipment for steel, electrical, glass, and textile industries; railway projects; oil exploration; technical training; and help with the agrarian reform program.[40] Russian technicians increasingly replaced the departing Americans and British. Meanwhile, a series of cultural exchanges took place. By 1959 there were almost eight hundred Iraqi students studying in the USSR, mostly at Soviet expense. Eastern bloc films and books were imported. Tourism to these countries was encouraged, as were exchanges of professional groups.

These cultural and educational exchanges were paralleled by arms deliveries, which would henceforth tie Iraq's military establishment to the Soviet Union rather than to the West. Late in 1958 a squadron of MIG-15 fighters was delivered, followed by later deliveries of MIG-17s and MIG-21s, transport aircraft, and helicopters. In February 1959 the first deliveries of 100 to 150 Soviet tanks took place. More followed. The Iraqi air force was reorganized and modernized under Soviet aegis.[41]

The Rupture with the West

Soviet help, however, did not entirely compensate for Iraq's alienation of the West. Both Britain and the United States were surprised and taken aback by the 1958 revolt, and both considered military action against the regime, urged on by regional allies such as Turkey, Iran, Jordan, and Israel. This was soon rejected as impractical, although both sent forces, temporarily, to the area—the United States to Lebanon, acting under the Eisenhower doctrine of 1957, and the British to Jordan. After the initial shock had dissipated, however, British and American reactions to the regime soon diverged. The British, still smarting from the Suez crisis and the failure of their 1956 tripartite action against Egypt, saw the main regional threat as an expanding Arab nationalism led by Nasser. They soon recognized that Qasim was an Iraqi—not a pan-Arab—nationalist and would not accept Arab unity if it meant subordinating himself to Nasser. In their view, Iraq could be a convenient buffer against expanding Egyptian influence.[42] While the United States also feared Nasser's brand of radical Arab nationalism, its fear of communism was greater, and it was slower than the British to recognize Qasim's independent policy. By the time it did, however, the rising tide of communism in Iraq had become Washington's major focus, supplanting Arab nationalism as a threat. Regardless of these Anglo-American differences, neither country was ever able to restore its previous position in Iraq, and in time, Britain too became increasingly disillusioned with Qasim. By 1961 acrimonious negotiations over oil, and Qasim's abrupt claim to Kuwait, had lost him what little British support he once had.

Tensions with Iran

Iraq's increased alienation from the West was matched by its deteriorating relations with its regional neighbors, especially Turkey and Iran. Turkey was concerned about the rupture of the Baghdad Pact, the increase of Communist and Soviet influence in Baghdad, and eventually, about rising Kurdish insurgency across its border. But relations with Turkey were less threatening than those with Iran, which deteriorated rapidly. The overthrow of the monarchy in Iraq, the leftward shift of Qasim's government, and the increased Soviet influence in Iraq worried the shah. Iraq's withdrawal from the Baghdad Pact all but ended cooperation between these powers on the Kurdish front, and as time went on, the Iranian and Iraqi Kurds began to cooperate across the border.

The first arena of disagreement, however, was over the Shatt al-Arab. Tensions rose along with accelerated border skirmishes.[43] In November 1959, Iran questioned the validity of the 1937 agreement, which had drawn the border at the low-water mark on the Iranian side and given Iraq control of the shipping channel. In December 1959 Qasim reacted to Iran's reopening of the dispute by nullifying the agreement. Iran then made a counterclaim to a boundary in the center of the channel along the entire Shatt. However, by April of that year the two powers had agreed to settle their differences by negotiation.

Qasim also asserted Arab interests in the Gulf, another shift of policy from the Old Regime. He began by laying claim to Arabistan (the Arab name for the province of Khuzistan in Iran), which contained a majority of Iranians of Arab descent, an action further alienating Iran.

Meanwhile, Qasim's domestic victory over Arif and the pan-Arabists had profound regional repercussions. Qasim represented a serious obstacle to Nasser's regional influence and even a threat to the recent Syrian-Egyptian union.[44] The open quarrel between Iraq and the UAR became a major feature of the Qasim period. Relations reached a point just as low as they had been under the Old Regime. The propaganda war began again, with Iraqis calling Nasser the new "Pharoah of the Nile" and Egyptians calling Qasim the "divider of Iraq," a pun on his name, which means "divider" in Arabic. The crowning blow came in 1961, when Qasim took one final step in foreign affairs that made his isolation virtually complete. This was the notorious Kuwait affair. In retrospect, this early episode was a forerunner and a warning of the much longer 1990 crisis, but there is little doubt that Qasim's handling of the affair was inept and hastened the demise of his regime.

The Kuwait Affair

The episode began in June 1961, when Britain and Kuwait agreed to terminate the agreement of 1899, which had made Kuwait a virtual British protectorate, and recognize Kuwait as an independent state.[45] While other countries hastened to send congratulatory cables, Qasim sent the Kuwaiti ruler an ambiguous message, making no mention of independence. In a radio announcement made five days later, on 25 July 1961, Qasim laid claim to Kuwait as an integral part of Iraq, citing as justification the fact that Kuwait had once been a district of the Basra *wilaya* (province) under the Ottomans. Qasim further announced the appointment of the ruler of Kuwait as a *qa'imaqam* (district ruler) of Kuwait, to come under the authority of the *mutasarrif* (governor) of Basra.

These claims harked back to the last quarter of the nineteenth century, when Kuwait had nominally come under the suzerainty of the Ottoman Empire. Iraq had previously made claims to Kuwait as early as 1938. However, it was not made clear how Qasim would enforce the claim. Although there were rumors of troop movements on Kuwait's border, no troops were actually sent, and military action was virtually ruled out with the bulk of the Iraqi army fighting the Kurds in the north. Scarcely a brigade was left in the south.

The repercussions were immediate. The Kuwaitis requested British protection, and on 1 July British troops entered Kuwait. Qasim's provocation and the resulting intrusion of the British into Kuwait increased Arab hostility toward Iraq, already inflamed over Qasim's stand on Arab issues. The matter was taken up in the Arab League in July, and the league decided to assemble an Arab force to replace the British. The first contingent arrived in Kuwait in September 1961, and except for the Egyptians, the Arab forces remained until 1962, when the danger appeared to be over.

Events then shifted to the diplomatic front. Kuwait applied to the Arab League for admission and on 20 July was admitted. Iraq thereupon ceased all cooperation with the league. Not content with this, on 26 December 1961 Hashim Jawad, Qasim's foreign minister, announced that Iraq would reconsider diplomatic relations with any country recognizing Kuwait. As the recognitions continued to pour in, Iraq began to recall ambassador after ambassador, though the remaining diplomatic staff was generally left behind. During 1962 the long list came to include, among others, Jordan, Tunisia, Lebanon, and the United States.

The Kuwait affair, although founded on long-standing Iraqi grievances and precipitated by events outside Iraq's control, was grossly mishandled. It isolated Qasim from all his Arab neighbors and solved no problems at home.

By the end of 1962, Qasim had no friends left inside Iraq except a weakened Communist Party and a handful of army officers, and none left outside except the Soviet Union, itself increasingly disturbed by the Kurdish war and far more concerned over Egypt than Iraq.

The promise of social revolution begun in 1958 had faltered. Land reform was in deep trouble, industrialization could make no headway, development plans could not be launched, and oil revenues were beginning to fall off. The state structure and the sense of national identity on which it was based had begun to unravel through a festering Kurdish war that could not be brought to conclusion. And political hopes for liberalization had died under the boot of an increasingly erratic dictatorship.

But while discontent was widespread and ran across a broad spectrum of political and social groups, the question was whether any of these had sufficient motive and means to displace the regime. Democratic-minded elements, such as the NDP, found dictatorship distasteful, but without any grassroots organization or foothold in the military, they were in no position to overthrow the government. Moreover, their views probably came closest to Qasim's. The Kurds were sapping the regime's strength but were unable to replace it on their own. Abroad, the United States and Britain, while alienated from Qasim, on different grounds, were not willing to intervene directly and by 1962 had lost any influence or ability to drive events inside Iraq.

What really undid the Qasim regime was the alienation of the pan-Arab groups, bitter over their failed attempts to gain power and the isolation of the regime in the Arab world. Unlike other opponents of Qasim, however, these had a foothold within the military and in organized, underground movements, like the Ba'th, with potential to mobilize against the regime and to strike it at key vulnerable points. By 1962 these forces, though still weak, were gathering strength and organizing; it would not be long before they would open a second, bloody chapter in the revolution.

The Qasim Regime in the Balance

The Qasim era has been variously estimated by opponents and supporters. Although the regime's record is decidedly mixed, there is little doubt that Qasim made fundamental changes in Iraq and the direction of its policy. The egalitarian thrust of the regime brought much needed social reform—in the landholding system, in Iraq's ownership of its oil resources, and in opening up the education system in a way that would strengthen the middle class. These wrenching changes could not have occurred without some turmoil, but the excesses of the left, especially the Communists, frightened conservatives and nationalists as well as outsiders like the United States, creating a backlash that would help to unseat the regime. The continual instability that resulted also contributed substantially to the establishment of an authoritarian regime.

Qasim also reoriented Iraq in the direction of an "Iraq First" policy and away from unproductive involvement in Arab unity schemes, a much needed corrective. He and his supporters also appeared willing, at least initially, to attempt a reorganization of domestic power-sharing arrangements. This should have had a beneficial effect in strengthening the nation-state project, but in fact it did not. Fear of Communist influence helped spark a religious revival among the *shi'a*. Far more serious was the return of Barzani and a resuscitation of the Kurdish movement. This gave impetus to the revival of Kurdish separatism and set off an intermittent, but long-running, Kurdish war that would plague the state for decades.

Qasim also changed the direction of Iraq's foreign policy away from the West and toward the Soviet bloc. The aim was greater Iraqi independence, a goal that was achieved in some measure. (Relations with the USSR were never as close as former ties with Britain.) But this new direction alienated the United States, fearful of the Communist threat, and eventually Britain, helping to isolate Iraq. Iraq's new orientation also alienated much of the Arab world and its domestic pan-Arab nationalists, who eventually mobilized to overthrow the regime.

In the end, the most important consequence of Qasim's four-and-a-half-year rule was negative: the failure to construct political institutions and processes to govern Iraq. Despite some feeble attempts at opening the political system, no constitution, no representative institutions, no elections emerged. Instead, Qasim governed, as prime minister, through a cabinet that he controlled, concentrating executive, legislative, and sometimes judicial powers in his hands. The Mahdawi Court made a mockery of justice and permanently damaged the concept and practice of the rule of law.

Above all, the Qasim era opened the door to direct military participation in politics. The military would thenceforth intervene again and again, creating more instability and increasingly authoritarian regimes. The result of this spiraling process was now seen in the next turn of the wheel, as the Ba'thists and Arab nationalists used the military to overthrow the Qasim regime in one of the bloodiest episodes of the revolutionary decade.

6

THE ARAB NATIONALISTS
IN POWER, 1963–1968

The coup that finally put an end to Qasim's regime came from a small but determined group of plotters able to draw on wider elements of disaffection in the military. Coming from diverse social backgrounds and shaped by different experiences, this group was united mainly by its members' common Arab nationalist orientation. As a result, the era that followed the coup shifted Iraq back in the direction of a more pan-Arab policy with renewed attempts at greater Arab integration. Based on high doses of ideology, too little tempered by reality, these attempts would founder just as badly as the attempts at radical social reform under Qasim. In the meantime, the foundations of the state and its collective identity would be further eroded.

The motives behind the coup were diverse but strongly held. Many officers, who had joined the revolution to achieve greater Arab unity, felt betrayed by Qasim and his leftist supporters. The exclusion of most Free Officers from decisionmaking positions had rankled, and some wanted this reversed. There was also bitterness over the failure of the Shawwaf rebellion and the subsequent execution and imprisonment of officers who had participated in it.[1]

The coup unfolded in a period when regional support for Arab nationalism and socialism was high and when Nasser was seen as a hero and a model. In retrospect, unity fever probably reached its peak between 1958 and 1961; the 1961 split in the UAR brought some disillusion, along with some realism, about prospects for Arab unity, but not enough to cool the general political climate. Many, especially in the younger generation, still fervently believed in the vision of unity and blamed Qasim for causing Iraq's isolation and its "split" from the Arab world. Because it was the dominant symbolic ideology of the time, Arab unity was an effective tool for mobilizing broader elements to counter Qasim and the left.

Even more potent as a motive was fear and dislike of communism. Although it is clear in retrospect that Communist influence had reached its peak by 1962 and was in decline, the movement still had considerable support at the popular level. The earlier excesses of the party—its mass demonstrations, its control and manipulation of popular and professional organizations, and above all its role in provoking civil disorder and bloodshed, both in the Mosul rebellion and indirectly in the Kirkuk slaughter of 1959—had left widespread anxieties among the population. Arab nationalists could also draw on support from conservative elements—whether landed proprietors or religious leaders—who feared that radical changes introduced by Qasim (such as land reform and the personal status law) would continue if he remained in office. The Arab *sunni* population, especially in the smaller cities and towns of northwestern Iraq, were strong supporters of these sentiments.[2]

The question has also arisen as to whether Arab nationalists had support or help from outside, specifically from the United States or Britain. That is possible, but to date no hard evidence exists one way or the other.[3] However, there can have been little doubt of US distaste for the left-leaning Qasim regime and its Soviet tilt. Whether or not the United States contributed directly to a regime change, those who perpetrated it could understand that the United States would not oppose a change.[4] Nor was Britain, engaged in contentious negotiations over IPC, likely to do so, either.

But the Arab nationalist contingent in Iraq, though the best placed to undertake a change, also had problems of its own. Its members had no real unity of purpose beyond their common desire to be rid of the "Sole Leader" and to reorient foreign policy toward some kind of union with other Arab countries. In fact, they were divided on ideological direction, on leadership, and on organization, all of which later impacted their ability to hold on to power once they had seized it. There were also differences in leadership style and experience. A number of the army officers who joined the movement not only were older but were used to positions of command. More pragmatic in outlook, they were primarily concerned with the task of getting and keeping power. The civilians, notably those in the Ba'th, were often young, inexperienced, and militant. Their main experience had often been as underground organizers and "street" mobilizers.

Lastly, there were organizational differences. Of the several groups constituting the Arab nationalist contingent, the two most important were the Ba'th and the Nasserites. The Nasserites did not constitute a political party; rather, as their name implies, they were a collection of individuals who looked to Nasser for leadership and desired some kind of unity with Egypt, although, even on this, there was no agreed formula. In any event, it was not the Nasserites who took the initiative in planning the overthrow of the Qasim regime but the Ba'th. Composed mainly of civilians who were long on zeal and short on experience, the Ba'th Party had a tight-knit, clandestine organization and a young militant leadership. It had branches in Syria, Jordan, and other Arab countries where it could draw on support. Its chief feature was an ideology that combined an almost mystic belief in Arab unity with a call for the social and economic transformation of society. Thus the party had succeeded in combining the two strains of thought that had divided the intelligentsia in Iraq since the 1930s.[5]

The Iraqi Ba'th in 1963

Although the party was first introduced into Iraq in 1949 by Syrian Ba'th students studying in Baghdad, it was in the early 1950s that it gained a real foothold in Iraq under the leadership of Fu'ad al-Rikabi. In 1951 the party had about fifty members; by 1952 its membership had doubled.[6] In the mid–1950s, it may have had about five hundred supporters in addition to full members. Between 1952 and 1958 the Ba'th made inroads in the schools and colleges, from which it drew much of its leadership and support. Many of these young men (a few were women) were *shi'a* whose families originated in the south; they were attracted by the party's nonsectarian character and modernizing ideology and, in general, favored the more radical, socialist ideas current at the time. After the revolution of 1958, membership increased, and new contacts were made in the officer corps. Not surprisingly, this military cohort was overwhelmingly *sunni* and drawn predominantly from the provincial towns north and west of Baghdad. Their interests in the party were pragmatic, even self-serving. They wanted to overthrow Qasim and needed a political base. The recruitment of Ahmad Hasan al-Bakr provides a good example. Bakr was a practicing Muslim from Tikrit and had qualms about joining a party led by a Christian (Michel Aflaq).

After the failed attempt on Qasim's life in 1959, the party went through a difficult period. Many members were in prison or in exile, and serious splits developed within the party. A struggle for power between the Ba'th and Nasser led some to support Nasser, while others supported the Ba'th. The party was also riddled with disputes over how radical a social program they should adopt. In 1961 the secession of Syria from the UAR left Syrian politics—and the Ba'th party—in considerable disarray. These internecine struggles indicate that the party was ill prepared to take over and run a government.

Nonetheless, by 1960 a new group of clandestine leaders had emerged in Iraq. They were mostly young and *shi'i*. Most important was Ali Salih al-Sa'di, of mixed Kurdish and Arab *sunni* stock. Tough, militant, even ruthless, he was a good organizer. A new Baghdad command was assembled, and a national front was organized with other Arab nationalist elements.[7] Though not a Ba'thist, Abd al-Salam Arif was associated with Sa'di's group. A military bureau of the party was also created to incorporate the new military members.

The 14 Ramadan Coup

During 1962 plans were laid for the coup. Some of those involved were retired officers; others were in active duty. A Ba'thist civil militia of several thousand was organized and armed. The coup itself was preceded by a long student strike at the end of 1962, organized by the Ba'th. In December, however, Qasim discovered the plot. When Qasim arrested some of the participants, the plotters decided they had to act, and on 8 February 1963—the fourteenth day of Ramadan—the coup took place.[8]

The 14 Ramadan action was no palace coup. Ba'thists and their Arab nationalist allies succeeded in gaining control of the government only after a bitter two-day fight with Qasim's forces that cost hundreds of lives. The coup began early in the morning of 8 February, when the Communist air force chief, Jalal al-Auqati, was assassinated and tank units occupied the Abu Ghraib radio station. Others moved toward Rashid Camp and the Ministry of Defense. Once again, a new revolution was announced over the radio, while supporters in the air force bombed the Ministry of Defense and a number of airplanes and the runway at Rashid Camp.

It was at the Ministry of Defense that the heaviest fighting took place. Qasim had taken refuge in the heavily fortified building with a few of his loyal followers. The battle at the ministry raged all day. Most of the army outside the capital apparently remained neutral. Meanwhile, the Communists took to the streets to resist for two days of bitter fighting. In encounters with the army, the Communist demonstrators were mowed down by tanks but not before killing a number of soldiers. Finally on 9 February Qasim asked for safe conduct out of the country in return for surrender. His request was refused. Instead, he was dragged before a hastily assembled group of military and party leaders and summarily interrogated about his failures. He and three associates were shot on the spot and their bodies displayed on public TV. The Qasim era had come to an end.[9]

The Ba'th Government

Soon after the coup's initial proclamation, the structure of the new government was announced. The Ba'th members, for the most part young and unknown, wished to have an older, well-established figure at the head of government—preferably one satisfactory to Nasser. For this purpose, Abd al-Salam Arif was made president and promoted to field marshal. Although his role was supposed to be more symbolic than authoritative, Arif had been friendly toward the Ba'th and was expected to cooperate with them. Military appointments were given to officers who had come out in support of the coup, Ba'thist or otherwise.

A cabinet of twenty-one members put Ba'thists in all key posts and gave the party an absolute majority of seats (twelve). Ahmad Hasan al-Bakr was made prime minister, and the party's civilian leader, Ali Salih al-Sa'di, was made deputy prime minister and minister of interior. But the cabinet also included some Arab nationalists (five) and Kurds (two), as well as a few respected professionals.

Behind the cabinet, however, real power was vested in the National Council of the Revolutionary Command (NCRC), established on 8 February. The NSRC was given the legal power to appoint and remove cabinets and to assume the powers of the commander in chief of the armed forces.[10] Membership in the NCRC was kept secret, but it clearly represented the Ba'th Party members who had collaborated in the coup.[11] (Only two, Abd al-Salam Arif and Abd al-Ghani Rawi, were not Ba'thists.) Of this group, the military dominated with ten members; civilians totaled eight.

This government was meant to establish a Ba'th Party state. But despite the party's numbers, Ba'th control of the government was more apparent than real. Several fault lines soon emerged in these hastily constructed structures. One was the cleavage between the young, civilian wing of the party, represented by Sa'di, and the older, military men, such as Arif and Bakr. There was also an ideological division between conservatives, or pragmatists, aware of the Ba'th's weak power base in the country and the need to compromise with others, and radicals, anxious to push forward rapidly with a Ba'th agenda. Soon a third divide appeared, as well, between Ba'th members on the party's Regional Command who held no official positions but were supposed to husband the party's interests and its policy, and those now in positions of authority, like Arif and Bakr, who could make and enforce decisions whether or not the party's Regional Command agreed. Sharp tensions surfaced right from the start. It was not long before the older, military men in positions of authority began to prevail over the young party militants. The young civilians on the Regional Command were no match for the more seasoned officer-politicians, backed by supporters in the military.[12] In this fluid atmosphere the military began to consolidate its hold on power by forming blocs based not on party affiliation but on tribe and locality. Those from Tikrit gathered around Bakr; those from Dulaim (Ramadi) around the Arif brothers.

Despite these frictions, the Ba'thists soon showed their ruthlessness in rooting out supporters of Qasim and persecuting the Communists, the one issue on which most could agree. The property of almost a hundred Qasim followers was frozen, and many of his ministers were arrested. Soon thereafter the execution of Communists began and continued for most of the regime's existence. Communists were unofficially sought out in their neighborhoods, arrested, and sometimes assassinated. Special investigative committees were set up, torture practiced, and random executions authorized by some of those in authority. These actions continued a vendetta begun earlier by the Communists who had persecuted Ba'thists under the Mahdawi Court. In their number, their extrajudicial illegality, and their use of torture, however, these Ba'th actions surpassed those of the Qasim period and boded ill for the conduct of politics in the future.[13] Ironically, although one of the principles of the Ba'th constitution was socialism, its first actions in government appeared relatively conservative. This was undoubtedly due to the increased influence of more conservative military elements in the regime. Faced with pressure from religious leaders, *sunni* and *shi'i,* one of the regime's first steps was to amend the personal status law, modifying the clause granting equality between men and women in inheritance. No socialist measures were passed.

Ba'th foreign policy was equally moderate. Relations with the West, specifically the United States, were strengthened, for example, and Qasim's policy toward the UAR (which no longer included Syria) was reversed. Even more significant was Iraq's new position toward Kuwait. The Ba'th described Qasim's attitude toward Kuwait as erroneous and in October signed an agreement recognizing Kuwait's sovereignty and independence. Even more remarkable, they agreed on a boundary, although no provisions were made for actual demarcation procedures. The quid pro quo for this recognition, apparently, was a long-term interest-free loan from Kuwait of ID 30 million, to cover increasing budget shortages in Iraq.[14]

Ba'th Failures

Despite these moderate beginnings, the Ba'th regime did not last the year. Its leaders' difficulties, mainly of their own making, began soon after the coup. One was the ongoing Kurdish war, which the Ba'th aggravated by their pan-Arab policy.

The Conflict with the Kurds
Initially, the KDP had been in touch with the Ba'th and had agreed to support the coup in return for a promise of autonomy. Shortly after the coup, contact between the Kurds and the government was established. From the first, the issue at stake was just how much self-rule the new government was prepared to offer the Kurds to achieve peace in the north, especially as the Ba'th, unlike their predecessors, were eager to achieve some kind of Arab unity. In March Barzani demanded, among other things, affirmation of the Kurdish right to autonomy, the formation of Kurdish legislative and executive authorities in the north, a Kurdish vice president in Baghdad, a Kurdish legion in the north, and the appointment of Kurds to all posts in Kurdistan. The Kurdish region was to include the provinces of Sulaimaniyya, Arbil, Kirkuk, and the districts in the Mosul and Diyala provinces in which Kurds were a majority. This was well beyond any concessions the Ba'th were prepared to make. Their reluctance became evident, although negotiations continued.[15] The real interest of the Ba'th lay in its negotiations with Nasser for

some kind of future unity, not in its accommodation of the Kurds. On 17 April an agreement in principle was concluded with Nasser on a future union. The Kurds had already made it clear that if Iraq were to join an Arab federation, they would demand greater autonomy.[16] After the agreement, the Kurds published a memorandum demanding virtually a binational state. From here on, relations with the Kurds rapidly deteriorated. By the end of April, aircraft and troops were deployed northward, and early in June the Kurdish delegation in Baghdad was rounded up and arrested. The war resumed. The situation in the north was serious. The Kurds soon had control of the entire northern region bordering Iran, and Barzani was receiving considerable aid from the Iranian Kurds. Abandoning the defensive strategy followed by Qasim, the government decided to recapture Kurdish territory and crush the Kurdish movement if possible. Iraqi forces bombarded villages with tanks, heavy artillery, and bombs dropped from the air; they bulldozed Kurdish villages under their control and began Arabization of strategic areas.[17] The toll taken on the Kurds was greater than previous losses, but the Ba'th policy was no more successful than Qasim's approach. By winter the Kurds had regained most of their position, and before long, moderates in the army began to turn against the government's policy. So did a number of ministers. The Ba'th inability to either find a solution to the Kurdish problem or win a military victory hastened its downfall.

Arab Unity Failures

The most serious problem resulted from the Ba'th regime's intense embroilment in Arab affairs. The pursuit of union, first with Nasser and then with the Syrians, distracted the leadership from internal affairs and brought few domestic benefits. The Ba'th coup in Iraq had been followed by a similar event in neighboring Syria; on 8 March the Ba'th came to power in Damascus. The Syrian Ba'thists were interested in a new union with Nasser. To strengthen their position in negotiations with Nasser, the Syrian Ba'thists needed the support of their Iraqi colleagues. In Iraq as well, there were reasons for engaging in the unity talks with Cairo. The ideology of the party called for pan-Arabism, and popular expectations for union were high. More important, however, was the need of the new Ba'thist government to propitiate Nasserites and other pan-Arab nationalists at home, who were restless because they had been given only a marginal role in decisionmaking.

On 19 March an Iraqi delegation went to Syria; on 6 April the delegates and the Syrians joined Nasser in Egypt for unity talks. These soon foundered on mutual mistrust between Nasser and the Ba'th. For a number of reasons, Nasser did not want unity with the Ba'thists in Syria and Iraq. He disliked the idea of sharing leadership in the Arab world with them, he distrusted their doctrinaire ideas, and he was unwilling to become embroiled in Iraq's numerous problems, especially the Kurds. In fact, the Iraqi Ba'thists were also unwilling to share power. In May a potential coup by Arab nationalist elements was forestalled in Iraq, and a number of civilians and officers were arrested. This event ended any prospects of power sharing with Nasserites.[18] By July, relations between Nasser and the Ba'th Party had deteriorated. From then on, Nasser encouraged the Ba'th opponents in Iraq to bring about a change of government.[19] With no real prospects for a union with Egypt, the two Ba'th parties in Syria and Iraq then turned to increased cooperation between themselves. In October a military agreement was concluded, followed by an economic pact. This growing rapprochement only increased Egypt's concern.

Party Cleavages

Ultimately, however, the critical factors responsible for bringing down the Ba'th were the deep splits in party leadership over policy as well as tactics, together with its inexperience and ineptitude in handling the task of governing. These differences soon crystallized around two factions, one dubbed "conservative" and the other, radical and more militant. The latter, led by Sa'di, was doctrinaire to the core, interested primarily in upholding party principles and maintaining party control. It adopted such Marxist ideas as socialist planning, collective farms, and workers' control of the means of production. This group was overwhelmingly civilian, young (mainly in their early thirties), and thoroughly committed to achieving their revolutionary agenda. They were not interested in gradual evolution or in sharing power, much less democratic institutions, and their inexperience—even naïveté—in the requirements of governing a complex society like Iraq's soon became glaringly apparent. One frankly stated: "We were not prepared for power. We had spent all of our time underground, preparing for conspiracy."[20]

The other, more moderate group was led by Talib Shabib and Hazim Jawad among the civilians but increasingly driven by military Ba'thists, such as Ahmad Hasan al-Bakr. Pragmatism was this group's hallmark. Realizing the weakness of the Ba'th position, it advocated some power sharing with sympathetic non-Ba'thists, especially the Arab nationalists. The group was more interested in keeping the Ba'th in power than in a purist, one-party state. The military contingent, in particular, was uninterested in ideology or rapid social change.

In October 1963 these issues all came to a head at the sixth Ba'th Party conference, held in Damascus.[21] In an election for the party's National Command,[22] Sa'di and his faction succeeded in winning most of the seats allotted to Iraq. He also succeeded in getting his more radical socialist ideas accepted, thereby alienating Michel Aflaq, the party's founder, and other moderates. Victory in Damascus, however, did not mean victory in Baghdad, where Sa'di's opponents were already preparing for his downfall.

Back in Baghdad, contacts among officers, Ba'thist and non-Ba'thist, had been underway for some time, aimed at ousting the radical faction of the party—and its civilian control. In November, at a Ba'th Party meeting engineered by the military Ba'thists, the moderates gained control. A new Regional Command then arrested Sa'di and four of his civilian supporters and exiled them to Spain.[23]

The reaction was not long in coming. Sa'di's supporters took to the streets and the National Guard, the Ba'thist militia controlled by the militants, went on a week-long rampage. Sa'di's supporters in the air force attacked the presidential palace. Baghdad appeared on the verge of anarchy. On 12 November Michel Aflaq and others in the National Command arrived in Baghdad to mediate. The arrival of Syrian leaders to help decide the issue of the country's leadership was considered by most Iraqis to be blatant foreign interference in their affairs and only worsened the crisis. In any event, they were in no position to rescue the party. Control of the local situation was in the hands of more radical elements who were demanding the removal of the two "moderate" civilian members of the Regional Command, Shabib and Jawad. A meeting held on 14 November declared the Ba'th election of 11 November null and void, and two moderates were exiled to Lebanon.

A more unfortunate set of circumstances for the party could not be imagined. The dispute had removed almost the entire leadership of the Ba'th Party that had carried out the coup of 1963, thereby easing the way for Arif and his Arab nationalist supporters in the army to take over. In one brief day of military action, Arif inaugurated a new regime.

On 18 November Arif announced that the armed forces would take control of the country and that a new government would be formed with himself as president of the republic and commander in chief of the armed forces. Arif also gave himself extraordinary powers for a year, renewable if necessary, to deal with the internal situation. The Ba'th Party militia was dissolved and a new cabinet established with his supporters in prominent posts. The military Ba'thists who had assisted in the coup were also rewarded with posts. It was not long, however, before Arif found ways of ridding himself of the key Ba'thists. In January 1964 Bakr's post was abolished and he resigned from the government; other Ba'thists were dismissed. Arif retired over four hundred officers, most of them Ba'th, and transferred others out of Baghdad, weakening Ba'thist ties to the military, particularly those of Bakr. By early 1964 the Ba'th had been thoroughly removed from power.

In the end, the Ba'th coup of 1963 succeeded only in putting power back in the hands of the military. But this brief, early Ba'th episode in power is important, less for what it accomplished than for the lessons learned by the Ba'th, especially Ahmad Hasan al-Bakr and his young aide and relative, Saddam Husain. Bakr remained a seasoned plotter, disdainful of party politics and thoroughly alienated from the ideological disputes that had split the ruling coalition. But he was bitter over his treatment and determined to get back in power. Both men appeared to have learned at least three lessons from the disaster of 1963. The first is that ideological divisions—or any other kind—are to be avoided at the top at all costs. Second, that potential military opponents must be moved out of power as soon as possible. Third, it is easier to gain power than to maintain it. In any future government, gaining control over the instruments of state would be paramount. For this purpose, a security apparatus would prove far more effective than a party or the military. These lessons would indelibly shape Iraq's future after the next Ba'th coup in 1968.[24]

The First Arif Regime, 1963–1966

The smooth execution of the November coup and the masterful manipulation of the Ba'th in its aftermath showed that Abd al-Salam Arif had emerged from the turbulent events of the past four years a somewhat different man from the Arif who had brashly led the coup of 1958. The lessons of his struggle with Qasim, his imprisonment, and his observation of the forces released by the revolution had tempered his impetuosity and given him a greater sense of realism and maturity. Arif was a relatively conservative Muslim and a staunch *sunni*, characteristics that would in time raise public accusations of sectarianism. But his conservatism and caution were largely in accord with the temper of the country. While hardly an intellectual heavyweight, his mastery of military politics, his newfound moderation, and his ability to govern in an open manner were to stand him in good stead in consolidating his power and giving the nation some relaxation from the tensions and clashes of the previous years.

Moderate Arab Socialism

Although the Arif regime went through several stages of development, in general it was dominated by the philosophy and tactics of Nasser's brand of Arab socialism. After removing the Ba'th, Arif relied heavily on the Nasserite elements in Iraq—at least at first—mainly to help consolidate his position internally and to win Nasser's much-needed support for his regime. The regime included many who were strong supporters of the Nasserite experiment and who wanted to be part of it. A number of these were military men in key positions, but the Nasserites also had a hard core among a group of civilians, young professionals, and technocrats with a much stronger commitment to socialism than their military counterparts. Much of the political dynamics of the regime can be understood only by examining the push and pull of the two remaining groups in power. On one hand stood a strong Nasserite element demanding unity and a more state-controlled economy; on the other were more pragmatic, "centrist" elements willing to accommodate nominal unity but more concerned with stabilizing Iraq's situation at home and achieving some reasonable balance between Iraq's foreign and domestic demands. Arif and his supporters clearly fell into the second category. This was apparent in his early actions, which were designed to calm domestic turbulence and normalize Iraq's relations with foreign powers. Although it was clear that the military would be in control, Arif was never as authoritarian as Qasim or as brutal as the Ba'th; greater freedom of speech and action was allowed. The first cabinet stated that it would institute a planned economy that would encourage both private and public sectors, stimulate industry and private investment, and carry out the agrarian reform that had been all but forgotten in the past few years—all on an equitable basis. Soothed by this start, many Iraqis who had been living abroad returned, and capital flowed into the country once again.

In foreign affairs as well, Arif's government followed a moderate policy, starting with an attempt to mend fences with the West. A proclamation on 24 December promised to settle disputes with international oil companies, and in February 1964 Abd al-Aziz al-Wattari, the oil minister, was appointed head of a committee containing several moderate technocrats to ad-

dress the problem. Between May 1964 and June 1965 they engaged in negotiations with IPC and arrived at several agreements that would have resolved
outstanding issues had they been implemented. Relations with the Soviet
Union were also improved without alienating the West. Arms deliveries were
resumed early in 1964; the USSR installed a surface-to-air missile system,
delivered three additional squadrons of MIG-21s, and provided Iraq's first
TU-16 medium jet bombers.[25]

It was not long, however, before the Nasserite elements in the regime began to push for more progress on a union with Egypt, and it was this policy
that tended to dominate the second phase of the regime, during 1964 and
1965. In January 1964 Arif visited Egypt and talked extensively with Nasser.
Neither leader appeared eager to rush headlong into union; both agreed that
preliminary steps should first be taken to harmonize their political and economic systems. In Iraq the impetus was seized by the Nasserites. Under their
influence, Iraq's internal structure began to be revised along Egyptian lines.
On 3 May 1964 a new provisional constitution, modeled on that of Egypt,
was announced. It provided that Iraq would be democratic, socialist, Arab,
and Islamic; a future National Assembly would be elected, but in the interim,
legislative power would be exercised by the president and the cabinet. The
chief difference with Egypt was that the Iraqi instrument gave more emphasis
to Islam and less to socialism. In June the government took a further step,
launching plans for the election of an Arab Socialist Union (ASU) on the
Egyptian model. The union was stillborn; only the young, ardent Nasserites
supported it. In May 1964 both countries signed an agreement providing for
a joint command. By September there were some 5,000 Egyptian troops on
Iraqi soil. Presumably there for joint maneuvers, the troops were meant in reality to bolster the regime in the wake of an attempted Ba'th coup.

The Nationalization Laws
These pan-Arab political and military measures were short-lived. Of far
more importance for Iraq's internal development were the nationalization
laws of 1964. Although passed mainly as a first step in coordinating the two
economies, the laws were also put forth for economic and social reasons.
Whatever the motives, they represented the regime's most substantial step
toward a socialist system, one that eventually had far-reaching effects, putting important productive sectors of Iraq's economy in government hands.

The chief architect of nationalization was a young, Cambridge-educated
economist, Khair al-Din Hasib, governor of the Central Bank. Hasib and

his cousin, Adib al-Jadir, who later became minister of industry, were representative of the pro-union technocrats who were impressed with Nasser's recent experiments in socialism and wanted to adapt them to Iraq. This group had examined the private sector and found it wanting. In their view, capital in private banks and companies was not being invested in economic development, foreign trade was dominated by consumer imports, and wealth was unduly concentrated in a small upper class. They advocated the nationalization of banks and key industries, the creation of a public sector to act as a catalyst for development, and the passage of laws designed to redistribute income.[26]

Published on the anniversary of the July revolution in 1964, the new laws nationalized all banks and insurance companies, all cement and cigarette companies, and some flour and textile industries. A later amendment made the import and distribution of pharmaceuticals, cars, tea, sugar, and other items a government monopoly. The shareholders of nationalized companies were to be compensated, and the capital of the banks and nationalized industries was to be converted into bonds payable in fifteen years at 3 percent interest. No individual was allowed to own more than ID 10,000 ($28,000) worth of shares in any company, and income and inheritance taxes were revised in a more progressive direction. To administer the new laws, the Public Establishment of Banks and the Economic Organization were created. Khair al-din Hasib was appointed head of both.

Opposed by conservative business elements, the nationalization laws unquestionably discouraged private investment. The suddenness of the decrees and the economic discontinuity they introduced created a climate of uncertainty. Arif felt it necessary to reassure the public that there would be no further nationalization.

The laws were controversial and assessments of their impact differ. Supporters claim that production and prices did not decline; detractors, that they caused a downturn in the economy.[27] Whatever the economic impact of the new laws, politically they marked a major step in converting the economy of the country from a free enterprise system (though an admittedly weak one), modified by concepts of the welfare state, to one based on a planned economy and on state ownership of the means of production in major industries. Whereas other aspects of the projected union with Egypt evaporated, this one remained. Although moderate in scope, the step placed the authority for directing the economy in government hands, where it would remain for the rest of the century. As in the case of the land reform, however, it proved easier to legislate change than to form a government cadre to take over the functions of the private sector. Problems of inefficiency were a result. As would soon be apparent, Iraq as yet lacked the skilled manpower to run such an establishment.

After the nationalization laws, the third phase of Arif's regime began. By the summer of 1965, Arif began to pull back from the union measures and felt strong enough to initiate a series of astute moves against the Nasserites. In this he was helped by discontent with the socialization decrees and by another failed coup attempt by a Nasserite officer he had appointed as prime minister. He was also able to secure his position by appointing his brother and loyal supporters from his own tribal group—the Jumaila from Ramadi—to key military posts.[28] This practice heralded the beginnings of a tribal policy in appointments that was to outlast the regime. With his position secure, Arif now appointed Abd al-Rahman al-Bazzaz as prime minister and gave him the authority to move in a new direction, one designed to civilianize the administration, marginalize the military (and thus circumvent more coups), and launch a modest return to a constitutional system.

Bazzaz: Another Attempt to Liberalize

Abd al Rahman al-Bazzaz was both a civilian and an Arab nationalist of long standing. As a lawyer with a degree from the University of London, and a mature man of fifty-two who had served in numerous legal and diplomatic positions, he would satisfy the moderates and wide segments of the population tired of military rule. More important, Bazzaz represented the potential for a return to the rule of law and even an elected assembly.

This new direction was made clear in a number of public statements and speeches by Bazzaz. First, the rule of law was stressed, especially an end to arbitrary arrests and extreme retribution for political opponents. Second was the promise to establish a permanent constitution, to promulgate an election law, and eventually to hold an election for a national assembly. Third, while adhering to agreements with Cairo, the government would now attend to Iraqi territorial unity, a reference understood to mean a renewed attempt to settle the Kurdish issue. Lastly, Bazzaz promised a retreat on the socialist front.

At the same time, the regime was increasingly civilianized. As prime minister, Bazzaz presided over a cabinet that had the fewest military members since 1963. The National Revolutionary Council, which had been an exclusively military group, was dissolved; its functions devolved on the cabinet.

Civilian technocrats continued to play an increased role. The relative openness of the regime as compared to its predecessors allowed for planning, discussion, and the normal processes of government to take place.

The Shi'i *Renaissance*

This modest attempt to liberalize, together with a concentration on Iraqi, rather than Arab, unity also brought some positive, if short-lived, results in the Kurdish and *shi'i* communities: more social peace in both areas. Indeed, under the Arif regime there was something of a *shi'i* renaissance. The s*hi'i* Islamic movements that had emerged under Qasim to confront the Communist challenge now took advantage of these relatively favorable conditions to expand their organization and influence. Arif, a *sunni,* was a practicing Muslim of conservative bent, and he supported public religious observances, including those of the *shi'a.* These moves not only reduced threats to the clergy, but provided *shi'i* movements greater political space to grow.

The s*hi'i* renaissance was encouraged by several factors. Muhsin al-Hakim, the chief *marji'* of the *shi'i* world, was interested in a campaign to Islamize society, and especially its youth, and he encouraged the *shi'i* renaissance.[29] The Da'wa, still underground, and other *shi'i* organizations used the new political climate to spread the *shi'i* movement widely in schools and colleges, in grassroots organizations like charities, in public rituals, and in the *hauza* (*shi'i* seminaries) themselves. Islamic schools and libraries spread not only in cities and towns of the south but in Baghdad and Kazimiyya as well. So successful were these efforts that some *shi'i* scholars and activists have seen the period between 1964 and 1968 as a "golden age" for the Islamic movement in Iraq.[30]

Not all of the results of the Arif regime were positive for the *shi'a,* however. The intrusion of the military into politics and its monopoly of positions at upper levels of power had greatly reduced *shi'i* participation in decisionmaking and increased the *sunni-shi'a* imbalance in government. (See Table A.2.) This increased "*sunni*-ization" of the political elite had been exacerbated by the removal of the Communists and the radical Ba'thists, both of whom had been predominantly *shi'i* in their leadership. This sectarian imbalance was further exacerbated by the nationalization laws, which disproportionately impacted the mercantile and financial sectors of the *shi'i* middle class. The increasingly *sunni* character of the regime brought to the surface the old issue of sectarianism and discrimination against *shi'a.* In response, the *shi'i* religious and intellectual community began to focus on its own sectarian identity and on creating a justification for it. They blamed outside forces (imperialism) for a permanent structural imbalance in the Iraqi state. The Da'wa movement directed much of its opposition to reaffirming the Arab character of the Iraqi *shi'i* community, emphasizing its majority in Iraq and therefore its right to govern. These sentiments would deepen in succeeding years.[31]

The Attempted Kurdish Accord

Kurdish separatism was a much more serious threat to Iraq's unity and the stability of the regime than were *shi'i* feelings of alienation, but here too Bazzaz was able to make some inroads despite unfavorable beginnings. Although the measures he took proved temporary, they indicated the direction the central government would have to take to achieve a modus vivendi with the north.

In February 1964 a cease-fire in the Kurdish conflict was announced. It called for recognition of Kurdish national rights, a general amnesty, and a reinstatement of Kurds in the civil service and the military. It did not mention autonomy and called for the return of the central government administration in the north.[32] This seemed to be a promising beginning, but it did not take into account emerging fissures among the Kurds.

Barzani's acceptance of the cease-fire had angered the hard-line leaders of the KDP because it had been concluded over their heads. Barzani now saw the cease-fire as an opportunity to settle his dispute with the urban intellectuals in the KDP once and for all. He had never favored their movement nor tolerated their challenge to his more tribally based leadership. In April 1964, when the KDP publicly condemned Barzani' position, he elected a new party committee, sent his forces to attack the KDP leaders, and actually forced many of them across the border into Iran.[33] The result was a serious split in the Kurdish movement, which had long been simmering beneath the surface but which now broke into the open.

The rupture had a number of serious and long-lasting effects. It created a continuing source of internal dissension that weakened the Kurdish movement and provided a dissident group that was frequently used by the government against Barzani's forces. Nevertheless, the split had one great virtue, which proved an overwhelming advantage in the short run: It enabled Barzani to put together a tough and seasoned fighting force, capable of confronting the government in the Kurds' mountain strongholds and able to take a coherent stance in negotiations.

By 1965 Barzani had unquestionably emerged as the strongest force within the movement. He had consolidated his hold over a wide stretch of territory in the north and had set up his own de facto Kurdish administration, consisting of a revolutionary council of fifty members (an embryonic parliament) and a smaller executive bureau (an embryonic cabinet). Barzani's control did not extend to the large cities, but it was virtually complete in the countryside. One authority has estimated that Barzani controlled about 35,000 square kilometers (13,500 square miles) and 1 million inhabitants.[34]

From his strengthened position Barzani felt able to make new demands on Baghdad. As early as October 1964 he submitted a memo to the government demanding the recognition of Kurdish rights on the basis of autonomy and the transformation of the Kurdish army (the *peshmergas*) into a regular frontier force. In January 1965 the minister of interior declared that there would be no further negotiations until the Kurdish army was dismantled, and there would be no autonomy in Kurdistan.[35]

In April 1965 the government began an offensive by occupying Sulaimaniyya and moving north to Raniyya; for the next year the two sides were engaged once again in hostilities. In April and May of 1966 the tide turned against the central government. In the fierce battle of Handrin, the Kurds scored a significant victory, forcing the Iraqi army to retreat from a strategic mountain pass and thus preserving their de facto autonomy. This event, together with the presence of a new cabinet with a moderate, civilian prime minister, Bazzaz, finally provided the impetus for an accord, which would prove to be pathbreaking.

Although the army was not eager for an agreement, it could not win the war on the ground; meanwhile, the conflict was weakening regime stability. At the same time, the Kurds now had a man in Bazzaz whom they could trust and whose politics—moderate, legal, and Iraqi oriented—matched that of Barzani. In two weeks of negotiation the two sides came to an agreement known as the June 1966 accord. Announced on June 29, it provided the Kurds with the most liberal recognition of their rights thus far.[36]

The June 1966 accord was a twelve-point peace plan that provided for recognition of Kurdish nationality to be specified in a permanent constitution, virtually promising a binational state; allowed a high degree of decentralized administration in Kurdish areas; recognized Kurdish as an official language; provided for proportional representation of Kurds in the institutions of state; reintegrated Kurds into the army and civil service; and appropriated funds to rebuild the north.

Unfortunately, this settlement was never implemented, although it calmed the situation in the north for a time and gave the regime a lease on life. It also set forth objectives to which future Kurdish negotiations could point.

Bazzaz's experiment with the Kurds, along with his attempts to liberalize, were brought to an abrupt end not by political or social forces but by an entirely unforeseen event that, in one blow, ended the regime of Arif the First. In April 1966 Arif had embarked on a speech-making tour of the country in an effort to develop popular support for the regime. On 13 April, after addressing a gathering at Qurna that lasted until dusk, he boarded a helicopter for Basra. Shortly after takeoff, the helicopter crashed, apparently because of poor visibility and a sudden sandstorm. All aboard were killed.

The Regime of Arif the Second, 1966–1968

Bazzaz temporarily assumed the office of president, and in accordance with the temporary constitution of 1964, the National Defense Council and the cabinet met to elect a new president. Three candidates were nominated. One was Bazzaz; the other two were military men. The key issue at stake was whether a civilian could be elected president. The military was unwilling to surrender power, and on 17 April 1966, Arif's brother, Abd al-Rahman Arif, was elected president. He was a congenial man of relatively weak personality whom the ambitious army officers believed they could manipulate. With the advent of the second Arif, the weaknesses of the regime became apparent and its difficulties mounted. Although Abd al-Salam Arif's short time at the helm had been marked by political twists and turns, he had a gift for keeping a coalition of forces together and a mastery of military politics, neither of which were shared by his brother. His decisiveness and his ability to learn from experience would soon be missed.

The Return of Military Politics
Bazzaz continued in office a while longer, but without a strong figure to keep the military in tow, military factionalism soon reasserted itself. The weakness of the regime manifested itself in yet another failed military coup in June 1966, which almost succeeded. Finally Bazzaz resigned. He was

succeeded by Naji Talib, who was a Free Officer, a moderate Arab nationalist, and more conveniently, a *shi'a*. But Talib was unable to solve any basic
problems. He reversed Bazzaz's stand on the Kurds, precipitating renewed
but desultory fighting on that front. He was unable—or perhaps unwilling—to bring about sufficient unity with Egypt to satisfy the Nasserites, and
he ran into economic difficulties over a pipeline dispute with Syria. By now,
however, pressures for a change—particularly from military officers anxious
for their turn in power—was too great for Talib, and on 10 May 1967 he resigned. However, no acceptable candidate could be found to replace him as
prime minister. Finally Arif himself became prime minister, and a coalition
cabinet was formed of various elements. The Arif government had by now
become little more than a collection of army officers balancing various interests and ethnic and sectarian groups. Like the new regimes before it, it had
failed to develop political structures or parties to support it or to create a
consensus or a framework for action. It had no parliament, and its power
base was in the middle class, but otherwise it increasingly resembled the status quo policies of the Old Regime.

   This lackluster coalition was unable to survive a series of events that radicalized the political climate in the region and culminated in the 1967 war.
One of these was the emergence in Syria of a new Ba'th regime under Salah
Jadid that had come to power in February 1966. Virulently anti-imperialist
and anti-Israeli, it soon undertook a series of actions that embroiled the rest
of the region in conflict. The new Syrian regime turned its attention to the
Arab-Israeli situation, initiating a disastrous series of events that eventually
led to the outbreak of war in 1967, which polarized the Arab world and
dragged other Arab states into an unwanted conflict.

   Iraq, saddled with a weak military government and involved in a renewed military engagement with the Kurds, could ill afford to withstand a
regional climate increasingly swept by animus against the West and Israel. It
is not surprising, therefore, that Iraq's participation in the 1967 war was
minimal, although it sent troops to fight with Jordan on the Jordanian front.
Like other Arab regimes, however, the government in Baghdad had to face
the responsibility for a humiliating defeat. This unquestionably added to the
unpopularity of the military politicians and played a role in eventually toppling a regime already seen as weak and incompetent.

   In the aftermath of the 1967 defeat, anti-Western sentiment was at a
peak. Not surprisingly, this feeling was now focused on the remaining vestiges of Western influence inside the country—the IPC. The government's

oil policy had long been a bone of contention between those oriented toward a pragmatic policy of increasing Iraq's financial benefits, and along with them its ties to the West, and those more concerned with Iraq's controlling its own resources and maintaining a more nationalist and anti-Western foreign policy.

The New Oil Policy

When it came to power, the first Arif regime inherited the unsettled oil problems of the Qasim era. It will be recalled that Public Law 80, passed by the Qasim regime, had expropriated almost all of IPC's concession area. However, the law had left open at least the possibility of IPC's future participation in the expropriated territory (in particular the rich Rumaila field), alone or in partnership with the government. From then on, it became a major aim of IPC to regain control over the northern extension of the Rumaila field, or at least to prevent its competitors from doing so.[37] From the Iraqi point of view, the issue was who was to exploit the expropriated territory and under what terms. This issue provided the backdrop for a struggle among various groups over oil policy and over the foreign policy intertwined within it, a struggle that continued right up to the overthrow of the Arif regime.

The process had begun shortly after the establishment of the Ba'th regime of 1963, when the new oil minister, Abd al-Aziz al-Wattari, who was a US-trained engineer and a moderate—one the West believed would be reasonable—took control.[38] In February 1964 Wattari established the Iraq National Oil Company (INOC) and drafted an agreement that provided for a joint venture between IPC and INOC in which IPC would be given a controlling interest. Most important of all, IPC was to have access to all important producing areas of Iraq, including Rumaila and other areas of proven reserves. In fact, this agreement was much the same as the final IPC offer rejected by Qasim. It left IPC in a very strong position within Iraq. It would have benefited Iraq, however, in providing immediate revenues and settling an outstanding dispute with the oil companies that had prevented exploitation of Iraq's rich resources and that had allowed competitors (Iran, Saudi Arabia, Abu Dhabi) to increase their production and market share at Iraq's expense.

Wattari's agreement produced a bitter reaction, especially from the Nasserite group led by Hasib and Jadir, and nothing was done about the agreement. However, when Tahir Yahya, a Nasserite supporter, returned as prime minister in July 1967, his cabinet passed Public Law 97, giving exclusive rights to INOC to develop the expropriated territory and prohibiting restoration to IPC of the Rumaila field. In April 1968 Adib al-Jadir announced that INOC would reject all outside offers to develop Rumaila and would proceed to develop the field itself.[39] With this statement, Iraq's future oil policy was clear. Those opposed to IPC and "imperialist monopolies" had won. Henceforth, the state would control the expropriated oil resources, although it would have to development them in cooperation with outside firms. This act also put more power in the hands of the state than ever before. However, a cloud still hung over the development of the field, for IPC did not recognize any of these acts as legal and announced its intention of taking legal action against anyone purchasing oil from the field.

Notwithstanding this liability, INOC began discussions with outside interests on further development of its oil resources. In November 1967 the government signed a service contract with Enterprise de Recherches et d'Activites Petrolieres (ERAP), the French state-owned oil company group, to develop areas outside Rumaila. In an even sharper departure from precedent, the government signed a letter of intent with the Soviets in December 1967 stipulating that the USSR would provide direct assistance to INOC for development of the Rumaila field. By April of 1968 drilling and exploration in the field had begun, but the regime was overthrown before much was accomplished.[40]

These steps affected not only IPC oil interests but Iraqi foreign policy as well. Once again Iraq was shifting away from a more pro-Western foreign policy toward the socialist bloc. The ground had already been prepared for this shift. Anti-Western sentiment had been building in Iraq for some time. The Americans were affected, as well. A US group, Pan-American, had been denied a contract to develop Iraq's sulfur deposits.

The Coup of 17 July 1968

The pro-Western forces were not the only ones dissatisfied with the regime. Many believed that Arif, a weak leader, had allowed things to drift. While more conservative forces were dissatisfied with the socialist trend, others wanted more decisive action in remedying the country's economic and social ills. Still others continued to want a more open political system and public elections. However, Prime Minister Tahir Yahya had a firm grip on the levers of political power that seemed to preclude future participation in government by a number of political contenders.

Against this background of rising discontent, a number of groups and individuals were jockeying for position on the political scene toward the end of 1967. On the left were two Communist movements. One was the central committee of the ICP; the other was a splinter group, the central command that had broken away from the party in September 1967 under the leadership of Aziz al-Haj. This group was fighting the regime in a guerrilla action in the south of Iraq.[41] The NDP was active, as well. Kamil al-Chadirchi had publicly asked for free elections and open political parties. On the right were a variety of groups, including the moderate nationalists previously gathered around Bazzaz but now in some disarray. Also arrayed against Abd al-Rahman Arif was a formidable group of military politicians, all determined to regain office. Most important among these were the military Ba'thists such as Bakr, Hardan al-Tikriti, and Salih Mahdi Ammash who had lost power in 1963 and hence had both political and personal reasons for desiring the fall of the regime. The Kurds and the *shi'a,* both with active opposition movements, could be relied upon to support the overthrow of a government that was predominantly Arab *sunni.* The Kurds, in particular, were dissatisfied with the government's failure to implement the 1966 agreement. Beneath these broader ideological groups were clusters of military cliques based largely on regional and tribal ties and aimed at protecting their personal interests and, where possible, enhancing their power.

The two different groups that, in an unlikely and uneasy coalition, would finally combine to carry out the coup were the Ba'th Party and a small contingent of disaffected supporters in Arif's inner circle. The latter group was led by Abd al-Razzaq al-Nayif and Ibrahim al-Da'ud. To a considerable extent these two men held the fate of the regime in their hands, Nayif by virtue of his position as deputy director of military intelligence, Da'ud as head of the Republican Guard, responsible for protecting the president and his entourage.

Whatever their motivations, the young officers had neither the stature, organization, nor public credibility to maintain a government after a coup. For this a political party or publicly recognized group with some grassroots support was needed. This was the role played by the Ba'th, which, independently of the officers, had been planning the overthrow of the Arif regime for some time.

The Ba'th Party of 1968
The Ba'th Party of 1968, however, was not the same party that had seized power in 1963. In the interim, the party had survived underground struggles, imprisonment of its leaders, and a bitter fight with the Syrian branch.

In September 1966 it broke decisively with Syria and elected a new National Command. As a result of these struggles, the leadership that emerged in 1968 was a more practical and seasoned group than that of 1963; it was also more ruthless, more conspiratorial, and above all, more determined to seize power and this time to hold it.

Once the new party command was in place, the leadership set about rooting out opposition and reorganizing the party's structure. It built up its local branches, developed a militia and an intelligence apparatus, and infiltrated mass organizations, especially those made up of students and professors.[42] Using its well-known military figures in the public sphere and its clandestine organization underground, the party was ready by 1968 to make another bid for power. But it was still not strong enough to do so without help from non-Ba'thists in the military. Indeed, both Bakr and Saddam Husain were planning to repeat the method of the military coup that had brought them to power in 1963.

The Making of the Coup

Early in 1968, if not before, the senior military Ba'thists began probing the military for dissatisfied elements willing to participate in a coup. Since Nayif was in a key military position, it is not surprising that he was drawn into such schemes. One such meeting may have taken place as early as February 1968. While these contacts were being made, the Ba'th Party was busy on other fronts as well, contributing to the climate that would help overthrow the regime. A student strike in January 1968 was largely its work, although the Communists participated. In March 1968 a demonstration was organized by Bakr and the Ba'th in favor of a change of government. The party was also making underground preparations.

These activities reached a climax in April 1968, when thirteen retired officers, including former ministers and prime ministers, submitted a memorandum to Arif calling for the removal of Tahir Yahya as prime minister and demanding, among other things, a coalition government of revolutionary elements and the establishment of a legislative assembly. Of the thirteen officers, five were Ba'thists. Bakr had taken the lead in organizing the group.[43] However, Arif refused to meet their demands. When Yahya was asked to form a new cabinet in July, it became clear to Nayif and Da'ud that the time had come to act.[44]

On the eve of the coup, Nayif and Da'ud presented themselves before Arif, demanding Yahya's removal and at the same time professing their loyalty. Whether this was a last attempt to change Arif's mind (as Nayif later claimed) or a ruse to cover up the impending coup is difficult to say, but Arif's refusal to dismiss Yahya clearly decided the issue. The contacts with Bakr and a few of his chosen colleagues were reactivated. In return for their participation in the coup, Nayif demanded to be made prime minister, and Da'ud, minister of defense. Bakr was to be president. The young officers believed that by controlling these posts, they would control the government and the army.

In the early morning hours of 17 July, the coup began. Nayif and his forces occupied the Ministry of Defense, while Da'ud, with members of the Republican Guard, occupied the broadcasting station. The critical action took place at the Republican Palace, where one of the Ba'th accomplices opened the gates to the Ba'thists. The Ba'th also called the militia and the Tenth Brigade into action. The air force also participated, making some cosmetic overflights. In the middle of the night, Arif was summoned, and after a brief confrontation, he surrendered. He was sent off to England and eventually into exile in Istanbul and later Cairo. (He returned to Iraq in the 1990s). Almost ten years to the day after the first revolution of 1958, the fourth major change of regime had been effected in Baghdad.

The Revolutionary Decade, Assessed

The revolutionary decade between 1958 and 1968 had a profound impact on Iraq at all levels—well beyond the political sphere. Beginning with Qasim and ending with the second Ba'th coup, the constant political instability ruptured the institutions of state, brought constant and dramatic shifts in policies and orientations, and eroded the country's still fragile national identity. While some change had been long overdue under the old regime, the revolutionary era was unable to create viable new policies or to institutionalize change. Parliament and political parties had been removed, considered by most of the new elites not as mechanisms of democracy but as vehicles of an outmoded class structure. In their stead, the military was made the main instrument of politics but, in the process, became hopelessly factionalized as it became permeated by the contending trends and interests within the larger society.

In the Arab nationalist period, 1963 to 1968, the direction of policy changed but not its methods or rule. Neither the short-lived Ba'th regime

nor the more moderate Arif regime could bring stability or coherent policies. The brief attempt to restore a constitutional process and the rule of law
under Bazzaz did not survive long enough to materialize. Meanwhile, the
Kurdish rebellion deepened and became more intractable. Even the Kurdish
movement, however, ended up split into ideological and social factions. The
shi'a also used the period of upheaval and declining central control to develop a new religious and communal identity at odds with the secular nationalism of the central government and to strengthen *shi'i* groups, like the
Da'wa and the clergy. Meanwhile, the Ba'th and the Arab nationalists in
charge of the government spent an inordinate amount of time and energy
in failed attempts to emasculate Iraq's identity and merge with the Arab
world.

Perhaps the greatest loss was a sense of civic responsibility, already weak
to start with, on the part of governing elites. Politics became a plaything in
the hands sometimes of inexperienced youth, more often of army officers
with coercive force at their disposal. Governments came to be toppled almost at a whim. In the brutal struggle for power and political survival, serious contenders for power were driven underground, where they were even
less likely to acquire the kind of experience necessary to govern Iraq.

The revolution of 1958 did put power in the hands of the new middle
class and spread Iraq's wealth—and access to middle-class status—more
widely. It also achieved a long-standing desire for greater independence from
the West and a better balance in Iraq's relations with both Cold War blocs.
But the period was so disruptive, over all, that these benefits could not take
root or bring substantial advantages.

In this environment of political disruption, loyalty to family, kin, and locality gradually began to fill the political and social gap, especially under the
Arifs. These ties did not yet supplant the modern institutions previously
built up over four decades—the military, the bureaucracy, the educational
establishment—but they became more important. Increasingly, Arab sunnis
came to exercise control over the country's levers of power and wealth.
Meanwhile, at the periphery, in the Kurdish north and the shi'i south, the
country faced competing cultural identities, while its "center" pursued will-
o-the-wisp Arab unity schemes. The seeds of the totalitarianism established
by the Ba'th regime were sown in this watershed decade of revolutionary
upheavals.

7

THE ERA
OF BA'TH PARTY RULE,
1968–1979

The coup of 17 July 1968 shortly brought the Ba'th Party to full power and inaugurated another, more permanent change in the structure and orientation of government in Iraq. This time the key Ba'th leaders instituted the kind of regime they had failed to achieve in 1963, and they managed to hold on to power, by draconian means, for the remainder of the century.

The early years of the new regime were precarious. The party's base was thin, and Ahmad Hasan al-Bakr and Saddam Husain—the two key figures—had challenges at home and abroad. Their dominance was secured only by instituting a reign of terror—a series of trials, executions, and arrests, reminiscent of the Stalin era—that became a hallmark of the regime.

By the mid–1970s, however, the party had stabilized its hold on power at the summit and was on its way to creating the foundations of a totalitarian state—establishing a mass-based, tightly controlled party, a ubiquitous secret police, a reorganized and Ba'thized military, and a burgeoning bureaucracy with virtually total control over society. Woven into this structure at the top were Tikriti family and clan ties. The regime's longevity was helped by a settlement of the Kurdish problem in 1975 that brought a period of stability in the north and by the oil price rise of 1973, which enabled Iraq, like other oil producers, to undertake a major development program. The party not only established a command economy, under the rubric of socialism, but undertook an industrial program—including extensive weapons development—and provided widespread health, education, and social benefits that went well beyond those of any previous regime. These measures enabled the regime to allay discontent and establish greater control over society. By the late 1970s, Iraq had begun to emerge from its earlier regional and international isolation. Thanks to the economic, social, and political developments mentioned above, Iraq also began to exercise a major influence on the Middle Eastern scene and even in the nonaligned movement, where it expected to play a leading role in the future.

Consolidation of Power, 1968–1973

Within two weeks of the 17 July coup, the Ba'th executed a series of maneuvers that completely removed Nayif, Da'ud, and their supporters from power and consolidated their position on the newly formed Revolutionary Command Council (RCC), the new fulcrum of power. On 30 July, President Bakr became prime minister and commander in chief of the armed forces; Hardan al-Tikriti was made minister of defense. The new RCC now included only five members, all Ba'th or Ba'thist supporters.[1]

Several features of this new government deserve mention. First, the RCC was completely military. Second was the predominance of Tikritis; three of the five members of the RCC were Tikritis and two were related to each other (Bakr and Shihab). To these must be added a third, Saddam Husain, related to Bakr. Husain was elevated to the second most important post in the RCC, that of Bakr's deputy. Last, the government was now completely dominated by the Ba'th. The new leaders had put into operation one key lesson from 1963—not to share power with non-Ba'thists.

Despite these steps, however, the party's position was still precarious. Ba'th support was thin; according to the party's own estimates, it had no more than 5,000 members in 1968.[2] Its support in the military was weak thanks in part to constant purges since 1958. The party faced several tasks if it was to retain power and avoid a repetition of its fate in 1963. It had to consolidate its hold over the apparatus of state; it had to avoid disruptive divisions among its leadership; and it had to neutralize—and then remove—the military from decisionmaking positions. Moreover, it had to undertake these tasks at a time when the regime was faced with domestic pressures (from the Kurds) and challenges from abroad (Iran). This difficult and delicate task was accomplished, almost wholly by Husain, between 1968 and 1973.

The consolidation process began in the military. Early on, officers of questionable loyalty were replaced by Ba'thists or Ba'th sympathizers. At the same time, many senior civil servants, including most directors-general, were also replaced by Ba'thists.

The Conspiracy Trials

The most important and dramatic mechanism for achieving Ba'th dominance was a series of trials that not only eliminated real or potential opponents but also cowed the political classes by introducing a reign of terror. The trials, which began only a few months after the Ba'th took office, involved a range of accusations, including spying for the United States, Israel, and Iran and conspiracy to overthrow the government. The validity of the charges were widely questioned, but they achieved their purpose. The convictions demonstrated the ruthlessness of the regime and made clear that no attempt to overthrow Ba'th rule would be tolerated. The first to be arrested were members of the previous government. They were charged with corruption and jailed. However, as fellow Arab nationalists and socialists, they were dealt with leniently. No charges were proved and all were eventually released.

Far more important, pro-Western elements were targeted. On 10 November 1968 Nasir al-Hani, former foreign minister, was murdered, and a number of Iraqi representatives of Western firms were arrested. Then came the arrest of several men accused of spying for Israel and supplying information to Central Treaty Organization countries, especially Iran and the United States.[3] The arrested men included a number of Jews as well as former ministers, including Abd al-Rahman al-Bazzaz. A number of the accused were tried by secret military court, and fourteen were executed. Amidst international outcry, they were hanged publicly in Baghdad's main square, where they were viewed at government urging by over half a million people. More trials and executions followed in 1969. Bazzaz did not confess and was given a prison sentence.[4]

No sooner had these trials ended than the regime faced a plot by just the right-wing pro-Western elements it most feared, one apparently supported by Iran and the exiled Abd al-Razzaq al-Nayif. In January 1970 thirty-seven men and women were executed on charges of attempting to overthrow the government, and a death sentence was passed in absentia on Nayif. In the same month, Iraq expelled the Iranian ambassador, closed Iranian consulates, and undertook wholesale deportation of Persians and

also Iraqis of Persian origin, making the point that the regime would tolerate no domestic interference from Iran.

Nor did the Ba'th spare the Communists. When the Iraq Communist
Party took a position of opposition in the spring of 1970, the regime began
arresting its members, and by June 1970 several hundred Communists were
in jail. The dissident Communist guerrilla group operating in the south under the leadership of Aziz al-Haj was also brought to heel, and Haj recanted
on television in 1969.

While the party was moving to eliminate or neutralize threats to its control, it also acted to broaden and institutionalize its power within the state.
The first step in this direction was taken on 9 November 1969, when the
five-member Revolutionary Command Council was enlarged to fifteen. All
those appointed were Ba'thists, and all but one of the new appointees were
civilians. Saddam Husain became vice chairman of the RCC, stepping out
of his strictly party role and officially becoming the second most important
figure in the regime after Bakr.[5] All the new appointees were members of the
party's Regional Command.

The Interim Constitution

The next step came in July 1970 with the formal publication of a new interim constitution. This instrument set the form of government that remained, with a few modifications, right up to the regime's overthrow in
2003. First, the constitution was a statement of the regime's ideology. It defined Iraq as a People's Democratic Republic aimed at achieving a united
Arab state and a socialist system. A provision aimed at the Kurds declared
that no part of Iraq could be given up. Islam was declared to be the state religion, but freedom of religion and religious practices were guaranteed. Iraq
was said to be formed of two principal nationalities, Arab and Kurd, with
recognition of Kurdish national rights.

The state was given the authority to plan, direct, and guide the national
economy for the purpose of establishing socialism on a "scientific and revolutionary basis." State ownership of natural resources and the principal instruments of production was stipulated, but private ownership was
guaranteed with some limitations on agricultural land ownership. Free education up to the university level and free medical care were guaranteed.
Work was not only guaranteed as a right but was required.

Second and more important, the constitution also defined the locus of
power in the new regime. Dominant power was given to the RCC, which

had the authority to promulgate laws and regulations, to deal with defense and security, to declare war and conclude peace, and to approve the budget.

The president, as the executive of the RCC, was made commander in chief of the armed forces and chief executive of the state. He was given the power to appoint, promote, and dismiss judiciary, civil, and military personnel. He was also responsible for preparing and approving the budget. The party's Regional Command was also to play a key role. Article 38 stipulated that newly elected members of the RCC had to be members of the Regional Command, thus enshrining the principle of the one-party state. The constitution put into practice another lesson from 1963—firm party control over the executive and legislative organs of state.

Neutralizing the Military

The second task of the party—preventing leadership divisions—proved more difficult. Both Bakr and Husain were anxious to reduce military influence in politics and to prevent the military Ba'thists from taking over the government once again. The enlargement of the RCC in 1969, which reduced the military component to a little more than a third and added strong civilian party figures, was a first step in this direction.

The next step was the removal of the two key military figures in the regime, Hardan al-Tikriti and Salih Mahdi Ammash, both of whom had ambitions and the constituencies in the party and the military to achieve them. Although there is little doubt that Bakr, who had an obsessive (and justified) fear of coups, desired the removal of both military rivals, it was a task he willingly left to Saddam Husain and his growing security apparatus. In October 1970 Hardan al-Tikriti was relieved of all his posts, ostensibly over a clash of policy with Saddam Husain on the Palestinian question but in reality to isolate a potential challenger. In March 1971 he was assassinated in Kuwait amidst rumors that he had been planning a coup. Next Ammash was dropped from the RCC in September 1971 and appointed ambassador to Moscow. He never again played an important role in Iraqi politics. These moves neutralized the military. Remarkably, by 1974 Bakr was the only former army officer left in a key post.

Equally significant was the gradual removal from the party command and the RCC of a number of Ba'th civilians with long-standing party credentials.[6] Again, this was largely the work of Husain in an attempt to remove any future rivals to himself or to Bakr.

This process finally met with a serious challenge, indicating how tenuous was the hold of Bakr and Husain on the sinews of power. In June 1973 Nazim Kzar, hand-picked head of the party's security system, attempted a coup that very nearly succeeded in ending Bakr's regime. Kzar, a *shi'a* who had worked his way up the party ladder, resented the growing monopoly of power by *sunnis* and Tikritis. The plot called for the assassination of Bakr at the Baghdad airport on his return from a trip. Earlier Kzar had taken both Shihab and Ghaidan as hostages. The plan misfired when Bakr's plane was late. Pursued by loyal Iraqi forces, Kzar fled toward the Iranian border. He was intercepted and captured, but both his hostages were shot. Shihab died but Ghaidan survived.

The Kzar episode further depleted the leadership at the top of the party.[7] Ironically, his removal from the scene, eventually strengthened the hold of the Tikritis on the security system, as Saddam Husain increasingly turned to his relatives to fill sensitive security posts. The removal of so many top party figures paved the way for the unquestioned domination of two men—Bakr and Husain. Their ability to work together would keep the party in power for decades.

Bakr and Husain

From the first, the relationship between Bakr and Husain was complementary. Bakr, the only senior politician in the regime who had previously held high office, conferred on the party a certain legitimacy. More important, he brought support from the army. Bakr provided the regime with a paternal face, projecting himself as a "father figure" who could reassure a public increasingly shocked by brutal purges and public executions. But Bakr also had his weaknesses, including a personal dislike of confrontation. He was, thus, content to leave the operational details of removing his rivals to someone willing and able to undertake the task, including the violence and unpleasantness it often entailed.[8]

In Saddam Husain, he found the perfect counterpart. Saddam's personality and background have been analyzed by many authors, who see in his upbringing and early life the forces that shaped him and his policies.[9] He was born into a poor, illiterate peasant family, and his early upbringing was harsh. The environment in his village, Auja, was one in which ties of kin and clan, as well as traditional bedouin values of honor, courage, and even revenge predominated, explaining his later reliance on tribal practices and ideas. His father died before he was born, and his stepfather reputedly abused him. These factors provided Husain with an early instinct for survival as well as cunning in the face of adversity; they also nourished a remarkable degree of persistence and patience and probably contributed to his penchant for cruelty.

At the age of ten, Husain went to Tikrit to live with his uncle, Khair Allah Talfah, previously imprisoned for participation in the Rashid Ali movement, who passed his strong nationalist and anti-British feelings on to Saddam. While attending high school, Saddam plunged into nationalist, anti-regime activities and in 1957 joined the Ba'th Party. He also had an early history of problems with the law, landing in jail with his uncle for six months for a political murder, never proved. These activities contributed to his reputation as a "tough" and a man to be feared. After the failed 1959 assassination attempt on Qasim, Husain took refuge in Cairo until 1963, where he finished high school; this is the only lengthy foreign exposure he has ever had. On his return to Baghdad in 1963 he married his cousin, Sajida Talfah, and they subsequently had five children—two boys, Udayy and Qusayy, and three girls, Raghad, Rana, and Hala. The marriage to a member of the Talfah family was a step up socially within his clan, and he used the ties and the period to cement ties of loyalty to Bakr, then prime minister. After the collapse of the Ba'th government in 1963, Husain went underground and spent several years in prison. He escaped in 1966 and then worked underground to establish the party's apparatus. According to many, he was in charge of the special security forces, which became his forte. It is these underground conspiratorial activities that were most influential in shaping Husain's outlook and mentality. His secretiveness, his suspiciousness, and his distrust of outsiders spring from years of being hunted—and hunting others—and from his own considerable talents in organizing conspiracy.

In 1968 Husain was a man too young to constitute a challenge to Bakr and with no military links. Although Husain began very early to gather the threads of power into his hands, he was careful not to challenge Bakr's leadership. Indeed, Husain's main avenue of advancement in the party—and the state—was through Bakr and his kinship relationship. Husain's organizational ability, ruthlessness, willingness to take risks and, above all, instincts for survival were to prove invaluable for Bakr and the party in this early period of challenge. Both men were nonideological. But Husain was the better organizer and political tactician, able to build mass institutions, to borrow and use the socialist ideology of the left to create a broader constituency for the party, and to tackle tough issues like the Kurds and the nationalization of oil.

By 1969 Saddam Husain was clearly a moving force behind the scenes. But in these early years, when Saddam was still in his thirties, he could not do without Bakr's support and patronage. In the last analysis, however, Bakr needed him, and Saddam began gradually to overshadow his patron.

Ba'th Foreign Policy: The Radical Phase, 1969–1973

Not surprisingly, the first years of the Ba'th regime were turbulent externally as well as internally, with foreign and domestic problems constantly intertwined. The radical, new regime, vulnerable at home as it purged its ranks and attempted to stabilize its power, adopted hostile rhetoric against its foreign adversaries—chiefly Iran, Israel, and the United States, which it saw in collusion against it. The rhetoric was designed in part to generate domestic support, or at least to distract attention from some of the severe measures it was taking at home, but it also reflected the regime's perception, not entirely unjustified, that it was isolated internationally and threatened by neighbors anxious to exploit its fragile position at home.

Ba'th accession to power coincided with dramatic changes in the regional environment that worked to its disadvantage. On the Western front, Iraq had to deal with the aftermath of the Arab defeat by Israel in the 1967 war. Iraq's diplomatic relations with the United States, broken during the war, were not restored, cutting it off from the major Western influence in the region. At the same time, Iraq rejected UN Resolution 242, calling for Israeli withdrawal from Arab territory in exchange for peace. Instead, it called for a continuation of "armed struggle."

Iraq was isolated on other fronts as well. Interactions with the rival Syrian regime remained contentious and antagonistic even after the more pragmatic Hafiz al-Asad replaced the radical Jadid regime in 1970. Relations with Egypt also cooled after Nasser accepted the peace plan advanced by the US secretary of state, which called for a negotiated settlement with Israel. By 1970 Egypt and Iraq were engaged in heated press attacks.

Trouble in the Gulf

In the Gulf, Iraq also faced an entirely new situation. The British announcement in 1969 of its intended withdrawal from the Gulf (accomplished in 1971) was followed by the emergence of new and relatively weak states there—Bahrain, Qatar, and the federated United Arab Emirates (UAE). In March 1969 the United States announced the "Nixon Doctrine," which offered to furnish support to any regional power able to defend security in the region. Iran stepped forward. Not long after, the flow of US arms to Iran began. Between 1970 and 1977 Iran's defense budget rose by 1,100 percent, while its arms imports increased from $264 million in 1970 to $2.6 billion in 1977.[10] Saudi Arabia was soon added as the second Gulf "pillar" of US policy and also supported with military training and some arms. Gradually, the US military presence expanded in and around the Gulf—in Diego Garcia, Oman, and Bahrain. In time, Iraq came to feel surrounded, although it established diplomatic relations with the new Gulf states.

Iraq's most serious difficulty, however, came from Iran. Confrontation began over the perennial problem of the Shatt al-Arab. In February 1969 Iran announced that Iraq had not fulfilled its obligations under the 1937 treaty and demanded that the boundary between the two countries be drawn along the *thalweg*, the deep water channel in the middle of the river. Iraq refused. On 19 April the shah publicly abrogated the treaty, and Iran proceeded to pilot its own ships through the Shatt without paying dues to Iraq. The Iraqi reaction was swift. A number of Iranians were expelled from Iraq, a propaganda war ensued, and Iraq began to aid dissidents against the shah's regime. Iran responded with support to Kurdish dissidents.

Iran was not the only Gulf country disturbed by Iraq's radical stance. Saudi Arabia and the conservative Gulf shaikhdoms opposed Iraq's support for South Yemen, its ties to left-wing elements in North Yemen, and its aid to the Popular Front for the Liberation of the Occupied Arabian Gulf, a Marxist organization dedicated to the overthrow of the conservative regimes in the emirates. The most serious confrontation was with Kuwait, centered on the two Kuwaiti islands of Warba and Bubiyan, which had assumed increased significance to Iraq with the development of its southern oil fields and its plans to expand the port of Umm Qasr. Iraq demanded that the two islands be transferred or leased to it. When negotiations proved fruitless, Iraq decided to apply force. On 20 March 1973 Iraqi troops attacked Samita, a border post in the northeast corner of Kuwait. The attack killed two Kuwaiti border guards. Saudi Arabia immediately came to Kuwait's aid and, together with the Arab League, secured Iraq's withdrawal from the post but not from other positions inside Kuwait.[11]

Relations with the USSR

Iraq's isolation, the Iranian threat, and domestic instability, especially a renewal of the Kurdish rebellion in the north, caused the regime to turn to the

Soviet bloc as a counterweight to these forces. On 1 May 1969 Iraq became the first Arab country to recognize East Germany; in the spring of that year the government concluded a major contract with Poland to develop Iraq's rich sulfur deposits. Meanwhile, the USSR provided essential help in developing the Rumaila field, the first significant entry of the Soviet Union into the production of Gulf petroleum. In February and June of 1969 Soviet naval squadrons paid a visit to Umm Qasr and Basra, indicating their support for Iraq in the face of its "imperialist" neighbors.[12]

The high tide of Soviet-Iraqi cooperation, however, came with the conclusion of the Iraqi-Soviet Friendship Treaty of 1972. The accord called for cooperation in the military, political, and economic spheres and required regular consultations on international affairs affecting both parties. On the Soviet side this meant continued supplies of military equipment and training at a high level. On the Iraqi side it meant Soviet access to Iraqi ports and airports, but no base facilities.

From the Iraqi point of view, the treaty played a role in stabilizing the situation, in neutralizing Soviet support for the Kurds, and in balancing Iran. But the relationship soon cooled. Iraq was irked by the Soviet's sale of oil to Europe at much higher prices than it paid, and at the poor quality of the Soviet goods it received in exchange. There was little the Ba'th could do, however, to break its dependence on Soviet arms.

The One-Party State

By the end of 1973, the regime had reached a turning point domestically. Saddam Husain had, by now, eliminated key military and civilian competition and was ready to lay out, publicly, the new foundations of party and state. To this end, the party called a regional congress, which met from 8 to 12 January 1974. Organized by Saddam Husain, the congress made clear that its aim was a one-party state with centralized control over all key institutions.

First, the congress elected a new, thirteen-member Regional Command, adding eight new members to the previous five.[13] The party then took several steps to strengthen its hold over the government. In November 1974 eight new ministers were appointed, five of whom were new command members. Although ministerial reshuffles occurred with regularity thereafter, the Ba'th share of ministerial posts seldom fell below two-thirds, and key posts were always occupied by Regional Command members. In September 1977 all Regional Command members were appointed members of the Revolutionary Command Council, making these two bodies indistinguishable. Through the overlap of personnel on three essential bodies—the Regional Command, the RCC, and the Council of Ministers—the party could control policy formation, policy legislation, and policy execution.

Party Structure

Buttressing this centralization of power at the top was a grassroots party organization that had taken full shape by 1974.[14] The smallest unit in this organization was the party cell or circle *(khaliyya)*, composed of between three and seven members. Cells usually functioned at the neighborhood level, where they met to discuss and carry out party directives. Next on the hierarchical ladder was the party division *(firqa)*, made up of several cells and operating in small urban quarters or villages. Professional and occupational units similar to the divisions were also located in offices, factories, schools, and other organizations. Honeycombing the bureaucracy and the military, these units functioned as the party's eyes and ears. Above the division was the section *(shu'ba)*, composed of two to five divisions. A section usually had jurisdiction over a territory the size of a large city quarter or county. A branch *(far')*, composed of at least two sections, operated at the provincial level, and the Regional Command, elected by the party's congress, operated at the national level. Over and above the Regional Command was the National Command, headed by a secretary-general, Michel Aflaq, and including the party's representatives from other Arab countries as well as Iraqis. While the Regional Command developed the ideological agenda for Iraq, the National Command connected the Iraqi party to its friends and allies in other Arab countries.

Attached to this structure was a militia or popular army, composed mainly of new party recruits. Initially, its main function was to help defend the party in time of need, to keep order in the neighborhoods, and to give military training to members. Although the party began arming members in 1968, the militia was not established by decree until 1970. Reliable figures on its size are difficult to obtain. One source claims that the militia, about 50,000 in the mid–1970s, grew to 100,000 in 1977 and 170,000 by 1980. Another puts them at 50,000 in 1978.[15]

Careful attention was paid to the recruitment and indoctrination of party members. Potential recruits were known as party "friends" and "supporters" but technically were not inside party ranks. Such candidates were required to undergo a long probationary period, taking anywhere from five to eight years, during which they would perform party tasks under careful supervision and attend party seminars and courses, before admission to the party. The party grew rapidly in this period, at least at the lower levels. In 1968, party membership may only have been a few hundred. By 1976, there were about 10,000 full members and some 500,000 supporters. By the early 1980s, according to official party sources, full members numbered 25,000; followers about 1.5 million. This latter figure included supporters as well as those working their way up the party ladder.[16] The party also spread its tentacles to the school system, indoctrinating and recruiting students at an early age. By 1983 the Tali'a (Vanguard), at the elementary and intermediate level, had over a million members; the Futuwwa (Youth), for the early teens, reached 127,000; and the Shabab (Adolescents), for ages seventeen to twenty-one, had almost 72,000.[17]

The Security System and the Military

The party was not the only mechanism controlling the state and its citizens, although it was the most visible. Equally important was the security apparatus, which not only grew in the decade after 1968 but evolved into an elaborate network of institutions watching over one another and intertwined with all state institutions. These were increasingly brought under the control of Saddam Husain, who made security his special province. The history and development of these security organs, some of which predate the 1968 coup, is understandably murky, but by the end of the 1970s they included the Amn al-Amm (Public Security Directorate), the "official" government organization responsible for criminal investigation, traditionally attached to the Ministry of Interior; the Mukhabarat al-Amma (General Intelligence Service), in charge of watching party as well as nonparty political activities at home and abroad; Istikhbarat Askariyya (Military Intelligence), responsible for data on foreign military threats as well as the loyalty of Iraq's officer corps; and the party's Military Bureau, in charge of security in the military. By 1980 still another organization, the Maktab al-Amn al-Qaumi (Bureau of National Security), oversaw the Public Security Directorate, the Mukhabarat, and Military Intelligence officers. Overlapping and compartmentalized, intelligence units not only watched citizens but each other.

The military was also brought under party control. By the mid–1970s, the officer corps was rapidly being Ba'thized. Early in the regime's tenure, party members and trainees who had graduated from secondary school were put into crash courses in the military college ranging from six months to two years. The longer course produced lieutenants; the shorter, warrant officers.[18] A commissar system was established in the military, with Ba'th cells overseeing recruitment and indoctrination. Officers were not permitted to carry out orders on any important matters without consulting the party. In July 1978 Ba'thization of the military was made mandatory. A decree made any non-Ba'thist political activity in the military punishable by death, essentially transforming the military into an arm of the party—and its leadership.

The end of this process was the growth during the 1970s of a political monolith buttressed by growing economic wealth. The party not only developed and controlled the coercive organs of state but took over an existing network of popular organizations and used them to generate grassroots support. Some, like the associations for lawyers, engineers, and teachers were old and well established; others, such as the General Federation of Peasants' Associations, the General Federation of Workers' Unions, and the Women's Association had been created after the revolution of 1958. All were encouraged and dominated by the Ba'th. The party put special emphasis on education and control of the media. The curriculum, especially in the humanities and social sciences, was rewritten, and the party began to restrict admittance to a number of college faculties to party members.

The Emergence of Personal Rule

While this party institutionalization was under way, an important countertrend was also at work: a shift in the balance of power from Bakr to Husain. By the mid–1970s Bakr had begun to retire from an active political role. This was due partly to illness (which surfaced increasingly by 1974). More important was Husain's own ambitions to succeed him. Over time, Husain's office became the central focus of power and decisionmaking in Iraq; Bakr's position became more ceremonial. By 1977 the party bureaux, the intelligence mechanisms, and even ministers who, according to the constitution, should have reported to Bakr reported to Husain. Meanwhile Husain himself became less accessible. Ministers who were not on the Regional Command, for example, rarely saw him. The RCC and Regional Command were used less for collective discussions of policy than as instruments to ratify decisions already taken by Husain and a close group of his followers.

As power gravitated to Husain's hands, he exercised it in an increasingly paternalistic fashion. Several hours a week he had an open phone line to receive public complaints, often dealt with summarily on a personal basis. Meanwhile a cult of personality—even a mythology—grew up around him.

The press constantly displayed his picture; his virtues became part of party legend. Newborn babies were named after him, and young party members emulated his walk, his dress, and even his manner of speech. The film *The Long Days,* depicting his participation in the assassination of Qasim in mythic terms, was another example. Typical of this adulation was an advertisement in the *New York Times* in July 1980 that asked whether Iraq would "repeat her former glories and the name of Saddam Hussein link up with that of Hammurabi [and] Asurbanipal."[19]

The Kin and Clan Network

Buttressing Husain's party position and his personal rule was a network of kin and clan relations that was interlaced with and often cut across party lines. At the core of this network was the family relationship between Ahmad Hasan al-Bakr, Saddam Husain, and Adnan Khair Allah Talfah. In 1977 Talfah, Saddam's cousin and brother-in-law, was elected to the Regional Command of the party, appointed to the RCC, and made Minister of Defense, to keep an eye on the military. From the mid–1970s on, Husain's half brothers Barzan, Saba'wi, and Watban assumed increasingly important posts in the security system. At the same time, several members of the Majid clan (related to Saddam's paternal line), including Ali Hasan al-Majid and Husain Kamil al-Majid, were working their way up the security ladder. From this inner circle, family ties extended outward to include more distant kin in positions of influence.

The kinship network, drawn almost wholly from Saddam's tribe, the Albu Nasir of Tikrit, allowed Saddam to bypass the party and the military and keep personal control over these institutions.[20] In this parallel, but traditional, system of recruitment, loyalty was based on family and clan ties rather than on institutions or ideology. While this unquestionably contributed to the regime's longevity, it did create embarrassment and even hostility from party members. To cover its traces, the regime in 1976 made it an offense for public figures to use a name indicating tribal, clan, or regional affiliation; overnight, most of the leaders had to change their names.

Relations with the Kurds

When the Ba'th came to power in 1968, it inherited the Kurdish situation left from the Arif era. The promising settlement concluded by Bazzaz in 1966 had fallen into abeyance, partly because it was unpopular with a number of army

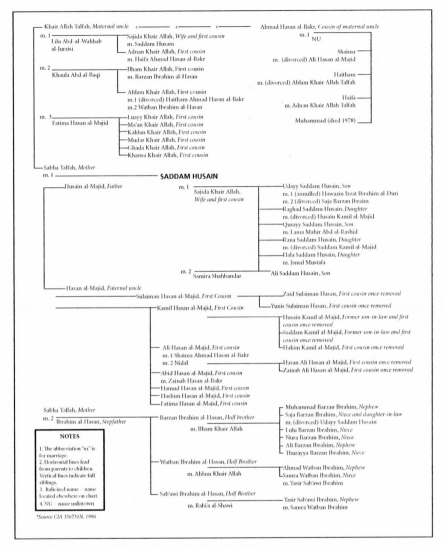

FIGURE 7.1   Saddam Husain's Family Tree

officers and partly because the Kurds under Barzani had hardened their stance. Although a desultory cease-fire had been maintained, Barzani had begun to consolidate his relations with Iran and had established contact with Israel, factors that did not augur well for a solution given the intense Arab nationalism of the Ba'th.[21] By 1968 he had acquired anti-aircraft weapons and field artillery. At the same time, intense factionalism continued within the Kurdish movement between the followers of Ibrahim Ahmad and Jalal al-Talabani on one hand and those of Barzani on the other; the latter now controlled the KDP.

The new Iraqi regime initially committed itself to implementing the 1966 agreement and offered cabinet seats to representatives of both Kurdish factions. But Barzani was doubtful of Ba'th intentions and refused to accept any positions in the cabinet. The Ahmad-Talabani faction, however, had no such qualms and, to bolster their position, accepted the offer. Before long the government was openly supporting them, and skirmishes between the Kurdish factions took place once again. Barzani now turned against the government, attacking some of the IPC installations in Kirkuk. Four divisions of the Iraqi army were now sent north and full-scale war ensued once more. Iran was soon heavily embroiled in the conflict. By 1969 Barzani was receiving extensive aid from Iran, and Iranian units were even fighting in Iraqi territory. This aid helped turn the tide in Barzani's favor. Recognizing the stalemate, the government reluctantly decided to negotiate with him.

In fact both sides had good reasons to come to terms. Barzani needed a respite in the fighting to deal with his opponents, who had gained some strength in the interim. As a quid pro quo, he insisted that the government abandon the Ahmad-Talabani faction and disarm the Fursan (pro-government Kurdish militia), consisting mainly of his tribal enemies.[22]

The regime had even stronger motives for concluding an agreement. In 1969 Saddam Husain was still preoccupied with consolidating control over the military wing of the party. He did not want a war that would strengthen the military faction, as had happened in 1963. Even more important was government concern over the shah's aid to Barzani in the midst of Iraq's intense confrontation with Iran over the Shatt. Better, the government reasoned, to grant some concessions to the Kurds on autonomy than to lose control of the Kurdish situation to Iran.

The March 1970 Agreement

In March 1970 an agreement was concluded with Barzani. From the first, the 1970 settlement was the work of Saddam Husain, who went north for discussions with Barzani in January. On 11 March the fifteen-point agreement was made public. It provided for Kurdish autonomy (the first official use of the word),[23] and it guaranteed proportional representation of Kurds within a future legislative body, the appointment of a Kurdish vice president at the national level, the expenditure of an equitable amount of oil revenue in the autonomous region, and the recognition of both Kurdish and Arabic as official languages in Kurdish territory. For his part, Barzani agreed to turn

over the heavy weapons of his fighting force, the *peshmergas,* and integrate
that force into the Iraqi army.

The agreement, which allowed both sides to claim a measure of victory,
was controversial from the start. Both sides doubted the sincerity of the
other. There is little doubt that the pact helped stabilize Ba'th rule and gave
the regime the capacity to deal with its enemies on other fronts, yet many
inside and outside the party felt the agreement allowed Barzani to control
too wide a tract of territory. Many Kurds were critical of the agreement, as
well, claiming that it failed to declare immediate autonomy. The agreement
would come into effect only in four years, after a census had determined areas in which the Kurds had a majority. Given these mutual misgivings, it is
not surprising that the agreement was to prove only temporary. In fact, the
main loser, as usual, was the dissident Ahmad-Talabani faction, which had
lost support from the government as well as the Barzani Kurds.

Breakdown of the Agreement

Between 1970 and 1974 the situation between the government and the
Kurds gradually deteriorated. In July 1970 the KDP nominated its secretary-general, Muhammad Habib Karim, as the Kurdish vice president, but
he was rejected by the Ba'th because of his Persian background. Worse, two
assassination attempts were made on Barzani, in 1971 and 1972.[24] Meanwhile, the government undertook an Arabization program in Mosul and
Kirkuk, deporting some 45,000 Faili *(shi'i)* Kurds to Iran and replacing
them with Arabs.

Barzani did not keep his part of the bargain, either. He refused to close
the border with Iran, continued to import arms, and in 1971, appealed directly to the United States for aid. President Nixon directed the CIA to sur-
reptitiously advance Barzani $16 million in aid. The shah followed with far
more massive support.[25] Barzani also resumed his contacts with Israel and
received some aid from this source as well. With this infusion of support, he
saw no reason to compromise with Baghdad.

By October 1973 the split between the Ba'th and Barzani was almost
complete, but one last attempt at a negotiated settlement was made. It
failed. The KDP demanded wide powers of autonomy in the Kurdish region
and the inclusion of Kirkuk in their sphere. These terms were unacceptable
to Baghdad. On 9 March 1974 the Ba'th gave the Kurdish negotiators two
days to accept the government's own autonomy plan. The Kurds rejected the
plan, and with this the rupture was complete. On 11 March the Ba'th

announced that their plan would become official government policy, and the pro-Barzani Kurdish ministers withdrew from the cabinet. By April the war had resumed.

The 1974–1975 War

At first, things went well for the government, and the troops demonstrated better fighting capacity than previously. By May government troops had occupied the great plains area of Kurdistan and consolidated their position in the cities of Kirkuk, Arbil, and Sulaimaniyya. By fall they had taken Rawanduz and reached Qal'at Diza. In response, Iran augmented its military aid, furnishing the Kurds with antitank missiles and artillery and intervening directly in Iraqi territory. Syria, also at odds with Iraq, likewise aided the Kurds. These activities slowed down the Iraqi offensive, and by spring of 1975 a stalemate had been reached. It was during this stalemate, with no further progress by the Iraqi army but with Iran becoming directly and dangerously involved, that talk of an agreement between Iraq and Iran, at the expense of the Kurds, began to surface.

The 1975 Agreement

By 1975 both Iran and Iraq had good reasons for seeking a solution. The Iraqi army had done better than expected on the ground, but Iranian intervention had made it clear that the Iraqi regime could not, on its own, win the military victory it needed to impose its own solution. Moreover, further escalation might well mean full-scale war with Iran, which Iraq could not win. More important, Saddam Husain had staked his future on solving the Kurdish problem and could not risk failure. Moreover, there was pressure from other Arab countries, which did not want to be distracted from the confrontation with Israel. Israel's support for the Kurds was another reason for ending the war.

On the Iranian side, the shah, although he wished to weaken the Baghdad government, did not want the rebellion to spill across his borders, nor was he himself ready to move to the level of open war with Iraq. Moreover, he was concerned over the Soviet commitment to Iraq. The Soviets were providing Iraq with sophisticated weaponry, including MIG–23s, and the use of Soviet pilots to fly the planes. In return for a cessation of aid to the Kurds, the shah wanted explicit recognition of Iran's boundary claims on the Shatt al-Arab and implicit recognition of his status as guardian of the Gulf. On 6 March the two sides finally negotiated an agreement.

The agreement did, in fact, accomplish most of the shah's goals. The official clauses specified that the frontier between Iran and Iraq would be governed by the 1913–1914 Constantinople Protocol but that the demarcation line on the Shatt would be the *thalweg*. In return, both parties agreed to exercise strict control over their frontiers to prevent subversive infiltration, in effect ending Iranian support for the Kurds. The Iraqis also renounced any Arab claims to the Arab-speaking province of Khuzistan, as well as to the islands at the foot of the Gulf.

For the Kurds supporting Barzani, the 1975 settlement was little short of a disaster. Within hours of its signing, the Iranians began to haul away their military equipment. On 7 March the Iraqi army moved into the remaining areas of the north, and on 2 April it reached the border, sealed off the area, and proclaimed the end of the revolt. For his part, Barzani, faced with the cease-fire, decided to give up the fight and fled to Iran, taking most of his *peshmergas* with him. (He died of cancer in Georgetown Hospital in 1979.) Under an amnesty plan, about 70 percent of his *peshmergas* eventually gave themselves up to the Iraqis. Some remained in the hills of Kurdistan to fight again, and about 30,000 went across the border to Iran to join the Kurdish civilian refugees settled there, then estimated at between 100,000 to 200,000. The result of the agreement was to leave the Kurdish national movement in a state of complete disarray with its leadership defeated and in exile.

The Aftermath of the Agreement

On 11 March 1974 the Ba'th regime began implementing its own autonomy plan, which stated that Kurdistan was to be autonomous, although forming an integral part of Iraq; that the administrative capital was to be Arbil; and that the region was to be governed by an elected legislative council and an executive council to be elected by a majority vote of the legislative council. The president of the executive council was to be appointed from among the members of the legislative council by the Iraqi head of state. The Baghdad government could dismiss the president and dissolve the assembly. The autonomous territory excluded Kirkuk and the districts of Sinjar and Khanaqin.

An appointed legislative council was convened on 5 October 1974, but in 1980, when a general law for the national assembly was promulgated, a new election law for the Kurds was also issued. The first elections for the new fifty-member council were held shortly thereafter. By 1981 the council was in operation.

In addition to implementing a degree of autonomy, the government took steps on the ground to change the political and social dynamics in the north, fundamentally. Some measures were positive; some, profoundly disruptive. On the positive side, the Ba'th moved to settle the refugee question. By the end of 1976, all but 30,000 refugees from Iran had been repatriated. A number of these were sent to the center and south of the country and kept there for a year; most, but not all, were returned to the north by 1976.[26] The government also moved forcefully to develop the north economically, aided by increased oil revenues. Much of this expenditure went into industrial projects, schools, hospitals, and tourist sites, as well as roads and communications networks, which improved the government's capacity to control the area. Between 1975 and 1979, textile, carpet, canning, and tobacco factories were built; the number of schools increased fourfold and student enrollment grew from 112,000 to 332,000. These actions did bring a measure of prosperity to the north and, in some areas, a new consumer-oriented society; some Kurds became rich, while a new middle class acquired a taste for stability and a higher standard of living.

The government also introduced land reform into the north in a more serious way. About 2.7 million dunams were distributed among Kurds; about four hundred cooperative societies were formed to replace the landlords.[27] While these measures weakened the *agha* class, especially those supporting Barzani, the government also revived the Fursan, the *agha*-led military forces willing to support the government. These grew in size, along with subsidies and favors for those tribal leaders willing to stand with the government.

However, these positive achievements were accompanied by drastic steps, taken to assure that no further organized rebellion would take place. These measures focused on large-scale relocation of Kurds as well as continued Arabization of Kurdish areas. By 1976 the Iraqi government had razed all Kurdish villages along an eight-hundred-mile border with Turkey and Iran ranging from five to fifteen miles deep. Some 1,400 villages had been razed by 1978 and some 600,000 villagers displaced.[28] Displaced Kurds were sent to newly constructed collective settlements near major towns, a policy bitterly protested by Kurds. In mixed Kurdish, Arab, and Turkman provinces such as Sinjar, Khanaqin, and Kirkuk, the Kurdish population was reduced and additional Arabs were introduced. In these areas Kurdish was not permitted as the primary language of instruction. The carrot-and-stick approach to the Kurdish area did bring a measure of quiet to the north, especially after 1975, and enabled the government to turn its attention to economic and social development—the second most important pillar of its regime. For this, the way was now prepared by the regime's nationalization of oil, perhaps its most popular act and one which helped legitimize an otherwise repressive regime.

The Nationalization of Oil

Despite its socialist aims, the Ba'th did not initially move toward nationalization of oil. Rather it allowed the ERAP agreement and other arrangements made by the Arif regime to continue in force. The regime undertook measures to exploit the southern fields previously expropriated by Qasim. In 1969 new contracts were signed with the Soviet Union for drilling in the northern Rumaila field; US and West German firms were enlisted in constructing pipelines and a new off-shore port, Mina-l-Bakr, to export the southern production. By April 1972 exports from the Rumaila field had officially commenced with 21,000 metric tons of crude.[29] Development of the southern fields, however, did not solve the government's continuing problems with IPC, including the company's refusal to recognize PL 80. In addition, there was underlying bitterness in Iraq over low levels of production from the Kirkuk fields in the face of increased production everywhere else in the Gulf. Iraq's share of Gulf production fell from 20 percent in 1960 to 10 percent in 1974, while that of Iran, Saudi Arabia, and even Abu Dhabi rose. Much of this imbalance, of course, was due to the lingering dispute with IPC.

Between March and May 1972 IPC dropped production from the Kirkuk field about 44 percent, an action that brought home to Iraq its dependence on the foreign oil company. The company maintained that the decision had been made entirely on economic grounds, but the Iraqis saw the move as a means of forcing concessions from them on other points of disagreement. When IPC failed to restore production, events then moved to a rapid conclusion. On 1 June 1972 Public Law 69 nationalized IPC. Despite dire predictions of what might befall Iraq as a result of nationalization, in February 1973 a final settlement was reached with IPC clearing the decks of all prior disputes and removing legal actions against purchases of Iraqi oil. Then, following the Arab-Israeli war of October 1973, all foreign oil concessions were put in government hands.

The Ba'th had finally accomplished a major aim of all revolutionary regimes since 1958. In the short term, nationalization had some negative

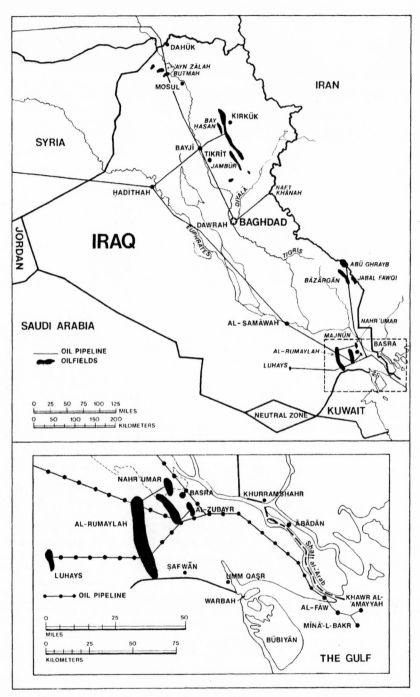

FIGURE 7.2   Oil Fields, Pipelines, and Ports

effects. It disrupted oil production and development programs and helped isolate the regime from the West. However, in the longer term, it had significant benefits. It gave the government complete control over its oil production and sales and paved the way for the regime to profit fully from the oil price rise about to shower bounty on the Gulf producers. It closed the books on a long-running dispute with the international oil companies that had frozen Iraqi oil production, reduced Iraq's global market share, and limited its income. Iraq quickly turned to expanding oil production and transport facilities as well as further exploration. By 1980 Iraq had doubled production and increased recoverable reserves fourfold. Iraq built a second pipeline, from Kirkuk through Turkey to the Mediterranean, and in 1975 completed the so-called strategic pipeline from Haditha south to Rumaila and then to Faw, designed to take Kirkuk oil south to the Gulf and Rumaila oil north to the Mediterranean, thus freeing it from Syrian interference.

Iraq's nationalization of oil coincided with the unprecedented oil price rise initiated by the Arab oil embargo of 1973. By 1974 oil prices had quadrupled, and they continually rose throughout the decade, with a second boost in 1979, after the Iranian revolution. This price rise, together with expanded production, provided a flood of wealth in Iraq. Iraq's oil revenues increased from $575 million in 1972 to $26 billion in 1980.[30] This bounty produced an era of unprecedented prosperity, as well as a new economic reality.

While nationalization gave Iraq greater economic independence from Western oil companies, it soon produced dependence of a different kind. Iraq's domestic economy became increasingly dependent on oil revenues and therefore on international oil markets. By 1979 oil production constituted almost 63 percent of Iraq's GDP.[31] The dramatic increase in income also turned Iraq into a consumer, instead of a producer, society. Although the government did make efforts to diversify, especially in the industrial sector, oil displaced the productive sectors as the chief source of national income. The government used the new income to spread services, especially health and education, to wide sections of the population, while the population became increasingly accustomed to state-supplied benefits.

Economic and Social Development

Increased revenue provided a brief period of prosperity unmatched in Iraq's previous history. It also enabled the Ba'th regime, which was now fully in

TABLE 7.1 Oil as a Percentage of Iraq's Gross Domestic Product, 1960–1979 (in current ID millions)

	Value in ID millions	% of GDP
1960	209.7	37.1
1965	285.9	33.0
1970	370.5	30.9
1975	2,287.7	57.6
1979	5,686.5	62.7

SOURCE: World Bank, *World Tables*, 3rd ed., vol. 1: *Economic Data* (Baltimore: Johns Hopkins University Press, 1983), pp. 90–91.

control of the government and the country, to make some impressive gains in economic development and social mobility. These were encompassed in three interrelated goals set out by the party. The first, adopted under the slogan of a "socialist" economy, was state ownership of national resources and state control over most of the economy. Second was a more broad-based distribution of wealth and services. The third aim was rapid modernization, particularly industrialization, as a means of diversifying the economy and achieving economic independence. Included in this was a military-industrial program designed to enhance Iraq's power. By 1980 the regime had taken significant steps in all these areas.

The Socialist Economy

Oil revenues gave great impetus to the socialization of the economy. Nationalization of the foreign-owned oil companies, which put control over the production and export of Iraq's major resource in government hands, was the most striking manifestation of this policy, but it was not the only one.

One new area into which government extended its control was agriculture, where the Ba'th began the development of collective farms (along with an extensive land reform program) with the intention of creating large-scale, capital-intensive agriculture. By 1976 seventy-nine farms, with an area of 534,000 dunams and 9,850 members, had been created.[32] However, by 1980 the leadership was disillusioned with collective farms as a panacea for agricultural problems. Despite substantial investments made by the regime in barrages, dams, irrigation works, and drainage systems, agricultural production, particularly in grain crops, continued to stagnate or decline. In 1981 the regime reversed its policies and abolished the collective farm program.

More significant was the socialization of industry. Much of the oil revenue went into developing large-scale industries, such as iron, steel, and petrochemicals. These were wholly owned and managed by the government, as were most medium-sized plants, manufacturing items such as textiles, food products, and construction materials. Trade likewise came under increased government control, through various mechanisms such as state trading organizations, state retail outlets, import licensing, and direct government purchasing.

Increased government control of the economy was reflected in the government's own statistics. The share of the socialist, or public, sector rose from 31 percent of domestic production in 1968 to 80 percent in 1977, although it varied from sector to sector. In foreign trade the increase was from 41 percent to 89 percent.[33]

Socialization was not without its drawbacks, however. It brought inefficiency, waste, and mismanagement, and there was no indication that the public sector was more productive than the private. Some of these drawbacks were recognized by the regime, but they did not outweigh the regime's commitment to government control.

Social Justice and the Welfare State

The regime's attempt to deliver social justice can best be seen in agrarian reform, one of the first areas it tackled. When the regime came to power in 1968, the overwhelming bulk of the expropriated lands remained in government hands, while peasants farmed the remainder under conditions not much improved from the days of the Old Regime. The Ba'th soon addressed this problem. In May 1969 Ahmad Hasan al-Bakr announced that peasants would no longer pay for the lands given to them and that landlords henceforth would receive no compensation for expropriated land, a considerable redistribution of income. Finally in May 1970, a new agrarian reform law was promulgated. It limited landholdings in rain-fed zones to a range of 1,000 to 2,000 dunams; in irrigated zones, from 400 to 600 dunams. Land distributed to peasants was to be limited to 100 to 200 dunams of rain-fed land; 40 to 60 dunams of irrigated land. Those receiving land had to join a co-op.

The Ba'th did not stop with legislation. It gave considerable impetus to land distribution, especially after 1975. By the end of 1976, 71.3 percent of state-held land had been distributed to 222,975 beneficiaries.[34] After the

1975 settlement of the Kurdish problem, as indicated earlier, land reform was rapidly pushed forward in the north. (See Table A.5.)

The egalitarian thrust of the regime could also be seen in its expansion of education and health services, measures that disproportionately benefited the poorer classes and improved living standards. Education up to the university level and health services, including hospitalization, were free. Between 1968 and 1980 the Ba'th more than doubled student enrollment in schools at every level. By 1980 Iraq had almost a million students in secondary schools and 100,000 students in higher education (see Table A.4).[35] Nonetheless, illiteracy remained high—53 percent in 1977. In 1978 Iraq mounted a massive literacy campaign. Similar progress was made in health services. The ratio of doctors to the population in 1968 was 1 to 4,200; by 1980 it had been improved to 1 to 1,790.[36] Life expectancy rose from forty-six to fifty-seven years. These expenditures brought rising living standards. Per-capita income rose tenfold, from ID 120 in 1970 to ID 1,181 in 1980. So did energy consumption and the use of TVs.

Some maldistribution of income remained, however, mainly in three areas: between rural and urban communities; between the central region of Iraq, focused on Baghdad, and the northern and southern regions; and within urban areas. In the central region, the average income was one-third higher than in the south and one-quarter higher than in the north.[37] The traditional agricultural sector contained the bulk of those at the bottom of the income scale.

Diversification and Industrialization

Diversification of the economy, as a means of achieving economic autonomy, mainly by industrialization, was the third aim of the Ba'th. Here results were mixed. The Ba'th regime was unsuccessful in lessening its dependence on oil, as were other Gulf producers in this period. The mammoth increase in oil revenues in 1973 and the second price rise in 1979 raised the share of oil revenues automatically in the budgets of all oil-producing states. Nevertheless, there was considerable development of industry in Iraq in this period.

In development allocations between 1975 and 1980, 30 percent—almost twice that of any other sector—went to industry. Much of the allocation to industry went into developing the nucleus of a heavy industry in Iraq, with a concentration on iron, steel, and petrochemical facilities. Among the new heavy industries constructed in this period were two sponge iron plants at Zubair; a companion steelworks in the same area; an aluminum company in

TABLE 7.2 Industrial Establishments and Employees, 1962–1980

	Large Establishments[a]				Small Establishments				Total	
	Number	%	Employees	%	Number	%	Employees	%	Number	Employees
1962	1,186	5.5	77,690	64.3	20,191	94.5	43,136	35.7	21,377	120,826
1965	1,243	5.5	88,343	63.3	21,333	94.5	48,344	36.7	22,576	131,677
1971	1,330	4.2	103,909	60.6	29,940	95.8	67,481	39.4	31,270	171,390
1975	1,349	3.3	134,600	56.9	39,275	96.7	101,993	43.1	40,624	236,593
1980	1,494	4.2	180,900	70.4	34,351	95.8	76,247	29.7	36,025	257,147

[a] Includes water and electricity establishments. Large establishments are those employing ten or more workers.
SOURCES: Iraq, Ministry of Planning, *Statistical Pocketbook, 1982*, pp. 29, 30, 32; *AAS 1978*, pp. 91, 118; *Statistical Pocketbook, 1976*, p. 40; *AAS 1973*, pp. 168, 169, 172, 173; *AAS 1965*, p. 150; *Statistical Pocketbook, 1960–1970*, pp. 88–89.

Nasiriyya; and a massive petrochemical complex in the Basra-Rumaila area, using the natural gas from the Rumaila fields. These included facilities for processing liquid petroleum gas, a fertilizer plant, and a plant to produce plastics and other chemical derivatives. Another fertilizer plant was located at Qa'im near the phosphate mines.

Meanwhile, lighter industries were added at a somewhat slower pace, among them a vehicle assembly plant and plants to produce electrical equipment, tires, and paper. The consumption of electricity increased almost fourfold. Infrastructure was also developed, as roads, railroads, ports, and airports were expanded and improved. Projects included the construction of the offshore port of Mina-l-Bakr, and the expansion of the ports of Umm Qasr, Khaur al-Zubair, and Ma'qal, near Basra.

Along with civilian industry went the construction of a military-industrial complex, expansion of conventional military infrastructure, and the development of a secret program for weapons of mass destruction (WMD). In 1974 a three-man Strategic Development Committee, headed by Saddam Husain, was formed with the aim of developing nuclear—as well as chemical and, later, biological—weapons. The same year, Iraq concluded an agreement with France for the purchase of a nuclear reactor, allegedly for research. In 1975 it purchased additional equipment from Italy capable of separating plutonium. The French agreed to sell Iraq two reactors, using enriched uranium—one large (Osiraq), the other smaller. To develop this program, Iraq relied initially on Arab expertise, importing hundreds, possibly thousands, of Arab scientists and engineers, and gave considerable impetus to training Iraqi scientists abroad.

Although the world knew of the reactor purchases, much of the program was secret. The secret program did not proceed smoothly and in fact received several serious setbacks. In 1979 Israeli agents destroyed reactor cores being shipped to Iraq from France as they were leaving a French port. In 1981 Iraq's Osiraq reactor was bombed and destroyed by Israel, setting back this portion of the program. However, Iraq continued the clandestine program, using other methods.

Iraq also used its oil money to import military equipment and construct military facilities, again with the aim of diversifying suppliers. The defense budget increased from $500 million in 1970 to $4.5 billion in 1975. Additional funds were used for the purchase of aircraft, tanks, air defense systems, surface-to-air missiles, airfields, and underground infrastructure to protect the equipment. At one point, Iraq purchased an entire electronics industry to be erected in Iraq.[38]

While these expenditures did provide an economic transformation in Iraq, they also produced some negative results. First, a disproportionate amount of resources was siphoned off on military expenditures. One source puts military expenditure as 30 percent of GNP by 1980.[39]

A second outcome was a relative decline in the productive sectors, especially agriculture. Its contribution to the GDP declined from 17 percent in 1970 to 7 percent in 1979. Meanwhile, agricultural imports increased tremendously. By 1977 Iraq was importing 33 percent of its agricultural supply.[40] Although industry grew, it could not keep up with the outsized growth of the service sector and government employment. Manufacturing accounted for 9 percent of GDP in the 1960s; only 7 percent in the 1970s.[41]

Third, the era of prosperity rapidly created a consumer society, dependent on government employment. One source estimates that government employment, exclusive of the military, doubled between 1972 and 1978.[42] Another claims that one-fifth to one-fourth of the population worked directly or indirectly for the government; in cities the figure reached one-third.[43]

The Social Transformation

Oil wealth also produced a more rapid social transformation and speeded up social mobility. Rural to urban migration, already under way, greatly intensified, permanently changing the demographic distribution of the population. By 1977 Iraq was an urban country with 64 percent of its people in cities.

TABLE 7.3 Civilian Government Employees, 1952–1990						
	1952	1968	1972	1977	1987	1990
Work Force (1000s)	n.a.	2324	2776	3010	4500	4900
Government Employees (1000s)	85	277	386	666	828	826
Percentage of Work Force	n.a.	12%	14%	21%	18.4%	16.8%

SOURCE: Faleh Abdul Jabbar, "The State, Society, Clan, Party and Army in Iraq," *From Storm to Thunder* (Tokyo: Institute of Developing Economies, March 1998), p. 12.

Of these, four cities—Baghdad, Mosul, Basra, and Kirkuk—had 61 percent of the urban population, 38 percent of the total population.[44] Massive domestic migration, however, may not have brought urbanization as much as ruralization of the cities, as village migrants clustered in poor, substandard satellite towns—like the Thaura township, now renamed Saddam City, in Baghdad—where they reproduced rural customs and practices.

Social change also brought the beginnings of a new class structure. A stratum of nouveaux riches—mainly contractors, entrepreneurs, and other intermediaries—flourished in a new semiprivate sector that fed off government distribution of wealth. A number of these new wealthy were related to leading Ba'th officials or had family ties to senior state officials.[45] The middle class, defined by education and a modern occupation, also grew. Much of the new middle class, especially at upper levels, was professional—doctors, academics, engineers, high-level civil servants—while others were white-collar workers in the middle levels of the civil service, teachers, and those in commerce. One study indicates that in 1977 this group constituted 35 percent of the urban population; a lower-middle class probably made up 20 percent.[46]

An urban working class also grew rapidly. These included semi- and unskilled workers in industrial establishments, as well as new migrants who found employment as police, in construction, and in other menial jobs. The changing social structure was reflected in the shift in Iraq's employment structure, particularly the decline of those employed in agriculture and the increase of those in services. In the 1960s, about half of the population was engaged in agriculture; by 1977, only about a third were. Employment in manufacturing rose from 7 to 9 percent, but the percent of the population in services rose from 12 to 15 percent in the 1960s to almost a third of the labor force in the 1970s. Most of these were in government employ, not in

productive sectors. These trends continued into the 1980s. The era of prosperity rapidly created a consumer society dependent on government salaries
(see Table A.3).

Iraq's Foreign Policy: The Pragmatic Phase, 1975–1980

Iraq's increased oil revenue and its desire for rapid economic development
were reflected, after 1975, in an increasingly pragmatic foreign policy, a
trend reinforced by the settlement with Iran on the Shatt and peace on the
Kurdish front.

The shift was most noticeable in the Gulf, where relations improved with
Saudi Arabia, and with the conservative Gulf shaikhdoms. In 1975 Iraq established diplomatic relations with Sultan Qabus of Oman. A series of bilateral agreements were concluded with Saudi Arabia, including an agreement
on the demarcation of the neutral zone on the countries' joint border. Relations with Kuwait also improved.

Meanwhile, relations with the Soviet Union took a downturn. The economic boom meant that Iraq turned increasingly to the West for purchases
of goods and services. During the late 1970s, Iraq's trade with Japan, Germany, France, and even the United States increased, while economic trans-
actions with the Soviet bloc declined to about 5 percent of total trade. The
Soviet share of Iraq's arms purchases also dropped from about 95 percent in
1972 to about 63 percent in 1979.[47] France was the main, but not the only,
Western beneficiary of this shift. Soviet actions in the region also alarmed
Baghdad, especially the establishment of a Soviet-sponsored Marxist government in Afghanistan in April 1978 and Soviet military support for Ethiopia
in its struggle with Somalia. When the USSR invaded Afghanistan in December 1979, Iraq-USSR relations reached a nadir.

Iraq's foreign policy was also affected by regional developments, especially
Egypt's move toward a peace agreement with Israel. More than any other factor, the Camp David Accords of September 1978, in which Israel and Egypt
agreed on a framework for peace, propelled Iraq into the mainstream of Arab
politics. In November 1978 the Iraqi regime took the initiative in organizing
a summit of all Arab governments (except Egypt) to counteract the Camp
David agreement. Although the summit did not halt Egypt's march toward a
peace agreement, it highlighted Iraq's new regional role in isolating Egypt and

moving to take its place. In March 1979, after the Egyptian-Israeli peace treaty was signed, the foreign and finance ministers of the Arab League met, again in Baghdad, to expel Egypt from the league.

These steps were accompanied by a mending of fences with Jordan and even with Syria. In June 1979 Saddam Husain paid a visit to Jordan, the first Iraqi head of state to do so since 1958, and a wide variety of agreements—military, economic, and political—were signed. By 1980 work had begun on a number of joint projects with Jordan. Chief among them were the expansion of the Aqaba port, which the Iraqis hoped to use to relieve their own Gulf ports, and the improvement of the road system between Amman and Baghdad.

Even more remarkable was the brief rapprochement with Syria. In an effort to shore up an Arab eastern front to counter the Israeli-Egyptian détente, Asad arrived in Baghdad for a meeting with Bakr and Husain. The outcome was a joint National Action Charter aimed at some kind of unity between Iraq and Syria and a joint committee to prepare for it. While this startling event was clearly an anti-Israeli effort, it temporarily eased mutual Syrian-Iraqi hostility. However, it soon collapsed.

Iraq's initiatives on the Arab front finally culminated in the pronouncement in February 1980 of an Arab Charter endorsed by most of the states that had attended the Arab summit. It rejected foreign bases on Arab soil (Soviet and US); rejected the use of force in Arab (but not non-Arab) disputes; and asked for Arab solidarity against foreign aggression, a clause directed against revolutionary Iran as well as Israel. By the end of the decade, Iraq had moved out of its earlier isolation into a potential leadership role. Husain's ambitions also lay beyond the Gulf and the Arab world to a broader, global stage. In the immediate future, he looked to the nonaligned nations' summit, which Iraq hoped to host in 1982, a position that would give him Third World, as well as Arab world, leadership. The new era of prosperity had brought Iraq—and its leader's expectations—a long way.

Iraq's New Ideological Stand

These changes in Iraq's economic fortunes and its new pragmatic foreign policy were accompanied by a perceptible shift in party ideology. This was most notable on the Arab nationalist front, where the emphasis on Arab unity was replaced by a focus on Iraq as a state and its leadership of the Arab world and beyond. The notion of integral Arab unity gave way to acceptance of individual states committed to gradual pan-Arab cooperation. Ba'th ideology moved to the idea of an Arab federative state in which each country would retain local institutions.[48] By the same token, Iraq's leadership role in this new Arab world was ever more pronounced. "The glory of the Arabs," stated one report, "stems from the glory of Iraq. . . . This is why we are striving to make Iraq mighty, formidable, able and developed, and why we shall spare nothing to improve its welfare and to brighten the glory of Iraqis."[49]

A second ideological feature was an attempt to draw different ethnic and sectarian groups in Iraq together under one ideological "tent." This was sometimes done by assuming that all Iraqis were part of Arab civilization, broadly defined. "The Kurds," Husain stated at one point, "have always been faithful to . . . the battles of the Arab nation to build the Arab civilization. When we talk about the Kurds, we mean the Iraqi Kurds who are a product of civilization six thousand years old."[50]

Another shift occurred in this period—a new emphasis not only on the leading role of a single party but on a single individual. This individual, Saddam Husain, was now melded with "society" as a whole as representative and leader of its collective aspirations. The report of the Ninth Regional Congress in 1982 divided the Ba'th revolution in Iraq into two phases, before and after Saddam Husain. Husain's speeches and pamphlets became the new ideological guide and the symbol of collective Iraqi consciousness and identity. By the close of the 1970s, the evolution of an ideology glorifying, not only the party but a dominant leader within it, was virtually complete.

Opposition to the Regime

Despite the imposing edifice created by the state and the ruthlessness of the party in dealing with dissent, by the end of a decade of rule, the Ba'th still faced opposition from a variety of sources. Some came from groups and parties dissatisfied with the regime's political or economic policies. More serious was the traditional opposition from ethnic and religious groups, most specifically, the Kurds and the *shi'a*.

Liberal Opposition
The regime still faced difficulties with the liberal end of the political spectrum. This contingent was far less organized and coherent than other

groups, but it was rooted in the professional classes and the intelligentsia, on whom the regime relied for its development program. The liberals were singled out for attention by the Ba'th as early as 1974, when the party report of that year stated: "School programs on all levels still fall short of expressing the principles of the Arab Ba'th Socialist Party and the socialist and nationalist revolution. They are still propagating bourgeois and liberal values."[51] To combat these tendencies, the party gradually exercised increased control over faculty and students, requiring courses on Ba'th ideology at the university level and replacing non-Ba'thist faculty with Ba'thists.

Many Iraqi intellectuals expressed their disaffection by leaving Iraq, as evidenced by the sizable number of educated Iraqis working outside Iraq. The intelligentsia also expressed its disaffection through passive resistance to government programs and policies. The poor productivity of the economy was sufficiently worrisome that in the autumn of 1976, the party held a series of seminars on the subject addressed by Saddam Husain himself. Among the complaints were protection of top-level administrators for political reasons and too many layers of decisionmaking.[52] These difficulties reflected a growing frustration on the part of an educated class, trained to lead, over its members' inability to control their professional lives.

The Communist Party
More significant than the liberal opposition was the Communist Party and the various left-wing elements that supported it. Friction between the Ba'th and the ICP was exacerbated by the Ba'th's deteriorating relations with the Soviet Union. The Ba'th feared internal subversion from the ICP supported by the USSR, particularly after the Soviet-supported coup in Afghanistan in April 1978. The very next month, to show that the Ba'th would tolerate no repeat of the Afghan situation in Iraq, it executed twenty-one Communists who had been imprisoned earlier for organizing cells in the army. By April 1979 most of the principal Communist leaders had left the country, and once again the party's leadership was driven underground.

The Kurds in Opposition
The measures taken by the government to end the Kurdish opposition after 1975 failed to do so. Indeed, the government's deportation and resettlement policy probably encouraged continued rebellion. In any event, renewed guerrilla acts in the north began as early as March 1976 as *peshmergas* infiltrated back into the region from Iran. However, without Mustafa-l-Barzani's

legendary stature to keep factions in tow, splits in the movement now deepened, especially the perennial divide between Jalal al-Talabani and the Barzanis, now led by his sons. In June 1975 this long-standing fissure was formalized with the establishment of a new party, the Patriotic Union of Kurdistan (PUK), under Talabani's leadership. The program of the PUK was clearly leftist and totally repudiated the leadership of the Barzanis.[53] The PUK was the first to return *peshmergas* to Iraq in 1976.

The old Kurdistan Democratic Party was also revived in the hands of Barzani's sons, Idris and Mas'ud. In October 1979 the KDP held a congress that officially elected Mas'ud the party's chairman, along with a new congress and political bureau. It called for continued armed struggle against the Ba'th through sustained guerrilla warfare inside Iraq. Unrelated to these factions, an Islamic group took shape in November 1978; eventually it would become the Islamic Movement of Iraqi Kurdistan (IMIK), although it did not announce itself until 1984. However, these guerrilla activities in the north were too weak to overcome the dominance of the Baghdad government. Internal conflict weakened Kurdish opposition to Baghdad and enabled the government to play Kurdish parties off against each other while relying for support in the north on the pro-government Kurds and the government-supported militias.

Shi'i *Opposition*

The Kurds were not the most serious opposition to the government in this period. By the late 1970s, the *shi'a* had superseded the Kurds as the major concern of the Ba'th. *Shi'i* disaffection was multifaceted.

The confrontation between the *shi'a* and the government began with a series of skirmishes shortly after the Ba'th came to power in 1968. Some of these were due to heightened tensions with Iran during which the regime expelled thousands of *shi'i* Iraqis of Iranian nationality and confiscated their property.[54] *Shi'i* opponents of the regime were also caught up in the spy trials of that year and Mahdi al-Hakim, son of the chief m*arji'*, was accused of spying and sentenced to death, although he was smuggled out of the country to safety. Several *shi'i* schools were closed. Finally, the regime put restrictions on the annual ritual processions in the holy cities. Hakim protested these actions, to no avail.

In June 1970 Muhsin al-Hakim was succeeded as chief *marji'* by Abu-l-Qasim al-Khu'i, a more traditional cleric who favored a "quietist" approach, avoiding confrontation with the government. As a result, in the early 1970s, *shi'i* opposition temporarily died down, although the government continued to monitor and sometimes harass the religious establishment.

Despite the surface quiet, however, organized *shi'i* forces were still at work. Chief among them was the Da'wa Party, now an international, not just an Iraqi, organization. By the early 1970s, the Da'wa had grown, forging contacts in the universities inside and outside Iraq, especially in Lebanon and the Gulf. Another group also took shape in this period, the Munazimat al-Amal al-Islamiyya (Islamic Action Organization, or IAO). Formed in Karbala by members of the Shirazi family, it was intertwined with the clerical establishment and had strong Persian affiliations. Gradually, the IAO was turned into a political as well as a religious movement. When the Shirazis were persecuted, the IOA turned militant, organizing cells and giving members guerrilla training. By the end of the 1970s, the organization was ready to begin operations against the regime.[55]

Given this underground organization and activism, it was not long before tensions between the *shi'i* activists and the regime erupted into political protests. These began during ritual ceremonies in November and December of 1974 when over two dozen *shi'a* were tried and sentenced for plots against the state. Five, all Da'wa leaders, were executed.

Far more serious and widespread were the *shi'i* demonstrations and riots of 5 and 6 February 1977, when the government tried to stop a ritual procession from Najaf to Karbala. A crowd of some 30,000 angry protesters, chanting anti-government slogans, was confronted by police. The government mobilized helicopter gunships and armored vehicles, and bloodshed ensued. At least sixteen demonstrators were killed and many more wounded; 2,000 demonstrators were rounded up and some 500 interrogated.

An urban mass demonstration of this size and kind was new for the regime and was worrisome. A revolutionary court sentenced eight participants to death, but this was considered too lenient by Saddam Husain, and two of the court's members were dismissed from the party. Nonetheless, Saddam did try to propitiate the *shi'i* community. More funds were sent to the south and more *shi'a* were introduced into the RCC and the upper levels of the party. By 1977 some 24 percent of the higher leadership levels and 17 percent of the lower levels were *shi'a*. But the Ba'th also tightened control on *shi'i* political activities, including continued restrictions on rituals. To secure party ranks, it was prohibited for any member of the party to have been a member of another organization or to have concealed such activity—by which the Da'wa was meant.

By the end of 1977, the regime may well have thought that these draconian measures taken against the activists had brought *shi'i* opposition under control. But such an assessment—if made—did not take into account the earthquake that was about to shake Iran. The onset of the Islamic revolution in Iran and its riveting example of a successful religious uprising soon changed these calculations. It also galvanized the *shi'i* opposition.

The Impact of the Iranian Revolution

As strikes and unrest escalated inside Iran in 1978, Baghdad became increasingly concerned that the disturbances could spill over into Iraq. Much of the unrest had been instigated by Ayat Allah Khumaini, the Iranian cleric who had fomented the Islamic revolution in Iran and who had been residing in exile in Najaf for thirteen years. When the shah asked for Khumaini's removal from Iraq in October 1978, the Ba'th regime complied. But if the regime had hoped to end *shi'i* unrest, it was soon disabused of this idea. With Khumaini's departure to Paris and his open leadership of the revolution, *shi'i* opposition in Iraq now entered a new phase. This time the leadership of the movement was taken up by Muhammad Baqir al-Sadr, who played a key role in the events to transpire.

On 1 February 1979 Khumaini returned triumphant to Tehran at the head of a successful revolution, and the impact of this success changed the political landscape in Iraq—as well as the rest of the Middle East. A wave of enthusiasm swept the *shi'i* community in Iraq. In March Sadr signaled clear support for the revolution in a telegram of congratulations to Khumaini, asserting that he looked forward to more Islamic victories. Sadr then published several essays on the projected new constitution in Iran, as his contribution to the revolution. To keep in closer touch with Khumaini, Sadr sent a close, personal representative, Mahmud al-Hashimi, to Tehran as Sadr's permanent envoy to Khumaini.

These steps were unquestionably a challenge—even a threat—to Baghdad. At one point, Sadr even went so far as to issue a *fatwa*—not made public at the time—against joining the Ba'th Party, a dangerous act of defiance well beyond any redline the regime might accept.

In May 1979 events reached a crisis over a visit Sadr was reputedly planning to make to Tehran. Whether he was actually going is not clear, but a telegram from Khumaini, publicly broadcast from Tehran on the Arabic service, asked Sadr to remain in Baghdad. This event precipitated a crisis of the first order and elevated Sadr to the rank of a leading challenger to the regime. Starting on 22 May, there were nine days of demonstrations, initiated by the Da'wa, organized around a *bay'a,* or oath of allegiance, to Sadr. *Shi'a* flocked to Najaf from all over Iraq. The regime allowed the demonstrations to escalate and then, on June 12, rounded up and imprisoned hundreds of Da'wa members. Sadr was arrested.

The detention of Sadr then set off a second reaction. His sister, known as Bint al-Huda, also a religious activist, exhorted the crowds to save her brother and secure his release. *Shi'i* activists responded with more massive demonstrations. Riots broke out in several cities. In fact, this uprising was the first popular mass movement of its kind in decades. There was also agitation abroad—in the UAE, in Lebanon, in Britain, and in France, where pro-Da'wa and pro-Sadr forces were situated. These protests finally achieved the release of Sadr. The rest of the activists did not fare so well. Although no full accounting exists, several hundred may have been executed or killed under torture. By the summer of 1979, the Da'wa organization had been virtually emasculated.

The 1979 demonstrations widened the fissure in the Ba'th leadership over how to deal with this challenge. One wing of the party, reputedly including Bakr, favored flexibility in dealing with Sadr and caution in handling the new Iranian government. Saddam Husain and his supporters took a hard line. Husain won out. No action was taken against Sadr until the spring of 1980, but on 1 April a bomb thrown in a public gathering slightly wounded Tariq Aziz and killed a number of others. A second attempt occurred a few days later with more deaths and injuries. Saddam blamed Sadr and the *shi'i* activists and, behind them, Iran. On 4 April 1980 Sadr was arrested for the last time. His sister, Bint al-Huda, was taken with him. Both were brutally tortured and executed.

Whether Sadr initiated the *shi'i* confrontation with the regime in 1978 and 1979 or was propelled into actions by others is less important than his death and the outcome of these events for the *shi'i* movement and for Iraq itself. Sadr provided the movement with a martyr but left the *shi'a* in Iraq leaderless and in disarray. In retrospect, the *shi'i* activists, Sadr included, appeared to have miscalculated. The Da'wa and other militant groups prematurely picked a violent quarrel with the regime before they were ready to withstand the reaction. The result was devastating for the movement itself. But the episode had created a mighty revival of *shi'i* consciousness and

revived religious opposition to the regime; both would go underground—
and abroad, mainly to Iran—to continue to bedevil the regime.

The Ba'th: The End of Its First Decade

The era of the 1970s ended for the regime on a mixed note. In the capital
and the central provinces, from which it drew most of its support, opposition
had been thoroughly cowed. The Kurdish insurrection in the north had
ended in 1975, and although brutal measures were taken with rural Kurds,
the benefits of economic development were already shaping the more urban
Kurdish areas, bringing prosperity and some quiet. In the south, it was clear
that the *shi'i* resurgence, initiated under the Arif regime, presented a worrisome problem. No longer merely domestic, it was now backed by a new and
increasingly militant *shi'i* regime in Iran. Domestically, however, by the summer of 1979, *shi'i* unrest in the south had clearly been brought under control.

Meanwhile, the massive inflow of oil wealth, spent not only in Baghdad
but the provinces as well, provided an aura of prosperity used to mitigate
tensions and distract attention from the harsh and brutal measures of the
regime. Social mobility also blunted discontent. New economic wealth provided the regime with the means to push rapid modernization and development and a new Ba'th vision of Iraq—strong, united, and under the
umbrella of a new Salah al-Din. Much of the wealth, of course, was put into
building the military sinews of the state and a nascent nuclear program that
would allow Saddam to fulfill the vision of Arab world leadership. Meanwhile, by 1979 the edifice of the monolithic, one-party state, in control not
only of the instruments of political and military power but of society as well,
was complete. Saddam had reason to feel more confident than worried
about the future and Iraq's place in it.

8

THE SADDAM HUSAIN REGIME, 1979–1989

In July 1979, eleven years after helping the Ba'th to power in a coup and after serving as second in command to Bakr, Saddam Husain became president of the republic. It was the first peaceful transition of power in over two decades. Despite the seemingly pedestrian nature of this event, in retrospect it heralded a new era in Iraq, one that was to have permanently damaging consequences and change Iraq's possibilities for the future.

The changing of the guard marked a decisive shift, already under way, from a one-party state to a personal, autocratic regime, dependent for security—and increasingly for decisions—on Saddam Husain and his close family members and cohorts. In the new political nexus, personal loyalty became critical. The party was weakened as an institution, and what little pluralism and balance had remained at the top disappeared. The brutal way in which Saddam accomplished this transfer of power left little doubt that his personal will would predominate. The party did not disappear, but what little independence it had was broken; it now became an organization subservient to Saddam Husain. At the same time, the party was both absorbed and displaced by another large, mass-based organization, an elected national assembly, which was convened for the first time since 1958.

These changes took place against the backdrop of a virulent and proselytizing Islamic revolution in Iran with potential threats to both regime and state in Iraq. Iran's extreme rhetoric, as well as its military mobilization and border attacks, played into Saddam's hands. With virtually no domestic checks on his judgment, he took the initiative in attacking Iran, thus beginning a disastrous

eight-year war that would shred much of the economic and social capital that
Iraq had built up in the previous decade. In the process, Iraq used chemical
weapons (CW), bombed Iranian cities, and succeeded in internationalizing
the conflict by bringing the United States into the Gulf on its side. These efforts finally brought Iran's acceptance of a cease-fire in 1988.

The war accomplished none of Iraq's stated purposes in beginning hostilities. The Iranian regime remained in power and was strengthened. Iraqi resources, human and economic, were drained. Above all, Iraq lost a large
measure of its economic independence through massive debts both to the
West and to the Arab Gulf states. A generation had been wasted. The war did
generate a brief period of patriotism, based on defending the homeland and its
more secular culture. An Iraqi identity appeared confirmed. But the Saddam
Husain regime remained in power and came through the war with a sense of
entitlement to benefits from the Arab world as its bulwark or "eastern flank."
The population meanwhile expected a "peace dividend." Unfortunately, these
assumptions were ill founded. In the aftermath of the war, its costs came due.
These new realities, and the misconceptions of Iraq's position in the postwar
period, set the stage for the second, and even more disastrous, Gulf War.

Saddam Becomes President

It had been widely expected for some time that Saddam Husain would take
Bakr's place. It came as no surprise, therefore, when, on 16 July 1979, President Bakr officially resigned and Saddam Husain became president of the republic, secretary-general of the Ba'th Party Regional Command, chairman of
the RCC, and commander-in-chief of the armed forces. There is little doubt
that Saddam was impatient to assume official title to the power he in fact already held and that he engineered the older man's retirement. In the cabinet
reshuffle that ensued, Izzat Ibrahim (al-Duri) was named deputy chairman of
the RCC and assistant secretary-general of the party's Regional Command,
and Taha Ramadan (al-Jazrawi) became first deputy prime minister, indicating
that these old party stalwarts had acquiesced in the change.

The Party Massacre
Much was made in public of the smoothness of this transition, but this was
a facade. Within days a bizarre episode revealed fissures within the leader-

ship and the potential for instability. An alleged coup attempt was revealed ten days after Saddam's inauguration, on 28 July, when the new president announced the discovery of a plot to overthrow the government by a number of Ba'thist leaders. An outside power (understood to be Syria) was said to be involved. The announcement of the plot had been preceded by the arrest, on 12 July, of Muhyi al-Din Abd al-Husain, a *shi'i* member of the RCC and the Regional Command.[1] He disclosed the names of the conspirators and the details of the plot. In an extraordinary session of the party's regional congress called for 22 July and televised in a large hall in Baghdad, Muhyi al-Din made a public confession of the plot, naming those involved.[2]

The accused, many of them sitting in the hall, were, in a chilling exercise of power, promptly taken into custody. An investigating committee and a court, both composed entirely of RCC members, were immediately set up, and ten days later death sentences were issued for twenty-two of the accused, including five RCC members. They were summarily executed. One of the accused escaped, and thirty-three others were sentenced to prison terms. Thirteen were acquitted.[3]

These events marked another sharp divide in Ba'th politics and ushered in a new era of personal rule. They also raised questions about the timing of the transition and motivations behind the drastic action taken by their main perpetrator, Saddam Husain. There is little doubt that Husain had been preparing for the transition for some time and that the way seemed propitious since Bakr had been less active over the years as real power shifted to Saddam. But there is no evidence that Bakr was yet ready to step aside or that he took any initiative in the formal transfer of power. This was Saddam's decision.

The troubles in Iran may have played some role in Saddam's decision to replace Bakr. Although unrest in Iran was still seen as manageable in 1978, it had worsened in 1979. Indeed, dealing with domestic *shi'i* disturbances had already caused splits in the leadership and appeared to put Bakr, a cautious man, on the side of those more interested in following a "flexible" policy, both toward local *shi'a* and toward Iran. Saddam, deeply suspicious of Iran, may have felt the time had come to move. It is also possible that Saddam wanted to put an end to the unity scheme with Syria, then under discussion. Bakr was slated to head the union, with Asad as second in command. This would have left Saddam Husain as third in rank—unacceptable to him.

But the reason for Saddam's actions appears to have been opposition to his rule from within the party command. Within the closed RCC meeting to arrange the transition, some made it clear they preferred Bakr to remain. And it is this opposition, as well as Saddam's aversion to tolerating any dissent, that explains the allegations of a "coup" and the massacre of party insiders that followed the announcement of Saddam's presidency.

The transition and the party massacre were a watershed in the regime's history. The succession of Saddam Husain to the presidency, though hardly a fundamental shift in power, did have a marked effect on the nature of the regime, its decisionmaking process, and the era of war that followed. The regime now became a more personal autocracy, focused on one man and his whims. The removal of Bakr eliminated a check and a balance on the actions of Saddam, one that was never restored. Although weak, Bakr had provided some shelter for those with opposing views—and possible rival ambitions; these were now destroyed in a chilling exercise of Stalinesque terror. The absence of such a check would soon become apparent in the decision to go to war with Iran. Meanwhile the party, which had previously had a modicum of independence, as represented by top-level officials, was reduced to an appendage of Saddam's personal rule.

The transition and the purge also reduced, temporarily, the power of the RCC and the inner circle. Saddam now undertook a modest restructuring of the political system. To command the heights of the military and the security system, he appointed himself field marshal, enhancing his authority to exercise more direct control over the military. His cousin, Adnan Khair Allah Talfah, was made deputy commander in chief. His half brother Barzan was put in charge of the Mukhabarat (Intelligence Service). At long last, too, the constitutional provisions providing for a national assembly were activated to provide a democratic facade.

The Establishment of the National Assembly

A law was promulgated in March 1980 that provided for an assembly of 250 members to be elected by secret ballot every four years. All Iraqis over the age of eighteen were eligible to vote and the country was to be divided into electoral zones of about 250,000 inhabitants each. A key provision stipulated that each district would have only a single electoral list, thus eliminating any competition among parties or groups. All candidates had to be reviewed by an election commission before receiving permission to run, thus assuring that only those favorable to Ba'th principles would be elected.

On 20 June 1980 elections were held, the first in Iraq since the fall of the monarchy. To no one's surprise, the results gave the Ba'th an overwhelming victory, although a number of independents were also elected. On 30 June the first session was held. Na'im Haddad, an RCC and Regional Command member, was elected speaker, putting a loyal party *shi'a* in a visible public position to help allay accusations of "sectarian" politics. The new assembly, while providing a safety valve—even a distraction—for public discontent, did little to obscure the increasingly personal and secretive nature of the autocracy now governing Iraq and the level of brutality that would face any who opposed it.

These decisions, particularly the removal of Bakr and the concentration of power in Saddam's hands, were to have critical effects on Iraq's future. They eliminated any possibility for dissent—modest though it may have been—or correctives to Saddam's judgment as Iraq faced a volatile situation on its border with Iran. Though that situation did pose some threats, containing the Iranian revolution would require cool judgment and a steady hand. Instead, Iraq now had a young man, relatively inexperienced in international affairs, willing—indeed eager—to substitute his own judgment for that of others and to use opportunities to advance his own visions of regional leadership. The result would be a serious miscalculation that would be costly for Iraq.

Iraq Goes to War

There is little doubt that the outbreak of the war between Iran and Iraq occurred against a background of longstanding grievances—even a state of permanent tension—between the two countries. Chief among these had been border disputes combined with a larger, even if intangible, Iraqi fear of Persian hegemony. In Iraqi minds, since the 1920s, Iran had been gradually encroaching on "Arab" land, including its absorption of the adjacent Arab territory of Khuzistan (formerly Muhammara) in 1925, the incorporation of the waters around Khurramshahr in 1937, and the 1975 agreement that gave Iran half the Shatt al-Arab.

Cultural differences, based partly on language and ethnicity, have always existed but were now brought into sharp focus with the Iranian revolution and Iranian attempts to spread the revolution to Iraq. The "cultural distance" between Iraq and Iran, however, has always been viewed differently by different communities in Iraq. For the *shi'a* in southern Iraq, especially those affiliated with the religious establishment, the differences have been muted, but among the power elite in Baghdad, especially those from small-town

Arab *sunni* backgrounds, traditional suspicion of and prejudice against Iran remained high.

Despite these ongoing tensions, it is unlikely that war would have occurred had the shah remained in power. To the contrary, there is no evidence that Saddam Husain intended to overturn the 1975 agreement while the shah was in power or even in the immediate aftermath of his overthrow. It was the Islamic revolution and the virulent attempt of Khumaini to spread its ideology, that shifted the regional balance of power and changed Iraq's calculations.

Provocation from Iran

The impact of the Iranian revolution on Iraq was first felt in the north among the Kurds. In the wake of the revolution, Iran ceased to police its northern borders and in July 1979 allowed the Barzanis to cross the frontier from Iran to Iraq with KDP forces in violation of the 1975 treaty. Kurdish activities escalated in the north, with the Iraqi KDP firmly supporting Khumaini and urging the overthrow of the Baghdad government.[4] In retaliation, the Iraqi government revived its support for dissident Arab groups in Khuzistan that were in open revolt against the Iranian government, making the point that if Iran did not observe the agreement in the north, Iraq would not observe it in the south.[5]

More serious than the Kurdish skirmishes, however, was Iran's open call for the spread of revolution to Iraq, where *shi'i* unrest, already apparent, was now deliberately stirred up by the new Iranian government. The hand of Iran was seen in the 1979 demonstrations in behalf of Baqir al-Sadr and in the April 1980 assassination attempt on Tariq Aziz. The regime responded by deporting up to 35,000 *shi'a*, allegedly of Persian origin.[6] The campaign also became a personal test of wills between Khumaini and Saddam Husain. Khumaini had no love for the man who had expelled him in 1978. Saddam, for his part, regarded the militant Islamic leader as a mortal threat to his own revolutionary credentials. Behind the personal struggle was a clash of ideologies, with the Iraqis championing secular Arab nationalism and socialism and Iran preaching the revival of a militant Islam.

Opportunism

Despite Iran's militancy, by the summer of 1979, Saddam Husain appeared to have the domestic situation under control. Thereafter, other, more aggressive aims increasingly came into play. Among these, opportunism undoubtedly played a role. As Iran sank deeper into chaos, as its military fractured and decomposed, as its international isolation deepened, the potential for Iraq to reverse its previous losses and even make new gains became irresistible. Chief among these aims was Husain's desire to reverse the 1975 decision on the Shatt al-Arab—impossible in the era of a powerful Iran. Iran's growing weakness also held out the possibility of ending the threat of revolutionary Iran once and for all by overthrowing the regime and replacing it with one more willing to come to terms with Iraq. There were even dreams of "liberating" the Arab population of Khuzistan and creating a new political entity at the head of the Gulf under Iraqi control.

As early as January 1978 a high-level military committee, including the chief of staff, was formed, and it worked for months on a contingency plan in the event of an Iran-Iraq war.[7] Military intelligence consistently reported the decline of Iranian forces, the collapse of the political system, and even a potential fracturing of the country from Azerbaijan to Khuzistan.[8] Such factors can only have fed Husain's aspirations.

Preemptive Defense

In the fall of 1979, Husain admitted to one of his officials that he would not rule out war, because the situation in Iran might provide the only opportunity in this century to regain Iraq's interests.[9] Indeed, as tensions and skirmishes between the two countries escalated, the idea of the necessity of a "first strike" appears to have grown. In the minds of some, if no preemptive strike were taken at a favorable time to rectify the border issue and, further, to preempt a future intervention from a reorganized but still militant Iran, the Islamic republic would constitute a far greater threat later.[10]

Iraq first tried to destabilize Iran by using Iranian opposition, such as Shahpur Bakhtiar, the last prime minister under the shah, and General Ghulam Ali Uwaisi, former Chief of Staff. Iraq funded their efforts to contact both tribal and military opponents inside Iran hoping to overthrow the regime from inside.[11] (These efforts were matched, of course, by Iranian support for Kurdish and *shi'i* opponents of the Baghdad regime.) In May 1980 pro-shah forces tried a military coup and failed; a second attempt, orchestrated and funded by Bakhtiar, also failed in July. This may have been a key turning point in Baghdad's decision to take the initiative itself.

Iraq was also encouraged by Iran's isolation. The American hostage crisis, initiated by Iranians in November 1979 and culminating in the disastrous US rescue attempt that failed in the Iranian desert in April 1980, ensured that the United States—and the West—would not come to Iran's aid in a war with Iraq. Whatever the mix of motives behind Saddam's decision, in the end, opportunity and a growing sense of confidence, rather than defense against a *shi'i* rebellion, appeared to dominate.

The Road to War

By late August the situation had escalated, with serious skirmishes on the borders. On 4 September 1980 Iranian armed forces used artillery to shell the Iraqi cities of Khanaqin and Mandali from the disputed border area of Zain al-Qaus, inflicting heavy losses of life and property among civilians. When the shelling was repeated on 7 September, the Iraqis delivered a protest but received no reply. Iraq then occupied the Zain al-Qaus district. On 17 September Saddam Husain officially abrogated the 1975 treaty and announced that the Shatt al-Arab was returning to Iraqi sovereignty. Iran rejected this action and the conflict shifted to the Shatt.[12]

On 19 September the Iranian government began to use heavy artillery and planes to bombard residential areas and vital economic installations on the Iraqi side of the Shatt. The Iranians also attacked foreign merchant ships in the river. This was the trigger Saddam had been waiting for. Three days later, the Iraqis carried the war to the heart of Iran with a bombing mission that raided ten Iranian air bases and two early warning stations. The attack was clearly modeled on the Israeli 1967 strike on Egypt.[13] On 23 September the Iraqis began their military advance into Iranian territory.

Iraq's strategic aims in the invasion remained unclear. Was it to regain the Shatt—and possibly all of Khuzistan? Was it to end the domestic threat from Khumaini's regime by ending the regime itself? Was it to force the revolutionary government in Tehran to negotiate with Baghdad on the latter's own terms? Whatever the aims, they failed. The war, instead of ensuring Iraq's domestic security or achieving territorial gains, much less ending the Islamic Republic, bogged down in a long, debilitating eight-year conflict that marked the beginning of a continuous downturn in Iraq's fortunes that would continue for the remainder of the century.

The Course of the War

The Failed Iraqi Offensive

Initially, the Iraqis made rapid advances into Iranian territory, occupying Qasr-i-Shirin, Mahran, and Musiyan on the central front and subjecting

Dizful to severe bombardment. In the south, their forces crossed the Karun River, advanced on Abadan, and after a bitter battle and enormous casualties on both sides, took Khurramshahr on 24 October. Meanwhile, the oil-producing centers of both countries were bombarded and oil exports temporarily suspended.

At this point the Iraqis' offensive ceased, and their army assumed a defensive posture, evidently expecting Iranian concessions in exchange for the territory won by these military victories. Cease-fire terms, announced by Saddam Husain on 28 September, included acceptance of Iraqi rights on the Shatt and noninterference in Iraq's domestic affairs. Misinformed, the Iraqis may also have expected the collapse of the Iranian government. This proved to be a critical error. The Iraqis had failed to take Dizful, a city in the north of Iran's oil region and a major transportation link between the Iranian capital and the south. This permitted the Iranians to resupply and reorganize their forces in the south. The Iraqis likewise failed to capture the key town of Abadan and thus did not gain control of the Shatt al-Arab—one of their main professed aims in the war.

One reason for the abrupt halt probably lay in Saddam Husain's reluctance to accept the high casualties that would surely have accompanied further advances. The morale of the Iraqi fighting forces was an unknown factor. Many Iraqis, civilian as well as military, opposed the risks and sacrifices involved in pursuing a war for purposes that might better have been achieved by other means. Moreover, the bulk of the soldiers were *shi'a*, who might be prone to defect.

Military capabilities may also have played a role in the decision. Iraq's capacity to sustain the long lines of communications and to absorb the inevitable losses was questionable. Whatever the reasons for Iraq's military strategy, it is clear that Husain made a catastrophic mistake in underestimating Iran's resources. Despite massive casualties, the Iranians put up an effective defense of their territory, consolidated, and mounted a counteroffensive. By October the Iranians had pushed the Iraqis back across the Karun River and had started their march on Khurramshahr, which they retook in May 1982. Rather than weakening the Khumaini regime, the Iraqi offensive provided the opportunity for more militant elements in Iran to gain control of the political system and, in the long run, helped consolidate the regime.

Putting the best face possible on these reversals, in June 1982 Saddam Husain announced an Iraqi withdrawal to the international borders, claiming that Iraq's objective—destroying the Iranian military apparatus—had

been achieved. He used the Israeli invasion of Lebanon as an additional justification. Few inside or outside Iraq were deceived.

The withdrawal announcement failed to contain the Iranian advance as
planned. The Iranians now attempted to carry the war to Iraqi territory,
with the professed aim of toppling Saddam Husain and his regime and supplanting it with an Islamic republic. Before long, it was apparent that Iran
was merely repeating the mistake that Saddam had made earlier. The fateful
Iranian decision to continue the war, rather than accepting Iraq's proffered
cease-fire terms, initiated the second phase of the war, lasting roughly from
1982 to 1986—a long war of attrition, fought mainly on land but also in
the Gulf, that depleted the resources and morale of both sides and, until a
sharp and sudden Iranian victory in 1986, was marked mainly by stalemate.

The War of Attrition

During the summer of 1982, Iran went on the offensive, making several
major but unsuccessful attempts to take Basra and to cut the main Basra-
Baghdad road, a key aim of their war strategy from then on. Holding well-
entrenched positions, the Iraqis held back the Iranian attacks and inflicted
heavy losses on their enemies. When fighting on their own soil, the Iraqis'
morale stiffened. From then on, the ground war bogged down in a stalemate
that was to persist almost to the end of the war. In a repeated pattern, Iran
would launch offensives not only in the south but in the center and north as
well, attempting to make breakthroughs, to wear down Iraqi morale, and to
overwhelm Iraqi forces with superior numbers in manpower. Despite some
minor territorial gains, Iraq's defenses held.

Throughout 1983 and 1984, there were repeated Iranian attacks on a
number of fronts using human waves of young irregulars, as well as up to
four divisions of the regular army. The Iranians also used dissident Kurdish
forces (the KDP) and Iraqi *shi'i* exiles. Iraq built huge earthworks and fortifi-
cations all along its frontier in the south and set up a static defense. In 1984
Iran captured Majnun, an artificial island created on the site of a recent oil
find near Qurna. Majnun gave the Iranians their first substantial bargaining
chip on the ground and a possible future source of oil.

It was during the battle for Majnun that reports reached the outside
world that the Iraqis were using chemical weapons. In retrospect, mustard
gas appears to have been used as early as August 1983. Although Iraqis officially denied it at the time, evidence mounted in subsequent battles that
chemical weapons were increasingly used. By the end of the war, they were

thoroughly integrated into war-fighting operations, and their use was widely known.[14] While controversy over their use came later, there was little if any protest from the West at the time.

Iran still had little to show for its efforts, except for Majnun and some pockets of Iraqi territory in the north, but the ground attacks continued. Kurdish guerrillas made inroads. The KDP may have controlled as much as a third of the north. Basra appeared increasingly to be a city under siege, fearing encirclement and losing population as its inhabitants fled north. By 1986, when the battlefield had stabilized, Iran held about three hundred square miles of Iraqi territory but had not been able to take Basra or any other major city.

The Economic and Diplomatic War

Although Iraq was able to fight Iran to a standstill on the ground, it had not been prepared to wage a long war of attrition and now had to compensate for economic losses, for its lack of strategic depth, and for its comparative disadvantage in manpower. Although Iraq had begun the war with a full treasury, the destruction of Iraq's Gulf port facilities in November 1980 and the closure of its pipeline by Syria in April 1982 had drastically reduced Iraq's oil revenue and its financial capacity to wage war. By 1983 the war was costing Iraq ID 312.5 million ($1 billion) a month.

In a major attempt to restore its finances, Iraq turned first to the Arab Gulf countries. By appealing to Arab solidarity and the fear of an Iranian victory, the Iraqis managed to gain financial support from these countries. Iraq then turned to Europe, where it was able to arrange for credits and a rescheduling of its debts. Even the United States extended agricultural credits to Iraq. At home the government introduced an austerity program. By slashing nonessential imports, obtaining new credits and loans, and deferring hard currency payments, Iraq managed to achieve a fragile economic equilibrium, although it had to go into debt to do so.

Iraq also bolstered its position by the acquisition of new armaments. In 1983 Iraq negotiated a loan of five French Super Etendard war planes, equipped with heat-seeking Exocet missiles and guidance facilities designed mainly for use against ships in the Gulf. More surprisingly, Iraq also repaired its deteriorating relationship with the USSR and was resupplied with Soviet arms.

Iraq also won the diplomatic struggle for world opinion, placing the blame for the continuation of the war on Iran. Even more important, Iraq managed to achieve a US "tilt" toward Iraq in the late summer of 1983 and a trip by US Special Middle East Envoy Donald Rumsfeld to Iraq in December 1983.

The United States, in a subsequent policy known as "Operation Staunch," put pressure on its allies and friends to stop supplying Iran with weapons. By 1983 the United States clearly saw a possible Iranian victory and an Iraqi collapse as not in its interests. In November of that year, it took Iraq off its terrorist list and in January 1984 put Iran on. Thereafter, the United States turned a blind eye to arms shipments to Iraq, as it attempted to stem arms flows to Iran. Except for the "Irangate" interlude from August 1985 to November 1986, when the United States allowed the secret resupply of some equipment to Iran, the Americans continued Operation Staunch to the end of the war.

Turning Points, 1986–1987

After four years of a grueling war of attrition, two events, one in 1986 and the other in 1987, marked turning points in the stalemate and, in retrospect, led to the end of the war the following year. The first of these was Iran's capture of Faw in February 1986. The second was its last unsuccessful attack on Basra in January 1987. Both eventually galvanized Iraq and the international community into taking steps to break the stalemate.

On 6 February 1986 Iran managed to capture Faw, giving the Islamic Republic a strategic foothold on Iraq's access to the Gulf. From Faw the Iranians were able to threaten Kuwait by launching silkworm missiles on the small Gulf shaikhdom.

Fearing further reverses, Saddam Husain was persuaded by his generals to relinquish some control over war operations and to delegate more authority to the military.[15] In July, an extraordinary Ba'th Party congress was held that confirmed several changes. First, more responsibility was given to the military command structure (although Saddam Husain retained final control). Second, the strategy of static defense underwent a revision in favor of preparation for a more aggressive offense. Third, to implement this strategy, a decision was made to enlarge the Republican Guard. By early 1987 the guard had grown from three brigades to twenty-eight.[16]

Buoyed by its success in Faw in January 1987, Iran mounted what it hoped would be its "final offensive" against Basra. In a fierce campaign during January and February, Iran pushed to within ten miles of the city, but by March it was clear that the offensive had failed and Iran could not take the city. In May and June 1987 Iraq counterattacked, making gains in the north in the Halabja area. In both attacks chemical weapons were used.[17]

The battle for Basra proved to be the turning point of the war. Though casualties were high on both sides, they proved to be insurmountable for Iran. Iran lost not only a large number of soldiers but also many experienced officers. An attempt to recruit for another offensive the following year collapsed in the face of shortfalls. Iran was also unable to replace lost equipment or resupply spare parts as Operation Staunch took its toll. As the 1987 offensive against Basra eventually made clear, Iran was suffering attrition beyond its capacity for replacement or repair.

Internationalization of the War

The ground war, however, was not the only factor moving the war to a close. Equally important was an escalation of the "tanker war" in the Gulf that had begun in 1984. Iraq attacked tankers bound for Iranian ports, attempting to interdict Iran's oil traffic. Iran then retaliated by striking tankers bound for Kuwait and Saudi Arabia, Iraq's Gulf allies. This sea war intensified in 1985 and 1986 and finally succeeded in "internationalizing" the conflict, bringing the US navy more deeply into the conflict and finally persuading the UN to exert more serious pressure (with US backing) on the combatants.

It had been a major aim of Iraq to involve the superpowers—especially the United States—in putting pressure on Iran to end the conflict. Progress in this direction was slow. Despite the US tilt to Iraq in 1983, American efforts to bring the war to an end had been inconsequential. In fact, the Irangate episode showed just how "neutral" the United States could be. But by 1987 the situation had changed. Public disclosure of the Irangate affair caused a huge public embarrassment in the United States and an outcry among the international community. More important, Iraq's defeat in Faw and the subsequent siege of Basra the following year once again raised the specter of an Iranian victory.

US Intervention

Increased US military involvement began with reflagging of Kuwaiti vessels to provide Kuwaiti tankers with US protection. This US decision was hastened, ironically, by another incident in the Gulf. On 17 May 1987 the US frigate *Stark* was hit by two Iraqi Exocet missiles, killing thirty-seven crew members. Iraq declared the attack an accident, officially apologized, and eventually paid compensation. However, some in the United States considered the attack deliberate, possibly as retaliation for Irangate, which the Iraqis bitterly resented or, as Iranians charged, a way of dragging the United States into the conflict.[18] Whatever the cause of the *Stark* attack, the result was to hasten the reflagging effort and to increase US involvement in the war.

On 16 October an Iranian silkworm missile hit one of the US-reflagged ships. The United States retaliated by hitting an Iranian offshore platform used by the Revolutionary Guards as a communications station. The United States was being drawn increasingly into direct conflict with Iran.

In April 1988 a US ship hit an Iranian-laid mine. The United States retaliated by striking two Iranian offshore oil platforms. Iranian speedboats responded by attacking UAE offshore oil platforms, and in return the United States sank two Iranian frigates, eliminating half of Iran's navy.

On 3 July an Iranian civilian airbus with 290 passengers left Bandar Abbas for Dubayy. The *Vincennes,* a US cruiser, misidentified the airbus as a military aircraft and shot it down, killing all on board. Although many in Iran persisted in seeing this action as intentional rather than accidental, it may have played a role in finally bringing Iran to the point of accepting an end to the war.[19]

By 1987 international diplomacy was working in the same direction. UN efforts, especially those of Secretary General Perez de Cuellar, had been under way since March of 1985, when he had put forth an eight-point plan for a cease-fire and a peace settlement. At that point, Iran was not interested, but in January 1987 de Cuellar called for a commission to determine who was responsible for the war, a concession to one of Iran's major demands. The result was UN Security Council Resolution 598, adopted in July 1987, calling for a cease-fire linked to a withdrawal to internationally recognized frontiers, a POW exchange, and an investigation into responsibility for the war. If 598 were not accepted by the combatants, the UN would take appropriate action to end the war. It would take another year to get final Iranian acceptance.

The Iraqi Offensive of 1988

By 1988 the tide began to turn in Iraq's favor. Economically, loans and credits had enabled it to import needed military hardware and spare parts for its equipment. The expansion of its pipelines had increased its oil revenues. By 1988 Iraq was fielding various armed forces of about 1.3 million troops in 130 divisions.[20] Iraq was also ready to go on the offensive, and with new tactics. It did so in February, first with a major bombardment of Iranian cities in a "war of terror" on civilians and then with a ground offensive in a series of actions that finally regained lost territory and decisively defeated Iranian forces.

The renewed war on the cities began 22 February with an attack on Tehran and lasted until 20 April. In these attacks Iraq used a modified SCUD B missile, the Husain, capable of reaching Tehran. Baghdad fired some two hundred missiles in all on a number of Iranian cities, including Isphahan and Qum, but the majority—some 150—rained down on the Iranian capital. Iran replied with a ground attack in the north of Iraq, seizing the town of Halabja. Deciding to counterattack, Iraq warned inhabitants of Halabja to evacuate, dropping leaflets specifying that it would use chemical weapons, and then it did use them.[21] On 16 March Iraq attacked the town using both mustard and nerve gas and killed an estimated 4,000. Partly because of this CW attack, the Iraqi missile attacks on Iranian cities, in particular Tehran, raised fears of chemical weapons use on civilians. Although chemicals were not used on Iranian cities, the missile attacks created a crisis of morale for Iran. In Tehran about 1.5 million residents eventually fled a city of about 8 million, posing serious problems for the Iranian regime.

The Iraqis now turned to Faw, their major objective. Attacking on 16 April, the beginning of Ramadan, the Iraqis took the Iranians completely by surprise. The Republican Guard and the Seventh Corps of the regular army, using amphibious landings—as well as CW—surrounded the Iranian forces. Within four days Iraq was in possession once again of the Faw peninsula. On May 25, one month later, the Iraqis followed up with an attack on Salamja, north of Faw. Iraq fought a ferocious nine-hour pitched battle. Iran counterattacked, but its losses were high and its forces were finally forced to fall back.

In June Iraq recaptured the Majnun oil fields and in early July advanced into Iranian territory—along with the Mujahidin al-Khalq, the Iranian opposition forces—briefly taking Dahloran. Thus, by July Iraq had achieved the upper hand in the war, and Iranian forces were in a shambles. These land offensives coincided with increased US naval actions against Iran, reinforcing an Iranian sense of isolation and hopelessness.

By 14 July serious discussions were under way in Tehran over accepting Resolution 598. Iran's official letter of acceptance was delivered to the UN Secretary General in New York on 17 July. The same day, Saddam Husain gave a speech offering a five-point peace program: a cease-fire, a return to international borders, an exchange of POWs, a comprehensive peace treaty, and a mutual commitment to noninterference in one another's territory. But Iraq also demanded direct, face-to-face negotiations with Iran in return for the cease-fire, an effort to compel Iranian recognition of its regime.

The Inconclusive Peace

Although the war came to an end, negotiations over the terms of peace, and the application of Resolution 598, were to prove too difficult to resolve. Iran wanted a cease-fire in place while the UN formed a commission to investigate the causes of the war; it intended to fix responsibility on Iraq and then demand reparations. Iraq wanted implementation of 598 in sequence: first a cease-fire, then withdrawal of forces, followed by an exchange of POWs, and finally a comprehensive settlement.

Although talks between the foreign ministers of both countries took place in Geneva in 1988 and 1989, under the auspices of Secretary General de Cuellar, there was little agreement between the two parties beyond the withdrawal of forces and a reopening of the Shatt al-Arab. By the time of Khumaini's death in June 1989, the peace talks had bogged down. Although the cease-fire held because both sides were too exhausted to resume hostilities, the eight-year conflict ended in a no war, no peace situation. Iraq still held Iranian territory, POWs had yet to be exchanged, no commission had been appointed to investigate "blame" for the war, and the boundary along the Shatt remained unresolved. Iraq had little concrete gain to show for eight years of war except defense of its territory. The river itself remained closed, full of ordnance and chemical weapons. Iraq was more landlocked than before and had to rely for export outlets mainly on Umm Qasr and the Khaur Abd Allah channel. This factor compelled Iraq to focus more intensely on Kuwait.

Although Iraq maintained its territorial integrity, its extensive—and increased—use of CW during the war gained it an unsavory reputation abroad that emerged almost as soon as the cease-fire took effect. While international criticism of CW use had been muted while the war was in progress, once this constraint was removed, various international groups in the West focused media attention on this factor. The unfavorable attention soon turned the international community against Iraq. Much of the advantage gained by an opening to the United States in the war was soon lost.

On the positive side, however, the war appeared to confirm the resilience of the Iraqi state. Despite eight years of a bitterly fought war, Iraq's forces and people had managed to defend their country and prevent occupation of their territory by a neighbor three times the country's size. Among most of the population, the war seemed to generate a greater sense of community, even of patriotism. This was truer for the Arab population than for the Kurds. Although most Kurds fought with—not against—Iraqi government forces, the war in the north strengthened and revived the Kurdish opposition. The most remarkable feat—though hardly positive—was that a repressive and autocratic regime, despite some close calls, came through the war with its hold on power strengthened.

The War's Impact on Foreign Policy

The Iran-Iraq war had a major impact on the regime's regional and international position and its foreign policy positions. In 1979 Iraq's position was stable and relatively secure; its economic wealth was growing, and it was able to maintain a high degree of independence in its international relations.[22] Baghdad had begun to play a leading role in the region and even internationally. Eight years later, this position was substantially altered. Much of Iraq's wealth had been dissipated and it was in debt. Its relative autonomy in the international arena had given way to dependence on regional and global powers.

Iraqi Foreign Policy in the Region

The first casualty of the conflict was Saddam's ambition to assume a leadership role in the region and in the global nonaligned movement. Owing to the war, the location of the nonaligned conference of September 1982 was changed from Baghdad to New Delhi, despite the elaborate plans and expenditure to prepare Baghdad for the event. Instead of Saddam Husain, India's Indira Gandhi assumed the leadership of the nonaligned world for the next four years. The war also ended Saddam's aspirations to play a dominant role in the Gulf. On the contrary, the destruction of Iraq's offshore oil terminals and its reduced income made Iraq heavily dependent financially and politically on the conservative Gulf states that were financing its war effort.

The most important evidence of the shift in the power balance, and the most significant for the future, was the formation of the Gulf Cooperation Council (GCC) in May 1981, not long after the start of the war. The six-member group included all Arab Gulf states (Kuwait, Saudi Arabia, Qatar,

Bahrain, the UAE, and Oman) but pointedly did not include Iraq. Although the idea of such a grouping had been entertained earlier, the Arab Gulf states had hesitated, partly for fear of Iran's reaction but also because of anxiety that Iraq would join and then dominate the group. The war eliminated both fears. The GCC institutionalized the distance between the Arab Gulf states and Iraq. Even more significant were the deepening military ties between the GCC and the West. Both the formation of the GCC and the US military presence greatly reduced Iraq's room for maneuver in the Gulf and virtually ended its ability to lead any Gulf alliance, even among the Arab states.

The war compelled Iraq to tilt toward the West and its supporters in the Middle East. This was most striking in the case of Egypt. Iraq had earlier taken the lead in ostracizing Egypt for its peace treaty with Israel, but war needs soon reversed Iraq's position. Once the war started, contacts between Egypt and Iraq accelerated. Egyptian munitions, tanks, and volunteers played a role in sustaining the Iraqi war machine. In return, Iraq helped smooth the way for Egypt's reintegration into the Arab world. In November 1987 Egypt was finally readmitted to the Arab League, and almost immediately thereafter Iraq restored diplomatic relations. Egypt's rehabilitation not only restored a more traditional balance of power in the Middle East but undercut Iraq's earlier tentative steps to supplant Egypt as Arab world leader.

Iraq also became more dependent on Turkey, a pillar of the North Atlantic Treaty Organization (NATO), not only because Turkey provided the sole outlet for its oil during much of the war but also because the Turks were policing the Kurds along Iraq's northern frontier while Iraq's troops were engaged with Iran. In 1984 Iraq agreed to let Turkey engage in operations across the border in "hot pursuit" of Turkey's own dissident Kurds. On at least two occasions—August 1986 and March 1987—the Turkish air force undertook raids on Kurdish strongholds in Iraq. Meanwhile, Turkish exports to Iraq increased from $135 million in 1980 to almost $1 billion by 1987; imports, mainly oil, averaged over $1 billion a year.

Relations with Jordan, another pro-Western country, were also greatly strengthened. Jordan provided routes to Aqaba, allowing Iraqi goods to be channeled through this port on the Red Sea. Jordan also helped with the war effort, seconding military officers, supplying tanks, and providing military volunteers. These close links with Jordan were to survive the war.

As relations with pro-Western neighbors improved, Iraqi-Syrian relations deteriorated to the lowest point in years. Despite pressure from Saudi Arabia,

Syria refused to end its collaboration with Iran, an act viewed in Baghdad as little short of treason to the Arab cause.[23] During the war, Syria constituted virtually a second political front for Iraq. In October 1980 Baghdad broke diplomatic relations with Damascus and began supporting the Syrian regime's opposition inside Syria and in Lebanon.[24] But Syria cut Iraq's pipeline in April 1982, eliminating half Iraq's oil exports and costing it $6 billion. Iraq closed its border with Syria. Syria and Iran negotiated a new oil agreement giving Syria 1 million tons of oil free and 2 million at reduced rates. This agreement, concluded in July 1986, was to last ten years—well beyond the conclusion of the Iran-Iraq war.

One of the most striking changes brought by the war was Iraq's moderation, at least officially, of its stand on the Palestine issue and Israel. In private statements in 1981, Iraqi officials affirmed their willingness to accept a negotiated settlement that was satisfactory to the Palestinians. In August 1982 in an interview with US Congressman Stephen Solarz, Saddam Husain went even further, stating that a condition of security for Israel was necessary for a resolution of the Arab-Israeli conflict. This unprecedented statement was followed by a declaration by Foreign Minister Tariq Aziz that Iraq was "not opposed to a peaceful settlement of the problem, and therefore negotiations with Israel."[25] This shift was designed to propitiate the United States and its regional allies, on whom Iraq was increasingly dependent during the war, but the changed foreign policy position persisted even after the war. The moderation in Arab-Israeli policy was even more remarkable in the wake of the Israeli bombing of Iraq's nuclear reactor in June 1981, which destroyed Iraq's incipient nuclear weapons program.

Iraqi Foreign Policy Toward the Superpowers

The war also affected the way in which Iraq dealt with the superpowers. As indicated, Iraq was compelled to draw closer to the United States as its difficulties with Iran and its need for superpower support increased. Tentative moves toward improved relations with the United States were made in 1981, and these soon bore fruit. In 1982 Iraq was taken off the US terrorist list, a major step forward for Iraq. The subsequent easing of Iraq's position on Israel made even more progress possible, such as the supplying of US satellite intelligence to the Iraqis during the war, as well as the extension of agricultural credits. In May 1984 the US government condemned Iraq for using chemical weapons in the war,[26] but even this did not prevent a renewal of diplomatic relations on 26 November. But relations with the United States remained fragile. In addition to protests over chemical weapons use, admittedly muted during the war effort, Irangate—the United States' ill-advised covert effort to sell arms to Iran in 1986—and the *Stark* episode in 1987 were blows to the relationship, indicating that it was uneasy and based on little more than strategic necessity and the need to contain a common enemy, Iran.

Relations with other Western European countries were likewise strengthened, with France singled out for special treatment. Iraq relied on France for much of its armaments, including Mirages and the loan of the Super Etendards. By 1983 Iraq was so deeply in debt to France that French financial circles worried about repayment problems, but the French government nevertheless decided to continue its support.

Despite its expanding ties to the West, Iraq was only partly able to reduce its dependence on the Soviets for arms. In 1985 Mikail Gorbachev came to power in the Soviet Union, and to get acquainted with the new Soviet leader, Saddam Husain visited Moscow in mid-December, for the first time in seven years. The meeting between the Soviet reformer and the troublesome Iraqi client was reportedly cool. Nonetheless, the Soviets agreed to maintain arms support. By 1987 Soviet policy was beginning to shift, as Gorbachev began to change the ground rules of the Cold War. But the real effects of this change came after the cease-fire and did not affect the war's end.

The War's Impact on National Cohesion

One intangible benefit that Iraq appeared to reap—one for which the war was ostensibly fought—was the continued ethnic and sectarian cohesion of the state. The war and its hardships seemed to forge a greater sense of national unity. Iraq had defended its territorial integrity and its more secular way of life against considerable odds, giving some credence to claims by the Iraqi government and many outside observers that the war had strengthened Iraqi nationhood. But this assessment, while not inaccurate, is incomplete. In fact the war had a differential impact on Iraq's various communities. Although the regime could generally count on the support of the Arab *sunni* population, who most closely identified with the Iraqi nationalist mission, the war put considerable strains on loyalty within the *shi'i* and Kurdish communities.

The Shi'a

Shi'i dissidence was the most worrisome for the regime, since the Islamic revolution in Iran was the proximate cause of the war and much touted by the Ba'th as its justification. Indeed, the war provided a test case of *shi'i* loyalty, not just for the regime but also for the state and the general direction it was pursuing. Although much has been made in the postwar literature on Iraq of *shi'i* loyalty, in fact the *shi'i* community exhibited mixed behavior. On one hand, there were no massive defections at the front, although there were some; Iraqi *shi'a* fought about as well—or as indifferently—as Iraqi *sunnis*. However, the war was not popular in the south, though it was not openly criticized. It is clear that Iraqi *shi'a* were not prepared to make common cause with the *shi'a* of Iran. Yet they probably fought because of a mixture of motives, among which positive attitudes of loyalty to the state may have been minimal.

In dealing with the *shi'i* population, Saddam used his usual carrot-and-stick policy. On the positive side, he moved to integrate more *shi'a* into political positions. The party congress held in June 1982 elected a new Regional Command; of the seven new members, a majority were *shi'a*.[27] When added to the *shi'a* already on the command, this produced a *shi'i* plurality, if not a majority, for the first time since 1968. However, these members were not included in the RCC, where most important decisions were made.

Greater inclusion was combined with generous public funding in the south for housing projects, hospitals, water and sewage works, electricity, and even the improvement and embellishment of mosques. The birthday of Ali, revered by the *shi'a*, was made a national holiday. Saddam also attempted to co-opt *shi'i* clerics, with limited success. In April 1983 the regime held a popular Islamic conference headed by Ali Kashi al-Ghita, who tended to support the regime, but members of the Khu'i and Hakim families refused to attend.[28]

These moves, however, were accompanied by continued severe persecution of any potential *shi'i* opposition. The Hakims, by now in open opposition, suffered extreme retribution. In 1983, after the Islamic Iraqi opposition in Tehran, headed by Muhammad Baqir al-Hakim, decided to constitute itself a government in exile, the Ba'th arrested about eighty members of the family still in Iraq and in May 1983 executed six, all *shi'i* religious leaders in good standing; three were brothers of Muhammad Baqir. In March 1985 a further ten members of the family were executed, and in January 1988 Mahdi al-Hakim, who headed a European-based opposition group, was assassinated in Khartoum.[29]

Major deportations of Iraqis of "Iranian origin," begun in 1980 at the time of Baqir al-Sadr's execution, continued. These included many wealthy *shi'a* as well as others from the south. At the war's end, this group may have totaled 200,000. These moves decapitated *shi'i* opposition inside Iraq and moved much of its support base outside the country to Iran. This growing number of alienated, bitter, and frustrated Iraqis provided an ideal resource to be organized by the Iranians and the exiled leadership of the Iraqi *shi'i* opposition.

The Formation of SAIRI

The chief Iraqi *shi'i* group opposed to the regime after 1980 was the Supreme Assembly for the Islamic Revolution in Iraq (SAIRI), formed in Tehran on 17 November 1982.[30] Iran took the initiative in its formation. Designed as an umbrella group composed of several *shi'i* parties, the movement was unified only after Iran made several attempts. In 1986 Muhammad Baqir al-Hakim became SAIRI's chairman and its moving force.

SAIRI evolved through various phases in an attempt to achieve some unity. Initially, influence was dispersed among component groups—the Da'wa, the Islamic Action Organization, SAIRI itself (essentially al-Hakim and his supporters), and some independents. The first assembly had fifteen members, a majority of them clerics. At a later stage, SAIRI's leading body was enlarged to encompass Kurds and one Arab *sunni*. In 1986 two tiers were created: an executive committee of fifteen and a general assembly of some eighty members. Real power, however, lay in the executive committee, whose members were Hakim supporters. At this stage SAIRI was committed to the establishment of an Islamic state in Iraq and embraced the key Khumaini concept of the *wilayat al-faqih* (rule of the theological jurist). Both concepts were alien to the majority of Iraqi *shi'a,* to say nothing of the *sunnis* and secularists.

Whatever its ideology, SAIRI's institutional foundation lay in the Iraqi deportees and POWs in Iran and in leadership and support from Iran. From its inception, it was tied to the Iranian war effort, particularly through its military arm, the Badr Brigade, several thousand strong in 1986. According to one analyst, this militia was under Iranian command in the war, although it had some Iraqi staff officers in the units.[31] In addition to fielding these political and military activities, SAIRI also engaged in destabilizing activities inside Iraq, including sabotage, bombings, and assassination attempts.

Despite its potential for disruption, SAIRI suffered from many shortcomings as a focus for *shi'i* loyalty. Its component groups—the Da'wa, the

Islamic Action Organization, and SAIRI's core under Hakim—had different constituents, organizations, and leadership. SAIRI's support was overwhelmingly in the exile community in Iran, with few roots or organizational ties in Iraq. Above all, however, SAIRI's collaboration with Iran doomed its efforts inside Iraq. Many *shi'a* who opposed Saddam and the Ba'th had no desire to be liberated by Tehran or incorporated in a new Islamic empire.

The Kurds

The impact of the war on Kurdish loyalty was more divisive. The war, and more importantly government policy, was devastating, not only for the Kurds in the north but in the longer run for the government in Baghdad as well. Kurdish loyalty to the state had always been problematic, but at the start of the war, the balance of forces in the north was in favor of the regime. The most serious danger to the state was posed by the continued armed opposition of the KDP, led by the Barzani brothers and by their active military alliance with Iran. The Barzanis, with many of their forces now located in Iran after their disastrous defeat in 1975, had forged close ties with the new Iranian regime and received support in return for their help in curbing the Iranian Kurdish movement (the Kurdish Democratic Party of Iran, KDPI).[32] However, in the first few years of the war, the Kurds spent more time fighting among themselves than fighting the government. Moreover, the institutions of self-rule and a continued high level of expenditures on economic development in the north helped blunt Kurdish activism.

In the war's early days, Kurdish conscripts and officers served at the front, although defections increased after the first few years. In the north, the Fursan were strengthened as Iraqi army forces were withdrawn to the south. However, this situation changed in October 1983 when the KDP joined forces with Iran to attack Banjwin and the Iranians seized Haj Umran, opening a second front in the northern area.

In retaliation, the government rounded up some 8,000 male members of the Barzani clan and sent them to an unknown destination; they were never heard from again. This event forced the government to send troops north and to support the Fursan, at a time when it was facing large numbers of Kurdish deserters.[33]

Under these new circumstances, the government turned once again to the Fursan. In 1983 a new National Defense Battalion was formed of Fursan, and it grew substantially thereafter. By the summer of 1986, it may have totaled 150,000, at least three times the number of *peshmergas* under arms.

The Fursan contingents, supplied by tribal leaders, were a volunteer force that included villagers and townspeople, farmers and shopkeepers—even some professionals. They helped stabilize the north, especially in and around the cities and communications routes.[34]

But the Fursan were not strong enough to hold the north, and by the end of 1986 and beginning of 1987, the regime faced real difficulties in the Kurdish area. In November 1986 Mas'ud al-Barzani and Jalal al-Talabani began coordinating a broad opposition movement. In February 1987 they issued a joint KDP-PUK statement, and in May 1987 an opposition umbrella came into being, including the KDP, PUK, KSP (Kurdish Socialist Party), ICP, and Assyrian Democratic Movement. This front spelled trouble for Baghdad. By 1987 the KDP had control of virtually the entire northern border with Turkey from Syria to Iran, while the PUK controlled the border with Iran from Rawanduz south to Banjwin.

The Anfal Campaign

It was in these circumstances that the government made the decision to take the drastic measures that would dramatically change its relations with the Kurdish population. These began on 28 February 1987, when Ali Hasan al-Majid was appointed governor of the northern provinces with "full powers" to take whatever measures necessary to end this insurgency. The problem was seen no longer as one of controlling the borders but of dealing with an insurgency that controlled much of the rural areas. The harsh actions previously taken by the government to control the borders in the mid- to late 1970s—razing villages and resettling several hundred thousand Kurds in *mujamma'at* (settlements), for which they general received compensation—now paled in comparison. The new scorched-earth policy had as its purpose to clear the region of guerrillas and remove the village environment that protected them. The campaign, generally known as the "Anfal" (spoils), reached a level of brutality and killing so high and wreaked such devastation on settled life, even for a regime widely known for its brutality, that it finally resulted in international outrage and charges of genocide.

The operation began in April 1987 with attacks on the KDP headquarters in the Dahuk area, on the PUK headquarters in the south, and in the PUK stronghold in the Balisan Valley north of Sulaimaniyya. In this attack, chemical weapons were used for the first time on the civilian population in the north.[35] The pattern to be followed later was established here. Villages were cleared, with CW if necessary, and villagers were transported to holding areas. The Fursan would follow, occupying the villages and often looting them. If there was resistance, villages were fired on and farms destroyed.[36] Many of those fleeing from detention centers "disappeared" or were killed.

The Iraqis then continued between April and June 1987 to raze villages in the lowlands and along main highways. After a lull, they focused on the highlands, putting thousands of villagers in holding camps and building new settlements. Over five hundred villages were destroyed in this period, two-thirds of them to the north and northeast of Kirkuk and Sulaimaniyya. In the new camps villagers were held under appalling conditions, and many did not survive. Despite this brutality, however, in this early period of the campaign, villagers were apparently given notice to evacuate and offered alternatives. Some went to relatives; others were resettled. It was those who resisted who were murdered or who disappeared.[37]

The unfolding "Kurdish solution" was so drastic that the policy backfired, creating greater Kurdish defections from the Fursan, who joined the *peshmergas*. But worse was to come.

In January 1988 the threat to Baghdad in the north deepened, with Iran's last attempt to break through the lines. In cooperation with the Kurds they reached Mawat and appeared to be headed for the plains. The government now responded with a series of planned and concerted military attacks— eight in all—between February and September 1988 on Kurdish guerrilla strongholds, designed to destroy and eradicate armed resistance and areas of *pershmerga* control once and for all. Building on the experience of the previous year, these attacks all had several characteristics that set them apart, at least in degree, from the drastic measures that had already taken place. First, they were focused assaults on targeted areas that all used CW and high-explosive air attacks to clear out *peshmerga* strongholds before ground troops entered. Second, once villagers were flushed out, men were separated from women, children, and the elderly; the latter were put in mass holding camps, where considerable numbers died. Many of the men were taken out of sight, where they were apparently indiscriminately shot and buried in mass graves. The villages they had inhabited were cleared and destroyed. It was this series of attacks to which the term *Anfal* has been applied.[38]

One attack in particular, in Halabja, has achieved notoriety. On 15 March the PUK and Iranian forces took the town, driving Iraqi forces out. Halabja was important because of its location near the Darbandikhan Dam, which controlled the water supply for the capital. Halabja then became the scene of one of the worst chemical attacks during the war. On 16 March

Iraq bombarded the city with a chemical cocktail; somewhere between 3,500 and 5,000 people were killed.

How many Kurds died in the scorched-earth campaign cannot be known for certain. Human rights investigators claim that at least 50,000 and possibly as many as 100,000 were killed in the Anfal attacks. By the end of the Iran-Iraq war, an estimated 4,000 villages and hamlets had been destroyed and some 1.5 million people forcibly displaced or resettled. The bulk of these displaced Kurds ended up in settlements outside major cities, such as Arbil, where they could be watched and controlled. But the operations also left a number of refugees across the borders—possibly as many as 250,000. By August 1988 there were reportedly 60,000 to 150,000 in Turkey and possibly 200,000 in Iran, some left over from 1975.[39] The Anfal marks one of the most brutal actions in Iraq's modern history and had a profound demographic, economic, and psychological impact on the Kurdish area.

While the government ended the war in control of its northern areas, the Anfal campaign polarized the Kurdish population. Even a number of the pro-government Kurdish contingents soured on the regime. Much of the north's agricultural production was damaged, making Iraq even more dependent on imports. Meanwhile, the government now had large numbers of hostile Kurds in settlements to watch. However, much of this cleansing campaign was visited on rural areas and the strongholds of the opposition. The urban areas, the stronghold of the government forces, on which considerable economic development had been lavished earlier, remained largely untouched and, in fact, at war's end appeared prosperous.[40] For the time being, the Kurdish insurgency, and the Kurdish nationalist parties that represented a separatist trend, had been defeated, but at an enormous price. One part of that price was deeper Kurdish alienation. Another was international opprobrium over the use of CW and the Anfal campaign. Although criticism was muted during the war, it resurfaced at its end, especially in the United States, where Congress began to take a more aggressive and hostile position toward the Iraqi government.

Economic and Social Effects of the War

Although Iraq's economic recuperation seemed possible at the war's end, in retrospect the war's huge economic bill and the regime's own unwillingness to face the costs, marked the beginning of a continuous decline for Iraq. By far the most serious blow to the economy was damage to Iraq's oil infrastructure and closure of the Persian Gulf to Iraqi oil exports. As a result Iraq lost much of its income for the duration of the war—and even beyond. The country's major offshore oil terminals in the south—Mina-l-Bakr and Khaur al-Amayya—were destroyed, making oil exports through the Gulf impossible. The Basra refinery was severely affected, as were the two fertilizer plants in the area. The petrochemical plant at Zubair, ready for commissioning when the war broke out, was unable to operate for the war's duration. The same was true of the nearby iron and steel plants.

More important than physical destruction was the cutoff of oil exports. When the war began in September 1980, Iraq was producing 3.5 million barrels per day. In the preceding year, it had earned export revenues of $26 billion. By 1982 exports were well under 1 million barrels per day, and by 1983, when OPEC prices began to fall, Iraq's oil revenues were reduced to about $10 billion per annum, roughly a third of prewar levels.[41]

For the first two years, the regime went to some lengths to insulate the population from the war's economic effects, mainly to guard against dissent against an unpopular conflict. As a result, it followed a policy of providing both "guns and butter." Until the fall of 1982, the regime continued its development program and indeed even expanded it. Visitors to Baghdad reported continued construction and plentiful consumer goods. A good example of wasted funds was the over $7 billion spent to refurbish Baghdad in preparation for the nonaligned conference (which was canceled) and the money invested in an elaborate state yacht that could not be delivered through Iraq's closed ports. The regime covered these expenditures by drawing down reserves at $1 billion a month and by borrowing from the Arab Gulf states at an estimated rate of $10 billion a year, putting it well into the red by 1983.

By mid-1982, however, it was apparent that expenditures would have to be curtailed and economic changes put into effect. Iraq simply did not have the resources to pay all its bills. The government took several steps. First, an austerity program was begun in November 1982. Most government employee benefits were reduced, imports were pared down by 50 percent, and the development program was cut back. By 1983 only those projects capable of aiding the war effort or expanding Iraq's potential for increased oil production and export were receiving funds.

Second, measures were taken to liberalize the economy. Although the new policy took effect all across the board—in agriculture, industry, trade, and services—it was particularly apparent in agriculture. Public Law 35 of

1983 allowed private individuals and companies to lease large blocks of land from the state. Most contracts called for large-scale mechanized farming in order to achieve immediate increases in productivity. Ironically, it was the large-scale private mechanized farms, particularly in the northern plains area, that had been eliminated in the early years of the land reform. In the course of the 1980s, the number of collective farms was drastically reduced and the numbers of cooperatives likewise declined, while agricultural loans to the private sector increased.[42] In 1987 new impetus was given to agricultural privatization with the selling of state lands and collective farms to private enterprise, including poultry and dairy enterprises. Privatization was also encouraged in industry and the trade sector. A number of state enterprises were sold to private entrepreneurs, including supermarkets, gas stations, and smaller factories. Even in the service area, the regime came increasingly to rely on private companies and individuals. In health services, critical to the war effort, the government turned to foreign hospital management companies and also encouraged doctors with previous experience in the state sector to establish private hospitals, a clear departure from socialism.

The results of this privatization appear to have been mixed in terms of productivity. In agriculture there was increased output of some food items, especially fruits and vegetables, and a better supply of foodstuffs to the capital,[43] but traditionally grown crops, such as cereal grains, declined.[44] The haste in selling off government enterprises without creating the necessary legal, economic, and financial underpinnings for a private sector led to abuses, creating a new and larger class of private landlords, entrepreneurs, and contractors tied to the regime and therefore inclined to support it. Moreover, despite this development, privatization did not really change the nature of the economic system; the state continued to play the preponderant role in the economy. Iraq then moved ahead on two fronts to sustain its economy— improving oil exports and borrowing to finance civilian and military imports. Left with only 650,000 barrels per day in exports via the Turkish pipeline in 1982, Iraq expanded its capacity to 1 million barrels per day through a connection to the Saudi pipeline to the Red Sea. By the war's end, oil exports were up to 2.1 million barrels per day. In addition, trucks carried oil through Jordan and Turkey. To pay for these improvements, as well as the costs of war, substantial loans were negotiated from Western Europe, Japan, and the United States; meanwhile, financial aid and loans of various kinds continued from Saudi Arabia and Kuwait. Iraq also became indebted to the USSR for arms sales. As a result, Iraq's foreign debt rose precipitously in this period, especially to Western and other non-Arab sources. As little of this was paid off during the war, the interest mounted, increasing the overall indebtedness.

Although these measures improved Iraq's economic situation somewhat by 1988, they could not make up for the losses. Iraq's modest improvement in oil exports was offset by a decline in the price of oil, especially in 1986. By 1987 Iraq was earning a mere $11 billion a year in oil revenue, still only a little more than a third of what it earned the year prior to the war.[45] The war also cost Iraq virtually all its reserves, roughly $35 billion.

Debt

Rather than paying for the war as it dragged on, Iraq had mortgaged its future by borrowing. Iraq came out of the war with an external debt—exclusive of that owed to Arab supporters—of at least $40 billion but more likely $50 billion. Of this, the Soviet bloc was owed about $8 billion, essentially for arms; Western governments and commercial establishments (mainly Germany, Japan, France, and the United States), about $27 billion; and developing countries, such as Brazil, Turkey, and South Korea, about $10 billion. At the start of the war, Iraq's debt had been miniscule—some $2.5 billion. During the war, Iraq followed a policy of pressing for a rescheduling, or a rollover, of the debt, along with a further, longer-term advance of credits. The creditors, with little choice if they wished to retrieve their debt, usually obliged. At war's end Iraq's annual payments, principal and interest, on debt to the West was estimated at a huge $7 billion. The overhanging debt and Iraq's new and far weaker credit rating were important impediments to rapid recuperation and development.

The loans and advances from Gulf states, primarily Kuwait and Saudi Arabia, have been estimated at another $30 billion to $40 billion. These sums would include oil sold on Iraq's behalf, payments through oil or cash to the USSR for weapons, and nominal loans. Iraq, however, considered these not as loans but as the Gulf contribution to the war effort. With the decline in oil prices in the later 1980s, these "contributions" had caused hardships in Gulf countries now facing their own financial difficulties. These difficulties—as well as the whole question of repayment—would set the stage for the tensions that followed the war.

Closure of the Shatt

At the war's end, Iraq also faced another paramount economic difficulty, the continued closure of the Shatt al-Arab—a real cause for concern since Iraq's control of the Shatt had been a major, if not the major, justification for the war. This situation also ended Basra's function as Iraq's major port. Before the war, the Shatt had carried almost two-thirds of Iraq's nonoil cargo. The river remained impassable because it was filled with war-related debris, some of it highly dangerous. The Shatt was also littered with over a hundred ships, some of substantial size and some sunk in the navigable channel. Lastly, the river had not been dredged for eight years, leading to massive accumulations of silt, some of it possibly contaminated with chemical weapons. The cleanup operation was expensive, highly technical, and estimated to take up to five years.

The closure of the Shatt and the difficulty of reopening it shifted Iraq's focus to its alternative port, Umm Qasr, on the Khaur Abd Allah waterway, and to a lesser extent Zubair, to its north. While expansion of these alternative ports was possible, Umm Qasr raised the perennial problem of Iraq's long-standing border dispute with Kuwait and, because of Iraq's desire for a secure seaward approach to the port, control over the two Kuwaiti islands, Warba and Bubayan, that lay at the entrance to the waterway. Thus the closure of the Shatt not only focused Iraq's attention once again on Kuwait but limited its ability to develop.

Differential Distribution of Destruction

Even more significant for the future political and social direction of the state was the uneven geographic distribution of war damage.

For example, physical damage to the city of Basra and its environs was extensive. In 1977 Basra had been Iraq's third largest province in population; by 1987 it was seventh, although it later regained population. The south—especially the Basra province, where much of the war was fought—sustained the greatest loss in damaged industrial plant. This was clearest in the case of the southern oil facilities but was also true of the major industrial complex in the south, so recently built up—the refineries, the petrochemical plant, the iron and steel factories shut down by the war.

Agriculture too was neglected, although this neglect predated the war. A trip by the author through much of the south in July 1987 revealed large areas left uncultivated and no evidence of agricultural development.[46] Agricultural destruction also took place in the north of the country, where guerrilla activities and the Anfal campaign had destroyed much of the countryside.

The center of the country was least affected. The concentration of new industry here, as well as population growth, was significant. These new industries included a fertilizer plant and a refinery at Baiji; a phosphate complex at Qa'im, near the Syrian border; cement plants at Hit, Mosul, Kirkuk, and Samawa (the last in the south); and a new industrial complex manufacturing steel construction materials at Taji, near Baghdad. The capital and its suburbs were the major recipients of most benefits and increased population. The city that benefited most was Tikrit, now completely changed from the 1950s. Modern roads and thoroughfares (including overpasses with escalators), new hospitals, government complexes, miles of middle-class housing, and luxury villas along the river all testified to the rapid development of the country's "heartland" and of the improved social status of its political elite.[47]

The Impact on Labor

The war also had significant costs on the labor front and greatly distorted Iraq's employment structure. As the huge and growing Iraqi army swallowed up available manpower, serious labor shortages occurred. According to one report, factories, state organizations, and government offices had their work-forces reduced by as much as 45 percent.[48] The military siphoned off much of the skilled and educated workforce, always in short supply, and wasted its potential productivity in eight years of war.

To ease the shortage, Iraq imported foreign labor on a large scale, a prac-tice it had previously kept to a minimum. Indians, Filipinos, and Koreans flooded the construction industry, while many positions in the bureau-cracy—and later in agriculture—were taken by Egyptians. Even menial jobs for unskilled workers fell into foreign hands. Some estimates in the early 1980s put the number of foreign workers at 2 million.[49]

One positive change came in rising employment for women, who also helped fill the gap. This was particularly true for Iraq's increasing numbers of educated women. The percentage of women in the nonagricultural work-force rose from about 17 percent in the 1970s to about 25 percent in the 1980s, a very high figure for the Arab world.

Social Costs

The war also had social costs, though these are more difficult to measure. The most important, of course, was the toll in human casualties. It has been estimated that total military casualties for Iraq were around 380,000, of which about 125,000 were deaths and about 255,000 wounded. Iraqi POWs totaled between 50,000 and 80,000; many of these did not return to Iraq for years after the war. To these casualties must be added the 50,000 to 100,000 of the Anfal campaigns. This would make a military and civilian casualty total over the eight-year period of at least half a million, or about 2.7 percent of the population.

In addition to the obvious human loss, casualties also represented a substantial loss of manpower and skill. The Iraqis attempted to preserve their skilled population, deferring students until they had finished their studies, but all had to serve at some point and many were lost. By the end of the war these losses bit deeply, eroding Iraqi morale and a sense of confidence in the country's future. The drafting of young men from school and work had become increasingly unpopular, and the loss of young lives weakened support for a regime that had gotten the country into an endless war from which it seemed unable to extricate itself. The war ended the sense of buoyancy that had characterized Iraq a decade earlier.

The war also began a change in the social structure. The slowdown in development, cutbacks in imports, and the resulting inflation—28 percent at the end of the war—bit deeply into the newly acquired prosperity of the middle class and impaired the social mobility on which the regime had based so much of its legitimacy. Many Iraqis were forced or pressured into giving up savings for the war effort, thus beginning a process of disinvestment. Many salaried civil servants, who depended on the government for jobs and income, saw their status and standard of living decline as wages failed to keep up with prices of food and housing. Many of these professionals resented the sale of government-owned industry and agricultural property to private interests, who then profited and became rich. The slow but unmistakable descent of Iraq's middle class and its salaried income base began during the war.

Even more striking than the gradual weakening of middle-class standards was the growth of an affluent and wealthy class of merchants, contractors, and businessmen as the government opened up the private sector. While this may have been the inevitable consequence of privatization, several features of this class became evident. First was the increasing discrepancy in wealth. While some merchants and landowners became merely affluent, others became conspicuously rich, with a high concentration of wealth and business in the hands of a few.

The second feature was the tie of this stratum of nouveaux riches to the regime and its allies. While the new commercial and entrepreneurial elite did cut across ethnic and sectarian lines (there were large Kurdish landlords and contractors as well as rich *shi'i* merchants and entrepreneurs), many were beholden to the regime for their prosperity, whether through the sale of lands, government-sponsored contracts, or the purchase of factories previously owned by the government.[50]

Eventually, the war even weakened some of the progress made in the status of women. The Ba'th position on women was relatively progressive to start with, encouraging their education, literacy, and professional advancement. Initially, the war encouraged this by providing jobs for women and integrating them further into the workforce, particularly professional and educated women. But as the war dragged on, even this Ba'th policy changed. To make up for losses at the front, the regime attempted to raise the birth rate by encouraging large families. Saddam Husain urged every family to have five children, including women in their forties and fifties. Far more important for women, however, was the toll of casualties on marriage and the family. Many women had to put off marriage for a decade for fear of becoming war widows. Even worse was the situation of the many widows or wives of handicapped men left to support families. Postponement of marriage, loss of manpower, and the decade-long delay in starting careers and work for both young women and men took a heavy toll on the family, still the bedrock of Iraqi society.

The War's Political Effects

These economic and social repercussions naturally spilled over into the political arena, raising questions about support for Saddam Husain and the survival of the regime. Saddam's fortunes shifted with the war, and so, too, did his responses. Initially the regime had support in the war, but the army's reverses and its retreat to the borders in 1982 unquestionably eroded loyalty to the regime. The first challenge for Husain was to maintain the allegiance of his inner constituency in the face of massive losses and to protect himself as the rightful leader of the state. The second was to maintain political control over an expanding army and prevent military leadership from acting as a countervailing center of power to himself. In the end, the regime survived, but it changed in several ways that strengthened the personal power of Saddam and his centrality to the system.

The Concentration of Power in the Presidency
Within the formal structure of government, the locus of power was gradually shifted from the party, especially the Regional Command, to the office of the

president, which Saddam now turned into his personal fief. The presidential office became the most important center for decisionmaking and the preferred route to power and position, reducing the party to an arm of the state.

Buttressing this structure was a full-blown personality cult. Already under way well before the war, it reached new heights. Saddam made himself not only head of state but symbol of the people. His picture, in multiple guises—as peasant, as educated official, as warrior, as religious penitent—became ubiquitous. The celebration of his birthday on 28 April became a national holiday, commemorated with processions from all over Iraq to his hometown of Tikrit. Radio, TV, and press were all saturated with coverage of his pictures, words, and activities. Iraq's revolutionary history was divided into two phases: before and after Saddam.

The party itself was transformed from a cadre of ideologically committed individuals to a mass-based organization designed to support the government. In the 1980s, party membership, including "supporters" and people in various stages of candidacy, represented about one member for each ten citizens.[51] But as membership in the party became a touchstone of loyalty, it also became a channel of mobility. Party membership became essential for employment, acceptance to elite schools, and professional advancement.

Elections for the National Assembly were also used to generate a popular base for Saddam's leadership rather than for the party. In fact it became a competing institution. The election of the first assembly, initiated in June 1980, after Saddam's assumption of the presidency, gave the Ba'th 75 percent of the seats. By the time of the third election, held in 1989, the Ba'th had been reduced to a slim majority. The assembly had no real legislative authority, but it did provide a voice beyond the party for the population at large.[52]

Ideological Shifts

As the political structure changed, so, too, did the ideology. Throughout the 1980s, Saddam experimented with different formulations designed to encourage national cohesion and support for the war and his own legitimacy. The metamorphosis from Arab nationalism to Iraqi patriotism was clear. Mesopotamian history and heritage were publicly emphasized in activities like the restoration of Babylon and the creation of the Babylonian Festivals. Saddam was repeatedly referred to as the modern day Nebuchadnezzar, the ancient Babylonian king who ruled over the Babylonian Empire at its height. But Iraq's central role in Arab and Islamic history was also emphasized, particularly to counter the penetration of Khumaini's religious propaganda from Iran. Saddam even invented a family lineage that tied him to Muhammad and, in a particular attempt to appeal to the *shi'a,* to Ali.[53] The war was known as "Qadisiyyat Saddam," in commemoration of the famous battle in which the Arab Muslims of the seventh century defeated the infidel Persians. All of these ideological myths were designed to generate a greater identity with the state, but even more to justify the legitimacy of the regime personified by Saddam.

Impact on the Military and Security

Meanwhile, the military was kept under control by tight surveillance. The war saw an increase in the security apparatus as well as the army. No figures have ever been published on the size of the security force in Iraq, and estimates vary. One source considers that this group may have risen as high as 200,000, some 15 percent of government employees.[54] Others give a much more modest figure of 60,000 to 80,000.[55] Whatever the figure, the network of informers and overlapping security organizations increased. To the three major security organizations present before the war—the General Security (Amn al-Amm) under the Ministry of Interior, the Military Intelligence (Istikhbarat) under the Ministry of Defense, and the Security Directorate (Mukhabarat) under the party— was now added the Special Security Organization (SSO, or Amn al-Khass), essentially under the president. Headed by Husain Kamil in the 1980s, it protected not only the regime but also its WMD program. The surveillance of the military was constant, as were executions for "failures" at the front and purges.

Kinship ties were also used to cement control of the military. Adnan Khair Allah Talfah, Saddam's cousin and brother-in-law, was maintained as minister of defense during the war. The upper echelons of the expanding military were liberally seeded with Tikritis and related clans. By the war's end, clan-based control at the commanding heights of the military and security systems was well established.

These steps enabled Saddam to surmount crises and even strengthen the regime during the war. But they did not end tensions or opposition. Within Iraq the security apparatus kept the opposition underground, but it was not entirely cowed, as sporadic bombings and assassination attempts indicated. Most groups operated from headquarters in Syria, Iran, or Europe. Among the secular groups, the most important were the Communists, several Kurdish organizations, and a pro-Syrian Ba'th splinter party led by Hasan al-Naqib, a former army colonel.

Even within the party, opposition took root. Dissatisfaction with the party's capture by Saddam Husain and his family led to movements in party ranks to reform. Most of these were reflected in pamphlets circulated outside the country.

The dissatisfaction of those in the center was more than matched by disaffection from the two traditional poles of regime opposition—the *shi'a* and the Kurds. But both of these opposition forces were dealt with brutally. Having surmounted tensions and opposition from within and from without, the regime now faced an entirely new challenge: coping with the outcome—and the costs—of the war.

The Aftermath of the War

These difficulties, however, were not uppermost in the minds of most Iraqis at the time of the cease-fire. To the contrary. Iraqis came out on the streets to celebrate with a sense not only of relief but also of victory. Along with the relief, went expectations of a fairly rapid economic revival and renewed possibilities of development. These expectations were encouraged by the government, which took a number of immediate steps to erase war damage and stimulate a sense of economic improvement. First, it initiated a three-month crash program, costing $4 billion, to rebuild Basra. Faw, a much smaller town, was rebuilt along with a museum to commemorate its reconquest. At the same time, the port of Umm Qasr was expanded and the industrial complex in the south revived.

The encouragement of the private sector, begun earlier, was given ever greater impetus. The sale of state assets increased, tourism was privatized, and in 1988 alone, the private sector was allowed to import billions of dollars of goods, equal to almost half of government imports.

Even on the political front, steps were taken to raise popular hopes for some reform. In November 1988 Saddam floated the idea of a new, permanent constitution, purportedly including the dismantling of the RCC and direct election of the president and allowing political parties other than the Ba'th to contest elections to the National Assembly.

These economic and political steps were accompanied by a major propaganda campaign designed to cement the idea of an Iraqi victory in the popular mind and to encourage expectations that Iraq's prosperity would soon return. Iraqis hailed the cease-fire as "a great victory which Iraq scored in the name of all Arabs and humanity."[56] But the propaganda, which deliberately exaggerated Saddam's achievements and concealed the damage to the country, was to cause him difficulties before too long.

In regional affairs Iraq soon moved to assert its leadership. One of the first efforts in this direction was the establishment of a new Arab bloc, the Arab Cooperation Council (ACC). Formed of Iraq, Egypt, Jordan, and Yemen, the ACC signed its founding agreement in February 1989.[57] The overarching aim of the organization remained unclear, and it did not survive Iraq's occupation of Kuwait.

In November 1988 Baghdad publicly supported the Palestine Liberation Organization's (PLO's) decision to recognize Israel and to bow to a negotiated settlement.

These early postwar steps, together with the "victory" propaganda, projected an image of strength and early recuperation. Both were illusions. They could not long disguise the real costs of the war and dissatisfaction among Iraqis with the regime that had brought them. Gradually, these problems began to surface once the euphoria of the cease-fire had dissipated. For example, the regime attempted to demobilize, releasing about 200,000 troops, but the process was halted when soldiers, with no employment available, vented their anger by attacking Egyptian workers who had been hired to take their places. A number of Egyptians were killed and wounded, and many left Iraq.

These underlying discontents were soon focused on the major political changes that had taken place since the start of the war—the dominance of political life by Saddam Husain and his family and their personal corruption and misbehavior. The misbehavior soon came into view in a stunning episode that occurred in October 1988. Although private in nature, it soon became widely known. During an official reception in Baghdad attended by Suzanne Mubarak, the Egyptian president's wife, Saddam's son Udayy, drunk and unruly, broke into the gathering and provoked a quarrel with Hanna Jajjo, a close aide and confidante of Saddam Husain. In full view of all assembled Udayy killed Jajjo, reportedly with a blow to his head.[58] The cause of the outburst, soon revealed, was purely personal. Udayy, and his mother, Sajida, blamed Jajjo for having introduced Saddam to Samira Shahbandar, wife of the head of Iraqi Airways, whom the president was rumored to be on the verge of marrying. The murder and the family feud behind it revealed the extent to which personal rule and family concerns had over-whelmed the process of government in Iraq. Saddam responded by briefly imprisoning his son, then exiling him, then pardoning him.

Not long after, family cohesion suffered another blow. On 5 May 1989 Adnan Khair Allah died in a helicopter crash near Hatra on a return from a tour of the Kurdish area. Although his death was attributed to a sudden and violent sandstorm (which actually did occur), his demise was widely attrib-uted to Saddam Husain. Whatever the truth, Khair Allah's death intensified popular dismay at the behavior of Saddam and his family. It also removed a key element of family control over the military.

This trouble from inside the regime was accompanied by problems from abroad, especially from the United States, which had been instrumental in providing political and military support for Iraq during the last years of the war. Opposition to the regime from the US Congress and some of the media, most of it stemming from Iraq's use of CW and other brutal measures against the Kurds in the war's aftermath, was a harbinger of things to come. The at-tacks on the regime began almost as soon as the cease-fire went into effect. On 8 September 1988 the US Department of State announced it had conclu-sive evidence of Iraq's use of CW against the Kurds, and Secretary of State George Shultz warned that such use would affect US relations with Iraq. Whatever support Iraq could expect from the United States was evaporating.

These early signs of trouble pointed to the dangers that lay ahead for Iraq in adjusting to the postwar environment. The elation at the end of a long and debilitating conflict, the false impression of "victory" relentlessly publi-cized by the regime, and the superior military posture of Iraq at the end of the war all masked a harsher reality. It was not long before the difficulties and the challenges would emerge with a vengeance.

Saddam's First Decade

Saddam Husain had managed to survive the first decade of his "new" regime. However, by concentrating all power in his own hands and silencing even modest dissent, he had made Iraq vulnerable to a seriously flawed deci-sion—to go to war with Iran. Though Iraq was undoubtedly challenged by a new, radical regime in Iran, the new Iraqi president appears to have made his decision for war not to ward off a threat but on calculations of long-term gains and an overestimate of his own capabilities. The result was a long and debilitating conflict that eroded much of the physical and human capital built up in the previous decade. The war was not a total loss. It had generated a sense of cohesion—even patriotism—among many Iraqis, and the country had been able, despite its losses, to protect some of its human assets and begin rebuilding. But these modest accomplishments could not mask for long the deeper problems. The question was whether Saddam and the regime he now led were ready to recognize the new reality or would believe the myth of victory and strength they were now propagating.

9

THE GULF WAR AND ITS
CONSEQUENCES, 1990–1991

Like the Iran-Iraq war, the occupation of Kuwait and the ensuing Gulf War were largely the result of miscalculations by Iraq's leader. Again, the motives behind the leader's actions were a mixture of defensiveness and fears for Iraq's domestic stability—as well as his own political survival—combined with a calculated opportunism and a willingness to take risks to achieve political advantage. The threats to Saddam's position this time, however, came less from external sources than from domestic problems and the difficulty of managing them.

Although Iraq had emerged from the Iran-Iraq war with its state intact and with some sense of national pride in having outlasted its adversary, the strength of this national cohesion was more apparent than real. The vast bulk of the *shi'a* remained loyal to their country, but they were weary as well as profoundly alienated from the regime. National cohesion was even more precarious in the north, where the Kurdish area had been brought under central government control but only through extraordinarily repressive measures. Within the central core of the regime's mainly *sunni* supporters, there were also rumblings of dissatisfaction, especially among the military. Most significant of all, Iraq was operating with a depleted treasury. Meanwhile, there was still no peace with Iran, little demobilization, and no opening of the Shatt al-Arab. Rapid attempts to expand the port at Umm Qasr focused attention once again on the perennial and increasingly intractable border problem with Kuwait. Iraq also had to deal with changes in the international environment—the end of the Cold War, a deterioration in relations with the

United States, and a sudden collapse of the oil market—that weakened domestic stability.

These accumulating problems produced a gathering storm that became apparent by late spring 1990 and resulted in the development of a bizarre conspiracy theory that increasingly came to dominate Iraqi counsels. This contributed to the disastrous decision to invade Kuwait. The invasion brought decisive international action, leading to a second war that ended in defeat and harsh and humiliating cease-fire terms for Iraq. The war was followed by widespread rebellion in the north and south of the country, which revealed the alienation of broad sections of Iraqi society from the regime and the state. The domestic challenge not only weakened the regime but undid much of the social and political cohesion achieved in the previous decade. Most serious, it tore at the fabric of the state by loosening the control of the central government over a substantial portion of its territory in the north. In the end, it produced a regime even more narrowly based and repressive than it had been.

The Occupation of Kuwait: Causes and Motivations

The Iraqi decision to invade and occupy Kuwait was so astonishing that it has given rise to much speculation and analysis about why it was made.[1] The most plausible explanation is one that takes account of several strands of Iraqi policy that had converged by the late spring of 1990, all eventually focusing on Kuwait.

The Kuwaiti Border Issue
The first strand focuses on Iraq's long-standing dispute with Kuwait over borders, which became increasingly acrimonious in the aftermath of the Iran-Iraq war. Baghdad was anxious to expand its territorial access to the Gulf, on land around the port of Umm Qasr and in the Khaur Abd Allah channel. The Iraqis wanted a border that would give it control of the waterway and over the islands of Warba and Bubayan, which dominate access to the channel.[2] Kuwait had no intention of giving up this territory. (See Figure 7.2, p. 160.)

Even before the war, Iraq had serious port problems. In Iraq's economic plan for 1975–1979, a huge number of financial resources had gone to the expansion of Umm Qasr and the port of Zubair, farther to the north. The closure of the Shatt after the Iran-Iraq war now gave this problem considerable urgency.

Commercial traffic was not the only Iraqi aim in expanding Umm Qasr. Iraq was also interested in developing a substantial navy, virtually nonexistent in 1988, and even expanding it into a blue-water fleet. Umm Qasr would be an important base for this incipient navy.

Although Kuwait was interested in getting a final settlement of the border issue, evidence shows that it was Iraq that took the initiative—repeatedly and ever more aggressively—in attempting to get a revision of the status quo. The Iraqis raised the issue officially at least three times in 1989, in February, September, and November, to no avail. By this time they likely concluded that the Kuwaiti position was immovable and that little could be achieved by negotiation. They may have considered more forceful means at this early stage, but Iraq's economic problems intervened and overshadowed the border problem.

Iraq's Economic Problems

The victory propaganda and the early postwar flurry of rebuilding could not disguise Iraq's growing economic problems. Most important was the shortage of money to pay expenses. A year after the end of hostilities, Iraq was earning only $13 billion from oil revenues, but its civilian imports were about $12 billion, military imports over $5 billion, and debt repayments $5 billion.[3] The regime would need an extra $10 billion per annum just to balance its current budget.

Instead of austerity, the regime once again used a "guns-and-butter" policy to disguise the cost of the war. By 1990 its problem was greatly exacerbated. The list of projects outlined in development plans between 1988 and 1990 called for, among other things, the Baghdad metro, the Mosul airport, 1,900 miles of railroad, six-lane expressways to Turkey and Jordan, two large dams, power stations, and chemical plants.[4] Eventually most of these were scaled back or eliminated. Meanwhile, expenditures on military industry, covert WMD programs, and other weapons technology continued.

The inability to demobilize troops, beyond some 200,000 to 300,000 men, hung like a cloud over the regime and its economic policy. Shortages of revenue made job creation difficult. While the regime wanted to expand oil production, in the short run it found difficulties in producing much more than 2 million barrels per day without more investment in the industry and repair of its facilities. Moreover, one of the most promising fields—

Majnun—was near the Iranian border and could not be developed before a peace settlement.

The result of these policies was a worsening domestic situation. The middle-class population, the regime's major base of support, was grumbling and unhappy about its future prospects. Inflation was persistent and rising.[5] There were also some early signs of the regime's inability to deal with the situation. Early in 1990 Saddam himself admitted a budget shortfall but indicated he expected rising oil prices to cover it. Instead, prices fell. For much of the population, as well as Iraq's leadership, it was becoming increasingly apparent by 1990 that little economic development was in sight. These perceptions were not lost on Saddam Husain.

The Debt

Although Iraq faced several economic problems, none was as serious as its debt. By 1990 Iraq owed over $50 billion to Western creditors and to Russia. The problem was less the size of the debt as Iraq's debt policy. Iraq refused to pay the debt, rolling over interest payments in return for new loans, using the bait of future oil benefits for Iraq's creditors. As a result, the debt mounted. In fact, Iraq could have rescheduled its debt payments over a longer term, thus easing its short-term credit crunch, but it refused to do so. Western creditors would have insisted on greater transparency and control over Iraq's finances. These were anathema to the regime. As a result, foreign credit began to dry up and the absence of long-term foreign investment slowed much-needed revitalization of Iraq's productive sectors.

To solve its problem, the regime focused its attention not on its Western creditors but on its neighbors in the Gulf, and on Kuwait in particular. These states were now portrayed as the source of Iraq's problem, as well as the potential solution. The loans from Kuwait and Saudi Arabia were portrayed as payment to Iraq for protecting the region. Worse, in the emerging Iraqi view, the Gulf states had benefited from the war by increased oil sales and a greater share of the market. Saudi Arabia had doubled its oil production, relieving the pressure on the international community to step in and put an end to hostilities. This act had prolonged the war and bled Iraq; Iraq had earned its new status as the "protector" of the Arab Gulf states. It was now the duty of these states to help restore Iraq to its previous condition.[6]

Although Saudi Arabia was willing to write off the debt, Kuwait was not, probably because it wanted to tie any such concession to a settlement of Iraqi claims on the border. In February 1990, at an ACC meeting in Amman, Jordan, Saddam privately asked both King Husain and President Mubarak to inform the Gulf states that they must put a moratorium on wartime loans; in addition, he wanted an immediate infusion of funds in the neighborhood of $30 billion, a sort of Arab Marshall Plan to rebuild Iraq and cover its growing financial crisis. The request was accompanied by a threat. The Gulf states should know "that if they do not give this money to me, I will know how to get it."[7] By this time, money had superseded borders as the main issue with Kuwait.

The Oil Pricing Crisis

By February 1990 Iraq was facing an additional financial crisis it had not bargained for—a drop in oil prices that drastically compounded its financial shortfall and drove the situation into a real crisis stage. In January of 1990 Iraq had been selling oil at $21 a barrel; by March the price was below $18, and by summer it was down to $11.[8] At $11 Iraq would be bankrupt without a bailout. The cause, in the Iraqi view, was refusal of some OPEC producers to stick to their assigned oil quotas, thereby flooding the market with petroleum and drastically reducing prices.[9] Kuwait and the UAE were identified as the culprits.

In fact, the claim was not invalid. At the start of 1990, instead of adhering to the OPEC quota of 22 million barrels per day, OPEC was producing 24 million. Kuwait and the UAE accounted for 75 percent of the excess. In February 1990 Iraqi oil minister Isam al-Chalabi, went to Kuwait to urge Kuwaitis to stick to their quotas, evidently to no avail.[10] Far more dramatic were the warnings of Saddam Husain at the extraordinary Arab summit meeting held in Baghdad at the end of May. At a closed session attended by the Amir of Kuwait, among others, Saddam claimed: "War is fought with soldiers, . . . but it is also done by economic means. . . . This is in fact a kind of war against Iraq."[11] This stern warning had no effect on Kuwait. The amir, according to one source, merely drummed his fingers on the table and said nothing.[12]

Iraq's WMD Program

There were other threads in the crisis, not directly related to Kuwait, that also came to play a role in the crisis. One was Iraq's renewed attempt to develop weapons of mass destruction. Iraq's attempts to create an indigenous nuclear weapons capacity, as well as experimentation with biological weapons, had not ceased during the Iran-Iraq war, but they had increasingly been hampered by the absence of funding. With the end of the war and the expectation of more available funds, these programs escalated. It is estimated that Iraq spent some $3 billion on missiles and up to $10 billion on various means of developing nuclear weapons between 1980 and 1990.[13] Iraq was also experimenting with a "supergun," designed by the Canadian ballistics expert Gerald Bull. In its nuclear program, there were at least eight sites dedicated to nuclear weapons development and dozens of major processing facilities. In February 1990 Iraq activated its first uranium enrichment plant at Tarmiyya.

Not surprisingly, this renewed interest in WMD and covert attempts to buy materials outside Iraq gave rise to suspicions—and active interdiction efforts—both by the West (especially the United States and Britain) and by Israel. And these actions created fears in Baghdad of a new Israeli strike on its facilities, similar to the one on Osiraq in 1981.

These fears were not misplaced. On 22 March Gerald Bull was found dead in a Brussels hotel. While the assassin was never apprehended, it was widely assumed that Mossad, Israel's intelligence agency, was behind it. Not long after, British customs officials seized several crates containing large steel tubes manufactured in England and destined for Iraq; they were presumed to be components of Bull's "supergun." In the next few weeks more tube shipments were intercepted. Finally, on 28 March, in a joint US-UK operation, customs agents in Heathrow Airport confiscated a number of electrical capacitors, called krytons, used to trigger implosions in nuclear weapons. These actions were clear indications of increased Western and Israeli surveillance of Iraq's nuclear and missile programs.

These events soon provoked a reaction in Baghdad. On 2 April, in a speech to officers, Saddam disclosed that Iraq had binary chemical weapons and that he would use them to "burn half of Israel" should Israel try to attack Iraq.[14] Although the speech was directed at a local audience, it was clearly meant as a deterrent to Israel. The statement had a major negative impact in the West and in Israel. But in the Arab world, almost instantly, Saddam was proclaimed a hero for standing up to Israel. Indeed, the Arab reaction was so positive that Saddam repeated the deterrent threat again in June, this time extending it to the rest of the Arab world. Although Saddam's public bravado generated increased fervor in the Arab world, it was accompanied by private assurances from the Iraqis to the United States that the statement was completely defensive.

The Israeli issue proved to be a sideshow, but the growing publicity provided Iraq with increased Arab support not only on the Israeli issue but on

Kuwait as well. And as popular support grew, especially in the Arab "street," it fed Saddam's growing conception of his role as an Arab leader and his pique at the intransigence of a country like Kuwait for thwarting his goals.

The Changing International Balance of Power

The emerging problems with Kuwait and Iraq's worsening economic situation also played out against the dramatic changes in the international balance of power as the Soviet empire collapsed and the newly created states of Eastern Europe took shape. This remarkable development not only weakened the power of the former Soviet Union—Iraq's chief arms supplier and political supporter—but ended the former bipolar world. The new, truncated Soviet state not only was too reduced in power to counterbalance the United States but—worse—had joined the West in a new policy of détente. So, too, had former Soviet client states, such as East Germany and Rumania, previous suppliers of Iraq's technology and training in security and intelligence. These remarkable events also affected the Middle East balance of power, strengthening the West's moderate clients and reducing the room for maneuver by radical states like Iraq.

This rapidly changing international situation was compounded by an equally dramatic regional challenge for Arab states—a sudden and massive wave of Jewish immigration to Israel. Arab fears of Israeli expansion grew. These events in the Arab-Israeli sector fed a growing sense of paranoia in Baghdad. At the same time, they also provided an opportunity for Saddam to play a leadership role on an issue on which it was always easy to gather Arab support. Saddam's speeches threatening Israel with chemical weapons added to his prestige. Indeed, much of the growing adulation in the Arab press may well have contributed to Saddam's misconceptions of his own strength in the Arab world.

Deteriorating US Relations

Meanwhile, Iraq also had to face a deterioration in its relations with the United States. The end of the Iran-Iraq war and the Cold War relieved pressures on the United States to support regional clients and allowed domestic anti-Iraqi forces to surface. By the beginning of 1990, criticism of US support for Iraq in the Congress and the media was vocal and this time centered on the regime itself. Newspaper articles and then the Voice of America itself, on 15 February, suggested that Saddam Husain, like Ceauçescu in Rumania, should be overthrown. This was followed by a State Department Human

Rights Report criticizing Iraq's human rights record. US officials made various statements criticizing Baghdad's aggressive new rhetoric even as they continued to seek a constructive relationship with Baghdad. But the US administration was clearly under attack from domestic opponents of Iraqi policy and had to tread warily.

The Conspiracy Theory

By May of 1990 these various stands of Iraq's policy had coalesced in Iraqi thinking into an elaborate conspiracy theory that became the basis of Iraq's policy, at least as officially enunciated. In this theory Iraq emphasized Kuwait's responsibility for Iraq's financial crisis. Kuwait had refused to cancel Iraq's war debts or to extend the kind of financial help that would contribute to reviving Iraq's economy and covering its budget shortfall.[15] Kuwait was also accused of tapping into the southern tip of the Rumaila oil field, which straddled the border with Kuwait, and of stealing Iraqi oil. Most important of all, it was manipulating oil prices to cause Iraq harm.

With respect to demarcation of the border, Iraq now put forth a new claim—that it was Kuwait which had encroached on Iraqi land, not the reverse. These areas were now demanded as rightful Iraqi territory.

These specific charges against Kuwait were now put in the context of the collapse of the USSR and the emergence of the United States as the sole superpower. The United States was depicted as solidly allied with Israel and as showing increased hostility toward Iraq—in press campaigns against Saddam Husain, in falsehoods about Iraq's nuclear program, and in attempting to thwart Iraq's general technological advance. Meanwhile, Israel's regional power was increasing. This joint US-UK-Israeli campaign was clearly directed at curtailing Iraq's domestic development and its role as Arab world leader. Since this triumvirate could not thwart Iraq militarily, it would now do so by economic means. Falling oil prices were part of this conspiracy. Kuwait, in this view, was not acting alone but was in collusion with the United States and Israel in this effort to weaken Iraq.

One can detect, underlying the theory, the worldview of Saddam Husain and his personal vision—for himself and for Iraq. The theory projected yet another myth for the Iraqi state. In it Iraq's rightful position and status as a large, important, military state, well endowed with resources, is emphasized. Iraq, by rights, should be able to command respect and concessions from Kuwait. The new line was also designed to generate a theory of collective

Arab guilt for not supporting Iraq after it spent so much upholding Arab— and of course Kuwaiti—aims in the Iran-Iraq war.

These themes were laid out publicly in several meetings but most specifically at the Arab summit meeting in Baghdad on 30 May, where Saddam equated Kuwaiti actions to a "kind of war against Iraq."[16] This meeting laid down a clear warning to Kuwait and marked a key turning point in the conflict.

The Final Decision

In the secretive world of Baghdad, it is difficult to determine exactly when and how the final decision to invade Kuwait was made. However, it seems certain that only a few in Saddam's inner circle were involved in formulating the idea, which may have been germinating for some time, and that others were brought in only gradually and marginally. The threat at the May summit indicates that the idea was already in play by then. Another turning point may have come at the end of June 1990, when Sa'dun Hammadi made a tour of the Gulf in an effort to shore up OPEC prices and convince all parties, especially Kuwait, to stick to their quotas. The meeting with the Kuwaitis did not go well. When Hammadi reported back to Saddam, he indicated that the meeting had been a failure. The following day, 27 June, an RCC meeting was held to consider the Kuwait issue. According to one report, Tariq Aziz suggested that, unlike other Arab states, Iraq was in a position to advance its aims by force rather than just rhetoric. If true, Saddam came out of the meeting with formal acquiescence for whatever military action he might chose to take.[17]

Events soon moved rapidly in that direction. On 10 and 11 July the oil ministers of the five Arab Gulf OPEC states met in Jidda to address the quota issue. The ministers agreed to hold the line. Three days later, however, the Kuwaitis made a statement to the effect that they would reconsider their decision in October. This statement confirmed the Iraqis in their forward march, and they shortly took a series of steps that virtually locked in a military response, beginning with a letter on 15 July to the Arab League laying out Iraq's case against Kuwait.

On 16 July the movement of Republican Guard units to the Kuwaiti border began, and on 21 July these deployments were made public. By the last week in July, Iraq had in place the military capability of invading and occupying all of Kuwait. The divisions mobilized were the tough, battle-hardened veterans of Iraq's reconquest of Faw, indicating Saddam's seriousness. Equally important, they were the most politically reliable troops, and all were under the command of a trusted Tikriti member of Saddam's inner circle, allowing Saddam to bypass all of the command channels of the regular military.

Several sources have claimed that in fact there were two plans for the use of force.[18] Plan A called for an Iraqi occupation of Warba, Bubayan, and a strip of northern border territory to a depth of about thirty to fifty kilometers. Plan B called for a total occupation of Kuwait. The problem with the occupation of the northern strip and the islands, however, is that it would only solve the border problem, not the whole range of economic problems facing Iraq. For that, a more "comprehensive" operation would be required.

It is the reconstruction of this second plan that is murky and difficult to pinpoint, but as the idea took shape among the inner circle, it appeared to be modeled on an old idea familiar to Ba'th veterans—a coup against the Kuwaiti regime, instigated inside Kuwait by those friendly to Iraq, in which Iraqi assistance would be sought. Iraq's military force would then come to their assistance and install a regime to Iraq's liking, after which Iraq could withdraw most of its forces and control Kuwait—and its financial activities—from Baghdad. The Iraqis had a model for this scenario close at hand—the Syrian "occupation" of Lebanon. Syrian indirect control over Lebanon, which relied on a modest occupation force but exercised the levers of political control from Damascus, provided an example—and a justification—for what Iraq could do in Kuwait.

How the decision was made is not yet clear, either, but all evidence points to a process that kept the decision in the hands of Saddam Husain and a few close family associates and cohorts he could trust. These probably included, in addition to Saddam Husan, Husain Kamil, Ali Hasan al-Majid, and General Ayyad Fatih al-Rawi, commander of the Republican Guard. There was no prior consultation with the minister of defense, the chief of staff, the head of the air force, or most civilian leaders. At some point others, such as Sabir al-Duri, head of Military Intelligence and a member of a clan close to the Tikritis; the president's secretary; and Sab'awi Ibrahim, Saddam's half brother and then head of the Mukhabarat, came to be included. By 29 July at the latest, under Sab'awi's supervision, over thirty Mukhabarat agents were put in place in Kuwait, at oil installations in Ahmadi, and in Kuwait city, while Tariq Aziz, Latif Jasim, and Hammadi were charged with preparing the announcement of the coup.[19] This group of names, even if incomplete, suggests how narrow was the scope of those consulted and how heavily the selection was weighted in favor of family and clan ties.

The threats and troop movements took most observers, whether inside or outside Iraq, by surprise. The US State Department warned Iraq against such threats and asked for "clarification." Both King Husain of Jordan and Palestinian leader Yasir Arafat attempted to mediate the dispute. Husni Mubarak of Egypt made a sudden visit to Baghdad to talk to Saddam Husain on 24 July and then went on to Kuwait. The interpretation of what was said in these discussions differs in Cairo and Baghdad, but Mubarak apparently returned to Cairo thinking the crisis had been defused, at least temporarily.

The Glaspie Interview

The same impression was apparently conveyed to the US ambassador to Iraq, April Glaspie, in an interview with Saddam Husain on 25 July that has become extremely controversial.[20] The Iraqi transcript of the meeting reiterates Iraq's complaints against Kuwait and the United States and warns the United States not to push Iraqis to a point that injures "their pride and their high standard of living." It ends with Saddam's assurances that a meeting would be held in Jidda to be followed by more serious bilateral negotiations in Baghdad and that nothing would be done until these meetings. A few days later, Glaspie left Baghdad, assuming the situation was under control.

The Glaspie interview has been subject to a myriad of interpretations. The one advanced by Iraq and widely believed in the Arab world is that Saddam's main purpose was to probe potential US reaction in case Iraq decided to invade Kuwait and that Glaspie's failure to strongly warn against this contingency was interpreted by Saddam as a green, or at least amber, light.

A second interpretation takes the view that the meeting was held because of Saddam's apprehension of US interference in the crisis and to warn the United States to stay out of the conflict. The threats and bluster in the interview were normal instruments of Saddam's diplomacy.[21] A third, even more cynical view sees the meeting as designed for deception. The key objective was to keep US intervention at bay and to provide some time. If this was the purpose, it succeeded.

The Jidda Meeting

On 31 July Iraqi and Kuwaiti delegates met in Jidda for negotiations, as agreed. There is no indication that Iraq expected anything to come out of this meeting to reverse its course; indeed, real movements on any of the issues at stake would have caused real difficulties with its plans for Kuwait. The Iraqis went to Jidda unwilling to bargain on their major demands—territorial concessions, compensation for oil "stolen" from the Rumaila field, forgiveness of debt, and an economic package to compensate Iraq for losses in the war. The Kuwaitis were willing to show some flexibility—possibly a financial package, concessions on Warba, and debt forgiveness—but only in return for a final agreement on borders. Unlike Iraq, Kuwait appears to have considered the Jidda meeting the first step in a longer negotiating process during which it could bargain its way to a solution.[22]

The Jidda meeting was, not surprisingly, short and unproductive. At its conclusion, the Kuwaitis asked for a joint statement; the Iraqis refused, saying the conference had not been a success.

At 10:00 P.M. on 1 August the Iraqi RCC and the Regional Command of the party met at a concealed location in Baghdad to hear the report of the delegation from Jidda. There was little doubt about the outcome. The assembled group heard a report from Duri, who claimed that Kuwait had refused Iraq's requests and that further meetings and discussions would not produce a different verdict. Shortly before midnight, orders were given to Iraqi forces to cross the Kuwaiti frontier, which they did at 2 A.M., 2 August. The occupation of Kuwait, one of the most fateful decisions in Iraq's modern history, was under way.

The way this decision was made clearly illustrates the weaknesses of the political system developed under Saddam Husain. The dependence on the personal whims and perceptions of one individual, the narrow base of consultation, the absence of any organized planning, and the isolation of Iraq from the international community all go far toward explaining its failure. Iraq entered Kuwait (much as it did Iran a decade earlier) under one set of expectations but soon encountered a very different reality. Rather than a quick conquest, at relatively minor cost, it found itself facing a major international confrontation and devastating long-term costs and consequences.

Iraq Moves South, August 1990

Republican Guard units moved rapidly toward Kuwait city while special forces secured several key sites, including the two islands of Warba and Bubayan, Kuwaiti air fields, and the palaces of the amir and the crown prince. There was some Kuwaiti resistance around the amir's palace and elsewhere, but these were soon extinguished by overwhelming Iraqi force. On 4 August planeloads of Mukhabarat and security units under Sab'awi Ibrahim's control were flown in to control the population and to establish in Kuwait the kind of security system familiar in Baghdad.

The initial occupation was far more successful than the attempt to establish a temporary government. At 9:30 A.M. on 2 August, as scheduled, Baghdad radio announced the "coup" and the establishment of a provisional government in Kuwait, which had allegedly asked for military support from Iraq. But the amir, the crown prince, and the rest of the ruling family had just enough advance warning to escape to Saudi Arabia. Here they were able to appeal for international support and within hours were broadcasting to the population urging it to resist. Not only did the Iraqis fail to capture or annihilate the ruling family as planned, but a surprisingly vigorous underground resistance to the occupation emerged.

Just as significant was the Iraqis' obvious inability to establish a provisional Kuwaiti government. Despite efforts by Tariq Aziz and others to find well-known Kuwaitis willing to associate themselves with the "coup," none would cooperate.[23] Finally Husain Kamil came up with the name of Ala Husain Ali, a junior officer in the Kuwaiti army, who had cooperated with the Iraqis in 1981, when he had been a student at the College of Administration and Economics in Baghdad. He was promoted to colonel, made prime minister of the new government, and sent to Baghdad to meet Saddam Husain.[24]

Iraqi failure to eliminate the Kuwaiti ruling family and to find any credible government replacement as a fig leaf inside Kuwait, removed Iraq's "indirect control" option in dealing with Kuwait almost immediately and revealed the operation for what it was—blatant seizure and occupation of a small, rich country by a larger and more powerful neighbor. The harsh suppression of the local resistance and the beginnings of a looting spree also revealed its brutality.

International Reaction

The reaction of the international community to the occupation was immediate and hostile. Both the swiftness of the response and its magnitude were unexpected in Baghdad, clear evidence of Iraqi miscalculations. On the very day of the invasion, the UN Security Council (UNSC) passed Resolution 660, the first of many, unequivocally condemning the aggression and calling for Iraq's withdrawal. The same day, a joint US-USSR statement was issued also condemning the invasion. The United States took immediate steps to deny Iraq access to its own—and to Kuwait's more substantial—overseas assets; other countries followed suit. These and similar pronouncements by other countries, including those in the Middle East, indicated a clear international—and regional—desire to reverse the action. It took longer to organize a cooperative response, but in the next few weeks, the response took shape under the leadership of the United States. From the first the effort revealed underlying differences, especially in the Arab world, on how to react.

The Saudis immediately recognized the danger, but their initial position was rather equivocal. Prior to the invasion, they had been somewhat sympathetic to some of Iraq's economic demands. But the occupation changed the Saudi situation and the ruling family's perceptions dramatically. The attempt to remove the Kuwaiti regime and replace it with a provisional "republican" government was a radical challenge—indeed a major threat—to the legitimacy of all Gulf ruling families. Moreover, Iraq's control of Kuwait's oil resources and assets would not only rival Saudi Arabia's financial dominance in the Gulf but its position as the chief "enforcer"—as swing producer—of OPEC oil prices. The continued presence of Iraqi troops in Kuwait would, in fact, give Iraq military and economic hegemony over the Arab Gulf.

Egypt was also taken aback by the occupation and had no qualms about insisting on its reversal. Iraq's occupation of Kuwait and its new strategic position in the Gulf would challenge Egypt's own regional role, while Saddam's increasingly radical statements on the Arab-Israeli issue were threats to Egypt's moderate posture. This perception was enhanced by Mubarak's personal feeling of betrayal by Saddam who, he claimed, had personally assured him of a negotiated solution only days before.

King Husain of Jordan had the most ambivalent Arab response. Jordan's economic ties with Iraq were strong and had been considerably developed during the Iran-Iraq war. Even more important was the Palestinian influence. Not only did Jordan have to deal with a Palestinian majority, overwhelmingly sympathetic to Iraq and its "Arab" stand, but it was also facing tense relations with Israel. King Husain could not condone the invasion, but he wanted it handled without foreign interference.

The United States, despite concerns over Iraq's mobilization on Kuwait's border, was still surprised by Iraq's action and was caught unprepared. But within days, the United States developed a rather firm stance and began to explore the means to act on it.

A resolution on sanctions—a total economic embargo against Iraq, including oil—was put before the UN and was finally passed by the UNSC on 6 August. This resolution, 661, was one of the most sweeping ever produced by the UN; it prohibited all trade with Iraq and any transfer of funds except for food, medicine, and necessities of life.

On the military side, the United States had long viewed both Iran and Iraq as long-term potential threats and had developed military contingency plans to deal with such an eventuality. But the plans required a force posture that was not in place, and any military action, even a defensive posture to protect Saudi Arabia, would require Arab, and of course, Saudi approval. For the Saudis, a decision to host such forces was akin to crossing the Rubicon. Even here, though, the Saudis were willing to make this dramatic decision very early in the game. On 6 August, after a meeting in Riyadh with a high-level US delegation, King Fahd agreed to a deployment of US forces to protect the kingdom. Not long after, Egypt and Morocco agreed to participate, as well.[25] By 7 August the first deployments—the 82nd Airborne Division and the first fighter squadrons—had been dispatched.

Thus, within a remarkably short time, an international coalition had taken shape, led by the United States; stiff economic sanctions had been put in place; and an unprecedented military option, involving the landing of massive numbers of troops on Saudi soil, had come into being. The aim of this coalition was clear: a reversal of the Iraqi occupation.[26]

Iraq's Response

Saddam's reaction to these events was continued defiance. On 7 August Iraq declared Kuwait a republic and made the Kuwaiti dinar equal to that of Iraq's. The following day, Iraq annexed Kuwait. An RCC decision stated that Iraq had decided "to return the part and branch, Kuwait, to the whole and the root, Iraq, in a comprehensive, eternal and inseparable unity."[27] On 10 August a full Arab League summit was held in Cairo to address the issue. It was stormy and ended by irrevocably splitting the League. Egypt, Saudi Arabia, the Arab Gulf states, Syria (Iraq's old nemesis), and Morocco were clearly aligned with the West in an effort to reverse the occupation. Nonetheless, antipathy to foreign troops and a desire to Arabize the solution were strong sentiments and had the support not only of the Jordanians and Palestinians but also of Yemen, Sudan, and Algeria.

In the end, a vote by a simple majority of twelve (out of twenty) called for Iraqi withdrawal, the return of the ruling family to Kuwait, and support for sending troops to defend Saudi Arabia.[28] Saddam's rebuttal linked a solution of the Kuwait problem with an end to Israeli occupation of Palestine. The solution should include Israel's withdrawal from Palestine, Syria, and Lebanon; Syrian withdrawal from Lebanon; and the mutual withdrawal of Iran and Iraq. Only then could "provisions relating to the situation in Kuwait" be arranged. (The word *withdrawal* was never mentioned.) This linkage proposal had no hope of acceptance.

Agreement with Iran

In the meantime, Iraq was busy finalizing an agreement with Iran on the Shatt al-Arab. This diplomatic initiative indicated a willingness by Saddam to burn his bridges behind him on Kuwait, with potentially serious consequences for his support base in the military. This agreement now made clear that gains in Kuwait would substitute for a loss on the Shatt. Iraqi control of the Shatt was virtually the only tangible accomplishment that could have been rescued from a fruitless eight-year war with Iran. This would make the preservation of Iraq's position in Kuwait, or some other long-term gain from the Kuwait occupation, essential.

On 30 July, even before the invasion, Saddam had proposed to President Ali Akbar Hashimi Rafsanjani that, though Iraq would retain sovereignty over the Shatt (in theory), the *thalweg* would apply (in practice); in return, Iraq would withdraw its remaining forces from Iran. Rafsanjani responded by insisting on Saddam's firm adherence to the 1975 accord.[29] On 14 August Saddam agreed to the Rafsanjani letter, essentially relinquishing Iraqi claims. This agreement now released Iraqi troops in Iran for the Kuwaiti theater and allowed Iraq to concentrate on this front.

The End of Kuwaiti Sovereignty

Finally, on 28 August Iraq took the step of ending any question of remaining Kuwaiti sovereignty, by announcing that Kuwait had become the nineteenth province *(wilaya)* of Iraq. The new governorate was divided into three districts *(qadas)*. More dramatic was the incorporation of the top third of Kuwait, down to the Mitla Ridge, along with both Warba and Bubayan, into Iraq's Basra governorate. Thus, the northern strip of disputed territory, over which Iraq had haggled for years, was now directly made a part of Iraq, suggesting that in any "final" solution of the problem, this was the territory Iraq intended to keep.[30]

Crisis Stalemate, September 1990–January 1991

By September the crisis had settled into a stalemate that persisted right up to the outbreak of war. The coalition insisted on Iraq's unconditional withdrawal from Kuwait and focused on keeping its loose alliance together while using the tools of a harsh economic embargo and the ultimate sanction of military action to achieve Iraqi withdrawal. Iraq remained intransigent. It hinted at withdrawal of its troops and some ultimate solution in return for unspecified concessions to be agreed on in negotiations. Indeed, to keep his support at home, Saddam could not now withdraw without something to show for his efforts.

Saddam's tactics in a crisis that was to stretch into months, not weeks, became clearer. The first and most elemental was to dig in and to absorb Kuwait. Second was the attempt to weaken and, if possible, break up the Western alliance. Third was the attempt to stir up the Arab "street" against the regional members of the coalition. While the "street" proved too ineffective to remove any regimes, popular opinion did provide pressures that may have hastened the decision for war.

The Manipulation of Hostages

In the standoff with the coalition, Saddam had a weak hand to play, but he was not without some leverage. One such lever was an attempt to manipulate foreign hostages. The occupation of Kuwait had created enormous numbers of refugees, mostly expatriate workers. While the bulk of these were non-Western and were sent home, the Westerners were soon treated differently. Though some managed to get out of Kuwait and Iraq, many more were not allowed to leave; indeed, some were flown from Kuwait and kept in hotels in Baghdad. Although the numbers varied over time, they were measured in the thousands. Very early on, Iraq made it clear that these "guests" would be used as a safeguard against attack. On 28 August Saddam did allow all women and children to leave, if they desired, but shortly thereafter he sent a number of males to military installations and military-industrial sites.

In fact, however, the policy backfired by stiffening Western resistance and worsening Iraq's reputation. Finally, after hostage manipulation seemed to have outlived its usefulness, Saddam decided to release the remaining foreigners. By 6 December all "guests" were sent home.

Tightening Control over Kuwait

Meanwhile Iraq tightened its grip on Kuwait. The task of subduing opposition and imposing control was given to Ali Hasan al-Majid, Husain Kamil, and Sab'awi Ibrahim, who had the support of Mukhabarat units, and the popular militia brought into Kuwait. Key opponents were arrested and executed; it is estimated that these totaled over 1,000 in the first few days of the occupation alone. The early Kuwaiti resistance was quickly subdued, although it was never entirely snuffed out. Most important was systematic looting of Kuwait's wealth and a dismantling of much of its infrastructure. Economic exigencies had been the main reason for Iraq's invasion, but the plunder went beyond the seizure of Kuwait's financial assets. The process began with the assets in Kuwait's central bank, apparently a meager $2 billion, less than anticipated. The far larger assets in foreign banks, estimated at over $200 billion, eluded Iraq when the international community froze them.[31] From the first, the security apparatus was under orders to take valuable electronic, communications, and industrial equipment, which it did, but the looting was much more extensive, involving orders to various institutions in Iraq to identify and remove equipment and valuables from their counterpart organizations in Kuwait. As a result, the Iraqi market was flooded for months with all sorts of goods, from household staples to luxury items, that helped sustain an economy sinking ever further into a morass under sanctions.

Nonetheless, the costs of occupation were becoming ever more apparent. Both the Saudi-Iraqi pipeline and the pipeline through Turkey were closed. Within a short time, more than 90 percent of Iraq's imports and almost 97 percent of its exports were shut off. The result was soaring prices, and in September Iraq was compelled to introduce rationing.

The October Decision in the United States

By October several factors began to tip US considerations in favor of a military solution. Iraq's continued intransigence was one. The toll taken on Kuwait was another. Fear of the inability of the coalition to hold out for months, particularly with US troops on Saudi soil, was a third. Perhaps most important was a practical consideration of timing. If the coalition had to go on the offensive to force Iraq out of Kuwait, the force level in Saudi Arabia would have to double. On 30 October the Bush administration made the decision to double its forces, giving it an offensive capability.

With this decision, the likelihood of military action against Iraq increased, but so, too, did the qualms of those in the alliance uneasy about going to war. The United States went to the UN for international authorization to use force. The result was Resolution 678, authorizing the use of force to compel Iraq to withdraw from Kuwait but giving Iraq a grace period of forty-five days to accomplish the withdrawal. The date of 15 January 1991 was set as the deadline.

Despite last-minute attempts by others to mediate a withdrawal and avoid a war, Saddam refused to budge.[32] Virtually all analysts agree that some flexibility by Saddam, even at this late point, would have severely strained the coalition, probably avoided a war, and even allowed him to come through the episode with come concessions. The key to his intransigence lay in his own perception that he could not politically survive a withdrawal without some gains, especially after such serious concessions to Iran. Relying on a Vietnam syndrome in the United States, he also assumed that the United States would have difficulty bringing its people into a ground war and that if it did, it could not last long under the kinds of casualties he intended his forces to inflict.[33] In the end, overconfidence may also have led him to miscalculate the time he had available for his brinksmanship. When the allied air attack came at 3:00 A.M. Kuwaiti time on 17 January, Iraqis seemed genuinely surprised.

The Gulf War, 17 January–28 February 1991

The Gulf War, which began with an air attack on 17 January (Iraqi time) and ended on 28 February, was unlike anything Iraqis had experienced before in eight years of war with Iran.

The Air Campaign
Within twenty-four hours the allies had control of the skies. Thereafter, they turned to their strategic targets. These included command and control facilities (including Saddam's palaces, Ba'th Party headquarters, intelligence and security facilities), power stations, hydroelectric stations, refineries, military-industrial targets, and Iraq's WMD and missile facilities. The country's communications system was essentially incapacitated and its electrical supply reduced by 75 percent. The coalition then turned to the military targets

critical to the ground campaign—roads, bridges, and storage facilities. Lastly it turned to Iraqi troops in the Kuwaiti theater.[34]

On 18 January Iraq launched missiles, mainly from mobile launchers, against Israeli and Saudi targets (Riyadh and Dhahran). The impact in Israel was mainly political; the missiles generated fears of a chemical attack, causing some disruption in Tel Aviv and other cities. Iraq had made the point that Israel was now vulnerable and had been hit at home by an Arab state, and the attack was now added to Saddam's propaganda arsenal. The main purpose of the attack failed, however. That was to induce retaliation by Israel, thus bringing it into the war on the coalition side and thereby weakening Arab support for the coalition.

Meanwhile in Iraq, the bombing campaign was taking its toll. In Baghdad the lights went out at the beginning of the war and did not come on again until its end. Although civilians were not targeted, inevitably a number were hit and killed. (The most precise figures given by the Iraqis claim 2,280 killed and almost 6,000 wounded.)[35] The most publicized civilian casualty figures came from the unfortunate hit on the Amiriyya shelter, which the alliance took for a communications and intelligence node; over three hundred were killed in that incident, over half of them women and children.

The damage was not just to infrastructure. The air campaign brought the war home to the population, especially the urban middle-class inhabitants in Baghdad who provided some of Saddam's political base. Daily life was becoming unbearable. There was no electricity or running water in most of Iraq's major cities. Vehicular traffic almost came to a halt for lack of fuel, and medical epidemics were feared.[36]

By the end of January, Saddam faced an increasingly tenuous position. His strategy had been to absorb the air attack but to draw the coalition into a ground war that would inflict casualties and that would produce enough pressure at home to compel negotiations with a favorable end for Iraq. Iraq had absorbed the bombing—but it was degrading its ability to wage war—and there was no ground war in sight. Meanwhile, the morale, equipment, and fighting ability of the Iraqi forces who would have to face the coalition in the "long war of attrition" was eroding to a point of no return.

The Attack on Khafji

On 29 January Saddam took the initiative and ordered a multipronged attack on the coalition forces situated in the Eastern Province of Saudi Arabia. Although the Iraqis did surprise the Saudis at Khafji, the other advances were repelled and the Iraqi units involved virtually demolished, mainly by fierce air action. Iraqi units did capture Khafji and hold it for forty-eight hours, but the coalition forces, mainly the Saudis, rallied and expelled the Iraqis the following day. The destruction of Iraqi forces under the full weight of allied air power and modern technological weaponry was devastating. For the first time, Saddam had to face the fact that a ground war could mean defeat, a loss of his military, and possibly an inability to survive as a result. A negotiated solution began to look more attractive.

Last-Minute Bargaining

Once again the negotiating process was revived, this time by the Russians. On 12 February Yevgeni Primakov, Russia's premier Middle East expert, traveled to Baghdad to arrange some kind of solution that would involve Iraqi withdrawal. Saddam Husain now admitted the possibility of withdrawal for the first time, but without a specified timetable. Rather, the Iraqis asked for a lifting of sanctions after withdrawal was only two-thirds complete. When this proposal was announced on 21 February, using the word *withdrawal,* it raised a red flag for the Iraqi military. If a withdrawal was to be the outcome, why had it not been agreed to earlier, before a damaging bombardment? And if no deal was concluded, why should troops fight and die when they knew that withdrawal was to be the outcome? The United States rejected the new Soviet-Iraqi offer and instead presented an ultimatum. There would be no lifting of sanctions, and Iraq was given one week to withdraw.

This intensive last-minute haggling with the Soviets clearly shows that Saddam had already decided to withdraw—mainly in return for the release of obligations in the UN resolutions (especially sanctions) and to retain control of the military; by this time all thoughts of retaining Kuwait were gone. Any doubt of this was dispelled by his actions on 22 February, when he began to set alight the Kuwaiti oil fields. Within days, as many as eight hundred wells, storage tanks, refineries, and other facilities had been blown up,[37] creating an environmental disaster of the first order in the region. But this did not stop the coalition attack.

The Ground War

The ground war, begun on 24 February, was over in one hundred hours—four days later—on 28 February. It was never a contest. The coalition military strategy involved action on several fronts. The least important militarily was a feint by forces from the sea designed to deceive the Iraqis, encouraging them to think that the main attack would be an amphibious assault, and then to move to take Kuwait City. Surprisingly, Iraqi forces did take these preparations seriously and had concentrated forces to meet the attack. The second prong of the attack was a direct assault on the defensive perimeter around Kuwait after probes for weak spots. After making a breakthrough, this group was expected to liberate Kuwait City. Although this was originally considered the most difficult operation and likely to produce the most casualties, given the degradation and poor morale of the Iraqi fighting units, the breakthrough was achieved quickly and relatively easily. The third prong of the attack was the wide left hook, an enveloping movement on the west that bypassed Iraqi forces in the Kuwaiti theater and moved across the desert into Iraq to envelop and cut off the Republic Guard forces from behind. This was the most imaginative and, as it turned out, unexpected part of the attack and was designed to close the gate on and capture Saddam's most effective forces.

Rather than encountering fierce fighting and high casualties, the coalition was surprised by the rapidity of its conquest, especially through the main lines of Iraq's defense around Kuwait. As a result, these forces failed to coordinate and link up with the western flanking movement as they were supposed to do. Coalition forces—with Arabs allowed to take the lead—reached Kuwait City and had liberated it on 28 February. Meanwhile, the flanking movement, which moved almost five hundred kilometers in four days, was not yet in a position to close the gate on the retreating Republican Guard forces in Iraq when the cease-fire was declared. Some, though not all, got away with their equipment. This failure has since come under severe scrutiny and criticism as an opportunity lost.[38] The capture or collapse of more Republican Guard units would have further weakened Saddam's support system and possibly contributed to his overthrow. Nonetheless, the victory was swift and stunning. By 28 February Iraqi forces were defeated and in retreat. Kuwait had been liberated.

At midnight on 25 February, about forty-eight hours after the start of the ground war, Baghdad Radio finally announced a withdrawal order for Iraqi troops. "Our armed forces," the broadcast said, "have proven their ability to fight and stand fast."[39] Among the military, this late and ineffective withdrawal order caused considerable bitterness; in fact, it left them to the mercies of the advancing coalition forces, which did not accept the "withdrawal" and dealt with them as an army in retreat. Meanwhile, in Moscow and within the UN Security Council in New York, bargaining continued as Saddam refused to accept the humiliation of public defeat.

The war now became a race between the coalition's determination to destroy as much of Iraq's forces, especially its Republican Guard, as possible and Saddam's need to get a cease-fire to preserve his Republican Guard. On 26 February Aziz finally announced a willingness to end official annexation of Kuwait and pay reparations in return for a cease-fire and an end to sanctions. The Security Council refused this offer and insisted on Iraq's unconditional acceptance of all UN resolutions. This finally came on 27 February.

Military Defeat

Regardless of the last-minute failure to "close the gate" on portions of Saddam's Republican Guard units, the extent of Iraq's defeat and its military losses were enormous. Its regular army was broken and scattered. The losses in military equipment, especially in the air force, were severe. Barely 10 percent of Iraq's prewar artillery survived. Iraqi casualties are harder to estimate but were probably in the area of 10,000 to 30,000 dead, many fewer than originally thought.[40] The numbers of POWs who gave themselves up or were captured was 86,000 to 90,000. Morale was shattered. But despite their disarray and the relative disorder of their retreat, much of the Iraqi army and especially the key Republican Guard units in the south of Iraq, were able to get away. Some would shortly regroup to help save the regime from its rebellious citizens.

The Cease-Fire and UN Resolution 687

On 2 March the UNSC passed Resolution 686, setting forth the conditions Iraq would have to meet before a cease-fire would be declared. Iraq would have to accept, in their entirety, all of the twelve resolutions previously passed on the Kuwait issue, including sanctions; payment of reparations for war damages; a rescission of all laws and regulations relating to the annexation of Kuwait; the release of all POWs, allied and Kuwaiti; and a return of all the property stolen from Kuwait. On 2 March Tariq Aziz accepted all UN resolutions, and on 5 March the RCC formally rescinded all laws on Kuwait's annexation and agreed to pay reparations and return Kuwaiti property.

Although the cease-fire ended hostilities, it did not yet result in troop withdrawal. The action now shifted to the UN, where a final termination resolution was drawn up and passed on 12 April. Resolution 687 was the longest and most comprehensive in UN history, and its provisions were to place much of Iraq's economy and its military under international control. Although not anticipated in April 1991, this control would remain—even deepen—over the coming decade.

Under 687 Iraq had several obligations. First, it had to accept the inviolability of the Iraqi-Kuwaiti border, which was to be demarcated by an international commission in which Iraq was expected to participate. Second, Iraq had to accept a UN peacekeeping force on the border. Third, it would have to demolish its weapons of mass destruction and long-range missile capacity and refrain from reviving their production. To accomplish this end, it was required to submit to the Security Council a full list of all nuclear, chemical, and biological materials and missiles with a range over 150 kilometers, together with its manufacturing capabilities. These would then be destroyed. To verify the validity of the list and to prevent future acquisitions and production, there would be on-site inspection teams. Lastly, Iraq would have to facilitate the return of Kuwaiti property and to agree to a level of reparations agreed on by the UN. Until these measures were fulfilled, the full trade embargo was to remain in place, except for imports of food, medicine, and other necessities of life. Sanctions would be reviewed every sixty days. In the meantime, no oil could be sold.[41]

These terms were accepted by Iraq, and on 9 May the last coalition forces were withdrawn from Iraq. At the same time, the regime propagated the new myth of the war—already underpinned by the conspiracy theory elaborated earlier. The war had not been a defeat but a victory. Iraq had fought "the mother of battles" by standing against thirty-one armies, including the most technologically advanced forces in the world, and triumphed. Iraq had demolished the United States' aura of invincibility and showed Americans and Europeans as cowards. The coalition would never have accepted a ceasefire if it had not feared the fist of the Republican Guard. Iraqis were commended for their fortitude and steadfastness in the face of imperialism.

The Costs of the War

But rhetorical claims of victory could not disguise the real outcome of the Second Gulf War for Iraq and its people. Its economy had sunk to depths that Iraq had not yet had time to appreciate. The economic problems left by the Iran-Iraq war would look manageable by comparison. Sanctions had cut off Iraq's major source of income, oil, and shut down almost all trade. Inflation had already started its upward trajectory. Coalition bombing had also destroyed a good deal of its industry and infrastructure, making the restoration of a normal peacetime economy a distant dream. Its military had not only had its morale destroyed but seen its size and its equipment drastically reduced. Iraq's army was scattered and in retreat (or had deserted and was sitting at home). The latter outcome, however, may have had a silver lining for the regime. Demobilization had been a major problem prior to the war. This problem no longer existed. At least half of the soldiers and many of the officers had simply vanished into their towns and villages. Nonetheless, the most serious potential threat to the regime came from angry officers and men, outraged at the leadership that had thrust them into such a foolhardy venture, mismanaged it from the start, and left them no orderly withdrawal at the end.

In foreign relations too, the cost of the war was high. The war, and the long crisis leading up to it, isolated Iraq as never before. Prior to the crisis, Iraq had had an uneasy relationship with the United States but one that was functioning after years of severed diplomatic relations. The Kuwait occupation and the Gulf War had now made an implacable adversary out of the world's only superpower. Iraq's relations with Europe were hardly better. All of the coalition members had cut diplomatic ties with Iraq and were participating in the sanctions regime authorized by the UN.

These enormous costs came with no new gains for Iraq. To consolidate his efforts in Kuwait, Saddam had publicly given up the one potential gain from the Iran-Iraq war, control over the Shatt. And he was left with no gains in Kuwait; indeed, in return for the occupation, Iraq would now be saddled with economic reparations. Meanwhile, it had to endure sanctions and the imposition of wide-ranging restrictions on its sovereignty in the form of weapons inspections.

By March 1991 it was apparent to all, inside and outside Iraq, despite rhetoric to the contrary, that the occupation of Kuwait had been a miscalculation of breathtaking proportions and that the Gulf War—utterly avoidable if withdrawal instead of intransigence had taken place—had been the most damaging act in Iraq's modern history.

The *Intifada,* March 1991

The Iraqi response to the disaster of the Gulf War and Saddam's miscalculations was the *intifada* (uprising) of March 1991. Although lasting only about a month (roughly from 1 March, when it began in Basra, until 1 April, when the northern cities of Zakhu and Sulaimaniyya were brought under government control), it was so widespread that it decisively shaped the subsequent political dynamics in Iraq. Ignited by the spark of a humiliating defeat in Kuwait and the war's toll on the Iraqi soldiers and civilians, it soon spread like wildfire through both the south and the north of the country. At its peak, rebels controlled substantial portions of fourteen of Iraq's eighteen provinces. The rebellion was unruly, unorganized, and at points almost as brutal as the regime. While not successful in overthrowing the regime, the *intifada* was a defining moment in Iraq's modern history in revealing attitudes toward the regime and the state.

Motives and Participants

The motives behind the uprising were mixed but nonetheless fairly clear. Opposition to the regime and its repression had been evident for years—indeed the regime's repressive apparatus was itself testimony to the extent and degree of opposition; to political factors had now been added years of war and economic hardship. These underlying issues were now intensified by Saddam's extraordinary Kuwait venture, culminating in a calamitous military defeat for his regular army and a dangerous and disastrous retreat. The *intifada* was essentially begun by soldiers, defeated, humiliated, and angry, supported by a population back home that had had enough.

At the same time, the Gulf War had already taken a toll on the civilian population. This was particularly true in Basra and its environs, which had been at the war's front and had suffered destruction of a good bit of its infrastructure. The sanctions regime, introduced by the UN at the start of the crisis, had also begun to bite. The levels of inflation and shortages brought by the economic embargo had necessitated rationing for the first time in Iraqi history.

There were also positive inducements for the *intifada*. One was the opportunity created by the coalition defeat of Iraq and the evidence of regime weakness. For the first time during the war, broadcasts were heard from "free" radio stations in neighboring countries, detailing Saddam's crimes and urging his replacement. The clear evidence of the defeat presented by the fleeing troops created, perhaps, the greatest impetus to revolt—destruction of the "wall of fear" that had surrounded Saddam's regime. All evidence suggests that as the rebellion spread, it was fed by the assumption he would not survive. It was also fed by the United States and calls from President Bush for both the military and the population to rise. These unquestionably played a role in encouraging participants to think they would get support from the coalition and the United States. The failure of the United States to respond with any help left deep bitterness and frustration.

One force that might have been expected to play a role in the *intifada* was the exile opposition. The main opposition parties included various *shi'i* groups, the Kurdish opposition parties, the Iraq Communist Party, and some liberal and nationalist groupings in the region and in Europe. Although these groups did have some constituencies inside Iraq, their support was drawn mainly from various regional powers, each with its own, competing interests. The Gulf War galvanized efforts of these opposition forces to unite, but the attempts to overcome deep divisions in theirs ranks over ideology and power sharing proved unsuccessful. A meeting of over three hundred Iraqi oppositionists in Beirut in March 1990 failed even to agree on a second meeting. As a result, with the exception of a few components, outsiders played virtually no role in the *intifada.*

There were two exceptions. One was the *shi'i* exile movement in Iran. The degree and extent of its role in the *intifada* has been controversial. SAIRI, for example, did send some forces into Iraq, most likely after the rebellion began.[42] However, the role played by SAIRI and its forces was subsidiary and, in fact, may have been negative. The second exception was the Kurds in the north, where the role of the organized parties was much greater. Even here, however, local spontaneity—and the defection of the pro-government Fursan—played a major role in the rising in the north.

It is also noteworthy which groups did not seem to play a major role: the established upper- and middle-class population of the cities; the organized units of the military; and even the religious establishment, the *marji'iyya*. Much of the rural, tribally organized population appears to have remained passive, as well. The rebellion was mainly an urban phenomenon and was led primarily by youth.

The Rebellion in the South

The story of the soldier returning with the defeated army to Basra and, in a fit of anger, turning the gun of his tank on an outsized portrait of Saddam in the city's central square has been repeated and embellished in Iraq as the spark that started the rebellion. Although there is no reason to question the episode, it is doubtful that the rebellion can be limited to a single act. Rather, the uprising had multiple foci that rapidly gathered momentum in an incendiary environment.

Whatever its antecedents, by 1 March rebellion had clearly broken out in Basra and probably in Suq al-Shuyukh as well. It then spread to Najaf, Kufa (4 March), and Karbala (7 March) and from there to Diwaniyya and Hilla, and then to Amara and Kut on the Tigris. Although chaotic and unorganized, by the end of the first week, rebel groups of various kinds had seized control of most of the provincial towns south of Baghdad province.[43]

The nature of the rebellion varied from place to place.[44] In Basra it was led by retreating soldiers. Between 10 and 20 February, soldiers started to return to Basra in large numbers, straggling back barefoot and hungry and in dirty clothes. After the ground campaign, the numbers accelerated. One retreating officer has described the scene: "Remnants of various military vehicles were burning up [with] the corpses of our heroic martyrs in them. . . . There were whole regiments of soldiers who were barefoot. . . . There were injured and wounded on the side of the road. . . . Telephone and electric lines were either dangling from poles or lying on the ground. . . . Fires were consuming everything."[45] It was in this incendiary atmosphere, in Sa'd Square, that the tank fired on the mural of Saddam Husain. Armored vehicles then attacked the key points of the regime's authority—the mayor's office, the Ba'th Party headquarters, and security centers. Security men were killed, files were destroyed, and for twenty-four hours there was shooting. Here, as elsewhere, there was looting; people broke into shops, hotels, and even houses. However, by the third day, the military began to regroup and reorganize, and by 17 March the *intifada* in Basra was over. Fighting was fierce and many took refuge across the Shatt in Iran. Thousands were killed or executed, with bodies left in the street.[46]

In Nasiriyya the rebels emerged from the marshes. They arrived in the town around noon—in dusty tattered clothes, with Klashnikovs slung over their backs, and soon took over the party and security headquarters. Rebels, backed by marsh tribes, soon attacked Iraqi regular army units. A battle ensued, the Iraqi military collapsed, and the town fell.

Further north, in Diwaniyya, the uprising began when some young people from the city took control of weapons and tanks located in one of the military camps near the city. They then took up positions around the headquarters of the governorate, the party, and the security apparatus. Here, there was considerable resistance. Some officials and party members were killed, while others fled. It took nearly half a day, but by the afternoon, the rebels had control of the city. Other districts in the governorate also fell, including Daghghara.[47] Here, however, there was cooperation between tribal notables and some military officers.

While rebels succeeded in securing Diwaniyya, they were not so successful in Hilla, much closer to Baghdad and more strategically located. Here, youth and local people took over government offices, polices stations, and the party headquarters as well as an infantry training center. The military intelligence headquarters put up stiff resistance, fearing annihilation and retribution. Nor did the rebels have enough organization to occupy the Mahawil camp, about twenty-five miles from the city. Remarkably, the rebels in Diwaniyya made an attempt to recapture Hilla on 15 March. Several officers and tribal leaders were killed after a fierce battle that ultimately failed.[48]

In Najaf the *intifada* took on a different complexion. Accounts of the *intifada* here all point to some organization beforehand.[49] This time the slogans were distinctly *shi'i:* They called for a *shi'i* ruler and an Islamic revolution. A tremendous clash soon ensued. There was considerable bloodshed, looting, and destruction of property, with bodies left in the streets. Here and in neighboring Karbala, there were clearer signs of influence from SAIRI and Iraqis coming from Iran.

The rebellion was not, initially, encouraged by the chief *marji',* Abu-l-Qasim al-Khu'i, but rebels urged him to take a leadership role. He issued two *fatwas,* one calling for order and the second forming an administrative council of nine *ulama* to oversee affairs; a second committee of army officers was associated with the council. When Republican Guard units regained control of the city, Khu'i was captured, taken to Baghdad, and compelled to go on television and support the government.

Despite differing localities, there were striking similarities. Rebels everywhere focused on the symbols of the regime and the seat of its power, especially the party and the hated security forces. Indeed, rebels had considerable success in forcing the collapse of the security system and the party in some areas of the south. Many of these elements were killed or fled. It is equally clear, however, that the uprising was spontaneous and had virtually no planning beforehand.

The Collapse of the Intifada *in the South and Its Causes*
The *intifada* in the south failed to take hold and to withstand a concerted government attack when it came. Four factors appear to have been of paramount importance in contributing to its failure.

One is the role the Badr Brigade and SAIRI played in the revolt. Although they came in numbers too few to make a significant impact, Iraqi exiles crossed the frontier in the collapse of order after the Gulf War. Both the Badr Brigade and the Tawwabin (Repentants), the latter a force made up of Iraqi POWs, came, in organized formations, to join—even to lead—the rebellion. How many organized fighters were present is not entirely clear, but the best estimate is in the low thousands, possibly 3,000 to 5,000. More to the point, the fighters came with banners and pictures—of Baqir al-Hakim and Ayat Allah Khumaini—and slogans from the Islamic revolution, demanding a *shi'i* government. The slogans, reported by both regional and Western media, gave rise to fears of sectarianism and of "outside organization" from Iran. They gave the revolt a narrow ideological cast that belied its much broader base and provided an ideal propaganda ploy for the regime to use in garnering support against the rebellion. It also worried the coalition, especially Saudi Arabia and the United States.[50]

In fact, however, the Iranians gave very little support to the revolt. Rafsanjani, attempting to fend off more radical elements at home, was busy in Tehran negotiating with emissaries from Baghdad to improve relations. This act greatly angered opposition leaders, some of whom publicly protested.

Second, the chaos, destruction, and retribution of the *intifada* were also factors in its ultimate failure. Although there were some local attempts to establish order and get killings under control, it was the image of retribution and disorder that frightened the populace in Baghdad and the country's center and helped convince the more stable elements of the population to stay at home.

A third, and the most critical, weakness of the rebellion was the failure of the military to join. Greater participation by the military, particularly organized military units under structured leadership, might have made a difference. Some military men—soldiers and officers—did join the rebellion, but they did so as individuals, not as units. There are few, if any, accounts of army units at the company or battalion level turning their guns on Republic Guard or security units. Organized defections from the army to the rebels did not take place.

Rather, the response of the military was more ambiguous. Here a distinction must be made between the Republican Guard units that had not seen action in Kuwait and most of the regular army, still withdrawing haphazardly. The latter, depleted of foot soldiers and in varying stages of disarray, were trying to reassemble back in Iraq, and they behaved, for the most part, in accordance with their military training and instinct. Above all they feared for their own safety and distrusted a rebellion that could turn against them. One of the generals retreating with his unit has given a vivid account of his feelings when confronted with a band of rebels:

> Some of the men tried to stop us . . . and I knew I had to save myself. . . . I was faced with young men who were rebelling against a regime that had been tyranni-cal, . . . and their hatred of it extended to all the government establishment, espe-cially the military. And because I was an officer, they might kill me. . . . Should I draw my weapon in the face of those I considered brothers? . . . How could I save myself? . . . Was I against the regime, or was I in favor of [the uprising,] or should I surrender to people not in control of their emotions?[51]

In the main, it was not the regular army that was used to restore order and repress the rebellion—their loyalties were suspect by the regime—but Republic Guard units and special security forces, considered more reliable.

Fourth, the rebellion in the south received no support from abroad, ex-cept in a very minor way from Iran. The United States and the Western forces occupying Iraq were not prepared to provide such support, despite numerous public calls from President Bush for both the Iraqi military and civilians to overthrow the regime. The most serious failure of support was the decision of General Norman Schwarzkopf to allow the Iraqi military to fly helicopters in Iraqi territory not occupied by coalition forces. Schwarzkopf apparently took the Iraqis at their word when they asked to use the helicopters for transport and communications in the absence of roads and bridges, now bombed out.[52] The regime immediately used helicopter gunships—in addition to ground forces—to put the rebellion down.

The helicopter decision was only one of several key decisions that indi-cated that the coalition would not get involved in or support the rebellion. The most significant of these may have been the cease-fire itself. Many rebels and returning soldiers have indicated that they knew, once they heard that there was a cease-fire, that the Allies would not continue fighting and, thus, the chances of a successful overthrow of the regime were slim. It was also clear from Schwarzkopf's statements that the coalition would withdraw its forces from Iraqi territory as soon as possible, ruling out a longer occupa-tion, which could have been used to pressure Saddam. The failure to "close the gate" on the Republican Guard units in the south also played a role in the rebellion's fortunes. Numerous attempts by rebels to solicit arms and help from the coalition from across the cease-fire lines were turned down.[53] In short, the coalition indicated in numerous ways that it would not support the rebellion, thus depriving it of hope and material help.[54]

The Rebellion in the North

The uprising in the north began in Raniyya on 5 March and quickly enveloped major cities and towns in the Kurdish region—Sulaimaniyya, Arbil, Dahuk, and territories in between—reaching its peak on 20 March with the siege and capture of Kirkuk by the Kurds. In many respects, the *intifada* in the north was similar to that in the south. The population in cities and towns rose spontaneously, the rebellion spread rapidly within days throughout all Kurdish areas, and it ended just as suddenly, when the regime mobilized its military forces, especially the Republican Guard units, once the rebellion in the south had been quelled.

Despite the similarities, however, there were some striking differences as well. In the north, there was a much higher degree of organization and leadership from the traditional Kurdish political parties. There was more planning and coordination with the Kurdish militias supporting the government—the Fursan. When the time came, their almost wholesale defection from the government was of crucial help. Kurdish handling of the regular military was also more politically astute and paid dividends in widespread surrender and desertion of military formations in the north. Most critical of all, however, was the contact between the Kurdish parties and the West, which ultimately laid a basis for internationalizing the plight of the Kurds and securing a measure of support from the coalition for their aims.

In the north, three distinct forces were involved in the *intifada*. The first was the local population, stirred by news, often brought by soldiers deserting from the front, of the rebellion in the south and the defeat and collapse of the Iraqi army. The people massed in demonstrations, grabbed weapons, and helped storm the centers of power in their cities and towns. As in the south, they committed atrocities on Ba'th Party and security personnel and undertook some looting, but these disorders were far fewer and more focused than in the south. The population was responsible for creating the spontaneity of much of the rebellion in the north, just as it had been in the south.

A second group, the Fursan, played a critical role. The Kurdish parties and their leaders, especially Mas'ud al-Barzani and Jalal al-Talabani, had been in contact with the tribal leaders and the *mustashars* who led these units, with a plea to bury the past and move toward unity. The outreach to the Fursan struck home. They too had been alienated by the Anfal campaign and government confiscation of their land, and they must have calculated, like others, that the regime was likely to collapse. In cities and towns across the north, Fursan joined the rebellion. Indeed, in many areas, they led it. Their massive defection from within government-controlled territory accounts for the ease with which much of the area fell to the anti-government forces.

The third force, as expected, was that of the Kurdish parties, the KDP and the PUK, which had been working in a common front with five smaller Kurdish parties and a portion of the Assyrian community. At this point, the party leaders were operating from outside Iraq, mainly in Iran and to a lesser extent in Syria. The parties had the organization, the experience, and the leadership to provide backbone to the rebellion and to help administer the region after the initial revolt. Most important, from earlier planning, they were able to provide a strategy and a sense of direction.

The motives behind the uprising in the north were also much clearer than in the south. Loyalty to the central government had always been more tenuous in the north. Repression had been severe and recent in the Anfal campaign and depopulation of rural areas. However, in contrast to the south, the Kurdish Front's commitment to change in Baghdad, while not absent, was second to its desire for Kurdish self-government.

The motives of the Fursan were more ambiguous. In a number of cases, they and their villages had also been hurt and damaged by the Anfal and the ravaging of the rural areas. But they had been empowered by the regime and had more at stake in the outcome. In their case, they must also have made a calculation on the shifting balance of forces, as they saw the army crumbling and the uprising spreading in the south. If an uprising was coming north, now was the time to join it.

In the north the rebellion began on 4 March in Raniyya, a town of about 50,000, situated north of Dukan Lake. Although KDP members in the town had been discussing an uprising beforehand and had been in contact with the local Fursan tribes, they were not the prime movers.[55] The spark for the revolt was provided by a deserter who was chased into the mountains and shot. The next day, the townspeople rose, protesting the action by closing their shops. When the military came to confront them, the townspeople attacked them. They were joined by the Fursan, who had weapons. They targeted the security forces, the Ba'th Party, and the military intelligence. The 24th Division of the military had its headquarters south of Raniyya, and fearing an army attack, the Fursan went south and managed to secure its surrender.

News of Raniyya soon spread. On 7 March Sulaimaniyya rose in what was primarily a popular uprising. When gunfire was heard, people rushed out in the street. They attacked the Ba'th Party headquarters, the Mukhabarat, and the security headquarters; the regime's supporters had crowded into the security building, and it was here that the real battle took place. Some reports put the number of Ba'th killed at four hundred, the number who died in the final assault at seven hundred.[56]

Sulaimaniyya was followed in rapid order by Qal'at Diza, Dukan, Darbandikhan, Halabja, Kalar, and Shamshamal. In these towns the Fursan took the lead in seizing army camps, arms depots, and weapons. By 19 March Kurdish forces held a line in the north parallel to the Kirkuk-Baghdad highway, including the southern Kurdish cities of Kalar, Kifri, and Tuz Khurmatu. Earlier, on 13 March, the Kurdish Front had announced the establishment of an executive and legislative council for regional self-government. Thus the Kurdish Front quickly established a civilian administration for the north, promising something more permanent for the future.[57]

The rebels then turned their attention to the prize—Kirkuk. There was no uprising in this mixed Arab-Kurdish-Turkman city, and advancing forces had to put up a fight. On 20 March the Kurdish Front and Fursan began their attack. After a considerable battle, they were able to take the town, but it reportedly cost them 3,000 casualties. In doing so, however, they acquired several airports, broadcasting and TV networks, oil wells, and the facilities of the oil companies, as well as a large cache of arms and government files. They also took the base of the 1st Army Corps, which surrendered.

Silence in the Center

In the end, one of the most important outcomes of the *intifada* was where it did not spread. There was no rebellion in the five central provinces of Baghdad, Anbar, Salah al-Din, Ninawa, and Diyala (except for the partly Kurdish towns of Kalar and Kifri in the latter). During the *intifada* itself, there were some reports of unrest, demonstrations, and even clashes with authorities and deaths in some sections of Baghdad, all *shi'i* concentrations. But whatever unrest took place in Baghdad and other towns in the center, it was marginal and swiftly contained. By all accounts, neither the city nor the central provinces were of a mind to revolt. As news spread of the rebellion, especially in the south, the mainly *sunni* urban population thought not of rebellion but of survival. Radio reports from abroad depicted the killing of regime supporters and the destruction, looting, and increased disorder.

In the regime's reports, the *intifada* was called "sedition" and the rebels "mobs." Iran was blamed for its instigation and sectarian slogans were exaggerated. The result was that the center greeted the *intifada* not with hope but with fear of a bloodbath and a desire to protect itself and its property. In the end the *intifada* stopped at the frontiers of the *sunni* triangle. The failure of the *intifada* in the center showed not only the strength of the regime but the passivity and ambivalence of its population toward a government it did not like but was unwilling to move against.

Repression of the Rebellion in the South

Two factors are noteworthy about the repression of the rebellion: the rapidity with which the regime was able to reorganize itself and the brutality with which the uprising was put down. Given the regime's resounding defeat in the war and the collapse and disarray of its military, the swiftness with which it was able to recoup its losses and quell an uprising that had spread to both the north and south of the country surprised many.

The regime sent not only its family and key Tikriti commanders to restore order but members of the party's military branch and the military intelligence to insure obedience to headquarters command.[58] The turnaround began 6 March in Basra, and by 17 March the balance of power had shifted in the south. By 29 March the uprising in the south was finished and the regime could concentrate on the north.

The repression was brutal. In Basra, for example, there was shelling of houses and buildings, and thousands of bodies were left in the streets. The most difficult battles, in Karbala and Najaf, went on for days. Women and children were used as human shields; thousands were rounded up and killed. Tens of thousands fled across the border to Iran. By 1 May these refugees totaled 68,000.[59] Many also fled across the front lines to coalition forces, eventually ending up in camps in Rafha in Saudi Arabia. There was serious destruction in the shrines and cemeteries in Najaf. The ties of the holy cities to the rebellion and the strong presence of SAIRI in these towns brought strong retribution from the regime.

There is no accurate death toll for the *intifada* in the south. While those killed by the rebels can probably be numbered in the thousands, those killed by the regime ran into the tens of thousands.[60] The number may have been well over 30,000. It is likely that the *intifada* as a whole took at least twice as many lives as the war itself. In addition, there were many more refugees. Tens of thousands fled across the border to Iran to swell the ranks of Iraqi exiles already there.

The results of the *intifada* in the south were devastating. The death and departure of substantial portions of the population, especially its youth and some of its local leadership, weakened a region of the country that had already borne a heavy burden from two wars. This was particularly true of Basra. A city of commerce, of intellectual life, and of close ties to the Gulf and Kuwait, Basra was badly damaged by the uprising, as well as the Gulf War. Cut off from its natural hinterland—the Arab Gulf—it was now under suspicion by the government.

Among the *shi'i* population of the south, alienation from the regime was higher than at any time since the founding of the state. Regardless of whether the population had participated in the uprising or not, its cities and towns and its youth had undergone a devastating experience in brutality. It was not likely to be forgotten soon. Alienation against the West—and especially the United States—was also high. However ephemeral, the *intifada* clearly represented a deep and widespread hope for political change, openly encouraged by the American president. While the *intifada* was domestically driven, the failure of US and coalition forces to provide any aid when asked left an indelible impression on Iraqis. The decision of Schwarzkopf, backed by the US administration, to allow the regime to fly and operate gunship helicopters against the population, however inadvertently arrived at, convinced many Iraqis that the United States supported the regime, and not the rebels, mainly out of fear of *shi'i* separatism or dominance. Much bitterness was also directed against Iran as well, mainly for Iran's failure to provide more support. In the end, the *shi'a* of the south, who had for the most part led a genuine domestic revolt against a repressive regime, were left brutally repressed and politically and intellectually isolated.

Repression of the Rebellion in the North

By the last week in March, the government was ready to turn its attention from the south to the north. By 26 and 27 March there were fierce battles on the road between Khanaqin and Jalaula, with the government using troops and helicopters, and by 28 March the attack on Kirkuk began. The government shelled the town, used aircraft and helicopter gunships, and dropped phosphorous bombs. Though no CW were used (the coalition had issued a serious warning against it), there was widespread panic over its possible use. The government then moved on to Sulaimaniyya and Arbil. And within a few days Zakhu and Dahuk also fell. By the beginning of April, the *intifada* had ended in the north, with the Iraqi forces in control of all major Kurdish cities.

The reasons for the collapse were similar to those in the south. Despite better organization and a fighting force with weapons, *peshmergas* and Fursan were no match for a regular army. The Kurds had poor command, control, and communications; in some cases they were communicating by written notes. As in the south, although they appealed for coalition support, as yet they received none. Most important of all, however, may have been their faulty misperceptions. Given news of the government's defeat at the front and the uprisings in the north and the south, the Kurds could not envision regime survival, much less a major counterattack in the north.[61] In the end, the government's counterattack produced panic and the greatest exodus of people in Iraq's modern history.

The State Unravels in the North

Despite the collapse of the Kurdish rebellion and the reassertion of government control over the north, the ultimate outcome of the uprising in the north was very different from that in the south. Due to entirely unforeseen circumstances, the result was to loosen—not restore—the state's control over the Kurdish population.

The Kurdish Exodus

The government's attack and recapture of the cities of the north led to a mass exodus of Kurds to the borders of Turkey and Iran and a refugee problem of such scope that it rapidly took on international proportions. Eventually it involved an estimated 2 million people, roughly half the Kurdish population. The flight was made in appalling conditions. The Kurds suffered not only air attacks from Iraqi forces but cold and snow in the mountains and inadequate food, clothing, and shelter. One report estimates the death toll at 500 to 1,000 a day at its peak.[62] Although the overwhelming majority of fleeing Kurds took refuge in Iran, the problem arose mainly on the Turkish frontier. Turkey, which already had absorbed some 60,000 Iraqi Kurds from the Anfal operation, was unwilling to exacerbate its Kurdish problem by absorbing more.

The size of this exodus has raised questions about its causes. The Iraqi government contends that the Kurds themselves encouraged the exodus, but there is no real support for the claim. The evidence is that the exodus, like much of the *intifada* itself, was spontaneous. It was driven by fear, by the severity of fighting in Kirkuk, and by the reputation of the regime for brutality and the use of CW. In fact, most of the Kurdish leadership, including Barzani and Talabani, made clear they did not want the territory and their support base depopulated.

Whatever the causes of the human stampede, it caused major problems for the Kurdish leadership, the Iraqi government, and the coalition. The Kurds, of course, faced a humanitarian disaster of the first order. Although they could call for international intervention, they could not be certain of getting much help or recognition. To salvage the situation, the Kurds had two options: to work for international support or to negotiate with the government. The Kurds chose both, successfully using both the West and the Baghdad government to achieve some political gains.

The Baghdad regime also found itself in a dilemma. Although it wanted control of the north and an end to the rebellion, the size of the flight was undoubtedly a major headache. It brought unwelcome international attention. Indeed, it might have brought renewed coalition military action at a time when Iraq was ill prepared to deal with it. Although the coalition was not operating in the north, coalition troops were still on Iraqi soil in the south and the government faced tough cease-fire resolutions.

The coalition likewise faced an unpleasant dilemma, which it was never adequately able to resolve. It now had a major humanitarian crisis on its hands that it could not avoid addressing. Yet the solution would likely require violating the principle of Iraq's sovereignty, intervening in a domestic civil conflict, and sending its troops into northern Iraq, all of which it wished to avoid. In the end, it managed to address the humanitarian issue but left the other questions in abeyance.

Operation Provide Comfort

In the solution that now emerged, the Kurds, unlike the *shi'a* in the south, owed much to having Western friends they had cultivated for years. Some, including influential journalists, were even on the scene. The harrowing pictures of fleeing Kurds on TV screens created instant public demand for some action, especially in Europe. In the United States, the Bush administration was more reluctant, but the US ambassador in Ankara, anxious to shift the responsibility for the refugees from Turkey to Iraq, put pressure on the US administration to take some action. The outcome was Operation Provide Comfort (OPC), an effort to provide the Kurds with humanitarian aid and sufficient protection to induce them to go home. The legal and political basis of the operation was ambiguous, but it provided a structure and a protective framework for the Kurds in northern Iraq that would persist for over a decade. Most important of all, it internationalized the Kurdish problem in Iraq and provided some modest support for the Kurds in their ongoing struggle with the central government. However, without actual protection from coalition forces on the ground, Kurds were not likely to return to the north of Iraq. In the end, the coalition responded by placing some troops on the ground, though under very fuzzy legal authority from the UN.

Designed as a means to protect initial relief efforts, OPC was to remain for years. On 5 April President Bush ordered US military airdrops to Kurdish refugees in the mountains, which began on 7 April. They were not very effective, often failing to reach their targets and even killing and injuring Kurds who were in their path, but the operation required air cover. As a result, the United States ordered Iraq to cease all military activity, including the flying of aircraft, north of the thirty-sixth parallel. This No Fly Zone protected aircraft delivering supplies and, later, ground troops operating in northern Iraq in the safe haven, but it also restricted Iraqi sovereignty over its air space in a wide region, including major cities such as Mosul and Arbil.[63]

Another step was the creation of a "safe haven" for the Kurds in northern Iraq, under UN control, where refugees would be free from attack. It was agreed to secure an area adjacent to the Turkish border to which refugees could return. On 16 April Bush agreed to send ground troops into northern Iraq to secure the haven. Eventually, a Military Coordinating Committee (MCC) composed of US and coalition forces was set up in Zakhu to administer the operation. Iraq, of course, was opposed, but under the circumstances could do little. In fact, in an effort to defuse the situation, it had earlier issued an amnesty for Kurdish rebels. On the ground, Iraqi government troops controlled Zakhu, Dahuk, and much of the area envisioned for the haven. On 18 April the UN negotiated a memorandum of understanding (MOU) with the Iraqi government that would allow humanitarian centers in the north.

The MOU negotiated with the Iraqi government anticipated that coalition forces would be replaced by a small UN police force once Kurds were resettled. By June, soothed by the coalition military presence, virtually all the Kurds who needed to be repatriated had returned from the Turkish border, and by the end of June, Iran had announced that 600,000 Kurds had also returned from Iran, a remarkably successful humanitarian effort. On 7 June UN forces began taking over the operation of refugee camps in Iraq and the relief program. By 15 June the last allied forces withdrew from northern Iraq, leaving only a small force in Zakhu to oversee relief operations. However, the disposition of forces between the Kurds and the central government outside the haven had not been settled.

Kurdish Negotiations with the Regime

If securing Western protection was one arm of Kurdish strategy, negotiating with the central government was another. Here too the Kurds provide a contrast with the *shi'a*. In undertaking these discussions, the Kurds were apparently driven by several realities. One was the massive depopulation of their area and the need to do something about it. Second was uncertainty over foreign support. Nonetheless, the Front could begin negotiations with the regime with some points in its favor. Thanks to the relief effort, its people—and its fighting forces—were returning to the area. Even if the international forces were eventually withdrawn, UN "police" would remain and so, too, would the No Fly Zone, a force preventing air attacks on the Kurds. The exodus had permanently internationalized the Kurdish issue, which would henceforth be watched from abroad. Under these circumstances, the Kurds might be able to consolidate gains through negotiation with Saddam, while he was weak. A third reason may be more cynical: to buy time to strengthen their position.

What was the government strategy in dealing with the Kurds? Having brutally repressed the *intifada* in the south and rapidly reconquered cities in the north, and with much of the population in flight, why negotiate with the troublemakers? One answer was the weak position of the government. The Fursan, on which it had relied to hold much of the region, had gone over to the other side and were not available. The regular army forces ringing the area had also largely collapsed. And now it also faced a No Fly Zone over an enormous swath of territory, which would hamper actions on the ground. Negotiations with the Front might help loosen Western control, give the appearance of good faith, and speed the termination of OPC. This was certainly preferable to continued guerrilla action by *peshmergas* in the mountains. Negotiations would buy time for Baghdad as well.

The negotiations followed a path similar to those that had gone before and predictably ended in an impasse. They continued from April until August 1991 and were finally broken off by the Kurds in January 1992. Disagreements arose first over the area of self-rule. The Kurds insisted on Kirkuk or at least administrative control of the province; despite earlier rumors that the government might concede this, there was no such concession. There was also disagreement over the extent of self-rule, in particular the disposition of the government's military and security forces in the north. The government insisted that Kurds break their ties with the international community. On behalf of the opposition as a whole, the Kurds pressed for a multiparty system and elections in Iraq. Not surprisingly, the government rejected this outright.

In fact, it was on the ground that the struggle over control of the north would take place. This occurred in the months after the establishment of the safe haven in a series of skirmishes—even battles—in the north between the *peshmergas* and government forces. These skirmishes began as early as May 1991, even while allied forces were in the region. Kurds attacked Iraqi police posts in Zakhu and Dahuk, displacing Iraqi security forces in both towns. More skirmishes occurred in July, mainly in Sulaimaniyya, as the last allied forces withdrew from the north. Casualties mounted into the hundreds and the flight of Kurds reached thousands, but the Kurds managed to take and hold Arbil and Sulaimaniyya and to capture Iraqi army POWs. Both sides, of course, were testing the coalition and its commitment to the Kurds as well as each other. It was the outcome of this ground action and the unpleasant prospect of renewed guerilla war in the north that probably account for the government's next action, its most striking and ultimately most significant in shaping the post-*intifada* period.

Government Withdrawal from the North

Toward the end of October 1991, the Iraqi government decided to withdraw its forces behind a defensible line in the north. It reached a cease-fire with the Kurds and withdrew from Sulaimaniyya, Arbil, and the major towns on the plains. It focused on Kirkuk, however, which it continued to hold. The government had now left much of the Kurdish region in Kurdish hands, retreating behind a new, internal front. The line was soon fortified by mines with Iraqi divisions behind them.

At the same time, the government informed all its employees in the north that to maintain their salaries and pensions they would have to relocate south of the line. A small group at the upper edges of the system, possibly 5 to 10 percent of the administration, as well as some worried about supporting their families, now made the choice to leave. This unprecedented action left Kurds, for the first time, in control of much of the territory (except for Kirkuk) they desired to control. It would not be long before they would seize the initiative in establishing a new Kurdish government independent of the central authority in Baghdad in all but name. At the same time, however, the central government foisted additional hardships on the region by imposing an internal economic blockade on the area. Sealing the main roads leading to the north, it clamped down on trade, attempting to isolate the north and cripple it economically.

In retrospect, this dramatic step by the government raises questions of its motives. The Iraqi army, with poor morale, did not want another guerrilla war on its hands. The government likely felt it was better to give up what was not essential and keep what was—Kirkuk—behind a defensible line. It was also clear that keeping the Kurds under central government control was less important to the regime than controlling the *shi'i* population in the south, where the regime continued to fight a low intensity conflict in and around the marshes. Baghdad probably estimated that both the government and the economy of the north would collapse and the Kurds would, perforce, eventually come back to the fold on their own. In time, the coalition would weaken, and as the government's situation improved, it would have a freer hand to deal with the area. Neither assessment was to prove correct.

In the end, it was the Kurdish Front—especially the two Kurdish parties, the KDP and the PUK—that would end up in control of the territory in the north, eventually consolidating its hold through elections and the establishment of a more formal regional government.

The Repercussions of the War and Rebellion

The short nine months between August 1990, when Iraq invaded Kuwait, and April 1991, when it accepted the final UN cease-fire resolution, 687, were not only fateful for Iraq but almost totally destructive—to the regime itself, to the state it had been building, and above all, to the population and society, already badly weakened by the Iran-Iraq war and the regime's own repression. Iraq now faced limited options for the future.

Although the regime and the central government had survived a major defeat and a widespread rebellion, it was left truncated and economically, militarily, and politically weak. It faced not only the costs of a second war, but harsh cease-fire terms—especially the economic sanctions and substantial disarmament, both intrusive infringements on its highly prized sovereignty. The military, the backbone of the state structure, was in disarray and in need of reorganization. The legitimacy of the regime had manifestly been shredded. And it was isolated internationally and domestically.

At home, the most serious result of the war was the erosion of the state structure, an indirect and unintended consequence of the conflict and its aftermath. The government's support base was now clearly limited to the center, although much of that support could be considered mere acquiescence. In the north, it had been compelled to yield administrative control to the Kurds. The south remained under its control, but its population had just revealed widespread hostility to the regime.

However, not too much should be made of the threat to the regime from the *intifada*. The regular military did not split or turn against the regime. The uprising was sporadic, unorganized, and unable to hold its ground, either in the north or the south, in the face of an organized military attack. Rather, the uprising showed a society and a political structure badly in need of rebuilding along new lines and under different management. In the end, the regime's major challenge would be the economic burden placed on Iraq by the cease-fire terms and the contest with the West that would now ensue over disarmament and its loss of sovereignty. The regime would spend the final years of the century attempting to extricate itself from these coils.

10

THE SADDAM HUSAIN REGIME, 1991–2003

The destruction wrought by the Gulf War and the rebellion profoundly marked Iraq—economically, socially, and psychologically. The regime survived—barely—but the steps it had taken to do so emphasized its worst features: its narrow power base, its reliance on security institutions, and its brutality in repressing its population.

Politically, the regime gained strength over time, but it faced continual opposition. In the north, the Kurds managed to carve out a self-governing enclave. Though they proved unable to establish a unified, cohesive government, the Kurds underwent an economic and cultural revival, making their future reintegration in the Iraqi state more difficult. *Shi'i* opposition continued in the south, where the *shi'a* remained a largely neglected and alienated population.

In foreign affairs the main feature of the decade was the struggle over removal of the cease-fire terms. Iraq kept up its effort to end sanctions, weapons' inspections, and the No Fly Zones. However, it was only partially successful. Its sovereignty remained compromised and its development stunted.

The Regime's Survival, 1991–1995

One of the most remarkable outcomes of the war was the survival of the regime. Even before the revolt was quelled the regime began to reorganize and to marshal its support in the four essentially Arab *sunni* or mixed provinces of the central triangle—Anbar, Salah al-Din, Ninawa, and Diyala—the "white provinces," so called because they had remained loyal during the war and the rebellion. (Baghdad was more problematic because it had a majority *shi'i* population that had to be kept under control.)

Talk of Reform

Following the war and the *intifada,* the regime did make some modest attempts to propitiate the disaffected. The government called for reconstruction and even suggested it would lay a new foundation for a democratic society. In April 1991 the RCC pardoned Iraqis who had taken part in the rebellion, lifted the ban on international travel, and disbanded the popular militia. The last move was particularly welcomed by the public.

On 23 March a new cabinet was formed under Sa'dun Hammadi, a long-time Ba'thist but an educated *shi'a* regarded as more amenable to reform. In July the National Assembly legalized opposition parties, and in August the Ba'th Party held an election at all levels, including the Regional Command. In fact, restructuring the party was a necessity; its cadre in the south had collapsed and positions needed to be filled.

It was not long, however, before talk of reform evaporated. The Assembly had already made clear that the parties it had legalized were not permitted to have a platform that was regional or sectarian and that parties could be dissolved if they undermined national unity or security. In September Hammadi was removed as prime minister. The RCC remained the chief legislative, executive, and judicial authority in the state, and its seats continued to be filled with old-line Ba'th stalwarts and Saddam's family. This ended any further discussion of political reform inside Iraq for the remainder of the decade. This feeble attempt is noteworthy only to indicate how far Iraq had traveled down a totalitarian path.

The Revival of Tribalism

As a substitute for the collapsing party, Saddam now turned increasingly to tribal groups in the countryside for governance. Those tribes that had supported the regime or remained neutral during the *intifada* were now enlisted to keep order in their regions. In a remarkable reversal of policy, *shaikhs* were rearmed—even in some cases with rocket launchers—in return for keeping law and order in their region. Benefits to *shaikhs* and their tribes included redistribution of land previously confiscated, as well as sizable sums of money for personal use.[1]

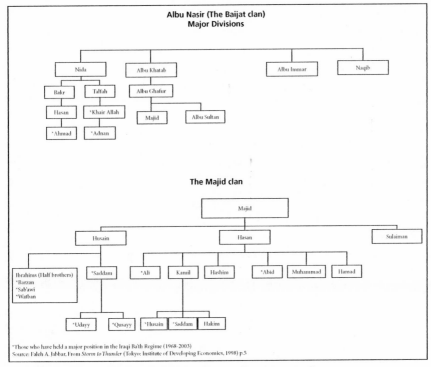

FIGURE 10.1   Major Divisions of the Albu Nasir Tribe

The revival of tribalism also included restoration of many aspects of tribal justice. In 1990, for example, the legal code was modified to allow leniency to male relatives (though not the husband) of an adulterous female who kill the woman in order to restore family honor.[2]

Above all, the new tribal policy restored tribal legitimacy and prestige. A clear indication of the new tribal status was public use of tribal names and affiliations by party, military, and regime figures, a practice outlawed in 1976. In 1995 some 60 percent of delegates to the National Assembly were either tribal leaders or their representatives.[3]

Reliance on Family and Clan

Meanwhile, at the top of the structure, the regime relied even more heavily on family and clan. Two members of the Majid clan were given key posts: Ali Hasan al-Majid, first as minister of interior, then as minister of defense; and Husain Kamil, as minister of industry and military industry. One of Saddam's half brothers replaced Majid in the post of Interior; the other was appointed head of the Directorate of General Security. More distant relatives manned various security and military posts.

The emerging profile of leadership had become clear. Leaders were overwhelmingly drawn from the *sunni* center, in particular the smaller, poorer, and more provincial towns of the northwest triangle. Reliance on the Albu Nasir and related tribes and clans was striking. Although neither the military intelligence nor the armed forces were closed to non-*sunnis*, there is little doubt that sensitive positions were increasingly filled with loyalists from these provinces and from known and trusted clans.[4]

Restructuring the Military and Security

The regime's survival was not accomplished without major purges and executions within the military, party, and security services. By one calculation, of the twenty division commanders in the regular army, six were executed on charges of conspiracy in March 1991, four were jailed, and six were forced to retire.[5] The same was true for the party, where hundreds from the south were expelled on charges of dereliction of duty.[6] A list was drawn up of military personnel who had been present during the Gulf War and the rebellion. In fact, however, the Gulf War counted for little; what mattered was active participation in repressing the rebellion. Those who had not demonstrated loyalty in this way were passed over for promotion or weeded out; those who did, were rewarded.[7]

The regime then concentrated on rebuilding its multiple and overlapping security and intelligence networks, especially those designed to protect the regime. A new organization created in 1992, the Military Security Service, was made responsible for dealing with dissent in the military and reported directly to the Presidential Palace.[8] Key security agencies were put under family control. By 1993 the SSO, responsible for thwarting potential coups, was headed by Saddam's son Qusayy. The Special Republican Guard, the only heavily armed force permitted inside Baghdad, was headed by a member of the Majid clan. At the pinnacle of this system was the Himaya (Protection) Force, a small group of thirty to forty men recruited wholly from tribal groups loyal to Saddam.

By 1992 the regime had drastically reorganized its military, strengthening the regime. Much of the regular army, especially its large and bloated infantry, had already evaporated through desertions. By 1993 Iraq's military forces were down to about 400,000 from a prewar total of about 1 million. The reorganization relied heavily on the Republican Guard (RG) as the backbone of the military. Many RG officers were transferred to regular army units, not only raising military standards but helping to ensure loyalty.[9]

Finally, a new ideological formulation gave this reorganization focus. By 1992, after the failure of most of the Arab world to support Iraq in the war, adulation of Arab nationalism was gone. Speeches and the press now focused on Iraq's new role as a "victim" of an international conspiracy, led by the United States and its Zionist allies, and Iraq's heroic struggle to survive. Steadfastness and patience was urged. Saddam also wrapped the regime's policy in religious rhetoric, claiming Iraq as a "representative of God . . . in the Mother of Battles."[10]

The Imposition of Foreign Control on Iraq

The cease-fire the United States and its coalition allies fastened on Iraq was one of the most intrusive since the Second World War. The most important element of the cease-fire regime was UN Resolution 687, which provided for a permanent boundary settlement between Kuwait and Iraq; elimination of Iraq's weapons of mass destruction and long-range missiles, together with a monitoring system to assure that they were not rebuilt; a return of Kuwaiti property and citizens seized by Iraq; and payment of reparations for the war. To ensure compliance, sanctions were to continue in force. Member states were specifically authorized to use "all necessary means"—that is, military force—to ensure compliance with 687, if needed.[11]

In addition, Resolution 688, requiring Iraq to cease repression of its population, had been used as the main justification for prohibiting Iraqi air flights north of the thirty-sixth parallel in order to protect the Kurds; in August 1992 a second such zone was established south of the thirty-second to protect the *shi'a.* (This line was later extended to the thirty-third parallel.) These zones restricted Iraq's control over much of its airspace.

The regime avoided compliance with resolutions where possible and acquiesced only where necessary. Saddam calculated that he could outlast the international community. To that end, the regime attempted to erode coalition solidarity by promising coalition members future benefits from oil in return for help in removing sanctions. Saddam also conducted a campaign to convince his population that his survival was synonymous with the survival of the nation-state. Although Saddam had some success with this policy, it is also clear that he misjudged what lay ahead. He did not expect the degree of intrusiveness that would ensue from inspections nor the persistence and determination exhibited by the coalition.

The West too was in for a surprise. The coalition was unprepared for the degree of intransigence it met in Iraq and the skill and organization the regime was to show in deception and resistance. On the contrary, the West, the United States in particular, apparently expected the regime to collapse. Second, the victors, though they had some knowledge of Iraq's WMD efforts, were unprepared for the scale and magnitude of what they found.

Recognition of Kuwait and Its Borders

One of the key elements in the cease-fire settlement—and the earliest to be tackled—was securing Iraqi recognition of Kuwait and its border and the return of missing Kuwaiti persons and property. By May 1991 a demilitarized zone had been established on the Kuwait-Iraq border and an unarmed UN observer force, UNIKOM (UN Iraq-Kuwait Observation Mission), sent to the area. In April 1992 a UN border commission recommended a return to the line established in a 1963 agreement between Iraq and Kuwait. Though Iraq's National Assembly rejected the recommendation, a new UNSC resolution was passed strengthening UNIKOM and turning it into a genuine peacekeeping force. By May 1993 the Kuwaitis had begun fortification of the frontier, mainly by digging a trench three meters deep, five meters wide, and two hundred kilometers long.

The border commission then turned to the offshore boundary, an even more contentious issue. Here there was no previous agreement to work from, and as was the case with the Shatt al-Arab, Iraq wanted complete control over its access to the Persian Gulf in the Khaur Abd Allah channel. However, the commission drew the boundary down the middle of the channel. (The parallel with the Shatt al-Arab and the border dispute with Iran is clear.) This finding was bitterly protested by Iraq, which claimed it had been made a landlocked country.

In October 1994, in an act of defiance, Iraq mobilized some 80,000 troops on the border with Kuwait, but the action backfired, bringing military retaliation from the coalition and punitive action from the UN. Iraq relented, and on 10 November 1994 the Iraqi National Assembly finally accepted the border specified in UN Resolution 833. This brought one important issue in the Gulf War to a close.

The Struggle over WMD

The second and ultimately most contentious issue in the cease-fire agreement was elimination of Iraq's weapons of mass destruction, an issue that came to define the postwar period. This struggle was critical for Iraq's domestic situation since removal of sanctions hinged on UNSC agreement that all WMD and long-range missiles had been eliminated in Iraq.

The clash over removing Iraq's WMD program began early.[12] In June 1991 a UN inspection team caught Iraqis smuggling nuclear processing equipment out of a site it was inspecting. Despite Iraqi denials, the UN now had eyewitness evidence of a full-blown Iraqi nuclear program. From then on, there were few illusions on the coalition side either about Iraq's weapons program or about getting Iraqi cooperation to eliminate it.

By the end of June, Saddam Husain had set up a high-level concealment plan to destroy, in secret, much of the forbidden weaponry in order to hide and preserve those elements Iraqis considered essential. Faced with demands to produce lists and evidence of what had been destroyed, Iraq continued to insist that nothing was left. The result was a long-running cat-and-mouse game punctuated by periodic and sometimes spectacular confrontations, including several military strikes on Iraqi sites, that lasted for most of the decade.[13] Iraq, when compelled, would make partial disclosure. There would be further investigation, further discoveries, and then more incomplete admissions. The UN Special Commission (UNSCOM) and the International Atomic Energy Agency (IAEA) made semiannual reports to the UN on their progress, but without a final, satisfactory report, the damaging sanctions regime remained in effect.[14]

Notwithstanding these difficulties, UNSCOM and the IAEA went a long way toward unmasking Iraq's WMD program. Between 1991 and 1994 IAEA and UNSCOM uncovered a network of about forty nuclear-research facilities using three clandestine uranium-enrichment programs. The key nuclear installations were dismantled in 1992, and by 1994 the IAEA had declared Iraq's nuclear program ended.

In the chemical field, UNSCOM had destroyed over 148,000 tons of chemical warfare agents (including mustard gas, sarin, and tabun). However, it was subsequently revealed that Iraq still had a VX nerve agent program, which UNSCOM was not able to detect and destroy. In the biological field, Iraq admitted that it had a biological weapons program but said it had destroyed all agents. Despite inspections of a number of suspected facilities, no biological stockpile was discovered. The long and frustrating process generated a climate of mutual hostility and distrust on both sides that, by the mid–1990s, made any substantial changes in foreign policy either by Iraq or the United States and the United Kingdom very unlikely. It also made removal of sanctions more difficult.

The cease-fire terms also imposed some constraints on Iraq's conventional military. Although Iraq was permitted to retain a conventional military force for defense, including missiles below the 150-kilometer range, the embargo included a prohibition on the sale and supply of weapons and other military equipment to Iraq. Without significant military imports or high-technology equipment, Iraq's military capability and readiness were steadily reduced. The No Fly Zones also continued in effect, seriously limiting Iraq's freedom of action and its military ambitions.

Sanctions

The most serious constraint imposed on Iraq by the UN was the sanctions regime. The application of sanctions for over half a decade had by 1995 fundamentally changed Iraq's social and economic structure and the welfare of its population for the worse. Oil production dropped 85 percent between 1990 and 1991 and began to increase again only after sanctions relief in 1997. The fall in Iraq's national income and gross domestic product (GDP) were equally dramatic. Iraq's per-capita income, which had stood at just over $2,000 in 1989 before the Gulf War, had fallen to $609 by 1992.[15] Those most affected were members of the middle class on fixed incomes. Iraq suffered a hemorrhage of its educated and technocratic elite.

Although there was no outright starvation, the oil embargo created a mounting humanitarian crisis. Before the war, food imports were estimated to be about 70 percent of Iraq's consumption. These were now drastically reduced. Famine was avoided by an effective rationing system, but calorie intake fell from an average of 3,000 calories a day to about 2,250, most of these provided through a ration "basket" provided by the government. While food was available on the market, skyrocketing prices made most items unaffordable for average families.[16] Infant mortality and mortality of children under five rose steeply. By 1995 the UN secretary general noted that the humanitarian situation in Iraq had deteriorated in all respects and that living conditions had become precarious for an estimated 4 million people. The Food and Agriculture Organization (FAO) claimed that child morality had risen nearly fivefold.[17] With drugs and essential supplies lacking, health services were nearing a breakdown.

The most serious sanctions problem was inflation. The rise in prices was continuous during and after the war, but it grew increasingly worse after 1993 until Iraq came to suffer from chronic hyperinflation. The dinar in prewar times had been worth $3.20; by 1996 $1 was worth ID 2,600.

TABLE 10.1 Crude Oil Production and Export, 1976–2001 (millions of barrels per day)

	Production	*Export*
1976–1980	2.69	2.5
1981–1986	1.26	.961
1995	.550	.150
1996	.580	.180
1997	1.15	.840
1998	2.11	1.795
1999	2.52	2.203
2000	2.57	2.243
2001	2.36	2.030

SOURCE: Economic Intelligence Unit, *Iraq, 2002–2003*, Country Profile (London, 2003), p. 31.

The coalition had expected sanctions to bring Iraqi compliance on WMD, possibly even a demise of the regime. Iraq's ability to manage the sanctions crisis and to withstand the economic hardships was remarkable and, like much else in the war's aftermath, unexpected. One factor that helped was the stockpile of goods it had purloined from Kuwait. Though some of the military equipment was returned over time, the consumer goods were absorbed by the population.

Iraq used other mechanisms as well. One was its effective rationing system, instituted during the war. The government provided every citizen, properly registered, with a subsistence package of basic staples. Another was its ability to smuggle oil. By 1995 Iraq was producing more than half a million barrels per day. It consumed a little over half and exported about 70,000 barrels per day of crude oil to Jordan, 20,000 to 30,000 barrels per day of refined products through Turkey and Iran, and about 10,000 barrels per day of crude through the Gulf.[18] Much of this oil was sold at discount prices and netted Iraq less than $1 billion a year.

Iraq also relied on its own economy, especially for food production. It attempted to raise prices for farmers in an effort to increase production, and initially had some success. But farmers, like industrialists, suffered from lack of raw materials and spare parts for machinery and fertilizer, which inhibited production. Iraq also received some aid from the UN and private donors. Between 1992 and 1995 these funds averaged a little over $100 million a year.[19] Iraq also sold off fixed assets, drew down its gold reserves abroad, and used up private savings of individuals.

Despite these palliatives, however, by 1994 the situation became increasingly dire, creating a political and moral problem for the coalition. In fact, this circumstance had been recognized by the coalition soon after the war, and it had tried to address it. In August 1991 the UN had passed Resolution 706, allowing Iraq to sell $1.6 billion worth of oil over a six-month period (renewable) for the import of food, medicine, and other essential civilian needs. The funds would not go directly to the Iraqi government but into an escrow account maintained under international supervision. The UN Sanctions Committee would be charged with reviewing sales contracts by Iraq to make certain they were for humanitarian needs.

However, Iraq rejected the resolution outright, almost wholly on the grounds that it compromised its sovereignty. Iraq did not accept the legality of the sanctions regime and would not cooperate with it; rather, its aim was not to alleviate its economic situation through incremental, humanitarian measures but to end the sanctions regime in its entirety.

In 1995 the UN tried again. It passed Resolution 986, which would come to be known as the "oil for food" resolution. Iraq also rejected Resolution 986. It presumed that a favorable report would be forthcoming soon from UNSCOM that would remove sanctions. That was a miscalculation. In the meantime, the economy continued on its downward trajectory, with implications for the regime's stability as well as the West's international position.

Opposition to the Regime, 1991–1995

Despite the regime's survival, Saddam Husain continued to face opposition from inside and outside Iraq. While none of this opposition was sufficiently well organized to overthrow the regime, it posed a constant challenge to the regime's legitimacy and even its stability.

Opposition from the Center
Most significant and potentially troubling for the regime were continual attempts at coups and assassination from within the center, the *sunni*-dominated area on which the regime relied for support. Information, although sparse, indicates that this disaffection reached into the highest levels of the regime's apparatus. Eventually defections even reached into the heart of Saddam's nuclear family.

Among the first to give Saddam trouble were the Juburis, a key tribal confederation spread over a wide area from Mosul to Hilla. Many Juburis had
reached senior positions in the military and the security system. Juburis were
behind an attempted plot on 6 January 1990 to assassinate Saddam during a
military parade.[20] In August 1991 and, reportedly, in June 1992 they tried
again. The attempt in June 1992 reportedly led to the execution or dismissal
of nearly 150 midlevel Republican Guard officers.[21]

In July 1993 a coup attempt led by well-known Tikriti families was revealed.[22] The group had made contact with opposition elements in Amman
and London and even with US intelligence. The incipient plot showed how
deeply opposition had penetrated the president's Albu Nasir tribe and key
Republican Guard units.

In November of 1994 the regime faced an alleged coup attempt in the
Dulaimi tribe. The Dulaimi tribal confederation, spread across the *sunni*
heartland in the Anbar province and even into Syria, controlled much of the
trade with Jordan, and its members staffed key military and security posts.
In November Major General Muhammad Mazlum al-Dulaimi was arrested
on coup suspicions; his body, reportedly mutilated, was returned to his
home in Ramadi in May 1995. This act resulted in a localized uprising
among some Dulaimi clans that took several days to put down.

Despite reorganization of the security service, individual opposition from
within the security apparatus continued to surface. In November 1994
Wafiq al-Samarra'i defected from his post as director of military intelligence.
Samarra'i then joined the opposition in the north and in March 1995 led an
attack on Iraq's regular forces that resulted in the collapse of several brigades.
According to Samarra'i's own memoirs, he had been in touch with the opposition for several years before he left.[23]

The Defection of Husain Kamil

These difficulties, however, paled in comparison to the split in Saddam's
own family that burst into the open in the summer of 1995 and resulted in
the flight from Baghdad to Amman of Husain Kamil, Saddam's son-in-law.
Husain Kamil took with him his brother Saddam Kamil, their two wives
(Saddam Husain's eldest daughters), another brother, and over a dozen
members of their retinue. This event delivered the worst shock to the regime
since the *intifada*. In several ways the incident and its repercussions proved
to be a turning point for the regime, but they also illustrated the regime's
survival skills.

Husain Kamil's defection was hardly based on disillusion with the regime; rather its motivation lay in a struggle for power and money within the family itself. Such feuds, involving collateral competition between branches of Saddam's extended family, especially the Ibrahims and the Majids, were long-standing. But recently the family struggle had shifted to Saddam's own sons, Udayy and Qusayy, who were emerging as political players desirous of their own place in the sun. Udayy, in particular, was anxious not only to move ahead as successor to his father but to carve out his own economic and political empire. Udayy's flamboyance, indiscretion, and undisciplined behavior, however, constantly put the family in jeopardy.

Husain Kamil, the most promising young member of the Majid clan, had risen rapidly from a lowly position to that of the second or third most important person in the country. In 1983 Saddam gave him his eldest daughter, Raghad, in marriage. Kamil then moved rapidly ahead, making his mark by supervising Saddam's prized military industries, including his weapons of mass destruction. He was also instrumental in furthering the Kuwait occupation and in putting down the *shi'i* rebellion, thereby proving his value to the regime. His brother, Saddam Kamil, was married to Saddam's second daughter, Rana, further cementing family ties.

But the rise of Husain Kamil threatened the future of Udayy. In 1994 Husain Kamil went to Amman for an extended period, where he reportedly underwent brain surgery. In his absence Udayy moved quietly to incorporate parts of Kamil's military procurement network into his economic empire. When Kamil returned, he challenged Udayy. In this family struggle, Saddam appeared to be supporting Udayy, or at least not curbing him. On 7 August Husain Kamil and his party left for Amman.

The defection was a stunning blow to the regime. Rapidly sensationalized in the international media, it laid bare for all to see the family basis of the regime and its economic and political corruption, as well as its apparent inability to manage its family affairs. Domestically, it caused embarrassment for Saddam not only because of the obvious disloyalty of several close family members but, more important, because two of his daughters had joined in the "treason." Under the tribal code in which Saddam operated, inability to control the women in one's family was the ultimate dishonor and, by inference, a reflection on his ability to control the country. From the day the Kamils left, Saddam worked to retrieve his daughters, preferably with their husbands but, if not, alone.

The defections also had serious international repercussions. UNCSOM had been moving, gradually, in the direction of a report indicating some Iraqi cooperation with inspections and possibly some progress on sanctions. The defection ended any hope of movement in this direction, as the Iraqi government, and Kamil himself, soon revealed how much of the WMD program had been concealed from the inspectors. The regime then had to divert time and energy to damage control.

The episode marked something of a turning point in Udayy's fortunes as well. Saddam rightly blamed the episode on his son. Added to the defection was another transgression. Udayy was responsible for wounding his uncle, Watban, during a shoot-out at a party in a family compound on the same night as the defection. Watban was left permanently incapacitated. Saddam finally moved to discipline his son. Udayy was stripped of several powerful positions in the security apparatus, including command of Saddam's Fida'iyyin, a new militia that had given Udayy a private army. In fact, from that time on, his younger, quieter brother, Qusayy, succeeded Udayy as the most likely family heir.[24]

Opposition from Abroad

The regime also faced opposition from Iraqis outside the country. These opposition groups had their roots in the growing exile community. Complete statistics are not available, but estimates indicate that the number of exiles may have reached 1.5 million prior to the Gulf war. The war, the rebellion, and the ongoing sanctions regime may have pushed this figure to 2 million, possibly 3 million, by the mid–1990s. The largest number of exiles were in Iran, where they numbered half a million to a million.[25] Others were in neighboring Arab countries, especially Jordan, Syria, and the Arab Gulf. In Europe the major concentration was in England, which housed hundreds of thousands. Some were scattered across the United States. While some of these exiles were poor, uprooted refugees, often inhabiting camps on the Iranian border, many more were from Iraq's educated and skilled middle class.

It was mainly within this middle-class exile community that Iraq's numerous opposition parties took root. The main groups comprising this outside opposition included the two Kurdish parties, the Democratic Party of Kurdistan (KDP), and the Patriotic Union of Kurdistan (PUK); the main *shi'i* groups—SAIRI, with its headquarters in Iran, and the Da'wa, with many members scattered abroad; and the venerable Iraqi Communist Party (ICP). To these must be added a few new groups. Most important were Arab nationalists, located in Syria, and the Wifaq al-Watani (Iraq National Accord) (INA), consisting of disaffected members of the Ba'th Party. The INA, led by Ayyad Allawi, a *shi'a,* with headquarters in London, had ties to those in the center.

The weaknesses of this exile opposition had been repeatedly demonstrated. Deep ideological divisions within its ranks prevented effective collaboration. Even more significant, the exile groups often had little or no foothold inside Iraq, especially in the center, where the regime had to be displaced. Only the Kurdish parties had managed to reestablish themselves within the borders of Iraq. But their ability to operate against the government—and even more, their willingness to do so at risk to their own position in the north—was limited.

In an attempt to overcome their difficulties, a number of these groups met in Vienna in June 1992. The chief outcome of this meeting was the formation of a new umbrella group, the Iraq National Congress (INC), which incorporated some, but not all, of the existing parties.[26] The INC then transferred its operations inside Iraq. In September a second conference was held, this time in northern Iraq. Out of these meetings came an executive committee directed by Ahmad Chalabi, a Western-educated mathematician from a wealthy *shi'i* banking family. A thorough secularist and an articulate spokesman, Chalabi had some drawbacks that would make him controversial. He had not lived in Iraq for years, he was under a cloud for allegations of banking fraud in Jordan, and he was seen to be heavy-handed in dealing with his colleagues. But his organizational abilities, tenacity, and ability to deal effectively with Western politicians soon made him a leading spokesman for the opposition in the West.

For a time, the INC made some headway in establishing its presence on Iraqi soil. It acquired a headquarters in Salah al-Din, in northern Iraq; it operated a radio station that reached into Iraq proper; it had printing facilities that it used to distribute leaflets and a newspaper; and it acted as a magnet to attract defectors, especially from the military. These were housed, fed, and trained as the beginnings of a militia to be added to the Kurdish *peshmergas.* In the course of time, it became apparent that the United States (in fact the CIA) was funding these activities and that it had sent some midlevel operatives into the north to help manage the operation. This connection alienated a number of INC members, who left the group.

Nonetheless, by 1995 the INC decided to push forward with an attack on Iraqi forces in two directions—Mosul and Kirkuk. A key element in its potential success—in the view of its perpetrators—was air support from the United States. Although there is no doubt that high-level officials in the United States were informed of the operation, there is no evidence that it received official support. One of the skeptics was KDP leader Barzani, who contacted Washington himself and received a denial. Already in a struggle with the PUK over territory, Barzani refused to join the operation.

Despite these setbacks, however, the INC, the PUK, and Samarra'i went forward. On 3 March 1995 the group attacked the regular armed forces in the Kirkuk area and had some success. Some seven hundred Iraqi troops surrendered to *peshmergas,* and the opposition forces occupied a few square miles of Iraqi territory. The equivalent of two Iraqi brigades collapsed, wrecking the best part of an Iraqi division. Although the military collapse was not serious enough to threaten the regime—or Kirkuk—the defeat revealed, once again, weakness in Saddam's army. It also gave the opposition a boost in morale.[27] Despite this outcome, the results of the operation showed how far the INC had to go to achieve its goals. Effective US support failed to materialize, and so, too, did the participation of the KDP, one of the two main pillars of the INC in the north. There was no supporting revolt in the military nor any *shi'i* activity in the south. Significantly, an attempt by the INA, also with the support of the CIA, to undertake a coup at this time was also unsuccessful.

Nevertheless, the outside opposition was not without impact. The very presence of the INC in northern Iraq, as well as the political, financial, and staff support that opposition groups were getting from the United States, constituted a reminder to Saddam Husain of the limits of his control inside his country and represented a continuing challenge to his legitimacy.

Opposition from the Shi'a *in the South*

Shi'i opposition to the regime continued in the wake of the *intifada.* Although the regime maintained control of the south, its position there was weak, as evidenced in numerous hit-and-run episodes against Ba'th and military posts and against high-level regime figures traveling in the south. The main area of activity, however, was in the marsh region, which constituted a refuge for dissidents, and the chief connecting link across the border to Iran.[28] Once the government had quelled the rebellion, it turned its attention to those in the marshes, sending some 40,000 troops south to build new roads and bases in the area and to slash and burn their way through areas with ten-foot-high reeds and palm thickets.[29] By August, it was reported that the government had five to six divisions engaged in the operation, including Republican Guard units, employing helicopters and fixed-wing aircraft in their pursuit. It was at this point, in August 1992, that the United States, the United Kingdom, and France, under UN auspices, instituted the southern No Fly Zone. Nonetheless, ground actions against the *shi'a* continued. By September 1995, the UN estimated that 200,000 to 250,000 former inhabitants of the marshes had been driven from the area. Some of these villagers were resettled by the Iraqi government in camps; others were moved to the Kirkuk region in an effort to Arabize Kurdish and Turkman territory.

The government did not rely wholly on military operations to eliminate the marsh area as a refuge for dissidents. It also employed massive—and controversial—drainage schemes to dry up the marshes. These involved a huge canal—the "Third River," running south of Baghdad to Basra, and a "Fourth River" between Kut and Basra—completed in record time. These large schemes were accompanied by huge embankments designed to block tributaries from flowing from the Tigris and Euphrates into the marshlands. By 1994 aerial photos showed near-total destruction of the marshes.[30] As the marshes were drained, the government's ability to move into the area and to control the population increased, but so, too, did opposition from the local population.

Opposition continued to emanate from the traditional centers of *shi'i* religious leadership. The regime attempted to control the selection of the chief *marji'* by imposing its own candidate, Sayyid Muhammad Sadiq al-Sadr, an Arab cleric related to the famous Muhammad Baqir al-Sadr. Sadr was expected to be malleable, but if the government had thought it was getting a "tame" *marji'*, it was soon to be disillusioned. In the course of time, Sadr came to speak for the *shi'i* community and eventually came to cause the regime considerable problems.

Notwithstanding this pent-up animosity, the ability of *shi'i* opposition to mount an organized challenge to the regime from within Iraq had been contained. The three most important *shi'i* opposition movements—SAIRI, the Da'wa, and the Islamic Action Organization—all had their headquarters and most of their cadre outside Iraq. All three groups faced multiple difficulties. Except for the Da'wa, they appeared unable to move beyond clerical leadership. Control by powerful clerical families gave *shi'i* opposition movements some benefits—a strong, informal organization, financial resources (through religious taxes), and a degree of independence from Baghdad. But it also brought drawbacks. Such leadership rested on a narrow sectarian background and was difficult to expand. It had a traditional outlook that often did not sit well with a younger generation educated in secular schools, and a small pool of qualified leaders from which to chose. Added to these difficulties were two other problems. One was Iraqi resistance to following the Iranian political model of putting clerics in control of the polity. As the aura of revolutionary success receded in Iran, so too did the appeal of the Islamic Republic. If clerical rule had less and less appeal for *shi'a*, it had none for *sunnis* or Christians, who still constituted at least 40 percent of the Iraqi population. More important was the obvious tie of these movements to a foreign country, Iran. As a result, organized *shi'i* opposition movements, though potent, were unable to mobilize an effective, domestic challenge to the regime, despite widespread discontent in the south.

The Kurds in the North

The government in Baghdad also faced an evolving and troublesome situation among the Kurds in the north. The challenge to the central government from the Kurds was less the threat of overthrow than the successful establishment of a separatist regime in the north. While the Kurds failed at unity, they did manage to achieve a high degree of independence; in doing so, they defied and weakened Baghdad.

Kurdish Elections

In January 1992, when it became apparent that negotiations with the central government had completely broken down, the Kurds announced that they would hold an election for a new government. Although the announcement caused some regional concern, the Kurds managed the situation well and succeeded, under extraordinary circumstances, in persuading an international monitoring group to come in and observe the election. Held on 19 May 1992, the election offered voters a list of candidates for a parliament of 105 representatives. To allow an array of parties to participate, a system of proportional representation was used, but parties had to exceed a threshold of 7 percent to be seated. Five seats were set aside for minorities, mainly the Christian population. There was also a separate election for the chief executive—the putative leader of "Kurdistan." This was essentially a contest between Barzani and Talabani, although other candidates, like Mahmud Uthman, also ran.

Although the vote itself and the campaigning that preceded it demonstrated considerable political leadership and organization, as well as a willingness to move in the direction of Western democratic standards, the results themselves sowed the seeds for future controversy and showed the strains in the Kurdish Front. Of the one hundred nonminority assembly seats, fifty-one went to the KDP and forty-nine to the PUK; four of the five seats allocated to minorities went to the Assyrian Democratic Movement.

Barzani believed he had won the election; Talabani was unwilling to accept that conclusion. In the end, Barzani capitulated in the interests of Kurdish unity. He yielded one seat to the PUK, thereby splitting the parliament evenly between the two main parties—fifty seats for the KDP, fifty for the PUK, five for the Christian minorities. There was no runoff to determine who would be the leader of Kurdistan. This resolution left an ambiguous situation with neither group in charge.

Establishment of the Kurdish Regional Government

On 4 July the Kurdish Regional Government (KRG) came into being, with the establishment of a Council of Ministers and then a parliament. But the effect of the elections had been to split not only the parliament but also the executive branch. For every minister of one party, there was a deputy of the other to check him. The two party leaders themselves, Barzani and Talabani, took no office, preferring to remain outside the government, running the affairs of their respective parties; they were thus unaccountable for government actions. This arrangement was a formula for deadlock and a renewal of the clash between the two parties that had been the staple of Kurdish politics for decades.

Nonetheless, despite their difficulties, the Kurds had established a functioning government, backed by an election (however flawed in its final acceptance) in the areas vacated by the government. By mid–1992 the Kurds had accomplished something that had eluded them since 1920: They were governing themselves, albeit without formal international recognition, in the three northern provinces of Iraq and without any control from Baghdad. And they had done so by holding the first election on Iraqi soil since 1958.

It was not long before the Kurds felt increased pressure from Baghdad designed to bring about the collapse of the KRG. In addition to a separate trade embargo placed on the north, Saddam also reduced food rations going to the area. In May of 1993 the Iraqi government withdrew the ID 25 note, closing its border for six days while new dinars were issued in Baghdad. None were issued in the north, leaving the Kurds with a severe cash shortage. Although a temporary burden, over the longer term this proved beneficial. Since the KRG could not print currency, the limited supply of notes held inflation down in the north while it soared in the south. In August 1994 electricity supplies were cut to Arbil and Sulaimaniyya.

These economic pressures did cause difficulties in the north but not collapse. Aid from nongovernmental organizations (NGOs) and the UN helped sustain and improve the economy in the north. The World Food Program (WFP), for example, fed some 750,000 displaced persons.[31] Gradually, agriculture and livestock raising improved, especially in lowland areas, and the population began to return to abandoned villages. Nonetheless, resources were scarce and the economy poor.

Breakdown of the KRG

Despite this promising beginning, the Kurds were not able to maintain the unity of their new regional government, and the north began to descend into an incipient civil war. Although economic problems and pressures from Baghdad played some role in the breakdown, the most important reason for the split was the renewed struggle for power between the two main protagonists in the north, now fed by the unsatisfactory power-sharing arrangements resulting from the elections.

It was clear that this struggle was both political and personal. Both leaders aspired to dominate a new Kurdish state-in-the-making. Neither was accustomed to sharing power. Talabani—a man with decades of experience and a wide variety of contacts in the region, in Europe, and in the United States—was more at home in modern party politics. Barzani—younger, more reserved, and far more at home in the Kurdish north than in the salons of the West—was more interested in protecting his patrimony at home than in currying favor abroad but equally unwilling to accept second-place status in the emerging Kurdish entity.

The two parties, which had been competing since the mid–1970s, also had different constituencies and operating styles. The KDP, although it attracted a number of urbanites and intellectuals, relied for administration on the Barzani clan and for support on related tribal groups. The PUK, as a legacy of its former leftist origins, considered itself more modern and progressive. Barzani's stronghold was the north, the Bahdinan-speaking area straddling the Turkish border; mainly rural and tribal, it had few large urban centers. Talabani's strength lay in the south, in the Surani-speaking area, with Sulaimaniyya and its urban intellectuals at its center.

This geographic division also had important economic consequences. The territory controlled by Barzani contained much rich agricultural land, less affected by the Anfal campaigns. He also controlled the border crossing point with Turkey at Khabur, which was soon to prove a lucrative source of customs income once transit traffic began to flow again. Talabani's territory, bordering Iran, had received the brunt of the Anfal campaign, and hence its economic base was poorer. Trade with Iran was much less lucrative. Both factors put Talabani at a disadvantage.

These issues came to a head in May 1994, when a minor land dispute in Qal'at Diza ended in a serious military conflict between the KDP and the PUK, the first battle in a full-blown civil war. The land dispute itself was in-consequential and should have been settled by the KRG, but the govern-ment was too weak to do so. Instead, it slipped out of control and soon engaged local KDP and PUK forces. Once the party militias were involved, the precarious balance of forces was at stake, and fighting spread. By August there were 1,000 dead and over 70,000 local Kurds displaced.[32]

In the meantime, a third party, the Islamic Movement of Iraqi Kurdistan (IMIK), entered the fray. The IMIK had received the third largest vote in the election and was strong in a number of regions it shared with the PUK. When fighting broke out between the KDP and PUK, the IMIK took ad-vantage of the situation to seize the towns of Halabja, Banjwin, and Khur-mal. By the time the fighting died down in the autumn, the IMIK was in control of a wide swath of territory around these towns.[33]

The civil war caused the de facto partition of the Kurdish north into two administrations. Though boundaries would shift thereafter, a unified government would not return. By March 1995 the PUK controlled about two-thirds of the "liberated" Kurdish area, including the two main urban centers of Arbil and Sulaimaniyya; the KDP, about one-third. Most of the southeast was Talabani territory; the north and some of the west, including the Turkish border and a piece of the Iranian border, were Barzani territory. In addition, a small slice of territory on the Iranian border was already un-der IMIK control. In this atmosphere of contention, it is not surprising that the north could not offer coherent opposition to the regime in Bagh-dad, or even support the Iraqi opposition movement, the INC, which had settled in the north.

Consolidation of the Regime and Its Limits, 1996–2003

By the mid–1990s the regime had clearly managed to consolidate its power. It had reduced, although not eliminated, the diverse challenges from its opposition. In the north, though it had not been able to regain control over the territory it had itself relinquished, it no longer faced a united Kurdish government. In the south, it held uneasy control but faced no organized threat that could unseat it. The potential danger from clans and tribes embedded in the military and security structures in the center had been dealt with through ruthless but carefully managed purges, while key security positions were kept in family hands.

But Saddam had still not been able to undo the structure of the cease-fire and its restrictions. The No Fly Zones, covering about two-thirds of Iraq's airspace, were constant reminders of Iraq's loss of sovereignty. The UN inspection teams, though they had eliminated much of Iraq's WMD and missile programs, constantly intruded into the inner workings of its security system in search of more. Most important of all, the most onerous of these restrictions—the sanctions—remained in force despite numerous efforts to get them removed.

The sanctions demonstrated all too openly the regime's lack of control over its major resource—oil—always a sensitive point in Iraq. And they were a major impediment to Saddam's long-standing strategy for domestic control: the carrot and the stick. A constantly dwindling resource base made it difficult not only to buy off discontent at the periphery but also to provide generous benefits to his loyalists. By 1995 the complete removal of the sanctions became the regime's key goal.

Acceptance of Resolution 986

In April 1995, when the UNSC passed Resolution 986 (Oil-for-Food), Iraq emphatically rejected it, but this sanctions policy generated a modest debate behind the scenes in Baghdad. Opponents of rejection argued that the best route to sanctions removal was acceptance of humanitarian oil sales, which could then be used as an opening wedge to their gradual de facto elimination. However, this line of reasoning had not yet won out; to the contrary, Saddam Husain, appeared convinced that UNSCOM could be persuaded to give Iraq a clean bill of health on WMD, which would result in a final end to sanctions. But Baghdad's campaign of political pressure came to an abrupt end on

8 August, when the world learned of Husain Kamil's defection. The revelations on Iraq's WMD program that subsequently ensued convinced any doubters in the UN community that much more remained to be done and set back whatever thought there may have been, even in Baghdad, of a "clean bill of health." Moreover, by 1995 Iraq's economy had reached a virtual crisis stage. Saddam had to cut rations. By January 1996, inflation had driven the dinar down to its lowest point ever—ID 3,000 ID to the dollar.[34]

On 18 January 1996, then, the Iraqi government announced that it was ready to talk to the UN about 986. But talk did not mean implementation. It took almost a year of continuous negotiations with the UN on the terms of the resolution to reach full acceptance and a memorandum of understanding (MOU) to implement it. It was only in December of 1996 that oil began to flow, for the first time in years. The first food shipments did not reach Iraq until March 1997.

Modest Economic Revival

Implementation of the resolution represented a turning point for Iraq—politically and economically. Acceptance opened the door to oil exports, even if only a crack. It would not be long before the amount of oil Iraq was permitted to export would increase. Gradually—very gradually—the worst effects of the sanctions on the economy were mitigated—food shortages, inflation, a shortage of medicines—although the basic condition of the economy remained depressed. For the regime, 986 had some benefits. It stabilized the dinar and curbed the worst excesses of hyperinflation. It freed up additional billions for benefits and salaries for its supporters and created a miniboom in contracts for private entrepreneurs favored by the family. It gave the regime more leverage in the international community through its ability to offer oil and purchasing contracts to UN members.

Although 986 was renewed in July and again in December of 1997, it was clear that the plan was not working well and that Iraq desperately needed more humanitarian relief. On 20 February 1998 the UN passed an expanded version of 986: Resolution 1153. This resolution permitted Iraq to raise its oil exports from $2 billion each six months to $5.2 billion and allowed it to expand its imports from food and medicine to include infrastructure improvements for civilian needs, such as water purification and electricity. Finally, the futility of controlling oil exports was recognized, and in December 1999 the UN passed Resolution 1284, lifting all ceilings on Iraqi production and exports. A "smart sanctions" resolution, 1409, was passed in May 2002, greatly easing the import of civilian, but not military, goods.

TABLE 10.2 Growth of GDP, Population, and Per Capital GDP, 1997–2002

	1997	1998	1999	2000	2001	2002*
GDP (billions US$)	15.4	18	23.8	31.8	27.9	26.1
Population*	21.2	21.8	22.4	22.9	23.6	24.1
GDP Per Capita ($)	725	832	1,062	1,385	1,184	1.078

* Based on estimates.
SOURCES: London Economist, Economist Intelligence Unit (EIU), *Country Profile Iraq, 2002–2003* (London, 2003); EIU, *Quarterly Economic Report, Iraq*, 1 March 2003.

This easing of sanctions had several consequences. It softened but could not end, the acute humanitarian crisis so evident in 1995 and 1996, especially in food supplies and eventually in medicine, but some malnutrition remained and the fundamental causes of economic decline had not been addressed. For the regime, the adjustments were a boon, buying a lease on life. Many billions of dollars now flowed into Iraq, legally and illegally. The income helped stabilize the domestic situation by reducing inflation and easing domestic discontent. Iraq was also helped by an upturn in oil prices late in 1999. By 2000 Iraq was producing 2.5 million barrels per day and earning an estimated $31.5 billion. It was estimated that the regime was getting $1.6 billion in direct revenues to spend on supporters. By 2002, however, these earnings had dropped somewhat to a GDP of about $26 billion but were substantially ahead of what they had been in 1995. (See Tables 10.1 and 10.2.) Despite these gains, however, the ultimate goal—a return of Iraq's full control over its resources—had not been achieved.

In addition to increased oil revenues, the regime also managed, in succeeding years, to improve its political situation from the low point of Husain Kamil's defection. Although these gains, like those in the economy, were modest, they helped the regime survive but did not change the underlying political structure or dynamics.

Husain Kamil's Punishment

In one of the most bizarre episodes in the history of a family already replete with notoriety, Husain Kamil stunned much of the world by announcing in 1996 that he and his family were returning to Baghdad after having received a pardon from Saddam. Although the return was initially good news for the regime, repercussions from the subsequent "family punishment" would reveal once again the regime's brutality and its reversion to primitive customs.

There has been much speculation on why Husain Kamil returned, but most observers agree that the defector, a man used to power, wealth, and a high degree of control over others, was completely unable to slip into a quiet, obscure life of retirement. His situation in Amman also became increasingly untenable when it became clear that plans to rally the opposition around him would fail. Meanwhile, Saddam had exercised considerable pressure to reverse the defection and to get the Kamils—and especially his daughters—to return. On 20 February the party left by auto caravan for the border.

Whatever the arrangement and the expectations, the denouement was not long in coming. Both Husain and Saddam Kamil were summoned to the presidential palace in Baghdad, where Saddam Husain forced them to divorce his daughters.[35] Husain Kamil's relatives were rounded up and told that the stain committed by Husain Kamil and his family had to be expunged. They were then taken to Husain Kamil's family villa to witness the punishment. Inside the house were the two brothers—Husain and Saddam Kamil—their father, their sister, and her children. The security forces sent to exact the punishment consisted of relatives and members of Kamil's clan, so as to validate the claim that it was not a government action but family and tribal retribution, taken "privately."[36] Apparently the Kamils inside the villa had ample firepower, and beginning at sunrise, a battle ensued with periodic bursts of gunfire from inside and outside the villa. Two of the attackers were themselves killed as was everyone in the villa.

The Husain Kamil affair and the bizarre manner of its settlement shed public light once again on the "tribal" nature of the regime as well as its unsavory character. Although this settled the problem of the Kamil defection, it would not be long before another episode would focus more attention on the dysfunctional family governing Iraq.

The Assassination Attempt on Udayy

Early in the evening of 12 December 1996, Udayy drove through a major intersection of an upscale quarter of the city. While waiting at a stoplight, he and his escorts were attacked by a group in a carefully prepared assassination attempt. The group failed to kill Udayy, but they gravely wounded him and then sped away in a waiting vehicle.[37]

The attack removed Udayy from any public role for months and gave him permanent disabilities, virtually eliminating his prospects for succession to the top role in the state. He was released from the hospital in June 1997 and by 1998 had resumed his smuggling enterprises and management of his newspaper. In March 2000 he was elected to the National Assembly, but he had been effectively sidelined as successor. Instead, Qusayy more clearly moved into that position. Unlike Udayy, Qusayy was quiet, but he was equally ruthless and could be relied on to act behind the scenes without attracting public attention. By the end of the decade, Qusayy was essentially overseer of all key security functions, including Saddam's protection force, the Special Security Organization, and the Special Republican Guard. In all, Udayy's temporary removal from the political scene and the reduction in his influence probably helped regime survival, rather than the reverse.

Divisiveness Among the Kurds
The regime's lease on life was also helped by a series of events in the north during 1996 that enabled Saddam to drive a wedge between the Kurds and their US protectors and to put an end to the presence of the INC on Iraqi soil. While the Iraqi president was not the initiator of this process, he was well placed to take advantage of Kurdish divisiveness to achieve his ends and to strengthen his regime by reducing the Western presence in the north.

The opportunity arose in the context of continued fighting between the KDP and the PUK. This time outsiders intruded, stirring the already murky waters. The main culprit was a relative newcomer to the politics of northern Iraq, the Kurdistan Workers Party (Partiya Karkari Kurdistan, PKK), Turkey's radical Kurdish movement.[38]

By the mid–1990s, the PKK had become an important and destabilizing force in northern Iraq, occupying the high and inaccessible mountain territory along the northern border with Turkey. The PKK established relations with Iraq's Kurdish leaders, the KDP, and the PUK. After the KDP-PUK split, their ties with the PUK continued, despite attempts by Turkey and the United States to sever them.

The Iranians and the Syrians also entered the fray. The Iranians, like the Turks, had hostile Kurds based in northern Iraq, represented by the KDPI (Kurdish Democratic Party of Iran), based mainly in PUK territory near the Iranian border. Between 1992 and 1994, fighting between the KDPI and Iran had intensified, making PUK areas vulnerable to attack. In July 1995 the Iranians made a major incursion, in collusion with the PUK, into Kurdish territory. The incursion's ostensible purpose was to curb the activities of the KDPI. Some 5,000 Revolutionary Guard troops entered through PUK territory, advanced about forty miles inside the border, and stayed for seventy-two hours. When they departed, they reportedly left behind weapons for the PUK. These episodes were the prelude to serious renewed fighting between the two sides in mid-August.

In this fluid situation, the PKK moved decisively to disrupt the situation. In August 1995 it attacked the KDP. The attack was fierce and serious, across a wide front; it was supported logistically by the PUK, Iran, and Syria. Iran gave the PUK artillery support; according to the KDP, there was also participation by the Badr Brigade and some Revolutionary Guards.[39] In fact, the attack left Barzani in serious trouble and he was fearful he would be annihilated. This precipitated a definitive turn to Baghdad.

On 22 August Barzani wrote a letter to Tariq Aziz, openly asking the Iraqi government for help in removing the PUK from Arbil and easing the "foreign threat" (Iran) in the north. According to the KDP, it had given the United States previous warning it would turn to Baghdad if it did not get help, but the US administration did not take that threat seriously.[40]

The Attack on the North, 1996

On 31 August Iraqi forces, in conjunction with the KDP, attacked Arbil. Deploying mostly Republican Guard units, Baghdad succeeded in occupying the city. Under protection of the Iraqi forces, the KDP then routed the PUK. The Iraqis then rounded up hundreds of opposition forces and the army deserters the INC had been harboring. INC communications and electronic equipment was seized, as were the organization's files. Among these opposition prisoners, at least ninety-six were executed at a camp southeast of Arbil.[41] According to a PUK source, seven hundred opposition members were arrested.[42] About two hundred escaped to Salah al-Din.

For the PUK as well as the INC, the incursion was a major disaster. As the buildup of Iraqi forces had proceeded in the days prior to the attack, the PUK had been in touch with the United States and, according to PUK sources, had expected US support in stopping the Iraqi advance. This proved to be wishful thinking; none was forthcoming. As a result, the PUK deserted Arbil and the KDP took its place. One week later, KDP forces entered Sulaimaniyya. By 11 September the KDP controlled all of Iraqi Kurdistan to the Iranian border.

For the United States as well as the PUK, the Iraqi occupation of Arbil—though temporary—was a decisive defeat. It was a breach of the cease-fire, it brutally ended opposition operations by the INC and others in the north, and it set back US influence among the Kurds as well as stability in the north. Baghdad's move, at the invitation of the KDP, had given it a stronger foothold in the north, destroyed an opposition base, and positioned the regime for a "peaceful" return.

A coalition response was deemed essential, but it came not in the north but further south. An attack on the Iraqi troops advancing on Arbil was opposed by regional—and some international—allies since Baghdad was operating in its own country. Instead, on 2 September the United States launched forty-four cruise missiles on defense installations in the south. More important, the United States and Britain extended the No Fly Zone one degree of latitude north, up to the thirty-third parallel, virtually on the outskirts of Baghdad. However, the bombing and the extension of the No Fly Zone were controversial; the French refused to participate, and the Saudis and others in the Gulf refused to allow bombing from their territory, weakening the coalition position.

Even more important, US personnel and operations in the north were removed. As a result of the attack on Arbil and the shift in the KDP posture in the north, the Military Coordination Committee (MCC) was permanently evacuated from Zakhu, along with the American relief agency. With this exodus, the US presence in the north—civilian and military—ended. This represented a major victory for the regime, despite the expansion of the southern No Fly Zone.

In these circumstances, the United States needed to undertake some damage control in the north. At least it had to put a stop to further erosion and prevent Saddam from "creeping" back into the region. In mid-September Assistant Secretary of State Robert Pelletreau met in Ankara with Mas'ud al-Barzani. Both were interested in recouping their losses. An understanding was reached to keep Baghdad out of the north in return for renewed efforts of the United States and Turkey to keep the peace there.[43]

This new arrangement was conveyed to Baghdad. Not long after, the head of Iraqi intelligence went to Iran and talked to Rafsanjani. The result was a "green light" from Baghdad for the return of the PUK, together with all of the Kurds who had fled into Iran after the attack.

In a remarkable development, on 14 October 1996 the PUK recrossed the Iranian border in force, backed by the Iranians, and reached Sulaimaniyya's outskirts. The PUK pushed Barzani's thinly deployed forces back to Arbil. But the PUK received a strong warning from Baghdad to stop short of Arbil, which it did. When the cease-fire finally came into effect, the Kurdish area was effectively divided in two. This time the KDP had more territory, including the capital, Arbil. A meeting of the two combatants in Ankara, under US auspices, provided for a cease-fire.

Each of the parties, and its neighbors, got something out of the settlement. Iran had wanted to thwart US influence in the north. It was unable to achieve this, but the return of the PUK to its traditional area, and its subsequent dependence on Iran, balanced the US and the KDP influence. The Turks, more interested in supporting the government in Baghdad than in fostering any independent movement in the north, gained even more. Indeed, they now became the actual peacekeepers in much of the north, especially in KDP territory. The Turks, and their supporters in northern Iraq, became responsible for security, replacing the United States and the departing MCC. The United States, although it had lost the assets—human and physical—among the opposition it supported and had its credibility damaged in the process, was able to help stabilize the north and preserve a dominant influence in the Kurdish area that Baghdad could do little to reverse. Baghdad achieved a foothold in Arbil and rid itself of the INC and the US presence in the north.

The Foreign Dimension, 1996–2003

Events in the north strengthened Saddam and the regime—marginally. So, too, did acceptance of Resolution 986, which eventually brought more money into the government's coffers. But despite these positive developments, the onerous restrictions on Iraq's sovereignty and development persisted. For the remainder of the its life, the regime turned its attention to eliminating these constraints. Although it was not able to remove the No Fly Zones or sanctions, it finally had some success with inspections, at least until 2002, when it was obliged to reverse course.

The End of UNSCOM
By 1996 UNSCOM, according to its chairman, Rolf Ekeus, had found "all the big things,"[44] including most of the nuclear, CW, and missile programs. But there were numerous elements for which there was still no accounting,

including some missiles, some VX nerve agent, and the entire biological weapons program. Documentation on these elements, it was assumed, was hidden in private homes, palaces, and other places difficult if not impossible to discern—or to enter. UNSCOM focused, increasingly, on Saddam Husain's concealment mechanisms. This inevitably led to UNSCOM's probing of Iraq's inner sanctums of security. Not surprisingly, Iraqis increasingly accused UNSCOM of spying for the United States and Israel and threatening its security and survival.

In 1997 this controversy sharpened. Iraq, determined to protect its elaborate security system at all costs, now became more willing to engage in a confrontational approach. UNSCOM also became more confrontational as Ekeus stepped down as UNSCOM's director and was succeeded by Richard Butler, an Australian arms-control expert who was more direct and less diplomatic than his predecessor. By this time, Iraq was on a collision course with the United States and UNSCOM.

The final countdown for UNSCOM began in August 1998, when a month-long crisis began. On 5 August Iraq demanded a restructuring of the sanctions regime and stopped cooperation with UNSCOM. This episode precipitated a rising debate over inspections and US policy in the US media and Congress. In the course of this debate, the issue of espionage emerged in full view when it became apparent that UNSCOM had been cooperating with Israel on intelligence and using US intelligence intercepts. This admission added fuel to the fire. Finally, at the end of October, Iraq announced that its cooperation with UNSCOM was at an end.

The next confrontation was not long in coming. In mid-November another UNSCOM inspection was scheduled to test Iraqi compliance, and Iraq immediately balked at handing over documents. This time UNSCOM teams were evacuated from Iraq and on 19 December, the United States, supported by the United Kingdom, responded with a major bombing campaign, Operation Desert Fox.

Operation Desert Fox was the most massive military strike on Iraq since Desert Storm, but its targets were more political than military. It was aimed at Saddam's nerve center—his concealment and security mechanisms—and secondarily at some key military facilities. Most indicative of the political aims were the strikes on seven or eight of Saddam Husain's palaces. The real long-term military damage was probably limited, but the main message was political—an ability to target key regime facilities, including those inhabited by Saddam Husain. But the strike also revealed weaknesses in the coalition. While

Kuwait, Oman, and Bahrain allowed use of their bases for the strike, Saudi Arabia did not, and most of the Arab world opposed the strike. So, too, did Russia, France, and many other European states. Moreover, the strike effectively ended UNSCOM, a major setback for the arms-control program. After 1998, Iraq was left free of any inspection system, a major gain for the regime.

The gain was not to last, however. In retrospect, the absence of a satisfactory settlement of the WMD issue and the withdrawal of inspectors would prove to be the Achilles heel of the regime's foreign policy. The year 2001 brought an entirely new international environment. In Washington a new, more hard-line administration took power, and in September a terrorist attack on America would dramatically change US policy toward Iraq. In a new climate of vulnerability, the US administration now adopted "regime change" in Baghdad as its policy. Seeking a justification for such a shift, the new administration found it in Iraq's breach of UN resolution 687, on WMD. Had the inspection regime still been in place or had Iraq cooperated more fully on disarmament, the United States would have had more difficulty justifying its subsequent attack on Iraq; nor would its fears of Iraq's activities been so acute. But the events of September 11 and the successful US military campaign to remove the Taliban regime in Afghanistan turned US attention to Iraq, its possible collusion in terrorism, and its WMD capacity. By 2002 the United States and United Kingdom were pursuing a policy of regime change, using the breach in inspections as an opening wedge. In November 2002 the UN passed resolution 1441, which accused Iraq of a "material breach" of the cease-fire and demanded the return of inspectors and immediate and full cooperation. Attempting to stave off a worse fate, Iraq accepted, and in November UNMOVIC returned to Iraq. However, its work was short-lived, its findings inconclusive. Although Iraq extended some cooperation, it was not sufficient to satisfy the United States or to stave off the eventual attack in March 2003. Ultimately, the inspections issue ended by turning the cold war into a hot one.

Remaining Cease-Fire Constraints
Despite ending inspections, Iraq still faced the No Fly Zones, restrictions on air travel, and continued political isolation. Iraq had no success in challenging the No Fly Zones; indeed its challenges worsened the situation. From 1999 on, bombing attacks in both zones were frequent. By 2003 the No Fly Zones were being systematically used to degrade Iraq's air defenses and other military assets.

However, Iraqis did have some success in challenging the UN ban on air travel and in breaking down their diplomatic and political isolation. Iraq announced on 20 August 1997 that Iranians would be allowed once again to visit the holy sites in Karbala and Najaf, opening the country to pilgrim traffic. In December of the same year, the UAE asked for—and received—permission from the UN to open a shipping line in the Gulf between the two countries; the line carried passengers as well as goods. On 17 August 2000 Iraq announced that it was reopening Saddam International Airport. From then on, a stream of international carriers landed in Baghdad, with or without UN permission. Most carried humanitarian goods, presumably allowed under sanctions, but they also brought international celebrities, dignitaries, and sports figures, making the point that much of the world wanted to end sanctions on air travel and Iraq's isolation. By 2001 there were regularly scheduled flights between Damascus and Baghdad and unscheduled flights to Amman, clearly marking the end of any practical enforcement of an air travel ban on Iraq.

Civilian air traffic was accompanied by an upsurge in international business as the expanded Oil-for-Food program loosened the purse strings on money and goods flowing into Iraq. The pipeline through Syria opened in November 2000, and before long Iraq was exporting 100,000 barrels per day to Syria. Oil continued to flow to Jordan and Turkey. The increase in trade and travel and the number of high-level officials willing to visit Iraq and deal with the regime was a clear indication of the erosion of Iraq's isolation and the sanctions regime, as well as the near-total disintegration of the wartime coalition. By 2002, improving relations with the Arab world was a necessity in the face of an aggressive new US policy. An Arab League summit in Beirut in March 2002 seemed to reintegrate Iraq into the Arab community; even Kuwait and Saudi Arabia were willing to make accommodating gestures in return for Iraq's official promise to respect their sovereignty and territorial integrity. In the end, however, Iraq's ability to martial support from the Arab world against a concerted effort from the United States to isolate it failed.

The Domestic Situation, 1996–2003

Through all of the international challenges, the regime survived, but its health and long-term prospects were not good. This could be seen in three interrelated areas: its lopsided and ossified political system, as yet unreformed;

its stagnating economy and eroding social structure; and the weakening of Iraq's national cohesion.

Political Structure

The regime had consolidated its power at the top of the political structure, but it still rested on increasingly shaky pillars. One of these was its continued reliance on a network of kin and clan. By 2003 Saddam's clan occupied central positions in all key security and military institutions. The Special Protection Force, now several thousand strong, were almost wholly from the Albu Nasir tribe. No less than half of Republican Guard division commanders were from the Albu Nasir or allied tribal groups.[45] On the Regional Command of the party in 1998, seven out of seventeen members were Albu Nasir or clan allies.[46] Though less dominant in other areas, member of these tribal groups also occupied important posts in the bureaucracy. This gave the regime a kinship network of considerable depth, but it also brought the political system back to premodern modes of operating.

A second feature of the political structure was its narrow ethnic and sectarian base, unrepresentative of the country as a whole and even of its urban middle class. The leadership structure in 1998 provides a good snapshot of these imbalances. Among top leaders (the RCC and the Regional Command) some 61 percent were Arab *sunni*, 28 percent Arab *shi'i*, and 6 percent each Kurdish and Christian. This substantially underrepresented both *shi'a* and Kurds. There was better integration of *shi'a* and Kurds at lower levels of government, probably reflecting the actual mix of these communities among Iraq's middle class. But these were not the levels at which decisions were made. (See Table A.2.)

Not surprisingly, there was also an imbalance in the geographic area from which the leadership was drawn. In the RCC and the Regional Command of 1998, some 61 percent came from the Arab *sunni* triangle northwest of Baghdad. Almost a quarter came from Tikrit; only 6 percent came from Baghdad, Iraq's most integrated city. Few came from the northern (mainly Kurdish and Turkman) and the southern (mainly *shi'i*) areas.[47] By the end of the decade, the Ba'th leadership failed not only to represent broad regions of the country and certain ethnic and sectarian groups but to adequately incorporate the most important social force in modern Iraq—the urban, educated middle class that was modern in its outlook and aspirations.

The second pillar of the regime—its institutional structures—though rebuilt after 1991, still remained in a weakened state. The Ba'th Party provides a good example. Starting with the collapse in 1991 and continuing through the rest of the decade, the party saw a decline in its base in the countryside. By 2003 it may have lost as much as 70 percent of its membership, weakening its capacity as an instrument of control and social engineering.[48]

Nor had the party been able to replenish its leading ranks with new, younger members, despite several attempts to rebuild and recruit members. The Regional Command of 1998 shows an aging group: Almost all hailed from the generation that had joined the party just before or just after 1958. Their longevity in office was also striking: Some two-thirds had been on the command over sixteen years. In fact, by 2003 the party had clearly lost any appeal to youth or the population at large and was mainly an instrument for career advancement. In May 2001 the party made an effort at outreach, and a new Regional Command (RL) was elected at the twelfth party congress. However, the two most notable younger-generation members elected were children of top party leaders. One was Saddam's son and anointed heir, Qusayy, also made head of the party's military bureau, and the other was Dr. Huda Ammash, the first female on the RL and a professor of biology, reportedly connected to the biological weapons (BW) program. She was the daughter of the veteran military Ba'thist Salih Mahdi Ammash, ousted from power by Saddam in 1971.

The military arm of state was also far smaller and weaker than it had been in several decades, although it was still large by regional standards. By the end of the decade, Iraq had an active force of a little over 400,000, roughly 9.7 percent of the workforce.[49] However, much of that force was hollow. The chief backbone of the military was no longer the regular army but the better-equipped, better-trained Republican Guard, a seven-division corps of about 60,000 to 70,000. In addition to size reduction, other factors weakened the military. Chief among them was the international inspection system, which gradually destroyed much of its unconventional weapons. Over a decade of sanctions also took its toll on military modernization and the military's ability to acquire advanced technology. Morale and standards among the rank and file were reportedly low.

Moreover, it was clear that the military could no longer perform its chief function—defending the country's territorial integrity and its borders. In the north, it had been forced to withdraw from a substantial portion of Iraqi territory, leaving its governance to parties generally hostile to the central government. In this area, it had no control over Iraq's borders, which were crossed at will by both Turks and Iranians. In the south, the military was able to control its borders, but its control over the population was weak. In the air, Iraqi forces had lost control of two-thirds of Iraq's airspace. By 2003 the role of the military was reduced mainly to protecting the regime and the territory in the center. As repeated coup attempts had shown, its loyalty had to be constantly watched.

The bureaucracy also underwent considerable shrinkage. Figures show that in the 1990s, civil servants constituted 16.8 percent of the work force—the lowest number since the early 1970s. (See Table 7.3.) By the end of the decade there was ample evidence that the bureaucracy was crumbling. Incidents of petty—and not so petty—crime were rife. Corruption, usually severely punished under the Ba'th, grew apace, from the top of the bureaucracy to the bottom. Ordinary services, such as processing visas, securing passports, and getting licenses, required a bribe. The rapid fall in living standards meant that most civil servants and teachers now had to hold two and three jobs to make ends meet, with inevitable neglect of their official duties.

To supplement these deficiencies, the regime increasingly relied on the third pillar of its support system—the new economic elite that functioned in the gray area of the economy between legal and illegal economic activities. While this class was far smaller and more restricted than in the 1980s, by the end of the 1990s it had grown as more money flowed into Iraq under the Oil-for-Food resolution. In addition to entrepreneurs and those in the private sector, this class also included top-level members of the military, security, and civil service; the Ba'th Party; and the technocratic elite.[50] Not only was this elite well remunerated, but they skimmed profits from the system and engaged in economic activities in addition to their official duties.

Economic Stagnation and Social Decline

Decline in the political sector was more than matched in the economic and social arenas. The gradual elimination of oil export ceilings after 1996 increased the flow of goods and services to the public, but these gains were modest. They helped stem Iraq's economic downturn but could not reverse the decline that had taken place since 1990 (see Table 10.2). For example, by 2000, per-capita income (GDP) had risen to a little over $1,000, but it was still, at best, less than half of what it had been in 1990. The humanitarian crisis eased but did not end. In 2000 an FAO report found that Iraqis were averaging about 2,500 calories a day[51] but that 21 percent of children under five were still underweight, and 9 percent suffered from acute malnutrition, raising questions about the impact on their future ability to learn and acquire the social skills necessary to compete in the twenty-first century.[52] By 2003 the malnutrition trend had been arrested, but at a high level. It was half what it had been in 1996 but double the rates in 1991. Though slow, there was some improvement in medical care as well.[53]

The same was true throughout the economy: some modest revival but not enough to repair the decade-long ravages. In agriculture the government made some efforts to encourage farmers to expand production, but with mixed results. Farmers had shifted from cash cropping to subsistence, while privatization favored only a few. Infrastructure was badly neglected. Although there was some expansion in acreage, yields did not substantially improve, and in the last years of the 1990s, Iraq suffered from serious drought. Between 1997 and 2001, wheat production declined by half, and barley by almost as much, although livestock and milk production made modest gains. When oil revenues increased in 1996, Iraq once again turned to agricultural imports. Between 1995 and 2000, wheat imports shot up from 480 tons to 2,900; rice from 225 to 1,200.[54] By the 1990s, only 13 percent of the population was engaged in agriculture. (See Table A.3.)

Industrial production also continued to limp along at levels well below the 1980s, although by March 2003 there had been some increase in local manufacture of goods, such as tires, textiles, vegetable oils, and chemicals. Only 40 percent of installed electric power was available in 2000, with frequent blackouts throughout the country. Although oil production, for example, rose to about 2.4 million barrels per day by 2001, the reservoirs had suffered long-term damage from years of mismanagement (see Table 10.1). Infrastructure, including pipelines and pumping stations, were in poor shape. But continued exploration had revealed Iraq's enormous potential as a future producer, if its political problems could be solved. By 2003, Iraq's proven reserves had reached 112 billion barrels (11 percent of the world's total).

The damage to the education system was also severe. The schools suffered disrepair as did supplies, such as textbooks, computers, and lab equipment. One report claimed that of 250 primary schools in the center and south of the country, over 80 percent were in poor or critical condition.[55] Credible figures show that the literacy rate, which reached 67 percent in 1980, fell to about 57 percent in 2001.[56] In the same years, school enrollment fell from 67 to 50 percent. Thus one of the major gains of the early

Ba'th period, like industrial development, was dramatically reversed (see Table A.4).

These trends were accompanied by social erosion. Much of the egalitarian structure of the early Ba'th period had disappeared. By the early twenty-first century, income and status disparities within Iraq's social structure were much higher than they had been in the 1970s. A new upper and affluent class emerged but with a lifestyle out of reach of the professional middle class. Meanwhile those merely on salaries could not keep up. The ordinary teacher, middle-level bureaucrat, and lower-level officer saw their assets depleted and their status lowered. Unskilled workers simply sank deeper into poverty. Instead of upward social mobility, Iraq now saw downward mobility and the shrinkage of the middle class.

Regional disparities grew, as well, with political as well as social implications. Lopsided urbanization continued to benefit Baghdad and the central region. By 2003, Baghdad was a megalopolis of over 5 million; Baghdad province, essentially the city and its environs had over 30 percent of Iraq's population. In contrast, as a result of wars, sanctions, and neglect, the northern and southern provinces had lost population. By 2003 the three autonomous Kurdish provinces (Dahuk, Arbil, and Sulaimaniyya) had about 13 percent of Iraq's population; the *shi'i* provinces of the south, including Basra, had just about a third; and the central provinces, including Baghdad, Ninawa, Salah al-Din, Anbar, and Diyala, half. The ethnically mixed Ta'mim had about 4 percent. Through its control of the central provinces—and by weakening and neglecting the north and the south—the regime maintained control of the country. (See Table A.1.)

One of the most important sectors of the population to be affected by these developments was Iraq's youth. The 1997 census shows that over half of the population (56 percent) was below the age of nineteen, meaning that an absolute majority of the population had been born and raised after Saddam came to power as president in 1979. His is the only system they have ever known.

These young people, and the generation slightly older that came to maturity in the 1980s and 1990s, have known only wars and hardship; many feel they have been deprived of a future. With fewer tools than their predecessors, they are now faced with rebuilding a nation that has declined. Anecdotal evidence suggests that this generation may be much more opportunistic—even cynical—than its predecessors and, not surprisingly, mainly interested in survival. Schoolwork and academic achievement have been downgraded; corruption has taken a toll. There may also be alienation from the West, and especially the United States, the result of sanctions and the regime's propaganda. There is much evidence, especially among college students, of a turn to religion, including Islamic dress, not prevalent among the younger generation in the 1970s. This was encouraged by the regime, which allowed more fundamentalist views to take root among *sunni* as well as *shi'i* youth.

Eroding National Vision

Decline in the political and economic sectors was also reflected in the chief project of the Ba'th Party—creating a viable nation-state and the vision to go with it. Declining aspirations were seen in the regime's own ideology, directed mainly at the Arab population in the center. By 2003 the early Ba'thist drive to remake Iraq and the Arab world had disappeared. Instead, the regime's pronouncements, including Saddam's speeches, increasingly reflected Iraq's declining status and its "postponed" future. As an indication of how little the regime could offer its population, Iraqis were constantly encouraged to manifest "steadfastness" in the face of adversity. Pan-Arabism and Iraqi leadership of the Arab world were still given lip service, but in the absence of much meaningful help from the Arab world since the 1990 invasion of Kuwait, such leadership appeared increasingly illusory.

Iraq's public rhetoric as well as the regime's actions also tilted heavily in the direction of Islam. The struggle against the United States and the United Kingdom was referred to as a *jihad,* and the population was encouraged to turn to religion. The emphasis on Islam, begun during the Iran-Iraq war as a means of propitiating the *shi'a,* grew in the 1990s as the regime's policy and the sanctions regime required ever greater sacrifices. This may have been designed as an escape mechanism for a weary population or as a response to the growing strength of Islamic movements among youth. Better to seize control of the movement and help direct it than to have it turn against the regime. In 1994 the regime banned alcohol in public places and encouraged the building of mosques in a new "faith campaign." Murals began to portray Saddam praying. Money was set aside to construct the largest mosque in the world. By 2003 Islam was firmly embedded in the regime's ideology and symbolism.

But the main thrust of the regime's message to the center—and the rest of the country—was its control over society and the need to defend the country and the regime against foreign enemies. A typical fifth-grade text exhorted students to be loyal to the state, the "revolution," the party, and the "struggler" president, Saddam Husain.[57] The main vehicle for expressing national identity was the military, and students were exhorted to join paramilitary formations. Overall, patriotism was defined through the values of sacrifice, honor, and courage. This vision of Iraq's future, emphasizing sacrifices and defense against enemies, represented the siege mentality of the regime but was not likely to have widespread appeal to future generations.

If these weaknesses were apparent at the center, they were glaringly evident in the Kurdish north and the *shi'i* south, where erosion of the national consensus had reached a high point.

The Challenge to Consensus in the North

In the north, the Kurds remained separated from the rest of the country, with more self-rule than at any time in Iraq's modern history. In areas under their control, Kurds continued to strengthen the institutions—and the ideology—of self-rule, although their actual achievements often fell far short of their aspirations.

Although some civil strife continued between the KDP and the PUK during 1997, by March 1998 a new turning point was reached and the situation appeared to improve. Representatives met frequently to establish areas of cooperation and to coordinate education, administration, and other activities. Both parties continued to govern their separate areas.

The revenues from customs dues on truck traffic from Turkey were increasingly pumped into the KDP region, giving it an air of prosperity. Some of this money was also spent in Arbil on roads, sewers, and other public works. PUK territory still had less revenue and more difficulty in paying the salaries of bureaucrats, but it now received income from the Oil-for-Food program, supplemented by remittances from Kurds outside and trade with Iran. It made some modest advances in establishing local industry.

Halabja and the surrounding area in the eastern portion of Kurdish territory remained largely under the control of the IMIK and was the least developed. Eventually, the IMIK was split, and its hold over this area was undermined. At the end of the 1990s, the IMIK was increasingly radicalized by younger, more militant Kurds returning from *jihad* in Afghanistan. The formation of the Jund al-Islam (the Army of Islam) in August 2001, later renamed the Ansar al-Islam (Supporters of Islam) effectively demolished the IMIK. After 2001 remnants of the Afghan forces, some reportedly connected to Qa'ida, infiltrated the area on the Iranian border east of Halabja.

By this time the border territory was a no-man's land dominated by radical Islamic groups and, in a "failed state" syndrome, was totally out of PUK control.[58]

By 2003 the Kurdish area was doing better economically than much of the central and southern portion of Iraq. International aid groups and the UN, with direct access to the north, had done a good job in distributing aid. A decade after the *intifada,* many villages had been wholly or partially resettled, health facilities revived, and some trade installed. Three universities operated in Kurdish territory and statistics showed an infant mortality rate better than that before the Gulf War.

The north was also freer than areas under Baghdad's control. Kurds established their own Kurdish-language newspapers and TV stations. A new generation of Kurdish journalists emerged. More important, the Kurdish parties allowed cable TV from outside to be broadcast in their region, giving their population an unprecedented view of the outside world, unavailable elsewhere in Iraq. Both parties also maintained offices and representatives in Turkey, Europe, and the United States. This gave the Kurds a window on the outside world and crucial contacts with the West, which they used to good advantage.

Despite these advances, the situation in the north remained an anomaly. The Kurds, while governing themselves, had no independent status or international recognition. Their neighbors kept a tight clamp on their borders. Like the rest of Iraq, Kurds remained under the international embargo. Moreover, they had to rely on the protection of foreign powers for their continued separate existence. The Kurds also failed to attract a return of their exile population and continued to suffer an outflow of population.

Despite these difficulties, however, the decade of the 1990s, allowed a separate Kurdish identity to take root in the north. A good example of this was found in the curriculum of the school system, where new lessons in Kurdish culture and heroes were designed to instill loyalty to a new entity—Kurdistan. Although students were taught that they live in Iraq, the focus was on Iraqi Kurdistan, their real homeland, which included not only the three provinces of Dahuk, Arbil, and Sulaimaniyya but also Kirkuk, with its oil. By 2003 this curriculum was taught in Kurdish in most, though not all, schools, although Arabic and English were taught as second languages, increasingly raising the question of how well the new generation of Kurds would be able to communicate with Iraqi Arabs in a future, more unified state.

The Challenge to Consensus in the South

In the south, problems of identity were not as severe. The regime remained in control, but much of the population continued to be alienated from government. Clashes between the central government and dissidents continued right up to the end of the regime. The constant unrest—though at too low a level to threaten the regime—kept tensions alive.

Opposition from the clerics continued, as well, and also met with continued persecution. In 1998 two senior clerics were killed. Most significant was the killing of Muhammad Sadiq al-Sadr, the chief *marji'* who had been hand picked by the regime because it had reason to believe he would cause no trouble. He asked for the release of *shi'a* held as political prisoners, and his sermons became increasingly popular, drawing larger and larger crowds, always a danger for the regime. It was not long before these activities were considered an unacceptable threat, and on 19 February 1999 Sadr and two of his sons were killed in an unexplained attack by unknown assailants. This time the regime faced some serious *shi'i* uprisings in response, turning Sadr into a martyr for the cause. The Sadr episode revealed that even by the end of the decade, the embers of the 1991 rebellion still burned and could flare up at any time.

Nonetheless, the regime took some steps to propitiate the south. Pilgrim traffic to the holy cities was reopened by agreement with Iran in 1997. The flow of pilgrims helped the economic situation in the holy cities and gave a boost to the clergy. The economy of the south also saw some benefits from the flow of oil after acceptance of Resolution 986. But overall, the south—especially the once-flourishing port of Basra—remained relatively neglected, hard hit by war and sanctions.

Whereas *shi'a* inside Iraq could not express opposition views or set forth alternative visions of the state, those in exile could. Among these expatriates, a new, revisionist version of Iraqi history appeared in which the dominant theme was discrimination against *shi'a* by sunni-dominated governments based on false suspicions of their loyalty to the state. Most indicative of the new *shi'i* consensus was a *shi'i* gathering summoned by the Khu'i Foundation in London in 1993 that included Communists, secular liberals, clerics, and members of religious parties. This group made clear that several decades of repression had, indeed, created a new *shi'i* consciousness that would not easily submit to continued *sunni* political dominance. Within this diverse *shi'i* group, however, there was no single formula on which they could unite: Some were religious, others secular and liberal. They were united only by a common sense of oppression and victimization and exclusion from governance. Loyalty to the Iraqi state, however, was not in question.

As these different expressions of national identity indicated, the task of creating a common vision for Iraq—one that most of its diverse inhabitants could accept—had suffered setbacks, some of them severe, since 1990. The chief problem lay with the Kurdish parties in control of northern territory, although some Kurds continued to participate in the central government. Even among the *shi'a*, however, communal identity had sharpened in the face of persecution and an increasingly narrow *sunni*-based government in Baghdad. Indeed this government, as its own philosophy indicated, was increasingly on the defensive and almost certainly no longer represented the increasingly well educated middle class to whom its Ba'th ideology had been originally designed to appeal.

The Challenge from Opposition Abroad

The regime also had to be concerned about the exile opposition, now ensconced in the West. Although the INC continued to be controversial in the United States, Ahmad Chalabi proved more durable than expected. After his removal from the north in 1996, he turned to the US Congress, where he managed to get new support and new funding. In May 1998 Congress appropriated $5 million for the opposition to spend on media and other outreach activities, and in October the Iraq Liberation Act, authorizing $97 million to be drawn down from the defense budget, was signed by the president. These funds were to include military training. Gradually, the US administration shifted to a policy of "regime change" in Iraq, although support for this goal was still modest under the Clinton administration; indeed, very few of the funds appropriated were spent up until 2001.

This outside opposition also had its vision of a new Iraq, mainly grounded in liberal democratic ideals and the development of constitutional structures and processes, including federalism to accommodate Kurdish and possibly *shi'i* demands for cultural recognition. But the outside opposition still remained divided on power sharing and other issues. A number were opposed to taking Western help and did not want Western interference in Iraq's domestic affairs; others were still dependent on Iranian support. The very diversity of views within this opposition proved, if proof were needed, how difficult it would be to replace the Ba'th vision, as well as its organization.

A Decade of Stagnation

The aftermath of the Gulf War was the worst period in Iraq's modern history. The regime's repression, the harsh and long-lasting cease-fire terms, and the *intifada* and its outcome weakened state structures and the cohesion of the nation-state. In the north about 10 percent of the country—the self-governing Kurdish area—was left free of central government control. In the south, government control was weak and needed constant reinforcement. Continual dissidence in the center revealed intense unhappiness with the regime. The modest economic and social revival toward the end of the decade was insufficient to undo the damage of a decade of sanctions or to set the country on a path of future growth and normalcy.

Meanwhile, the sanctions and the regime's own policies eroded Iraq's wealth and its resources and set back its economic development for years. The exodus of millions of Iraqis and the depletion of the middle class have deprived Iraq of much of its best talent and experience, while leaving those who remain isolated and with lower standards of living, health, and education and little exposure to the outside world. Although the repressive regime survived through 2003, it rested on an exceedingly narrow power base, dominated by one community—Arab *sunnis*—and only a small portion of that community, at that. The struggle with the West—now narrowing mainly to the United States and the United Kingdom—continued. US policy, in its intransigence and hostility focused, until 2001, on maintaining key cease-fire restrictions on Iraq and, if possible, encouraging a change of regime. This was to change dramatically after September 2001. The terrorist attacks on the United States fundamentally altered its foreign policy, first toward Qa'ida and then toward Iraq. By the end of 2001, it was already clear that a new administration under George W. Bush would focus, not on containment of Iraq, but on regime change and that the long tenure of Saddam Husain's regime was seriously threatened. In the year and a half remaining to the Iraqi regime, Saddam attempted to make adjustments in foreign policy and at home in an effort to fend off the gathering storm from abroad, but they were to prove entirely insufficient. It would not be long before his regime would come to a swift end.

EPILOGUE

On 20 March 2003 the United States, Great Britain, and a small "coalition of the willing" launched a military attack on Iraq and, in three short weeks, ended the regime of Saddam Husain. An occupation of Iraq by Western—mainly US and UK—forces followed. This event, while not unexpected, opened an entirely new chapter in Iraq's modern history. The outcome of this dramatic change cannot be predicted—indeed Iraq's future is likely to be uncertain for some time—but it is clear that a long and largely destructive era has come to a close and that a new one has begun.

The forces that brought the war and the fall of the regime were largely external to Iraq. On 11 September 2001 attacks by small but well-organized groups of terrorists destroyed the World Trade Center in New York and damaged the Pentagon in Washington, DC, killing nearly 3,000 civilians and disrupting the global economy. The perpetrators, led by Islamic extremist Usama bin Ladin and his Qa'ida (Base) network, fundamentally changed the international environment and US foreign policy. In the wake of this shock, President George W. Bush declared a "war on terrorism." A new US strategy made preemptive military strikes against regimes that threatened the United States part of the US political arsenal. While the United States first turned its attention to Afghanistan and the removal of the Taliban regime, which had been protecting bin Ladin, it soon focused on Iraq and the potential threat that could be posed by weapons of mass destruction (WMD) in the hands of a hostile dictator like Saddam Husain. It made clear that it would seek regime change in Baghdad—by peaceful means if possible, by military action if necessary.

In seeking regime change in Iraq, the United States gave several shifting rationales. One was a link between Usama bin Ladin's network and the Iraqi regime, which would have implicated Iraq in the September 11 attacks. However, the administration failed to make a compelling case on this account and this rationale was soon downplayed. More convincing were arguments centered on Iraq's continued possession of WMD, which could not be verified or eliminated due to the absence of inspectors. A third argument cited the regime's appalling human rights record and the benefits that would accrue from a more peaceful and democratic leadership in Baghdad. Indeed, some put forth a new and ambitious agenda—creating a democracy in Iraq that would provide a model for the region and shift the very parameters of regional politics.

Inside Iraq, little changed. Iraq continued to deny possession of WMD and was cautious not to provoke the international community on this issue. Without inspections, however, no one could be certain what Iraq possessed. Meanwhile Iraq's human rights record was put under greater international scrutiny, as the United States, now joined by the United Kingdom, gave greater support to the exile opposition. But it was in the United States that the real change of policy took place.

The March Toward War

In his State of the Union address in January 2002, President Bush singled out Iraq—along with Iran and North Korea—as part of an "axis of evil" and a threat. However, it took over a year of preparation for the new Bush policy of regime change to materialize. Increasingly in public debates and the press, "regime change" in Iraq—even by military means and unilaterally, if necessary—became the dominant topic. A public hearing in the Senate in the summer of 2001 elevated the debate to a national level. In September Bush took his case to the UN General Assembly, and in November the UN Security Council unanimously passed Resolution 1441 demanding that Iraq restore inspections on rigorous terms. Meanwhile, the United States, in collaboration with the United Kingdom, began a quiet military buildup in the Gulf. As the troop mobilization grew, more was heard of the need for action sooner rather than later. Although outside the United States there was widespread opposition to the war, expectations of a military campaign mounted.

In an attempt to avoid military attack, Iraq accepted Resolution 1441, and in November 2002 a new inspections regime, led by Hans Blix, the head of UNMOVIC and a former IAEA director, began its work. Iraq cooperated with inspectors but its report to the UN added nothing new. Nor did those of Blix. Despite deep divisions in the international community between those wishing to continue with inspections (mainly France, Germany, and Russia) and those impatient to bring the issue to closure while forces were in place to accomplish this (mainly the United States and United Kingdom), the United States decided to act on the authority of UNSC Resolution 1441. On 18 March President Bush gave the Iraqi leader forty-eight hours to leave the country, a clear warning to all that war would follow. On 20 March the air attack on Baghdad began. Shortly thereafter, coalition forces landed in Basra and began their march to Baghdad.

The Three-Week War

Operation Enduring Freedom, as the US campaign was called, was over in virtually three weeks. Despite a few problems, the military action accomplished its mission with remarkable swiftness and relatively few civilian casualties. Precision air strikes on regime strongholds in Baghdad were accompanied by the rapid movement of ground forces from Basra north to Baghdad, essentially avoiding the cities. By 8 April US forces had entered the capital. The end of the regime was marked, symbolically, by the toppling of a bronze statute of Saddam Husain in Firdaus Square by enthusiastic crowds. Although it took some days longer to secure the city, the regime of Saddam Husain had effectively ended.

Not all went according to plan, however. Saddam Husain and his family disappeared and, at present writing, his whereabouts—even whether he was dead or alive—were unknown. Remnants of the regime, particularly in the *sunni* triangle, continued attacks on coalition soldiers after major military operations ceased. Although much of the population greeted the change of regime with immense relief, the attitude of the population toward their new "liberators" was decidedly cautious, leaving open the question of how much cooperation the Americans would get in reshaping the new Iraq.

The Aftermath

The immediate aftermath of the military victory bore out the immense difficulty of the task facing the United States and the United Kingdom in securing the peace and replacing the totalitarian dictatorship. The fall of Saddam Husain and his security apparatus was followed by widespread looting and rampaging. The damage was considerable. Priceless treasures from the National Museum, including world-famous antiquities, were stolen, and much of the National Library was burned and destroyed. In addition, substantial portions of Iraq's infrastructure—hospitals, schools, the electricity grid, oil facilities—were badly damaged, creating a major problem for reconstruction. The degree and spread of the damage—especially in intellectual property—revealed just how little sense of civic responsibility there was in Iraq after decades of misrule. A restoration of law and order in the aftermath was also slow in coming. Meanwhile, in local areas, a variety of new Iraqi leaders, from junior *shi'i* clerics to tribal leaders and former Ba'thists, emerged to claim a place in the new political order, indicating a revival of grassroots politics and a new struggle for power. They were now joined by leaders of the exile opposition, like Ahmad Chalabi, who returned to Baghdad to establish a base in the country. All of this activity indicated that without a relatively firm hand at the national helm in Baghdad, Iraq could soon begin to fragment into its regional and local components.

Iraq's New Chapter

At present writing, Iraq's future direction is uncertain. Whether Iraq as a country can take a new direction and begin to achieve some of its obvious potential or whether it will become mired, once again, in problems that have plagued it in the past is a question that cannot yet be answered. The fall of the Saddam Husain regime and the imposition of foreign rule, however, suggest that some change will come to Iraq. But the forces for change will have to contend with strong cultural and historical traditions and—at least in recent history—a sorry performance record. To bring about a more stable—and equitable—political and social system, the new rulers of Iraq, be they foreign or domestic, will have to address the three tasks that have bedeviled Iraqi politics since its founding and have been identified in this book.

The first will be the consolidation of Iraq's national cohesion based on a greater degree of consensus than has prevailed in the past. How Iraqis handle this issue will determine whether the nation-state will survive and move forward or a more decentralized polity—even a collapse of the state—will ensue. To recapture a sense of nationhood, Iraq's ethnic and sectarian communities, its tribal and clan groups, and its once vigorous urban middle class must rekindle a sense of common purpose and destiny.

The second task is one of renewed economic and social development. Because of Iraq's favorable resource base this problem is more manageable, but Iraq has seen substantial erosion of its physical and human infrastructure. The decline in Iraq's education system, its isolation from intellectual advances abroad, and the depletion of its skilled middle class may take decades to restore. Even more important is the question of economic policy. Iraq, like most Gulf states, has had an oil-based rentier economy, in which oil revenues are captured by the state and dispensed to citizens. Can a new, market-based economy be developed, one that encourages initiative, spreads ownership more widely, and reduces the economic importance of government? If some economic diffusion does not take place, reduction in the power of the central government will be more difficult.

Along with economic development must go the development of civil society. This could be accomplished by strengthening previously existing professional associations (lawyers, teachers, jurists, journalists), labor unions, and women's groups in ways that help them reestablish professional standards and make them a buffer against arbitrary government. Civil society will also need to find ways to restore a sense of individual responsibility and wean a population away from its passivity and its dependence on government.

Third and most critical, Iraq must deal with multiple problems of governance, which have been at the heart of its difficulties and which are responsible for its present parlous state. It must develop both national and local institutions capable of representing various communities and classes as well as differing ideas and programs. Representation, however, will not be enough; the new institutions, and the leaders within them, will have to develop some of the skills and attitudes associated with governing in a more open society. These have been sorely lacking in Iraq. The secular, liberal tradition that most strongly supports these democratic principles in politics has not been absent in Iraq, but as this narrative indicates, it has been weak and has frequently lost out in the political process. To be reasonably effective, any new government will have to learn how to mobilize constituencies behind programs; to compromise with opponents and to tolerate losses. This is a matter not simply of institutions but of political culture and values that will take time to develop.

Lastly, one of the most important issues for Iraq's future is both new and old. This is the role of the outside power in generating change and establishing new institutions and modes of governing. The United States—with some help from allies such as the United Kingdom—has assumed the classic role of an imperialist power. It now faces the same dilemma as Britain in 1920. On one hand, it must assure that a modicum of US interests are satisfied; this means producing a leadership in Iraq that is willing to satisfy at least some US aims and goals, on WMD, on terrorism, and on relations with neighbors, including Israel. On the other hand, the United States has stated that it intends to create a more democratic government and more freedom for Iraqi citizens. What if these two goals conflict? Greater freedom may result in a leadership anxious for an end to occupation and committed to goals at odds with US interests. In the end, the British put few resources into Iraq and left early, only to have to reoccupy the country later, in 1941. Will the United States be willing to put the time, resources, and energy into "changing" Iraq? Or will it try to realize its goals with an economy of resources, and end up with little change? Above all, how much opposition will it encounter in a country with a strong tradition of anticolonialism? And will this opposition obstruct Iraqi cooperation in developing the political institutions and the new direction that Iraq needs?

In the short term, the foreign factor will be dominant in setting the parameters and direction of change. In the long term, however, it will be the Iraqis themselves who determine the future of their country. The fall of the Saddam Husain regime has provided an opportunity for change, but it is the vision, perception, and leadership of Iraqis that will determine how extensive the change will be and what direction it will take.

APPENDIX

TABLE A.1 Distribution of Iraq's Population by Region, 1977–2002 (percentages)			
	1977	1987	2002
Central Governorates			
Total	47.5	48.8	50.8
Baghdad	26.5	23.5	32
Ninawa, Salah al-Din, Anbar, Diyala	21	24.4	18.8
Southern Governorates			
Total	35.8	36	31.8
Basra	8.4	5.3	8.1
Babil, Wasit, Karbala, Najaf, Qadisiyya, Maysan, Muthanna, Dhi Qar	27.4	30.7	23.7
Northern Governorates			
Total	16.5	16	17.4
Ta'mim	4.1	3.7	3.9
Dahuk, Arbil, Sulaimaniyya	12.4	12.3	13.5

SOURCES: Iraq, Ministry of Planning, *AAS 1978*, p. 26; *AAS 1992*, p. 43. London Economist, Economic Intelligence Unit, *Iraq, 2002–2003,* Country Profile (London, 2003), p. 18.

TABLE A.2 Ethnic and Sectarian Background of Political Leaders, 1948–1998

	Arab Sunnis	*Arab Shi'a*	*Kurd/ Turkman*	*Other[a] unknown*	*Total*
Old Regime 1948–1958					
Upper level[b]	24 (61%)	8 (21%)	6 (15%)	1 (3%)	39
Lower level[c]	17 (31%)	23 (43%)	12 (22%)	2 (4%)	54
Both levels	41 (44%)	31 (33%)	18 (19%)	3 (3%)	93
Military Regimes 1958–1968					
Upper level[d]	30 (79%)	6 (16%)	2 (5%)	—	38
Lower level[c]	57 (46%)	43 (35%)	16 (13%)	8 (6%)	124
Both levels	87 (54%)	49 (30%)	18 (11%)	8 (5%)	162
The Ba'th Regime 1977–1978					
Upper level[e]	10 (48%)	6 (29%)	—	5 (24%)	21
Lower level[f]	13 (52%)	4 (16%)	6 (24%)	2 (8%)	25
Both levels	26 (57%)	10 (22%)	6 (13%)	7 (15%)	46
1986–1987					
Upper level	9 (53%)	6 (35%)	1 (6%)	1 (6%)	17
Lower level	8 (38%)	4 (19%)	6 (29%)	3 (14%)	21
Both levels	17 (45%)	10 (26%)	7 (18%)	4 (11%)	38
1998					
Upper level	11 (61%)	5 (28%)	1 (6%)	1 (6%)	18
Lower level	7 (26%)	8 (30%)	3 (11%)	9 (33%)	27
Both levels	18 (40%)	13 (29%)	4 (9%)	10 (22%)	45

[a] Includes Christians.

[b] Includes the regent, prime ministers, deputy prime ministers, and the ministers of interior, defense, finance and foreign affairs.

[c] Includes all other ministers.

[d] Includes the president in place of the regent.

[e] Includes the RCC and the Regional Command of the Party (RL).

[f] All ministers not on the RCC and the RL.

SOURCES: Phebe Marr, "Iraq's Leadership Dilemma," *Middle East Journal* 24 (1970): p. 288; Amatzia Baram, "The Ruling Political Elite in Ba'thi Iraq, 1968–1986," *IJMES* 21 (1989): appendix 1; unpublished data collected by the author.

TABLE A.3 Employment of the Population by Economic Sector, 1967–1987 (in thousands)

	1967		1977		1987	
	No.	%	No.	%	No.	%
Agriculture	11,774	53.5	9,438	30.1	4930	13.0
Mining	145	0.7	368	1.2	451	1.2
Manufacturing	1,400	6.4	2,843	9.1	2669	7.0
Electricity, water, gas	126	0.6	231	0.7	362	0.96
Construction	591	2.5	3,216	10.3	3412	9.0
Trade[*]	1,350	6.1	2,241	7.2	2156	5.7
Transport./Commun.	1,370	6.2	1,778	5.7	2242	5.9
Services[**]	2,850	13.0	9,890	31.6	1,9881	53.0
Other	2,400	11.0	1,329	4.2	1678	4.4
Total	22,006		32,157		37,720	

[*]Includes restaurants and hotels.
[**]Includes finance, banking and insurance.
SOURCES: Iraq, Ministry of Planning, *AAS 1973*, p. 358; *AAS 1978*, pp. 38–39; Europa Publications, *The Middle East and North Africa, 1996* (London), p. 516.

TABLE A.4 Growth of Education, 1958–1994

	Number of Schools	*Students*	*Teachers*
Primary Schools			
1958	n.a.	416,000	n.a.
1973	4,594	1,297,756	54,979
1980	11,280	2,612,332	93,917
1985	8,127	2,812,516	118,492
1990	8,917	3,328,212	134,081
1994	n.a.	3,251,000	n.a.
Secondary Schools			
1958	n.a.	51,500	n.a.
1973	904	601,895	14,338
1980	1,891	950,142	28,453
1985	2,238	1,031,560	35,051
1990	2,719	1,023,710	44,772
1994	n.a.	1,103,000	n.a.
Universities and Scientific Institutes			
1958	3	5,679	n.a.
1973	7	49,194	1,721
1980	n.a.	96,301	6,515
1985	n.a.	136,688	7,616
1990	11	175,000	10,592
1994	n.a.	203,000	n.a.

SOURCES: Iraq, Ministry of Planning, *Statistical Abstract on Education, 1958* (Baghdad: Republican Government Press, 1959), pp. 6, 9, 14–16, 20, 21, 26; Iraq, Ministry of Planning, *AAS 1973*, pp. 508–510, 519–521, 528, 531, 545; *AAS 1983*, pp. 210, 214, 228, 231; *AAS 1986*, pp. 208, 212, 226, 229; *AAS 1992*, pp. 290, 294, 310; Iraqi Economists Association, *Human Development Report 1995* (Baghdad, 1995), p. 40.

TABLE A.5 Comparative Distribution of Landholdings, 1958–1973

Size of Holdings (in dunams)	Percentage of Total Holdings	Percentage of Total Area
1958		
Landless	n.a.	n.a.
Small holders (under 1 to 50)	73	6.3
Medium holders (50–500)	24.2	24.4
Large holders (500–2,000)	1.9	14.2
Very large holders (2,000 and over)	1	55.14
1973		
Landless	8.8	0
Small holders (under 1 to 40)	62.1	23
Medium holders (40–500)	28.6	59
Large holders (500–2,000)	.37	8.1
Very large holders (2,000 and over)	.08	10

SOURCES: Adapted from Hanna Batatu, *The Old Social Classes and Revolutionary Movements of Iraq* (Princeton, N.J.: Princeton University Press, 1978), p. 54; Republic of Iraq, Ministry of Planning, *AAS 1973* (Baghdad: Central Statistical Organization, n.d.) p. 71.

NOTES

Chapter 1: The Land and People of Modern Iraq

1. Georges Roux, *Ancient Iraq* (London: Allen and Unwin, 1964), pp. 302–305.

2. Abd al-'Aziz al-Duri, "Baghdad," in *Encyclopedia of Islam* (Leiden, The Netherlands: E. J. Brill, 1960), p. 925.

3. Yitzhak Nakash, *The Shi'is of Iraq* (Princeton: Princeton University Press, 1966), pp. 15–16; Pierre-Jean Luizard, *La Formation de l'Irak Contemporain* (Paris: Edition de Centre National de la Recerche Scientifique 1991), pp. 136–138, 145, 183–185, 189.

4. Sati'-l-Husri, *Mudhakkirati fi-l-Iraq* (My memoirs in Iraq) (Beirut: Dar al-Tali'a, 1967), 1:116.

5. M. S. Hasan, "Growth and Structure of Iraq's Population, 1867–1947," in *The Economic History of the Middle East, 1800–1914,* ed. Charles Issawi (Chicago: University of Chicago Press, 1966), pp. 155–157.

6. For convenience, the term *Iraq* will be used throughout the book to designate the territory constituting the modern state, even in periods prior to the twentieth century, when the state did not exist as such. Before 1920 parts of the country were known by various names. The most common was Mesopotamia, which in ancient times included the two river valleys. The early Muslim Arabs called the southern delta lands al-Iraq and the northern portion the Jazira (island). By the twentieth century, Europeans were again using the term *Mesopotamia* in its ancient sense as the lands between the two rivers. The country was named Iraq only when it became a state in the twentieth century.

7. Iraq, Ministry of Planning, *Annual Abstract of Statistics, 1992* (Baghdad: Central Statistical Organization, n.d.), p. 1 (hereafter cited as *AAS* with the appropriate year); Encyclopaedia Britannica, "Iraq," *2003 Book of the Year* (Chicago: Encyclopaedia Britannica, Inc., 2003), p. 440.

8. Because of the dispute between Iran and the Arab countries over the name of the Persian/Arabian Gulf, it will be referred to throughout this work as the Gulf.

316 *Notes*

9. U.S. Energy Information Administration, *Iraq* (www.eia.doe.gov) November 1998, p. 2.

10. *Middle East Economic Survey* [*MEES*] 24 (6 April 1981): 5.

11. The population figures on the Kurds vary widely depending on the source. These figures are taken from David McDowall, *A Modern History of the Kurds* (London: I. B. Taurus, 1997), pp. 3–4, and Mehrdad R. Izady, *The Kurds* (Washington, DC: Crane Russak, 1992), p. 116. A good list of figures is found in Gareth Stansfield, *Iraqi Kurdistan: Political Development and Emergent Democracy* (London: Routledge Curzon, 2003), p. 33.

12. Encyclopaedia Britannica, "Iraq," p. 440.

13. Although there is a rich oral tradition in the Kurdish language, no written literature from early times has survived. Some early written poetry in Kurdish dialects survives from the eleventh century onward (Izady, *The Kurds*, p. 176). A Kurdish literature, written in Persian, Arabic, and Turkish, especially from the thirteenth century on, also exists. For example Sharif Khan, of Bitlis, wrote the Sharif-nama, an authoritative medieval account of Kurdish history, in Persian (Joyce Blau, "Kurdish Written Literature," in *Kurdish Culture and Identity*, ed. Philip Kreyenbroek and Christine Allison [London: Zed Books, 1996], p. 21).

14. Richard Nyrop, ed., *Iraq: A Country Study* (Washington, DC: U.S. Government Printing Office, 1979), p. 67. Some Turkman sources estimate their numbers as far higher—some 2.5 million, or over 8 percent of the population, but this number is not accepted by most scholars.

15. Nyrop, *Iraq*, p. 63. The figures on the Persian-speaking population vary. Hanna Batatu estimated them at 1.2 percent of the population in 1947 (Hanna Batatu, *The Old Social Classes and the Revolutionary Movements of Iraq: A Study of Iraq's Old Landed and Commercial Classes and of its Communists, Ba'thists, and Free Officers* [Princeton: Princeton University Press, 1978], p. 40). Expulsions of Persian-speaking and native Iraqi *shi'a* with Persian citizenship since 1980 has probably reduced this population to well under 1 percent of the population.

16. The Lurs speak a dialect of Persian that some consider a separate language (Bruce Ingham, "Languages of the Persian Gulf," in *The Persian Gulf States*, ed. Alvin J. Cottrell [Baltimore: Johns Hopkins University Press, 1980], p. 329). Others consider the Lur dialect a variant of Kurdish and the *faili* Kurds merely *shi'i* Kurds. In the early 1970s tens of thousands of *faili* Kurds were expelled by the government, reducing their numbers in Iraq.

17. Lawless estimated the non-Muslim population at about 5 percent in 1972. R.I. Lawless, "Iraq: Changing Population Patterns", in ed. J.I. Clarke and W.F. Fisher, *Populations of the Middle East and North Africa* (London: University of London Press, 1972), pp. 101, 107. Nyrop gave a similar figure for 1977. Nyrop, *Iraq*, p. 67. Due to considerable migration in the 1980s and 1990s, non-Muslims were about 2.7 percent of the population in 2000. Encyclopaedia Britannica, "Iraq," p. 440.

18. Foreign Area Studies (American University), *Area Handbook for Iraq* (Washington, DC: U.S. Government Printing Office, 1969), p. 64.

19. Virtually all Yazidis speak the Kurmanji dialect of Kurdish.

20. Stephen Longrigg, *Iraq, 1900 to 1950* (London: Oxford University Press, 1953), p. 22.

21. Memorandum by King Faisal, cited in Abd al-Razzaq al-Hasani, *Ta'rikh al-Wizarat al-Iraqiyya* (The history of Iraqi cabinets) (Sidon: Matba'at al-Irfan, 1953–1967), 3:287.

22. Great Britain, Colonial Office, *The Arab of Mesopotamia* (London: H.M. Stationery Office, 1916), p. 4.

23. Great Britain, Naval Intelligence Division, *Iraq and the Persian Gulf* (London, 1944), pp. 353–354.

Chapter 2: The British Mandate, 1920–1932

1. The occupation was not without setbacks. An initial attempt to take Kut, in 1916, met with defeat and a retreat. The city of Mosul was occupied only after the armistice was declared and was challenged—for years—by Turkey.

2. Peter Sluglett, *Britain in Iraq, 1914–1932* (London: Ithaca Press, 1976), pp. 231–258.

3. For the 1920 revolt, see Pierre-Jean Luizard, *La formation de l'Irak contemporain* (Paris: Editions du Centre National de la Recherche Scientifique, 1991), pp. 403–413; Yitzhak Nakash, *The Shi'is of Iraq* (Princeton: Princeton University Press, 1994), pp. 66–72; Ghassan Atiyyah, *Iraq, 1908-1921: A Political Study* (Beirut: Arab Institute for Research and Publishing, 1973), pp. 326–338; Abdul Hadi Hairi, *Shiism and Constitutionalism in Iran* (Leiden, The Netherlands: E. J. Brill, 1977), pp. 125–126; Muhammad Mahdi al-Basir, *Ta'rikh al-Qadiyya-l-Iraqiyya,* 2nd ed. (London: LAAM, 1990).

4. Stephen Longrigg, *Iraq, 1900 to 1950* (London: Oxford University Press, 1953), p. 112, and 'Abd al-Razzaq al-Hasani, *al-Thaura-l-Iraqiyya-l-Kubra* (The Great Iraqi Revolt) (Sidon, Lebanon: Matba'at al-Irfan, 1952), pp. 124–170.

5. For diverse interpretations of the revolt, see Luizard, *La formation de l'Irak,* pp. 414–422; for an excellent summary of works on the revolt, see pp. 383–384. For the role of various groups in the revolt, Atiyyah, *Iraq,* pp. 270–354.

6. Philip Ireland, *Iraq: A Study in political Development* (New York: Macmillan, 1938), p. 273; Longrigg, *Iraq, 1900–1950,* p. 123.

7. For Husri's role on the curriculum and especially his clash with the *shi'a* and Kurds, see Sati'-l-Husri, *Mudhakkirat fi-l-Iraq* (Beirut: Dar al-Tali'a, 1967), 1: 79–80, 215–216, 271–277, 377–378, 401–402, 457–464, 585, 588–602; William Cleveland, *The Making of an Arab Nationalist* (Princeton: Princeton University Press), 1971, pp. 62–70. For criticism of that role, see Abd al-Karim al-Uzri, *Mushkilat al-Hukm fi-l-Iraq* (The problem of governance in Iraq) (London: n.p., 1991), chapter 5.

8. For the treaty see Abd al-Razzaq al-Hasani, *Ta'rikh al-Wizarat al-Iraqiyya* (The history of Iraqi cabinets) (Sidon, Lebanon: Matba'at al-'Irfan, 1953–1967), 1:94–98; for the agreements, see 1:223–258.

9. For an account of the tortuous British diplomacy on this issue, see McDowall, *Modern History of the Kurds*, pp. 163–171.

10. Edith Penrose and E. F. Penrose, *Iraq: International Relations and National Development* (Boulder, Colo.: Westview Press, 1978), p. 139.

11. Hilton Young, *Report on Economic Conditions and Policy and Loan Policy* (Baghdad: Government Press, 1930), p. 12.

12. Iraq, Ministry of Planning, *Report on Education in Iraq* (Baghdad: Government Press, 1959), pp. 20–21.

13. For this episode and its implications, see Nakash, *The Shi'is of Iraq*, pp. 75–88; Luizard, *La Formation de l'Irak*, pp. 440–493; Hairi, *Shi'ism and Constitutionalism*, pp. 131–134.

14. Iraq, *Majmu'a Mudhakkirat al-Majlis al-Ta'sisi-l-Iraqi* (Compilation of the proceedings of the Iraqi Constituent Assembly) (Baghdad: Dar al-Salam, 1924), 2: 659, 754, 1303, 1144.

15. Iraq, *Compilation*, 2: 793.

16. Sa'dun was a leading, pro-British politician until 1929, when, in a fit of despair over treaty negotiations, he committed suicide, paving the way for Nuri al-Sa'id.

17. For a succinct biography of Nuri al-Sa'id, see Louay Bahry and Phebe Marr, "Nuri Said," in Bernard Reich, ed., *Political Leaders of the Contemporary Middle East and North Africa* (New York: Greenwood Press, 1990), pp. 467–475.

18. Great Britain, Colonial Office, *Special Report on the Progress of Iraq, 1920–1931* (London: H.M. Stationery Office, 1932), pp. 289–292.

Chapter 3: The Erosion of the British Legacy, 1932–1945

1. Khaldun S. Husry, "The Assyrian Affair of 1933, I," *International Journal of Middle East Studies [IJMES]* 5:2 (1974).

2. This account has been drawn from Longrigg, *Iraq, 1900 to 1950,* pp. 229–237, and R. S. Stafford, *The Tragedy of the Assyrians* (London: Allen and Unwin, 1935). For a critical view of this perspective see Husry, "The Assyrian Affair of 1933, I" and "The Assyrian Affair of 1933, II," *IJMES* 5:3 (1974).

3. Khaldun al-Husri, interview with author, Beirut, 12 December 1967.

4. On this problem see Hanna Batatu, *The Old Social Classes and the Revolutionary Movements of Iraq,* chapters 5, 6; Samira Haj, *The Making of Iraq, 1900–1963* (Albany, N.Y.: State University of New York Press, 1997), chapters 1, 2; and Ernest Dowson, *An Inquiry into Land Tenure and Related Questions* (Letchworth, England: Garden City Press, 1932), pp. 16–39.

5. Iraq, Ministry of Justice, *Compilation of Laws and Regulations, 1932* (Baghdad: Government Press, 1933), pp. 42–43.

6. Nakash, *The Shi'is of Iraq*, pp. 109–111, 117–120; Ali al-Wardi, *Dirasa fi Tabi 'at al-Mujtama'-l-Iraqi* (A study of the nature of Iraqi society) (Qum: Matba'at Amir, n.d.), pp. 344–345.

7. Nakash, *The Shi'is* of Iraq, p. 113. For an exposition of *shi'i* views on this subject, see Hasan al-Alawi, *al-Shi'a wa-l-Daula-l-Qaumiyya* (The *shi'a* and the nationalist state) (France: CEDI, 1989), pp. 240–247, 252–253, 258; Uzri, *The Problem of Governance*, pp. 231, 260. For an exposition of the way this prejudice was taught at the popular level, see Sa'id al-Samarra'i, *Ta'ifyya fil-l-Iraq* (Sectarianism in Iraq) (London: al-Fajr, 1993), p. 84.

8. Hasani, *Iraqi Cabinets*, 3:220–221; Nakash, *The Shi'is of Iraq*, p. 114; Uzri, *The Problem of Governance*, pp. 215–239.

9. For the *mithaq*, see Hasani, *Iraqi Cabinets*, 4:48–49.

10. On these revolts, see Hasani, *Iraqi Cabinets*, 4:106–132, 139–144, 150–180; Nakash, *The Shi'is of Iraq*, pp. 120–125.

11. Longrigg, *Iraq, 1900–1950*, p. 246.

12. *Jaridat al-Bilad* (Baghdad), 25 June 1936.

13. Examples of this thinking were to be found in several newspapers but especially *al-Bilad*. See *al-Bilad*, 28 May 1936, and Sati'-l-Husri, *Ara wa Ahadith fi-l-Ta'rikh wa-l-Ijtima'* (Ideas and discussion on history and society) (Cairo, n.p., 1957). For German influence and the *futuwwa* movement, see Reeva Simon, *Iraq Between the Two World Wars* (New York: Columbia University Press, 1986), pp. 35–41, 110–114.

14. Abd al-Fattah Ibrahim, *Mutal'at fi-l-Sha'biyya* (Studies in populism), Ahali series, no. 3 (Baghdad: Ahali Press, 1935), cited in Majid Khadduri, *Independent Iraq, 1932–1958* (London: Oxford University Press, 1960), pp. 70–73; Kamil al-Chadirchi, *Mudhakkirat* (My memoirs) (Beirut: Dar al-Tali'a, 1970), pp. 49–50.

15. Hasani, *Iraqi Cabinets*, 4:192–194; Khadduri, *Independent Iraq*, pp. 78–82.

16. For the events of the coup, see Hasani, *Iraqi Cabinets*, 4:192–202; Khadduri, *Independent Iraq*, pp. 80–92; and Longrigg, *Iraq, 1900–1950*, pp. 245–250.

17. For a good analysis of the Bakr Sidqi coup and its subsequent government, see Mohammad A. Tarbush, *The Role of the Military in Politics: A Case Study of Iraq to 1941* (London: Kegan Paul, 1982), chapter 6.

18. "The Conflict with Iran," *Arab World File* 177 (1977): I i9; Majid Khadduri, *The Gulf War: The Origins and Implications of the Iraq-Iran Conflict* (New York: Oxford University Press, 1988), pp. 37–40. On the government's pro-Turkish orientation, see Tarbush, *Role of the Military*, pp. 139–141.

19. For this program see al-Hasani, *Iraqi Cabinets*, 4:265–267.

20. Among the officers were Muhammad Fahmi Sa'id and Mahmud Salman, both of whom later figured in the 1941 coup. (Hasani, *Iraqi Cabinets* 4:314, note 1).

21. The personal vendetta sprang, in part, from the killing of his brother-in-law, Ja'far al-Askari, a leading Iraqi politician and minister of defense during the Bakr Sidqi coup. Sidqi was undoubtedly responsible for his death.

22. For this version see Salah al-Din al-Sabbagh, *Mudhakkirati* (My memoirs) (Damascus: n.p., 1956), pp. 80–97; and Talib Mushtaq, *Awraq Ayyami* (Papers from my days) (Beirut: Dar al-Tali'a, 1968), pp. 314–325.

23. On the selection of Abd al-Ilah, see Hashimi, *My Memoirs, 1919–1943*, p. 305; Sabbagh, *My Memoirs*, p. 79; and Hasani, *Iraqi Cabinets*, 5:75–76. Information on Abd al-Ilah is taken from interviews with men who knew him well. An excellent assessment of his character is also found in Falih Hanzal, *Asrar Maqtal al-A'ila-l-Malika fi-l-Iraq, 14 Tammuz 1958* (Secrets of the Murder of the Royal Family in Iraq, 14 July 1958) (n.p., 1971), pp. 31–47.

24. Mahmud al-Durra, *al-Harb al-Iraqiyya-l-Baritaniyya, 1941* (The Iraqi-British War of 1941) (Beirut: Dar al-Tali'a, 1969), pp. 90–97.

25. For the background and views of these key officers, see Sabbagh, *My Memoirs*; for Yunis al-Sab'awi, see Khairi-l-Umari, *Yunis al-Sab'awi: Sira Siyasi Isami* (Yunis al-Sab'awi: Biography of a self-made politician) (Baghdad: Ministry of Culture and Information, 1980).

26. On the Rashid Ali movement, see Isma'il Ahmad Yaghi, *Harakat Rashid Ali al-Kaylani* (The Rashid Ali movement) (Beirut: Dar al-Tali'a, 1974); Hashimi, *My Memoirs, 1919–1943*, pp. 314–430; Durra, *The Iraqi-British War*, pp. 120–237; Sabbagh, *My Memoirs*, pp. 135–223; Taufiq al-Suwaidi, *Mudhakkirat* (Memoirs) (n.pl.: Dar al-Kitab al-Arabi, 1969), pp. 343–374; Uthman Haddad, *Harakat Rashid Ali al-Kailani* (The Rashid Ali al-Kailani Movement) (Sidon, Lebanon: al-Maktabat-l-Asriyya, n.d.); Hasani, *Iraqi Cabinets*, 5:121–231; Abd al-Razzaq al-Hasani, *al-Asrar al-Khafiyya* (The hidden secrets) (Sidon, Lebanon: Matba'at al-Irfan, 1958); Khairi-l-Umari, *Yunis al-Sab'awi*; and Khadduri, *Independent Iraq*, pp. 157–243.

27. For this aspect of affairs and for the German negotiations, see Naji Shawkat, *Sira wa Dhikrayat Thamanin Amman, 1894–1974* (Biography and memories through eighty years, 1894–1974) (Beirut: Matba'at Dar al-Kutub, n.d.), pp. 384–423, and Khadduri, *Independent Iraq*, pp. 177–189.

28. For an excellent analysis of the historical impact of the Rashid Ali coup, see the introduction by Khaldun al-Husry in Hashimi, *My Memoirs, 1919–1943*, pp. 21–40.

29. Durra, an ardent nationalist, claims there were over 1,000 (*Iraqi-British War*, p. 417). Talib Mushtaq, an internee, claims about 750 (*Papers from My Days*, p. 455). Pro-government sources put it at not more than 500, most of whom were released as early as 1942. Most were out by 1943. (Ali Mumtaz, interview with author, Beirut, 5 December 1967.)

30. For a good analysis of the texts and the role of education in creating a climate of nationalism, see Simon, *Iraq Between the Two World Wars*, chapter 4.

31. In the seven cabinets formed between March 1941 (after the Rashid Ali affair) and May 1946, Arab *sunnis* constituted half or less of the members, not the usual majority. In at least three of these cabinets—the one led by Nuri al-Sa'id (December 1943-June 1944), that led by Hamdi al-Pachachi (August 1944-January 1046); and that led by Taufiq al-Suwaidi (February–May 1946)—Arab *sunnis* were a minority, outnumbered, collectively, by *shi'a,* Kurds, Turkmen, and a Christian.

32. Iraq, *Statistical Abstract 1947,* p. 235.

33. Iraq, *Statistical Abstract 1947,* p. 211.

34. Hasani, *Iraqi Cabinets,* 6:72. Batatu estimates that the wages of unskilled laborers rose 400 percent between 1939 and 1948, while the price of food rose 800 percent, the salaries of lower-level civil servants rose less than 150 percent, and the wholesale price index rose to 690 (Batatu, *The Old Social Classes,* pp. 472–473).

35. Iraq, *Statistical Abstract 1958,* p. 123.

Chapter 4: The End of the Old Regime, 1946–1958

1. For the establishment of the Istiqlal and its program, see Muhammad Mahdi Kubba, *Mudhakkirati* (My memoirs) (Beirut: Dar al-Tali'a, 1965), pp. 108–208; Abd al-Amir Hadi al-Akam, *Ta'rikh Hizb al-Istiqlal al-Iraqi, 1946–1958* (History of the Iraqi Independence Party, 1946–1958) (Baghdad: Ministry of Culture and Information, 1980), pp. 11–70.

2. For the establishment of the National Democratic Party and its program, see Chadirchi, *My Memoirs,* pp. 53–103, 179–225; Kamil al-Chadirchi, *Min Awraq Kamil al-Chadirchi* (From the papers of Kamil al-Chadirchi) (Beirut: Dar al-Tali'a, 1971), pp. 101–145; and Fadil Husain, *Ta'rikh al-Hizb al-Watani-l-Dimuqrati* (The history of the National Democratic Party) (Baghdad: Matba'at al-Sha'b, 1963), pp. 29–49, 103–214.

3. The most authoritative study of the Iraqi Communist Party is Batatu, *The Old Social Classes.* For the early history of the party, see pp. 390–462. For the composition of Fahd's central committee in 1941, see pp. 494–495.

4. Hasani, *Iraqi Cabinets,* 7:221–224; Suwaidi, *Memoirs,* pp. 459–460.

5. For the events of the *wathba* see Hasani, *Iraqi Cabinets,* 7:219–233, 253–274; Suwaidi, *Memoirs,* pp. 473–477; Chadirchi, *Memoirs,* pp. 170–177; Kubba, *Memoirs,* pp. 223–233; and Akam, *Iraqi Independence Party,* pp. 210–228. In addition, the following material draws on interviews with several Iraqis, including Suwaidi, Taufiq Wahbi, and Yahya Qasim, the editor of *al-Sha'b* who accompanied the party to Portsmouth.

6. Michael Eppel, *The Palestine Conflict in the History of Modern Iraq* (Devon, England: Cass, 1994), pp. 187–191; Fred Khoury, *The Arab-Israeli Dilemma* (Syracuse: Syracuse University Press, 1969), pp. 68–109.

7. For the story of this exodus, see Yehouda Shenhav, "The Jews of Iraq," *IJMES* 31 (1999): 605–630.

8. Penrose and Penrose, *Iraq,* p. 167.

9. Charles Issawi and Muhammed Yeganeh, *The Economics of Middle Eastern Oil* (New York: Praeger, 1962), pp. 143, 147.

10. Abd al-Rahman al-Jalili, *al-I'mar fi-l-Iraq* (Development in Iraq) (Beirut: Dar Maktabat al-Haya, 1968), pp. 239–242.

11. Doreen Warriner, *Land Reform and Development in the Middle East* (London: Royal Institute of International Affairs, 1957), p. 118.

12. John Simmons, "Agricultural Development in Iraq: Planning and Management Failure," *Middle East Journal* 19:2 (1965): 131.

13. The figures are taken from James Salter's report, *The Development of Iraq* (Baghdad: Iraq Development Board, 1955), cited by Keith McLachlan, "Iraq: Problems of Regional Development," in Abbas Kelidar, ed., *The Integration of Modern Iraq* (New York: St. Martin's Press, 1979), p. 148.

14. Penrose and Penrose, *Iraq,* p. 177.

15. Ferhang Jalal, *The Role of Government in the Industrialization of Iraq, 1950–1965* (London: Cass, 1972), p. 8.

16. Hasani, *Iraqi Cabinets,* 8:276–277.

17. Khalil Kanna, *al-Iraq, Amsuhu wa Ghaduhu* (Iraq: Its past and its future) (Beirut: Dar al-Rihani, 1966), p. 172; Ahmad Mukhtar Baban, interview with author, Beirut, 21 December 1967.

18. *New York Times,* 25 September 1954.

19. For the constitution of the federation, see Hasani, *Iraqi Cabinets,* 10:211–223.

20. Suwaidi, *Memoirs,* pp. 583–585; Kanna, *Iraq: Its Past and Its Future,* pp. 297–299.

21. Suwaidi, *Memoirs,* pp. 594–597.

Chapter 5: The Qasim Era, 1958–1963

1. Falih Hanzal, *Asrar Maqtal al-A'ila-l-Malika fi-l-Iraq 14 Tammuz 1958* (Secrets of the murder of the royal family in Iraq, 14 July 1958) (n.p., 1971), pp. 61, 65; Kanna, *Iraq, Its Past and Its Future,* pp. 301–302; Abd al-Muttalib Amin, interview with author, Baghdad, 30 May 1968.

2. Majid Khadduri, *Republican Iraq* (London: Oxford University Press, 1969), pp. 17, 20–25; Hanna Batatu, *Old Social Classes,* pp. 773–783; Sabih Ali Ghalib, *Qissat Thaurat 14 Tammuz wa-l-Dubbat al-Ahrar* (The story of the revolution of 14 July and the Free Officers) (Beirut: Dar al-Tali'a, 1968), pp. 18–24.

3. The members of the committee were Muhyi-l-Din Abd al-Hamid, Naji Talib, Abd al-Wahhab Amin, Muhsin Husain al-Habib, Tahir Yahya, Rajab Abd al-Majid, Abd al-Karim Farhan, Wasfi Tahir, Sabih Ali Ghalib, Muhammad Sab', Abd al-Karim Qasim, Abd al-Salam Arif, Abd al-Rahman Arif, Abd al-Wahhab al-Shawwaf. Many went on to play an important role in the revolutionary period.

4. Ghalib, *Story of the Revolution,* pp. 44–45. Testimony of Naji Talib in Iraq, Ministry of Defense, Coordinating Committee for the Special High Military Court, *Muhakamat* (Trials) (Baghdad: Ministry of Defense, 1958–1962), 5:2093.

5. Hanzal, *Secrets,* pp. 126–130.

6. King Hussein, *Uneasy Lies the Head* (New York: B. Geis, 1962), pp. 197–201.

7. Muhammad Hadid (finance) and Hdaib al-Hajj Hmud (agriculture) represented the National Democrats; Saddiq Shanshal (guidance), the Istiqlal; Fu'ad al-Rikabi (development), the Ba'th; and Ibrahim Kubba (economics), the Communists. The Kurd was Baba Ali, son of Shaikh Mahmud, who took the Ministry of Communications; the Arab nationalist was Abd al-Jabbar Jumard, who became minister of foreign affairs.

8. Batatu, *Old Social Classes,* pp. 812–813.

9. For the temporary constitution, see Hasani, *Iraqi Cabinets,* 10:260–262.

10. The clash led to a possible attempt by Arif to shoot Qasim at point-blank range during a discussion. Fu'ad Arif, interview with author, Baghdad, 10 February 1968. See also testimony of Fu'ad Arif in Iraq, *Trials,* 5:1983, and of Abd al-Salam Arif, "Mudhakkirat Abd al-Salam Arif" (The memoirs of Abd al-Salam Arif), as told to Ali Munir in *Ruz al-Yusuf,* 30 May 1966, p. 29.

11. Khadduri, *Republican Iraq,* pp. 100–104. Whatever Rashid Ali's involvement, the real threat came from the Nasserite and Ba'thist army officers.

12. The plot itself was hatched by a number of nationalist groups, including midlevel nationalist officers, Free Officers, and civilian Ba'thists.

13. On the Mosul revolt, see Khadduri, *Republican Iraq,* pp. 104–112; Batatu, *Old Social Classes,* pp. 866–889. Details of the revolt are to be found in Iraq, *Trials,* vols. 8 and 9. A Ba'th view is found in Ali Karim Sa'id, *Iraq 8 Shabat 1963, Min Hiwar al-Mafahim ila Hiwar al-Dam. Muraja'at fi Dhakira Talib Shabib* (Iraq of 8 February 1963: From the dialogue of conceptions to the dialogue of blood: Reviews on Talib Shabib's memories) (n.pl.: Dar al-Kunuz al-Arabiyya, 1999), pp. 24–25. (Since this last work is both a memoir of Shabib and a commentary by Sa'id, it will henceforth be referred to with both authors' names, as Sa'id/Shabib.)

14. Efriam Karsh and Inari Rautsi, *Saddam Hussein: A Political Biography* (New York: Free Press, 1991), pp. 17–18.

15. See Iraq, *Trials,* vols., 20–22.

16. The Ba'th attempt on Qasim came after the Kirkuk events described below.

17. Uriel Dann, *Iraq Under Qassem* (New York: Praeger, 1969), pp. 55–56.

18. On the Kirkuk episode see Batatu, *Old Social Classes,* pp. 912–921.

19. Batatu, *Old Social Classes,* p. 704.

20. For a discussion of this subject, see Khaldun al-Husri, *Thawrat 14 Tammuz* (The 14 July revolution) (Beirut: Dar al-Tali'a, 1963), chapter 7. For a discussion of the USSR's relations with Iraq in this period, see Oles Smolansky with Bette

Smolansky, *The USSR and Iraq: The Soviet Quest for Influence* (Durham, N.C.: Duke University Press, 1991), pp. 13–16.

21. Ibrahim Kubba has described Qasim as "a man of strange personality" who lacked the mentality to be constructive. He was interested in insignificant things, on which he spent his time day and night (Ibrahim Kubba, *Hadha Huwa Tariq 14 Tammuz* (This is the way of the 14 July [Revolution]) (Beirut: Dar al-Tali'a, 1969), pp. 17–18. For a more favorable view of Qasim, see Penrose and Penrose, *Iraq,* pp. 288–292.

22. The text of the law is taken from Muhammad Hasan Salman, *Dirasat fi-l-Iqtisad al-Iraqi* (Studies on the Iraqi economy) (Beirut: Dar al-Tali'a, 1966), pp. 383–416.

23. For an account of these events and the Communist role in them, see Dann, *Iraq Under Qassem,* pp. 56–61; Rony Gabbay, *Communism and Agrarian Reform in Iraq* (London: Croom Helm, 1978), pp. 108–151. As Gabbay points out, the Communists were challenged in the countryside by the National Democratic Party and did not have the field wholly to themselves.

24. Gabbay, *Communism and Agrarian Reform,* p. 134.

25. John Simmons, "Agricultural Development in Iraq: Planning and Management Failure," *Middle East Journal* 19:2 (1965): 131.

26. J. N. D. Anderson, "A Law of Personal Status for Iraq," *International and Comparative Law Quarterly* 9 (1960): 542–563.

27. Office of the Iraqi Cultural Attache, *Education in Iraq* (Washington, D.C.: Embassy of Iraq, n.d.), p. 2; Arab Information Center, *Education in Iraq* (New York: Arab Information Center, 1966), p. 32.

28. Khair el-Din Haseeb [Khair al-Din Hasib], "Plan Implementation in Iraq, 1951–1967" (Beirut: Economic Commission for West Asia [ECWA], 1969), pp. 4,6.

29. Kathleen Langley, "Iraq: Some Aspects of the Economic Scene," *Middle East Journal* 18 (1964): 184.

30. For an excellent discussion of these negotiations and their outcome, see Penrose and Penrose, *Iraq,* pp. 257–269, from which the following section has largely been drawn. Parent companies of IPC included at this point British Petroleum (BP), the French Compagne Francaise des Petroles (CFP), Royal Dutch Shell, and two US companies, Mobil and Standard Oil of New Jersey.

31. On the role of Hakim in this revival, see Pierre-Jean Luizard, "The Nature of the Confrontation Between the State and Marja'ism," in Faleh Abdul-Jabar, ed., *Ayatollahs, Sufis and Ideologues* (London: Saqi Books, 2002), pp. 90–100. On the role of the *marji'* in shi'ism, see Abdul-Jabar, "The Genesis and Development of Marja'ism in the State," in Abdul-Jabar, ed., *Ayatollahs,* pp. 61–89.

32. Ali al-Mu'min, *Sanawat al-Jamr: Musira-l-Harakat al-Islamiyya fi-l-Iraq, 1957–1986* (Years of embers: The journey of the Islamic movement in Iraq, 1957–1986) (London: Dar al-Musira, 1993), p. 45; Falih Abd al-Jabbar, "Shi'i Islamic Movements" (Ph.D. thesis, Birbeck College, University of London, 2001), pp. 78–79.

33. Abd al-Jabbar, "Shi'i Islamic Movements," Chapter 3.

34. The group kept no public records. For various accounts of the founding, see Mu'min, *Years of Embers*, pp.32–36; Abd al-Jabbar, "Shi'i Islamic Movements," pp. 64–66; Shaikh Muhammad Rida al-Na'mani, *al-Shahid al-Sadr: Sanawat al-Mihna wa Ayyam al-Hisar* (The martyr al-Sadr: The years of his ordeal and the days of his siege), 2nd printing (n.pl.: Isma'iliyyan, 1997), pp. 145–147; Abdul-Halim al-Ruhaimi, "The Da'wa Islamic Party: Origins, Actors and Ideology," in Abdul-Jabar, ed., *Ayatollahs*, pp. 149–161. Information is also drawn from Sayyid Muhammad Bahr al-Ulum, interview with author, London, June 1991.

35. Sadr's participation in the party faced opposition from senior clerics as incompatible with his future status as a *marji'*. In 1960 he withdrew from the Da'wa, but he remained its intellectual inspiration (Na'mani, *The Martyr al-Sadr*, p. 175).

36. Chris Kutschera, *le Mouvement national Kurde* (Paris: Flammarion, 1979), p. 216.

37. Dana Adams Schmidt, *Journey Among Brave Men* (Boston: Little, Brown, 1964), pp. 62–63.

38. On the foundation of the KDP see Kutschera, *Mouvement national Kurde,* pp. 191–194.

39. For the Kurdish side of this story, see Ismet Cheriff Vanley, *le Kurdistan Irakien entite nationale* (Boudry-Neuchatel, Switzerland: Editions de la Baconniere, 1970), pp. 81–177; for the Iraqi central government side, see Mahmud al-Durra, *al-Qadiyya-l-Kurdiyya* (The Kurdish question) (Beirut: Dar al-Tali'a, 1966), pp. 175–304. Other sources include McDowall, *Modern History of the Kurds,* pp. 308–313.

40. For the text of these agreements, see Salman, *Studies on the Iraqi Economy,* pp. 417–440.

41. Roger Pajak, "Soviet Military Aid to Iraq and Syria," *Strategic Review* 4:1 (winter 1976), p. 52.

42. They may even have extended some help to Qasim in fending off Egyptian-backed Arab nationalist attempts to overthrow him (Malik Mufti, "The United States and Nasserist Pan-Arabism," in David Lesch, ed., *The Middle East and the United States: A Historical and Political Assessment,* 2nd ed. (Boulder, Colo.: Westview Press, 1999), p. 169.

43. Jasim Abdulghani, *Iran and Iraq: The Years of Crisis* (Baltimore: Johns Hopkins University Press, 1984), pp. 17–18.

44. Malcolm Kerr, *The Arab Cold War,* 3rd ed. (London: Oxford University Press, 1971), pp. 17–19.

45. The following account has been drawn largely from Richard Schofield, *Kuwait and Iraq: Historical Claims and Territorial Disputes* (London: Royal Institute of International Affairs, 1994), and Majid Khadduri and Edmund Ghareeb, *War in the Gulf, 1990–1991: The Iraq-Kuwait Conflict and Its Implications* (New York: Oxford University Press, 1997), pp. 6–67.

Chapter 6: The Arab Nationalists in Power, 1963–1968

1. One of the most useful records of this coup and its results is to be found in Sa'id/Shabib, *Iraq of 8 February 1963.*

2. Hani al-Fukaiki, *Awkar al-Hazima* (Dens of defeat), 2nd ed. (Beirut: Riad El-Rayyes Books, 1997), p. 118. Fukaiki's memoir is one of the best accounts of the Ba'th in this period, and its flaws.

3. For these suspicions, see Fukaiki, *Dens of Defeat,* pp. 269–270. He accuses a Lebanese professor at the University of Baghdad of being a Central Intelligence Agency (CIA) contact for the Ba'th through Talib Shabib. Shabib has denied any outside help from the United States (Sa'id/Shabib, *Iraq of 8 February 1963),* p. 271; interview with Talib Shabib, New York, 11 September 1980). However, claims of US help persist. The most recent rendition is Said Aburish, *Saddam Hussein: The Politics of Revenge* (New York: Bloomsbury, 2000).

4. Mufti, "The United States and Nasserist Pan-Arabism," pp. 163–182. Some sources allege that the United States gave the Ba'th lists of Communist Party members, who were then tracked down (U. Zaher, "Political Developments in Iraq, 1963–1980," in CARDRI (Committee Against Repression and for Democratic Rights in Iraq), ed., *Saddam's Iraq: Revolution or Reaction?* (London: Zed Books, 1986), p. 32; Penrose and Penrose, *Iraq,* p. 288.

5. A translation of the party constitution is to be found in Sylvia Haim, *Arab Nationalism: An Anthology* (Berkeley and Los Angeles: University of California Press, 1962), pp. 233–241.

6. Batatu, *Old Social Classes,* pp. 741–743.

7. Batatu, *Old Social Classes,* pp. 966–970; Fukaiki, *Dens of Defeat,* p. 175.

8. For an account of the coup planning, see Khadduri, *Republican Iraq,* pp. 188–190; Batatu, *Old social Classes,* pp. 968–973; Fukaiki, *Dens of Defeat,* pp. 231–235; Sa'id/Shabib, *Iraq of 8 February 1963,* pp. 45–59.

9. For an account of this end, see Fukaiki, *Dens of Defeat,* pp. 247–252; Sa'id/Shabib, *Iraq of 8 February 1963,* pp. 101–109. According to Shabib, who was present, there was no organized body or legal procedure; Qasim and several captured companions, including Fadil Abbas al-Mahdawi, were simply shot in a separate room by soldiers after a rough interrogation by the coup leaders present. A decree was subsequently issued claiming that he was sentenced by a martial law tribunal. Fukaiki, also present, supports this view.

10. Batatu, *Old Social Classes,* p. 1003; Khadduri, *Republican Iraq,* p. 197.

11. Because of the secrecy, there is some disagreement on the membership. Most sources agree on the following: Ali Salih Sa'di, Hazim Jawad, Talib Shabib, Hamdi Abd al-Majid, Muhsin al-Shaikh Radi, Hamid Khalkhal, Hani al-Fukaiki, Abd al-Salam Arif, Ahmad Hasan al-Bakr, Salih Mahdi Ammash, Abd al-Sattar Abd al-Latif, Tahir Yahya, Abd al-Karim Nasrat, Abd al-Ghani Rawi, Khalid Makki al-Hashimi, Hardan al-Tikriti, and Abd al-Qadir al-Hadithi (Batatu, *Old Social*

Classes, pp. 1004–1007). Some sources would add Mundhir al-Wandawi, Dhiyab al-Alkawi, and Sa'dun Hammadi; others would omit Karim Shintaf and Abd al-Ghani Rawi (see also Khadduri, *Republican Iraq*, p. 197; Sa'id/Shabib, *Iraq of 8 February 1963*, p. 177).

12. Hani al-Fukaiki gives a graphic description of the bitter civilian-military and generational divide in his memoirs. In one meeting, Ammash is reported to have told a young Ba'thist (Fukaiki) "that he did not take orders from secondary students, but his party colleague reminded him that he had obeyed the orders of secondary students when was given the rank of general and appointed minister of defense" (Fukaiki, *Dens of Defeat*, p. 275).

13. On the Ba'thist persecution of the Communists and disputes in the party over the killings, see Batatu, *Old Social Classes*, pp. 982–991; Fukaiki, *Dens of Defeat*, pp. 254–265, and Sa'id/Shabib, *Iraq of 8 February 1963*, pp. 176–194. Between 7,000 and 10,000 Communists were imprisoned, and 149 officially executed. The unofficial death toll was much higher.

14. Schofield, *Kuwait and Iraq*, pp. 110–111; Fukaiki, *Dens of Defeat*, p. 303.

15. Mahmud al-Durra, *al-Qadiyya-l-Kurdiyya* (The Kurdish question) (Beirut: Dar al-Tali'a, 1966), pp. 308–309; Fukaiki, *Dens of Defeat*, pp. 272–273.

16. For these discussions, see Dana Adams Schmidt, *Journey Among Brave Men* (Boston: Little, Brown, 1964), pp. 253–255, 260–265.

17. Kutschera, *Mouvement national Kurde*, p. 237.

18. Sa'id/Shabib, *Iraq of 8 February 1963*, pp. 287–289; Kerr, *The Arab Cold War*, pp. 85–86.

19. For this aspect of inter-Arab politics, see Kerr, *The Arab Cold War*, pp. 44–95; Kemal Abu Jaber, *The Arab Ba'th Socialist Party* (Syracuse, N.Y.: Syracuse University Press, 1966), pp. 75–95; and John Devlin, *The Ba'th Party: A History from Its Origins to 1966* (Stanford: Hoover Institute Press, 1966), pp. 239–271.

20. Talib Shabib, interview with author, New York, September 13, 1980.

21. For this historic congress, see Itamar Rabinovich, *Syria Under the Ba'th, 1963–1966* (New York: Halsted Press, 1972), pp. 75–108; Batatu, *Old Social Classes*, pp. 1020–1022.

22. The National Command of the Ba'th Party was pan-Arab and included party members from various Arab countries. The Regional Command, in Ba'th parlance, represented the leadership of the party within a single country, like Iraq.

23. Fukaiki, *Dens of Defeat*, p. 345–357; Sa'id/Shabib, *Iraq of 8 February 1963*, pp. 317–332. Those exiled were Ali Salih al-Sa'di, Hani al-Fukaiki, Hamdi Abd al-Majid, Muhsin al-Shaikh Radi, and Abu Talib al-Hashimi.

24. The assessments of the mistakes made were clearly laid out in the report of the Eighth Regional Congress (engineered by Saddam Husain) in Baghdad in 1974 (Arab Ba'th Socialist Party, *Revolutionary Iraq, 1968–1983* [Baghdad: Arab Ba'th Socialist Party, 1974], pp. 57–61).

25. Pajak, "Soviet Military Aid to Iraq and Syria," p. 52. The Soviets also constructed an atomic reactor, completed in 1964, and set other projects in motion.

26. Khair al-Din Hasib, *Nata'ij Tatbiq al-Qararat al-Ishtirakiyya fi-l-Sana-l-Ula* (Results of the application of the socialist decisions in the first year) (Baghdad: Economic Organization, n.d.), pp. 3–5.

27. For the positive view, see Hasib, *Results,* pp. 60–61. A negative view can be found in an unpublished report by Shukri Salih Zaki—an opponent of the program—cited in Batatu, *Old Social Classes,* p. 1033, note 20. For a more detailed analysis of the nationalization laws, see Penrose and Penrose, *Iraq,* pp. 460–467.

28. These included his brother, Abd al-Rahman Arif, as acting commander in chief; Sa'id Slaibi, commander of the Baghdad Garrison; and Abd al-Razzaq al-Nayif, in Military Intelligence.

29. Pierre Martin, "Les Chiites d'Irak: une Majorite Dominee a la Recherche de son Destin," *Peuples Mediterraneens* 40 (July–September 1987): 165.

30. T. A. Aziz, "Muhammad Baqir al-Sadr: Shi'i Activism in Iraq," *IJMES* 25:2 (1993); 211; Mu'min, *Years of Embers,* p. 68.

31. On sectarianism under the Arif regime, see Uzri, *The Problem of Governance,* pp. 249–261.

32. For the text of the government announcement, see Durra, *Kurdish Question,* pp. 351–353.

33. On this split in the Kurdish movement, see Kutschera, *Mouvement national Kurde,* pp. 245–253.

34. Vanley, *le Kurdistan Irakien entite nationale,* pp. 248–249; for the text of the Kurdish constitution and administrative laws of 17 October 1964, see Annexes 8 and 9, pp. 375–377.

35. For these negotiations and the demands of the parties, see Durra, *Kurdish Question,* pp. 358–387; McDowall, *Modern History of the Kurds,* p. 317.

36. The text of the government statement is to be found in Khadduri, *Republican Iraq,* pp. 174–276.

37. Khair al-Din Hasib, interview with author, Beirut, 16 June 1980.

38. The following material has been drawn mainly from Penrose and Penrose, *Iraq,* pp. 381–390, 394–397; Centre for Global Energy Studies, "Politics, Economics and Oil Policy," sec. 3 of *Iraq,* vol. 4 of *Oil Production Capacity in the Gulf* (unpublished report) (London: Centre for Global Energy Studies, 1997), pp. 74–75.

39. *Middle East Economic Survey* [*MEES*] 10 (11 August 1967): 1–5; 10 (24 November 1967): 1–4; 11 (12 April 1968): 1–5.

40. Penrose and Penrose, *Iraq,* pp. 426–427.

41. For this movement, see Abbas Kelidar, "Aziz al-Haj: A Communist Radical," in Kelidar, ed., *Integration of Modern Iraq,* pp. 183–192; and Batatu, *Old Social Classes,* pp. 1069–1072, 1100–1101. Haj later recanted.

42. The military branch was under the control of Bakr; Saddam Husain was in charge of the special security apparatus (Amin Iskandar, *Saddam Husain: Munadilan wa Mufakkiran wa Insanan* (Saddam Husain: The fighter, the thinker, and the man) (n.pl.: Hachette, 1980), p. 101).

43. *Middle East Record*, 4 (1968): 515.

44. *Middle East Record*, 4 (1968): 516–517.

Chapter 7: The Era of Ba'th Party Rule, 1968–1979

1. The members of the RCC were Ahmad Hasan al-Bakr, Hardan al-Tikriti, Salih Mahdi Ammash, Hammad Shihab, and Sa'dun Ghaidan.

2. *Economist* (London), 24–30 June 1978, p. 78.

3. The Central Treaty Organization (CTO) included the former Baghdad Pact countries; the pact was renamed the CTO after Iraq withdrew in 1958.

4. Bazzaz died on 28 June 1973, after an illness due to maltreatment during a long prison sentence. He was released from prison before his death.

5. The new members of the RCC were Saddam Husain, Abd al-Karim al-Shaikhli, Abd Allah Sallum al-Samarra'i, Izzat Mustafa, Shafiq al-Kamali, Salah Umar al-Ali, Izzat al-Duri, Murtada-l-Hadithi, and Taha-l-Jazrawi.

6. These included Salah Umar al-Ali, a relative of Bakr; Abd Allah Sallum al-Samarra'i, Shafiq al-Kamali, and Abd al-Karim al-Shaikhli, all removed by 1970. In 1973 Abd al-Khaliq al-Samarra'i was imprisoned.

7. The RCC was now reduced to six members: Husain, Bakr, Izzat al-Duri, Izzat Mustafa, Taha-l-Jazrawi, and Sa'dun Ghaidan. Four of these men were still in power thirty years later, in 2003.

8. For the relationship between the two men, see Sa'id/Shabib, *Iraq of 8 February 1963*, p. 344, and footnote 1, p. 353; Aburish, *Saddam Hussein: The Politics of Revenge*, pp. 79–80, 86.

9. For biographies of Saddam Husain, see Karsh and Rautsi, *Saddam Hussein: A Political Biography*; Aburish, *Saddam Hussein: The Politics of Revenge*, and Con Coughlin, *Saddam, King of Terror* (New York: Harper Collins, 2002). The two most important "semiofficial" biographies are Fuad Matar, *Saddam Hussein: The Man, the Cause and the Future* (London: Third World Center, 1981), and Iskandar, *Saddam Hussein: The Fighter, the Thinker and the Man*.

10. Arms Control and Disarmament Agency, *World Military Expenditures and Arms Transfers, 1970–1979* (Washington, D.C.: US Government Printing Office, 1982), p. 62, cited in Amirav Acharya, *U.S. Military Strategy in the Gulf* (London: Routledge, 1989), p. 29.

11. For this episode see Schofield, *Kuwait and Iraq*, pp. 114–117, and Majid Khadduri, *Socialist Iraq* (Washington, D.C.: Middle East Institute, 1978), pp. 154–156.

12. For these events, see Smolansky, *The USSR and Iraq,* pp. 16–17; George Lenczowski, *Soviet Advances in the Middle East* (Washington, D.C.: American Enterprise Institute, 1972), p. 142; and Shemesh, *Soviet-Iraqi Relations, 1968–1988,* pp. 32–33.

13. The Regional Command now consisted of Ahmad Hasan al-Bakr, Saddam Husain, Izzat al-Duri, Izzat Mustafa, Taha-l-Jazrawi, Na'im Haddad, Tayih Abd al-Karim, Muhammad Mahjub, Adnan al-Hamdani, Ghanim Abd al-Jalil, Tahir Taufiq al-Ani, Abd al-Fattah al-Yasin, and Hasan al-Amiri.

14. For the hierarchical structure of the party, see Falih Abd al-Jabbar, *al-Daula, al-Mujtama' al-Madani wal-Tahawwal al-Dimuqrati fi-l-Iraq* (The state, civil society, and democratic transformation in Iraq; hereafter *Democratic Transformation*) (Cairo: Ibn Khaldun Center, 1995), p. 82.

15. The first set of figures is taken from Abd al-Jabbar, *Democratic Transformation,* p. 74; the second, from Khadduri, *Socialist Iraq,* p. 40.

16. Abd al-Jabbar, *Democratic Transformation,* p. 80. *The Economist* (London) 24–30 June 1978, pp. 78–79, claims that there were 50,000 regular members and 500,000 followers in 1978. Batatu claims that "active" members, i.e., those at the highest level, numbered about 10,000 in 1976 (*Old Social Classes,* p. 1078).

17. Abd al-Jabbar, *Democratic Transformation,* p. 232.

18. Batatu, *Old Social Classes,* p. 1094.

19. *New York Times,* 17 July 1980.

20. The Albu Nasir tribe, located in the vicinity of Tikrit, was a small group of about 25,000. However, they were able to field about 2,000 to 3,000 males in active politics. Because of their small numbers, the Albu Nasir frequently made political alliances with neighboring tribes and clans, such as the Duris (from Dur) and the Rawis (from Rawa). For a study of this phenomenon, see Falih Abd al-Jabbar, "The State, Society, Clan, Party and Army in Iraq," in Faleh A. Jabbar, Ahmad Shikara, and Keiko Sakai, eds., *From Storm to Thunder* (Tokyo: Institute of Developing Economies, 1998), p. 6; Amatzia Baram, *Building Toward Crisis: Saddam Husayn's Strategy for Survival* (Washington, D.C.: Washington Institute for Near East Policy, 1998), chapter 2; Faleh A. Jabar, "Sheikhs and Ideologues," and Hosham Dawood, "The State-ization of the Tribe and the Tribalization of the State: The Case of Iraq," in Faleh A. Jabar and Hosham Dawod, eds., Tribes and Power (London: Saqi, 2003), pp. 61–135.

21. On contacts between Barzani and the Israelis and on Israel's economic and military aid, see Edmond Ghareeb, *The Kurdish Question in Iraq* (Syracuse, N.Y.: Syracuse University Press, 1981), pp. 142–145, and Jonathon Randall, *After Such Knowledge, What Forgiveness?* (New York: Farrar, Straus and Giroux, 1997), chapter 7.

22. For a good discussion on the development of the Fursan, see Martin van Bruinessen, "Kurds, States and Tribes," in Jabar and Dawod, *Tribes and Power,* p. 173.

23. Some have argued that the word used in the agreement was *self-rule,* something less than *autonomy* (Khadduri, *Socialist Iraq,* p. 103). The issue was not semantics but how much self-rule or autonomy would be granted the Kurds.

24. On these attacks, see McDowall, *Modern History of the Kurds,* p. 330 and footnote 26, p. 342.

25. Kutschera, *Mouvement national Kurde,* pp. 282–283. On the CIA aid, see the portions of the Pike report (made to Congress) that appeared in the *Village Voice* (New York), 16 February 1976, p. 88.

26. Estimates of the numbers sent to the south vary widely. Ghareeb claims there were only 10,000 hard-core insurgents sent south (*The Kurdish Question,* p. 176); Randall gives a very high figure—120,000 to 300,000 (*After Such Knowledge,* p. 173.)

27. Ghareeb, *The Kurdish Question,* p. 180.

28. McDowall, *Modern History of the Kurds,* p. 339.

29. The following section has been drawn from Penrose and Penrose, *Iraq,* pp. 408, 433–435.

30. Celine Whittleton, "Oil and the Iraqi Economy," in CARDRI, ed., *Saddam's Iraq,* p. 65.

31. World Bank, *World Tables,* 3rd ed., vol. 1: *Economic Data* (Baltimore: Johns Hopkins University Press, 1983), pp. 90–91.

32. Iraq, Ministry of Planning, *Statistical Pocketbook, 1976,* p. 29; Ministry of Planning, *Man: The Object of Revolution* (Baghdad: Government Press, 1978) p. 45.

33. Iraq, Ministry of Planning, *Man,* p. 34; *AAS 1978,* p. 135; Iraq, Ministry of Planning, *Statistical Pocketbook, 1982,* p. 46.

34. Iraq, *Statistical Pocketbook, 1976,* pp. 27–28.

35. Iraq, *Man,* p. 87; *AAS 1980,* pp. 225, 228, 240.

36. Iraq, *Man,* p. 98; World Bank, *World Tables,* 3rd ed., vol. 2: *Social Data* (Baltimore: Johns Hopkins University Press, 1983), p. 45.

37. Shakir Moosa Issa, "Distribution of Income in Iraq, 1971" (Ph.D. diss., University of London, 1978), p. 11.

38. Aburish, *Saddam Hussein: The Politics of Revenge,* p. 146.

39. Anthony H. Cordesman and Ahmed S. Hashim, *Iraq: Sanctions and Beyond* (Boulder, Colo.: Westview Press, 1997), pp. 218–221.

40. UN, Economic Commission for West Asia (ECWA), "Industrial Development in Iraq: Prospects and Problems" (unpublished paper) (Beirut: ECWA, 1979), p. 14.

41. These figures are taken from Phebe Marr, *The Modern History of Iraq* (Boulder, Colo.: Westview Press, 1985), table 9.6, p. 266, and table 9.7, p. 267. Similar trends with even lower figures are cited in Muhammad Ali Zainy, "The Iraqi Economy between Saddam Hussain and the UN Sanctions," in Iraqi Economic Forum, *Studies on the Iraqi Economy* (London: Iraqi Economic Forum, 2002), pp. 38–40.

42. Nirou Eftekhari, "Le Petrole dans l'Economie et la Societe Irakiennes, 1958–1986," *Peuples Mediterraneens* 40 (July–September, 1987): 53.

43. Batatu, *Old Social Classes,* p.1123.

44. *AAS 1978,* p. 26.

45. Petroleum Finance Company, "Iraq: Political and Economic Structures" (Country Report, unpublished) (Washington, D.C.: Petroleum Finance Company, December 1994), p. 31. Much of the report was authored by Joe Stork.

46. Marr, *Modern History*, p. 279.

47. Karsh and Rautsi, *Saddam Hussein: A Political Biography*, p. 95.

48. Report of the Ninth Regional Congress, June 1982 (Baghdad, 1983), p. 301, cited in Amatzia Baram, *Culture, History and Ideology in the Formation of Ba'thist Iraq, 1968–89* (London: Macmillan, 1991), p. 121.

49. Amatzia Baram, "Qawmiyya and Wataniyya in Ba'thi Iraq: The Search for a New Balance," *Middle East Studies* 19:2 (April 1983): 188–200, cited in Karsh and Rautsi, *Saddam Hussein: A Political Biography*, p. 100.

50. Saddam Husain, *Iraqi Politics in Perspective*, 2nd ed. (Baghdad: Dar al-Ma'mun, 1981), pp. 29–30.

51. Arab Ba'th Socialist Party, *Revolutionary Iraq*, p. 182.

52. *Al-Thaura* (Baghdad), 8–10 September 1976.

53. Vanley, *le Kurdistan Irakien*, p. 300.

54. The status of native Iraqis of Iranian origin is a controversial issue in Iraq. After the modern Iraqi state was founded, the population of Iraq was registered either as Ottoman or Persian (Iranian) subjects. A number of Arab *shi'i* families had previously chosen Persian nationality to avoid the Ottoman draft. The choice then carried over into modern Iraq, giving rise to controversy over citizenship and providing the pretext for the expulsions. Many sources say the numbers expelled reached over 100,000 (Mu'min, *Years of Embers*, p. 103.

55. Much of the following material has been taken from Abd al-Jabbar, "Shi'i Islamic Movements," pp. 170–192, and Mu'min, *Years of Embers*, pp. 163, 222–223.

Chapter 8: The Saddam Husain Regime, 1979–1989

1. Abd al-Husain was identified as one of those who had openly opposed Bakr's resignation. This disagreement is openly discussed in a semiofficial biography of Saddam, for which the main source was Saddam himself (Fuad Matar, *Saddam Hussein, the Man, the Cause, and the Future*, p. 54). Such opposition also appears in Shabib/Sa'id, *Iraq of February 1963*, p. 347.

2. For a good description of the proceedings, see Aburish, *Saddam Hussein: The Politics of Revenge*, pp. 171–172.

3. Iraq News Agency (Baghdad) (hereafter, INA), cited in Foreign Broadcast Information Service (Washington, D.C.) (hereafter, FBIS), 30 July 1979, pp. E1–E4; INA, 7 August 1979, cited in FBIS, 8 August 1979, p. E1.

4. FBIS, 8 October 1980, p. E8.

5. INA, 29 June 1979, cited in FBIS, 2 July 1979, p. E4; INA, 30 June 1979, cited in FBIS, 3 July 1979, p. E1; INA, 4 August 1980, cited in FBIS, 8 August 1980, p. E5.

6. *Middle East Economic Digest* (London) (hereafter, *MEED*), 24 (18 April 1980): 40.

7. Wafiq al-Samarra 'i, *Hitam al-Bawaba-l-Sharqiyya* (Shattering the eastern gates) (Kuwait: Dar al-Qabas, 1997), p. 33

8. Samarra 'i, *Shattering the Eastern Gates*, p. 41.

9. Salah Umar al-Ali, interview with author, London, July 2, 1998.

10. Ralph King, *The Iran-Iraq War: The Political Implications*, Adelphi paper 219 (London: International Institute for Strategic Studies [IISS], 1987), p. 10.

11. Dilip Hiro, *The Longest War: The Iran-Iraq Military Conflict* (New York: Routledge, 1991), p. 36; Simon Henderson, *Instant Empire: Saddam Hussein's Ambition for Iraq* (San Francisco, Mercury House, 1991), pp. 104–105.

12. Text of Foreign Minister Sa 'dun Hammadi's speech, UN General Assembly, 3 October 1980, cited in FBIS, 7 October 1980, pp. E1–E6.

13. Hiro, *The Longest War*, p. 40.

14. For confirmation of the use of chemical weapons in the war, see Samarra'i, *Shattering the Eastern Gates*, p. 153.

15. Samarra 'i, *Shattering the Eastern Gates*, p. 107.

16. Stephen Pelletiere and Douglass Johnson II, *Lessons Learned: The Iran-Iraq War* (Carlisle Barracks, Pa.: U.S. Army War College, 1991), p. 38. Although Hiro agrees on the expansion, he claims the Republican Guard grew from six to seventeen brigades (Hiro, *The Longest War*, p. 178). See also Shahran Chubin and Charles Tripp, *Iran and Iraq at War* (Boulder, Colo: Westview Press, 1988), p. 119, for the decision on the generals.

17. Hiro, *The Longest War*, p. 185.

18. Amatzia Baram, "Iraq Between East and West," in Efriam Karsh, ed., *The Iran-Iraq War: Impact and Implications* (New York: St. Martin's Press, 1989), p. 86.

19. President Ali Khamenei, in his letter accepting UN Security Council Resolution 598, referred to the airbus tragedy and a war that was engulfing even innocent civilians (*The Times* [London], 19 July 1988, p. 9, cited in Thomas McNaugher, "Walking Tightropes in the Gulf," in Karsh, ed., *The Iran-Iraq War*, footnote 77, p. 198.

20. Samarra 'i, *Shattering the Eastern Gates*, p. 107.

21. This chilling episode is described in Samarra 'i, *Shattering the Eastern Gates*, p. 110.

22. For an excellent analysis of Iraq 's foreign policy in this period, see Charles Tripp, "Iraq," in Yezid Sayigh and Avi Shlaim, eds., *The Cold War and the Middle East* (Oxford: Clarendon Press, 1997), pp. 186–215.

23. Relations with Syria had returned to their normal, strained position in 1979 after Saddam had accused Syria of the failed plot that led to the party massacre in Baghdad. Iraq broke relations with Syria in October 1980 because Syria was sending arms to Ira n. Syria, for its part, saw Iran as a regional balance against a hostile neighbor.

24. Syria likewise harbored Iraqi oppositionists, including the ICP, elements of the KDP and the PUK, Iraqi members of a pro-Syrian faction of the Ba'th Party, and even members of the Da'wa.

25. Fred Axelgard, "Why Baghdad Is Wooing Washington," *Christian Science Monitor*, 29 July 1983.

26. *Washington Post*, 13 May 1984.

27. FBIS, 29 June 1982, pp. E1–E2.

28. Hiro, *The Longest War*, p. 107.

29. Chubin and Tripp, *Iran and Iraq at War*, p. 101.

30. This group is sometimes known as SCIRI, the Supreme Council for the Islamic Revolution in Iraq, because of a different translation of the Arabic.

31. Abd al-Jabbar, "Shi'i Islamic Movements," p. 215.

32. McDowall, *Modern History of the Kurds,* p. 346; Chubin and Tripp, *Iran and Iraq at War*, pp. 105–106.

33. Much of this section is drawn from McDowall, *Modern History of the Kurds*, pp. 348–352.

34. The Fursan were heavily drawn from specific tribes. Some, like the Baradostis, Khushnaw, Surchis, Harkis, and Zibaris, had long been opposed to the Barzanis. Others, such as the Jaf and Pizhdar, were generally pro-government. Still others joined to avoid having their villages razed or their population displaced. Many also joined to avoid the draft and service on the southern front.

35. The organization Human Rights Watch conducted the most thorough study of the Anfal and related events. For their account, see Middle East Watch, *Genocide in Iraq: The Anfal Campaign Against the Kurds* (New York: Human Rights Watch, 1993), and Randal, *After Such Knowledge*, p. 228.

36. In this first episode in which CW were used, victims were treated in local hospitals, but a number, estimated between 225 and 400, died (Middle East Watch, *Genocide*, p. 70). There is no way to independently verify these figures, most of which are taken from interviews with survivors and other reputable evidence. Middle East Watch, *Genocide*, gives detailed descriptions of each of these attacks.

37. Middle East Watch, *Genocide*, pp. 73–74.

38. The term *anfal*, meaning "the spoils," is taken from the eighth *sura* (verse) of the Quran and refers to the first great Muslim battle with unbelievers in A.D. 624. The *sura* claims that the spoils of the battle belong to God and the Messenger (Muhammad). The *sura* says, in part: "I am with you. . . . I shall cast into the unbelievers' hearts terror . . . because they had made a breach with God and with His Messenger; and whosoever makes a breach with God and His Messenger, surely God is terrible in his retribution" (see McDowall, *Modern History of the Kurds*, p. 31; translation is from A. J. Arberry, *The Koran Interpreted* [New York: Macmillan, 1955], p. 198).

39. These figures are taken from Middle East Watch, *Genocide*, p. xiv, and McDowall, *Modern History of the Kurds*, pp. 357, 360.

40. This observation is based on a trip by the author to the area and a visit to three large cities, Arbil, Kirkuk, and Sulaimaniyya, in May 1989. These areas were living on the development of the region in the early 1970s (Stansfield, *Iraqi Kurdistan*, p. 44).

41. Eliyahu Kanovsky, "Economic Implications for the Region and World Oil Market," in Karsh, ed., *The Iran-Iraq War*, p. 233.

42. For an excellent study of this privatization policy, especially in agriculture, see Robert Springborg, "Iraqi Infitah: Agrarian Transformation and Growth of the Private Sector," *Middle East Journal (MEJ)* 40:1 (winter 1986): 33–52.

43. Chubin and Tripp, *Iran and Iraq at War*, p. 112.

44. Springborg, "Iraqi Infitah," p. 42.

45. Kanovsky, "Economic Implications," p. 238.

46. The trip included the areas around Najaf, Nasiriyya, Amara, and Kut as well as smaller towns such as Samawa and Suq al-Shuyukh.

47. Based on a trip by the author around the city in May 1989.

48. "Special Report: Iraq," *MEED*, 26 October 1982, p. 4.

49. Chubin and Tripp, *Iran and Iraq at War*, p. 110.

50. Petroleum Finance Company, "Iraq: Political and Economic Structures," p. 15. For a selected list of these families and their backgrounds, taken from Isam al-Khafaji, "The State and the Infitah Bourgeosie in the Arab Mashreq" (unpublished manuscript), see pp. 33–34.

51. Zuhair al-Jaza 'iri, "Ba'thist Ideology and Practice," in Fran Hazelton, ed., *Iraq Since the Gulf War* (London: Zed Books, 1994), p. 44.

52. Abd al-Jabbar, *Democratic Transformation*, p. 98; Keiko Sakai, "Tribalization as a Tool of State Control in Iraq," Jabar and Dawood, *Tribes and Power*, pp. 146–149.

53. For an excellent study of this Mesopotamian phenomenon and the rewriting of Ba 'thist ideology, see Baram, *Culture, History and Ideology.*

54. Aburish, *Saddam Hussein: The Politics of Revenge*, p. 208.

55. Abd al-Jabbar, *Democratic Transformation*, p. 72. See also Samir al-Khalil (Kanan Makiya), *Republic of Fear* (Berkeley: University of California Press, 1989), pp. 37–38.

56. *MEED*, 19 August 1988.

57. *New York Times*, 17 February 1989.

58. *New York Times*, 22 November, 1988.

Chapter 9: The Gulf War and Its Consequences, 1990–1991

1. For an excellent analysis of the decision process, see Gregory Gause, "Iraq's Decision to Go to War, 1980 and 1990," *Middle East Journal* 1:56 (winter 2002): 47–59.

2. For a good account of this phase of the dispute, see Schofield, *Kuwait and Iraq*, p. 116.

3. Lawrence Freedman and Efriam Karsh, *The Gulf Conflict, 1990–1991* (Princeton: Princeton University Press, 1993), p. 39.

4. Patrick Clawson, "Iraq's Economy and International Sanctions," in Amatzia Baram and Barry Rubin, eds., *Iraq's Road to War* (London: Macmillan, 1993), p. 72.

5. Although the official rate of the dinar was ID 1 = $3.20, in actuality it was trading at a rate of $1 = ID 2.5 –ID 4.

6. Sa 'd al-Bazzaz, *Harb Tulid Ukhra* (One war gives birth to another) (Amman, Jordan: al-Ahliyya lil-Nashr wal-Tawzi'a, 1992), p. 35.

7. Freedman and Karsh, *The Gulf Conflict*, p. 45; Roland Dannreuther, *The Gulf Conflict: A Political and Strategic Analysis,* Adelphi paper 264 (London: IISS, 1991–1992), p. 12.

8. Minutes of the meeting between Tariq Aziz and Secretary of State James Baker, 9 January 1991, in FBIS, 14 January 1992; Freedman and Karsh, *The Gulf Conflict*, p. 41.

9. Aziz-Baker meeting, FBIS, 14 January, 1992.

10. Freedman and Karsh, *The Gulf Conflict*, p. 45.

11. Speech by Saddam Husain at a closed session of the Arab summit, Baghdad, 30 May 1990, FBIS, 19 July 1990.

12. Bazzaz, *One War Gives Birth to Another*, p. 43.

13. Anthony Cordesman, *Iran and Iraq: The Threat from the Northern Gulf* (Boulder, Colo.: Westview Press, 1994), pp. 236, 262.

14. Amatzia Baram, "The Iraqi Invasion of Kuwait: Decision Making in Baghdad," in Baram and Rubin, eds., *Iraq's Road to War,* p. 13.

15. Carrying Iraq's debt on the books, even if Kuwait did not call it in, affected Iraq's credit position and its ability to get new loans.

16. Saddam's 30 May speech to the Arab summit, FBIS, 19 July 1990.

17. This account is taken from Bazzaz, *One War Gives Birth to Another,* pp. 41–51, and Sa'd al-Bazzaz, *al-Janaralat Akhir Ya'lim* (The generals are the last to know), 3rd ed. (London: Dar al-Hikma, 1996), pp. 41–53. Bazzaz, a former member of the regime, interviewed those involved inside Iraq. While the accounts of secret meetings cannot be verified, they are among the best we have and, in general, paint a plausible picture.

18. Baram, "The Invasion of Kuwait," p. 23; Bazzaz, *The Generals,* p. 48.

19. Bazzaz, *The Generals,* pp. 67–68.

20. The published version of this interview was put out by the Iraqis, who taped the proceedings. There is no official US version, but the Iraqi text has not been refuted by official US sources. This account is based in part on several interviews by the author with the ambassador, as well as the Iraqi tape.

21. He is reputed to have remarked to an aide, when departing the meeting, that he had given the ambassador a lesson in diplomacy the United States would not forget (Bazzaz, *The Generals,* p. 67).

22. Joseph Kostiner, "Kuwait: Confusing Friend and Foe," in Baram and Rubin, eds., *Iraq's Road to War*, p. 113.

23. Bazzaz, *The Generals,* pp. 90–94.

24. Bazzaz, *The Generals,* pp. 94–95.

25. Bob Woodward, *The Commanders* (New York: Simon and Schuster, 1991), pp. 266–273.

26. The best works on this effort are Woodward, *The Commanders*; George Bush and Brent Scowcroft, *A World Transformed* (New York: Alfred A. Knopf, 1998); and Michael Gordon and General Bernard Trainor, *The Generals' War* (Boston: Little, Brown, 1995).

27. Statement by the Iraqi RCC, 8 August 1990, cited in FBIS, 9 August 1990, p. 27.

28. Iraq and Libya voted against the resolution ; Mauritania, Sudan, and Palestine abstained; Jordan, Yemen, and Algeria did not vote; and Tunisia was absent. Those supporting the resolution were the Gulf countries—Egypt, Syria, Lebanon, Morocco, Somalia, and Jibouti. For a view sympathetic to the Arab attempt at a solution, see Khadduri and Ghareeb, *War in the Gulf.*

29. Shaul Bakkash, "Iran: War Ended, Hostility Continued," in Baram and Rubin, eds. *Iraq's Road to War*, p. 228; Schofield, *Kuwait and Iraq*, p. 131.

30. Schofield, *Kuwait and Iraq*, pp. 144–145.

31. Baram, "The Iraqi Invasion," p. 25.

32. Bazzaz, in *One War Gives Birth to Another*, discusses the failure of these attempts. They were extensive, including secret talks between French contacts and Tariq Aziz and efforts by the USSR's main Middle East specialist, Yevgeni Primakov, and King Husain of Jordan. They also included a last-minute meeting between US Secretary of State James Baker and Tariq Aziz in Geneva on 9 January. This latter meeting is notable for the veiled warning by the United States that if Iraq used WMD in the war, the regime was unlikely to survive.

33. Bazzaz, *The Generals*, pp. 120–121.

34. Dannreuther, *The Gulf Conflict*, p. 48.

35. Freedman and Karsh, *The Gulf Conflict*, p. 329.

36. These deprivations and the anger and shock they provoked are vividly described by Nuha al-Radi, a well-known painter and sculptor who kept a diary of life under siege. See Nuha al-Radi, *Baghdad Diaries* (London: Saqi Books, 1998).

37. Freedman and Karsh, *The Gulf Conflict*, p. 384.

38. For an excellent account of the reasons for the failure of coordination, see Gordon and Trainor, *The Generals' War*, chapters 7–8.

39. Quoted in Freedman and Karsh, *The Gulf Conflict*, p. 400.

40. These estimates are taken from Freedman and Karsh, *The Gulf Conflict*, p. 408.

41. United Nations, *The UN and the Iraq-Kuwait Conflict, 1990–1996* (New York: United Nations, 1996), pp. 30–33.

42. Some sources have maintained that Iraqis came across the border before the *intifada* (Bazzaz, *One War Gives Birth to Another*, p. 449). He claims that about 30,000 such forces crossed into Iraq in the first month of the war and began to destroy and burn government establishments forty-eight hours after the beginning of the ground war. Wafiq al-Samarra'i, the military intelligence officer responsible for

watching Iran, claims that the *intifada* was spontaneous in its inception; nonetheless elements of the Badr Brigade and some networks of SAIRI did enter Iraq to participate (Samarra'i, *Shattering the Eastern Gates*, p. 413.)

43. Falih 'Abd al-Jabbar, "Why the Intifada Failed," in Hazelton, ed., *Iraq Since the Gulf War*, p. 106.

44. Much of this account is drawn from a series of five articles written by Fa'iq al-Shaikh Ali on the *intifada* in *al-Hayat* (London), 22–26 March, 1996.

45. Najib al-Salihi , *al-Zalzal* (The earthquake) (London: Rafid, 1998), p. 83.

46. Adil Jamil, interview with author, Amman, 26 August 1999. Jamil was a professor at Basra University and an observer of events.

47. Salihi, *The Earthquake*, p. 321; Majid al-Majid, *Intifadat al-Sha'b al-Iraqi* (Rebellion of the Iraqi people) (Beirut: Dar al-Wifaq, 1991), pp. 37–38.

48. Salihi , *The Earthquake*, pp. 326–330; Majid, *Rebellion*, pp. 38–39.

49. See Kanan Makiya, *Cruelty and Silence* (New York: W. W. Norton, 1993), pp. 65–66; Salihi, *The Earthquake*, p. 273.

50. Abd al-Jabbar, "Why the Intifada Failed," p. 10. How much planning and organization was behind the SAIRI role has been disputed. Some previous coordination, especially between SAIRI and the Kurdish parties, apparently did take place in Tehran after the occupation of Kuwait, with a view to inserting the Badr Brigade into Iraq to spur revolt. According to these reports, SAIRI agreed not to raise slogans favoring an Islamic republic for fear of alienating local, regional, and international support, but these admonitions were not followed in practice (Makiya, *Cruelty and Silence*, p. 82).

51. Salihi, *The Earthquake*, pp. 108–110.

52. Bush and Scowcroft, *A World Transformed*, pp. 490–491.

53. Majid al-Khu 'i, son of the chief *marji'*, for example, made several trips to meet with coalition forces.

54. The reasons for this decision are best stated in Bush and Scowcroft, *A World Transformed*, pp. 484–485, 489.

55. Interview with leaders of the revolt, Raniyya, 21 July 1993.

56. Randall, *After Such Knowledge*, p. 47.

57. Ibrahim Nawwar, *al-Ma'arida-l-Iraqiyya wal-Sira'a-l-Isqat Saddam* (The Iraqi opposition and the struggle to remove Saddam) (London: Aurora Press, 1993), p. 94; Salihi, *The Earthquake*, chapter 6; McDowall, *Modern History of the Kurds*, pp. 371–372.

58. Ali Hasan al-Majid was in charge of Basra; Husain Kamil, of Karbala; Taha Ramadan, of Hilla; and Izzat Ibrahim al-Duri of Nasiriyya (Samarra'i, *Shattering the Eastern Gates*, p. 414).

59. Sarah Graham-Brown, *Sanctioning Saddam: The Politics of Intervention in Iraq* (London: I. B. Taurus, 1999), p. 21.

60. Peter Galbraith, *Civil War in Iraq*, Staff Report to the Committee on Foreign Relations, United States Senate, May 1991 (Washington, D.C.: US Government Printing Office, 1991), p. vi.

61. One Kurdish commander reportedly claimed he could not imagine Baghdad sending a corps-sized force to the north (Randall, *After Such Knowledge*, p. 46).

62. Graham-Brown, *Sanctioning Saddam*, p. 24.

63. Graham-Brown, *Sanctioning Saddam*, p. 28.

Chapter 10: The Saddam Husain Regime, 1991–2003

1. Amatzia Baram, "Neo-Tribalism in Iraq: Saddam Hussein's Tribal Policies, 1991–1996," *IJMES* 29 (1997): 13; Talib Suhail, tribal leader of the Bani Tamim, interview with author, Amman, July 1993; Sakai, "Tribalization," pp. 141–145.

2. Adeed Dawisha, "Identity and Political Survival in Saddam's Iraq," *Middle East Journal* 53 (autumn 1999): 563. Dawisha cites *MEED* (London), 30 March 1990, p. 16.

3. Dawisha, "Identity and Political Survival," p. 566. See also Sakai, "Tribalization," pp. 156–157.

4. For example, in the new Regional Command (RL), elected in 1991, there were fourteen *sunnis*, only two *shi'a*, and one Christian. Thirteen were from the *sunni* triangle, five from Tikrit alone. At least three and possibly as many as five were from the Albu Nasir tribe; six more were from allied tribes. The members were Saddam Husain, Izzat Ibrahim al-Duri, Taha Ramadan, Tariq Aziz, Abd al-Ghani Abd al-Ghafur, Muhammad Hamza al-Zubaidi, Sa'di Mahdi Salih, Mizban Khadr Hadi, Ali Hasan al-Majid, Kamil Yasin Rashid, Muhammad Zamam Abd al-Razzaq al-Sa'dun, Muhammad Yunis al-Ahmad, Khadr Abd al-Aziz al-Duri, Nuri Faisal al-Hadithi, Mazhar Awad al-Hardan al-Dulaimi, Fauzi Khalaf Arzuq al-Tikriti, and Abd al-Rahman Ahmad al-Duri.

5. Salihi, *The Earthquake*, pp. 423–425. According to Salihi, thousands of officers were discharged and hundreds court-martialed for not carrying out orders or neglecting to put down the rebellion (p. 425).

6. Salihi, *The Earthquake*, p. 426; London Economist, Economic Intelligence Unit (EIU), *Iraq*, no. 3 (1991): 11.

7. Salihi, *The Earthquake*, pp. 379–380.

8. Sean Boyne, "Inside Iraq's Security Network," part 2, *Jane's Intelligence Review* (August 1997): 365–367.

9. Michael Eisenstadt, *Like a Phoenix from the Ashes* (Washington, D.C.: Washington Institute for Near East Policy [WINEP], 1993), p. 50.

10. Army Day speech by Saddam Husain, 6 January 1992, FBIS-NES, 6 January 1992. For a good exposition of the use of religion in Saddam's discourse, see Ofra Bengio, *Saddam's Word: Political Discourse in Iraq* (Oxford: Oxford University Press, 1998), chapter 13.

11. Boutros Boutros-Ghali, Introduction to United Nations, *The UN and the Iraq-Kuwait Conflict,* pp. 30–33. This volume also contains a documentary record of the UN resolutions, reports, and other actions on Iraq.

12. This account draws on reports from IAEA and UNSCOM; numerous interviews with a number of inspectors; Andrew and Patrick Cockburn, *Out of the Ashes* (New York: Harper Collins, 1999), chapter 4; and Scott Ritter, *Endgame* (New York: Simon and Schuster, 1999). Much of the UN documentation on Iraq's disarmament can be found in United Nations, *UN and the Iraq-Kuwait Conflict.*

13. These missile strikes sometimes killed civilians; one killed one of Iraq's leading artists, Laila al-Attar.

14. UNSCOM was tasked with investigating chemical and biological weapons and long-range missile programs. The IAEA was to investigate the nuclear program.

15. Cordesman and Hashim, *Iraq: Sanctions and Beyond,* p. 127.

16. Food and Agriculture Organization/World Food Program (FAO/WFP), Food Supply and Nutritional Assessment Mission to Iraq, *Special Report* (3 October 1997), http/www.fao.org/giews/english/alertes/srirq 997.htm, p. 10.

17. Boutros-Ghali, *UN and the Iraq-Kuwait Conflict,* p. 60.

18. Cambridge Energy Research Associates (unpublished report), 17 February 1995, p. 2.

19. Boutros-Ghali, *UN and the Iraq-Kuwait Conflict,* pp. 59–60.

20. Interview with Dr. Husain Muhammad Abd Allah al-Juburi, *al-Wasit* (London), 19 April 1993, cited in FBIS-NES, 23 April 1993.

21. Eisenstadt, *Phoenix,* p. 9.

22. The key figure was a nephew of Maulud Mukhlis, the Old Regime figure responsible for placing Tikriti clans in the military in the first place.

23. Samarra 'i admits he left just as he was about to be apprehended (Samarra'i, *Shattering the Eastern Gates,* pp. 437–449).

24. For a good account of this defection, see Baram , *Building Toward Crisis,* pp. 10–11.

25. The EIU's *Profile of Iraq, 2002–2003,* gives estimated exile figures at one million to two million, with 500,000 in Iran (London: Economist, 2003). These are lower than others.

26. The Vienna meeting included the two main Kurdish parties, the KDP and the PUK, as well as Islamic groups, nationalists, and liberals. SAIRI, the Da 'wa, and the ICP boycotted the meeting. For a good article on the opposition, see Rend Rahim Francke, "The Opposition," in Hazelton, ed., *Iraq Since the Gulf War,* pp. 153–177.

27. This account is based on the author 's interviews (August 1998) with participants, including representatives from the INC, KDP, and PUK, and from Samarra'i, *Shattering the Eastern Gates,* pp. 445–453.

28. The marsh area in question comprised some 6,000 square miles of wet-lands and swamp, formed by the waters at the confluence of the Tigris and Euphrates that had overrun their banks on flatland surrounding the rivers; the area is defined by a triangle stretching roughly from Basra in the south, to Nasiriyya in the west, to Amara in the east. The two largest marshes were the Haur al-Hawiza, on the Iranian border between Qurna and Amara, and Haur al-Hammar, in the west near Suq al-Shuyukh and Nasiriyya.

29. Cordesman and Hashim, *Iraq: Sanctions and Beyond*, p. 103.

30. Cordesman and Hashim, *Iraq: Sanctions and Beyond*, p. 104.

31. Graham-Brown, *Sanctioning Saddam*, p. 222.

32. McDowall, *Modern History of the Kurds*, p. 386.

33. McDowall, *Modern History of the Kurds*, p. 387.

34. Cordesman and Hashim, *Iraq: Sanctions and Beyond*, p. 151.

35. This account has been taken from an interview with an eyewitness, Sami Salih, in the *Sunday Telegraph* (London), 27 September 1998, and from Cockburn and Cockburn, *Out of the Ashes*, pp. 209–210.

36. One study shows that those on the "hit team" involved five generations of Saddam's clan, which, according to tribal custom, is responsible for exacting retribution in cases of family honor (Baram, *Building Toward Crisis*, p. 13).

37. The assassins were never caught. Whoever did it probably had connections with those inside the regime and knew Udayy's personal schedule.

38. The PKK was established in Turkey in 1979 but came into public view in August 1984, when it began its insurgency campaign against the Turkish government. Led by Abd Allah Ocalon (known as "Apo"), the PKK was devoted to Kurdish independence but also to Marxism-Leninism. In the 1990s, the movement increased its activities in southeastern Turkey; at the same time, it made some progress in developing mass support.

39. Graham-Brown, *Sanctioning Saddam*, p. 232.

40. Hushyar Zibari, KDP representative, interview with author, Salah al-Din, 24 August 1998.

41. Graham-Brown, *Sanctioning Saddam*, p. 233.

42. Kasrat Rasul, then PUK prime minister, interview with author, Sulaimaniyya, 2 August 1998.

43. Interview with Zibari, Salah al-Din, 24 August 1998.

44. Rolf Ekeus, talk before the Council on Foreign Relations, Washington, D.C., 17 June 1997.

45. Amatzia Baram, "Saddam's Power Structure: The Tikritis Before, During and After the War," in Toby Dodge and Steven Simon, eds., *Iraq at the Crossroads: State and Society in the Shadow of Regime Change*, IISS Adelphi paper 354 (London: Oxford University Press, 2003), pp. 96–104.

46. These were Saddam Husain, Ali Hasan al-Majid, Kamil Yasin Rashid, Samir Abd al-Aziz, Najm al-Tikriti, and Adil Abd Allah Mahdi al-Duri —all Albu Nasir—together with Izzat Ibrahim al-Duri (Harb) and Muhammad Zamam Abd al-Razzaq al-Sa'dun (Sa'dun).

47. The upper levels of leadership in 1998 included all of the Regional Command (RL) and the RCC. Both bodies were overlapping except for one member of the RCC, the Kurd Muhyi al-Din Ma'ruf, who was not on the RL. They were Saddam Husain, Izzat Ibrahim (al-Duri), Ali Hasan al-Majid, Muhammad Hamza al-Zubaidi, Mizban Khadr Hadi, Kamil Yasin Rashid, Abd al-Ghani Abd al-Ghafur, Latif Nsayyif Jasim, Muhammad Zamam Abd al-Razzaq al-Sa'dun, Muhammad Yunis al-Ahmad, al-Radi Hasan Salman, Aziz Salih al-Nu'man, Samir Abd al-Aziz Najm (al-Tikriti), Fadil Ibrahim al-Mashhadani, Adil Abd Allah Mahdi al-Duri, Taha Yasin Ramadan, Tariq Aziz, and Taha Muhyi al-Din-Ma'ruf.

48. Falih Abd al-Jabbar, "Iraq Mutates into a Society of Tribalism," *Gulf News*, 3 August 2000.

49. Encyclopedia Britannica, *Book of the Year,1996* (Chicago: Encyclopedia Britannica, 1996), p. 632. These figures do not include the Kurds in the north, from which no military was recruited.

50. Petroleum Finance Company , "Iraq: Political and Economic Structures," p. 27.

51. FAO, *Assessment of the Food and Nutrition Situation* (Rome: FAO, 2000), p. 23.

52. FAO, *Food and Nutrition Situation*, p. 17.

53. EIU, *Quarterly Economic Review, Iraq 2003* (London: Economist, 2003).

54. EIU, *Iraq Profile, 2002–2003*.

55. EIU, *Iraq 2001*, p. 29.

56. EIU, *Iraq 2001*, p. 27.

57. Ministry of Education , *al-Tarbiyya-l-Wataniyya* (Text for fifth grade elementary) (Baghdad: Ministry of Education, 1994).

58. Gareth Stansfield, "The Kurdish Dilemma: The Golden Era Threatened," in Dodge and Simon, eds., *Iraq at the Crossroads*, pp. 142–143.

GLOSSARY

ABSP. Arab Ba'th Socialist Party. The official name of the Ba'th Party.

ACC. Arab Cooperation Council. A pan-Arab organization composed of Iraq, Egypt, Jordan, and Yemen and formed in the aftermath of the Iran-Iraq war; it did not survive the First Gulf War.

Agha. A tribal leader or landowner among the Kurds.

Ahali. "Popular, populist." The name of a reform movement and a newspaper active in the 1930s.

Albu Nasir. A tribal group in the vicinity of Tikrit to which Saddam Husain and his family belong.

Amn al-Amm. Public Security Directorate. The main Iraqi government organization charged with public security and criminal investigation.

Amn al-Khass. Special Security Organization (SSO). Was responsible for protecting the regime and its WMD program.

Anfal. "Spoils." The term is taken from the Quran, where it refers to the spoils of battle. In Iraq it is the code name for a campaign by the central government against Kurds in the north in the aftermath of the Iran-Iraq war, in which chemical weapons were used.

Ansar al-Islam. Supporters of Islam. A radical Kurdish Islamic party that had a sphere of influence in territory near the northern Iraqi border with Iran.

Arabistan. The name given by some Arabs to Khuzistan, a province in southwest Iran with a large Arabic-speaking population.

Badr Brigade. Militia formed of Iraqi exiles in Iran, generally associated with SAIRI.

Baghdad Pact. Security agreement made in 1955 by Turkey, Iran, Pakistan, Iraq, and Britain, with headquarters in Baghdad (hence the name). When Iraq dropped out of the pact in 1958, the organization became known as the Central Treaty Organization, or CENTO.

Ba'th. "Renaissance, rebirth." Refers to the Ba'th Party, a pan-Arab party founded in Syria in 1946 that took root in Iraq in the 1950s. It was in power in Iraq from 1968 to 2003.

BW. Biological weapons.

CW. Chemical weapons.

Da'wa. "Call or summons," in a missionary sense. The name of a *shi'i* religious party established in Iraq in the late 1950s.

Dunam. A measure of land equal to 0.618 acres.

ERAP. Enterprise de Recherches et d'Activites Petrolieres. A French state-owned oil company engaged in joint ventures with Iraq in the 1960s.

Faili. S*hi'i* Kurds.

Far'. "Branch." A committee; an administrative unit, composed of several *shu'bas,* within the Ba'th Party.

Fatwa. Formal legal opinion given by a qualified Islamic scholar; especially important among the *shi'a.*

Fida'iyyin. "Those who sacrifice." A special elite militia established to support the Ba'th regime.

Firqa. "Division." A committee; a lower-level administrative unit within the Ba'th Party.

Fursan. "Knights, cavalry." Kurdish irregular troops, recruited by tribal leaders who supported the government against the militias *(peshmergas)* of the Kurdish parties. The Fursan manned frontier posts in the Iran-Iraq war.

Futuwwa. "Youth; chivalry." A Ba'th Party paramilitary formation recruited from youth in high schools; the name of a similar movement initiated in the school system in the 1930s. Named after a medieval brotherhood devoted to chivalry.

GCC. Gulf Cooperation Council. A regional security organization formed in 1981 of six Arab Gulf states: Saudi Arabia, Kuwait, Bahrain, Qatar, the UAE, and Oman.

Himaya. "Protection." A small force recruited mainly from Saddam Husain's tribe, with responsibility to protect him personally.

IAEA. International Atomic Energy Agency. The United Nations agency responsible for inspections of Iraq's nuclear facilities after the Gulf War.

IAO. Islamic Action Organization *(Munazamat al-Amal al-Islamiyya).* One of several *shi'i* Islamic parties established in the 1970s.

IMIK. Islamic Movement of Iraqi Kurdistan. An Islamic movement established in the Kurdish area of Iraq in the early 1980s.

INC. Iraq National Congress. An umbrella group of Iraqi opposition parties formed after the Gulf War to replace the regime. It has been headed by Ahmad Chalabi.

Intifada. "Uprising." Refers to disturbances that took place in 1952, as well as the uprisings in the north and south of Iraq in 1991.

INOC. Iraq National Oil Company. The government-owned oil company established in 1964 to manage oil interests in the territory taken from the IPC.

IPC. Iraq Petroleum Company. Created after the First World War to operate and manage the Iraqi oil concession granted to several major international oil companies. It was dominated by the British.

Istikhbarat Askariyya. Military Intelligence; the organization in the military that collects information on foreign military threats.

Istiqlal. "Independence." A nationalist and pan-Arab political party founded after the Second World War.

KDP. Kurdistan Democratic Party. The mainstream Kurdish party in Iraq founded after the Second World War; led by Mustafa-l-Barzani until his death in 1979 and thereafter by his son Mas'ud al-Barzani.

KDPI. Kurdistan Democratic Party of Iran. The leading Iranian Kurdish party.

Khaliyya. "Cell." A small, underground unit in the Ba'th Party.

KRG. Kurdish Regional Government. The unified government established in the north by the Kurdish Front after the elections of 1992.

KSP. Kurdistan Socialist Party. One of several small Kurdish parties in northern Iraq.

Madinat al-Thaura. "City of the Revolution." An urban housing project for poor migrants on the outskirts of Baghdad, built by Qasim after the 1958 revolution; later renamed Saddam City, and after the fall of the Saddam Husain regime, Sadr City, after a leading *shi'i* cleric.

Maktab al-Amn al-Qaumi. Bureau of National Security. A higher-security bureau that coordinated the efforts of several intelligence and security services.

Marji'iyya. "Religious authority." Refers collectively to the body of religious scholars who act as religious authorities among the *shi'a.*

Marji'. "Authoritative religious source." For *shi'a* the recognized religious source on questions of faith and practice. The chief *marji'* is the senior *shi'i* cleric recognized as having precedence over others.

MCC. Military Coordination Committee. A group of Western, mainly US, military advisers established in Zakhu to oversee the Kurdish safe haven between 1991 and 1996.

Mukhabarat al-Amma. General Intelligence Service. Iraq's secret police, responsible for domestic and foreign intelligence on potential threats to the regime.

Mustashars. "Advisers." Kurdish tribal leaders who supported the central government and who were responsible for recruiting units for the Fursan; they were rewarded with subsidies.

Mutasarrif. Provincial governor. Head of one of Iraq's eighteen provinces.

National Command. The pan-Arab leadership of the Ba'th Party. Since the party considers the larger Arab world as "the nation," this command consists of representatives from Iraq, Syria, Jordan, and other Arab countries.

No Fly Zone. Area established under United Nations auspices in which Iraq was not allowed to fly noncommercial fixed-wing aircraft. There were two such zones in Iraq: one in the north, above the thirty-sixth parallel, and one in the south, below the thirty-third parallel.

OPC. Operation Provide Comfort. The name given by the US military to the operation that returned Iraqi Kurdish refugees to their homes in the wake of the 1991 rebellion.

OPEC. Organization of Petroleum Exporting Countries. Formed in 1960 by Middle East oil-exporting countries and a few others, such as Venezuela, Indonesia, and Nigeria, OPEC is dedicated to protecting the oil-price structure in the interests of exporters.

Peshmergas. "Those who face death." Irregular militias attached to Kurdish political parties, especially the KDP and the PUK.

PKK. Kurdistan Workers Party (Partiya Karkari Kurdistan). Radical Kurdish party formed in Turkey in the late 1970s, advocating an independent state and a Marxist social agenda.

PUK. Patriotic Union of Kurdistan. One of the two main Kurdish parties in the north. Founded in 1975 and led by Jalal al-Talabani, who broke away from the KDP.

Qa'imaqam. Local district administrator; the head of a subdistrict below the provincial level.

Regional Command. The leadership of the Ba'th party in a specific country (or "region," in Ba'th terminology). The party's regional command in Iraq was in charge of party (and government) affairs in Iraq.

Resolution 687. The United Nations cease-fire resolution that concluded the Gulf War and stipulated the requirements Iraq had to fulfill before troops were withdrawn. Chief among these was the destruction of Iraq's WMD; sanctions would be maintained until this was satisfactorily accomplished.

Resolution 688. The United Nations resolution that instructed Iraq to cease repression of its population and to allow the international community to assist Kurdish refugees in returning to Iraq.

Resolution 986. The United Nations resolution, known as "Oil for Food," that allowed Iraq to export a certain amount of oil, despite sanctions, to purchase food, medicine, and other essentials for its population.

RG. Republican Guard. Elite military units within the Iraqi armed forces.

SAIRI. Supreme Assembly for the Islamic Republic in Iraq. Also known as SCIRI, the Supreme Council for an Islamic Repulic in Iraq. An umbrella organization representing several Iraqi *shi'i* political parties. Established in Iran in 1982, SAIRI is led by Muhammad Baqir al-Hakim.

Shabab. "Adolescents." Ba'th Party paramilitary formation recruited from adolescents seventeen to twenty-one years of age.

Shaikh. Head of a tribe among Arabs.

Shaikhdom. Principality led by a tribal family. Most Persian Gulf states were founded as shaikhdoms.

Shu'ba. "Section." A committee; an administrative unit within the Ba'th party composed of several *firqas.*

Sirkal. The agent or manager for a landlord-*shaikh* in southern Iraq.

Tahrir. "Liberation." A shadowy, underground Islamic party with origins outside Iraq. It played a minor role in Iraq after the 1958 revolution.

Tali'a. "Vanguard." Ba'th party paramilitary formation recruited from youth in elementary and intermediate schools.

Tawwabin. "Penitents." An anti-regime militia formed by Iran from Iraqi deserters and POWs during the Iran-Iraq war.

Thalweg. Deepwater channel in the center of a river; used in a specific sense to denote the (disputed) boundary between Iraq and Iran in the Shatt al-Arab.

UAR. United Arab Republic. A political union formed by Egypt, Syria, and Yemen in 1958. The UAR lasted only until 1961.

Ulama. Islamic scholars knowledgeable in Islamic law and theology.

UNSCOM. United Nations Special Commission. A body created in 1991 to conduct inspections in Iraq for chemical and biological weapons and long-range missiles.

Wathba. "Leap, attack." Refers to the disturbances that broke out in 1948 in protest of the Portsmouth Treaty.

Wilaya. State or province; a unit of government under the Ottoman Empire.

WMD. Weapons of mass destruction, whether chemical, biological, or nuclear.

POLITICAL
PERSONALITIES

Abd al-Ilah, Crown Prince. Crown prince and regent of Iraq from the death of King Ghazi in 1939 until 1953, when King Faisal II came of age. He continued to be the dominant influence in the palace until he was brutally killed in the revolution of 1958.

Aflaq, Michel. A Syrian Christian, cofounder in 1946 and longtime leader of the Ba'th Party. Author of theoretical works on Arab nationalism, laying the foundations of the party. Lived in Baghdad for much of the period after 1968 and died there in 1989.

Ahmad, Ibrahim. Secretary-general of the Kurdistan Democratic Party from 1951 to 1961 and a leader of its intellectual wing; espoused leftist ideas and split with Mustafa-l-Barzani in 1961.

Arif, Abd al-Rahman. President of Iraq from 1966 to 1968. An army officer, active in Arab nationalist politics. Chief of staff, 1963–1966. Elected to the presidency after the death of his brother, President Abd al-Salam Arif. Overthrown in the 1968 coup.

Arif, Abd al-Salam. President of Iraq from 1963 to 1966. An army officer and a key figure in the overthrow of the monarchy in 1958. Ousted from power by Abd-Karim Qasim in 1958, but brought back as president by the Ba'th in 1963. He out-maneuvered the Ba'th and took full power the same year. Died in 1966 in a helicopter crash.

Al-Bakr, Ahmad Hasan. President of Iraq under the Ba'th from 1968 until 1979. An army officer and a Tikriti from the Albu Nasir tribe. Played a role in the Free Officers' movement and was prime minister in the Ba'th regime of 1963. Removed from power by Abd al-Salam Arif in 1964. Instrumental in bringing the Ba'th to power in 1968.

Al-Barzani, Mas'ud. Son of Mustafa-l-Barzani and leader of the Kurdistan Democratic Party from 1979 to the present. Holds paramount influence over the area of the north, from Zakhu to Arbil, controlled by the KDP since the mid–1990s. Rival of Jalal al-Talabani for leadership of the Kurdish movement.

Al-Barzani, Mustafa. Legendary leader of the Iraqi Kurdish national movement. Fought the central government in the 1940s, was in exile in Russia in the 1950s, and returned to Iraq in 1958. Assumed leadership of the Kurdistan Democratic Party and led it in a continuous military and political struggle for greater Kurdish self-government until his defeat in 1975. Died in 1979.

Al-Chadirchi, Kamil. A leading political intellectual and liberal of the post–Second World War period. Founder and leader of the reformist National Democratic Party from 1946 until 1961, when the party was disbanded under the Qasim regime.

Chalabi, Ahmad. Member of a wealthy *shi'i* family. Educated in the West and lived abroad after 1958. In the 1990s, assumed a leading role among exile Iraqis in opposing the Saddam Husain regime. Heads the opposition umbrella group, the Iraq National Congress, founded in 1992. Returned to Iraq in 2003, after the fall of the regime.

Faisal I, King. King of Iraq from 1921 until his death in 1933. A leading member of the Hashimite family of Mecca and active in the Arab revolt against the Turks in the First World War. Installed as monarch in Iraq under British auspices, he established the Hashimite dynasty there, which lasted until its overthrow in 1958.

Faisal II, King. Son of King Ghazi, grandson of Faisal I, and king of Iraq from 1953 until his murder in the revolution of 1958. He was too young to exercise much authority as king and Crown Prince Abd al-Ilah was the leading figure at the palace during his tenure.

Ghazi, King. Son of Faisal I and king of Iraq from 1933 to 1939. He assumed the position at a young age and was inexperienced. His nationalist sentiments caused anxiety among the British and senior Iraqi politicians. He died in a violent auto crash in 1939 that has been regarded with suspicion by many Iraqis.

Al-Hakim, Muhammad Baqir. Head of the Supreme Assembly for the Islamic Revolution in Iraq (SAIRI), a *shi'i*-based religious opposition group established in 1982 and headquartered in Iran until 2003. It draws support from Iraqi exiles in Iran as well as *shi'a* inside Iraq. A religious cleric and son of a former chief *marji'*, Muhsin al-Hakim. Returned to Iraq in 2003, after the fall of the regime.

Al-Hakim, Muhsin. Chief *marji'*, or religious authority for the *shi'a*, from 1961 to 1970. Active in furthering the *shi'i* cause. The *shi'a* in Iraq underwent a considerable renaissance during his tenure, including the formation and development of the *shi'i* political party, the Da'wa.

Husain, Qusayy. Younger son of Saddam Husain. Played a leading role in security affairs during the 1990s and until the regime's overthrow in 2003.

Husain, Saddam. President of Iraq from 1979 until his overthrow in 2003. Vice president of the Revolutionary Command Council from 1969 to 1979 and the architect of the Ba'th government and its policies after 1968. A Tikriti, a relative of

Ahmad Hasan al-Bakr, and a member of the Albu Nasir tribe, he used his tribal connections to get ahead and to maintain himself in power.

Husain, Udayy. Older son of Saddam Husain, known for his brutal, flamboyant, and irresponsible behavior. Head of youth and sports affairs and editor of *Babil* newspaper. Badly wounded in an assassination attempt in 1996.

Al-Husri, Sati'. Ottoman-educated Syrian intellectual who adopted Arab nationalism after the First World War. The leading figure in Iraqi education during and after the mandate, he shaped its curriculum in a secular, Arab-nationalist direction, to the consternation of many *shi'a* and Kurds.

Jabr, Salih. The first *shi'i* prime minister in Iraq in 1947–1948 and a leading politician in the post–Second World War period. Responsible for negotiating the unpopular Portsmouth Treaty of 1948, which was repudiated after it generated riots back home.

Al-Kailani, Rashid Ali. A leading politician under the monarchy. Prime minister in 1941, when he and four officers undertook an anti-British "coup," removing the pro-British regent. The coup caused the second British occupation of Iraq.

Kamil, Husain (al-Majid). A relative and son-in-law of Saddam Husain and a leading figure in the Ba'th regime during the 1980s and early 1990s. Responsible for overseeing much of Iraq's WMD program. Defected in 1995. He returned and was killed during a "family" shootout in 1996.

Al-Khu'i, Muhammad Abu-l-Qasim. Chief *marji'*, or religious authority among the *shi'a*, from 1971 until 1992. He represented the "quietist" school, avoiding politics, but still had difficulties with the Ba'thist regime. Captured in 1991 and taken to Baghdad by the Saddam Husain government during the *intifada*, he survived the ordeal but was under house arrest until his death in 1992.

Al-Khumaini, Ruhalla Ayat Allah. *Shi'i* cleric; leader of the 1979 Islamic Revolution in Iran and its most important religious and political figure until his death in 1989. As an opponent of the shah, he spent thirteen years in exile in Najaf, until his expulsion by Saddam in 1978. The religious foundations of the Islamic Republic of Iran are his creation.

Kubbah, Muhammad Mahdi. A *shi'a* and leader of the anti-British, nationalist Istiqlal (Independence) Party formed in 1946. Minister in the short-lived cabinet formed in 1948 after the *wathba*.

Al-Majid, Ali Hasan. A member of Saddam's clan and a leading figure in the Ba'thist regime from the 1980s until its overthrow in 2003. A member of the RCC and the party's Regional Command in the 1990s. Responsible for the Anfal campaign against the Kurds in 1988 and other atrocities.

Qasim, Abd al-Karim. Army officer, leader of the 1958 revolution that overthrew the monarchy. Prime minister from 1958 to 1963. Undertook radical social and economic reforms. Overthrown and killed by the Ba'th in 1963.

Al-Sadr, Muhammad Baqir. A cleric and leading *shi'i* thinker, considered the spiritual founder of the radical Da'wa party, established in the late 1950s. Author of several works attempting to reconcile traditional *shi'i* theology and modern social science. A moving force behind *shi'i* opposition to the regime in the late 1970s. Tortured and executed by the Ba'th regime in 1980.

Al-Sadr, Muhammad Sadiq. Chief *marji'*, or religious authority for the *shi'a*, between 1992 and 1999. Although originally supported by the Ba'th government, he was killed by the regime when he generated widespread support among the *shi'i* community.

Sa'id, Nuri. The most important politician in Iraq from the end of the mandate period in 1930 to the overthrow of the monarchy in 1958. Repeatedly prime minister and the moving force in numerous cabinets, he held the threads of power through shrewd manipulation of the parliamentary system. Pro-British and pro-monarchy, he steered Iraq's foreign and domestic policy in a pro-Western direction until his violent death during the 1958 revolution.

Salman, Yusif. Also know as Comrade Fahd, a Christian and founder of the Iraq Communist Party in 1941. Played an important role in organizing the party and spreading Marxist ideas among intellectuals. Executed in 1949.

Sidqi, Bakr. A Kurd, an army officer, and a key leader in the first military coup in Iraq in 1936. Also considered responsible for the Assyrian massacre in 1933. Assassinated by Arab nationalist officers in 1937.

Sulaiman, Hikmat. Ottoman-educated politician of the mandate period. With Bakr Sidqi and a group of liberal-left reformers, participated in the 1936 coup and led the government that followed.

Al-Talabani, Jalal. A leading figure in the Kurdish nationalist movement. Originally a member of the KDP and, with Ibrahim Ahmad, a leading member of its intellectual wing. Established a competing party, the Patriotic Union of Kurdistan (PUK), in 1975. Rivalry with Mas'ud al-Barzani broke into open warfare in the mid-1990s. Since 1995, head of a government in the southeastern portion of northern Iraq.

BIBLIOGRAPHY

The Land and People of Iraq

A good overview is still R. I. Lawless, "Iraq: Changing Population Patterns," in *Populations of the Middle East and North Africa*, edited by J. I. Clarke and W. F. Fisher (London, 1972). This work can be updated with the *Human Development Report, 1995*, published in Baghdad by the Iraqi Economists Association in conjunction with the United Nations Development Program, although their figures, taken from the Baghdad government, cannot be verified. The best description of the geography and population of Iraq in the early part of the twentieth century is Great Britain, Naval Intelligence Division, *Iraq and the Persian Gulf* (London, 1944). A good survey at the end of the 1970s is found in Richard Nyrop, ed. *Iraq: A Country Study* (Washington, 1979). C. J. Edmonds, *Kurds, Turks and Arabs* (London, 1957) has the best background on the Kurds during the mandate period. For a delightful firsthand account of village life and customs in the south of Iraq, see Elizabeth Warnock Fernea, *Guests of the Sheik* (Garden City, N.J., 1969). Other cultural and anthropological descriptions of groups are to be found in Philip Kreyenbroek and Christine Allison, eds., *Kurdish Culture and Identity* (London, 1996); W. Thesiger, *The Marsh Arabs* (New York, 1964) and Shakir Mustafa Salim, *Marsh Dwellers of the Euphrates Delta* (London, 1962). The classic work on Iraqi tribes is still Abbas al-Azzawi, *Asha'ir al-Iraq* (The tribes of Iraq) (Baghdad, 1956). An updated version can be found in Thamir Abd al-Hasan al-Amiri, *Mausu'a-l-Asha'ir al-Iraqiyya* (Encyclopedia of Iraqi tribes), 9 vols. (Baghdad, 1992), but this reflects the government manipulation and appointment of tribal leaders under Saddam Husain, including his manufactured genealogy going back to Imam Ali. For an excellent discussion on tribalism in contemporary Iraq, see Faleh Abdul-Jabar, "Sheikhs and Ideologues: Deconstruction and Reconstruction of Tribes Under Patrimonial Totalitarianism in Iraq, 1968–1998," and Hosham Dawod, "The State-ization of the Tribe and the Tribalization of the State: The Case of Iraq," in Faleh A. Jabar and Hosam Dawod, eds. *Tribes and Power: Nationalism and Ethnicity in the Middle East* (London, 2002). On the Kurds, three scholarly studies can be recommended: Mehrdad Izadi, *The Kurds: A Concise Handbook* (Washington, 1992); Martin Van Bruinessen, *Agha, Shaikh and State: On the Social and Political Organization of Kurdistan* (Rijswik, 1978); and "Kurds,

States and Tribes," in Jabar and Dawod, eds., *Tribes and Power.* The best recent study is Gareth R. V. Stansfield, *Iraqi Kurdistan: Political Development and Emergent Democracy* (London, 2003). On the *shi'a,* the best overview is Moojan Momen, *An Introduction to Shi'i Islam* (New Haven, 1985). In Iraq, the best recent studies include Yitzhak Nakash, *The Shi'is of Iraq* (Princeton, 1994), and Nakash's article, "The Conversion of Iraq's Tribes to Shi'ism," *International Journal of Middle East Studies (IJMES)* 26 (1994), and an excellent collection of articles in Faleh A. Jabar, *Ayatallahs, Sufis and Ideologues* (London, 2001). A good study on Iraq's Turkman population is Aziz Qadir al-Samanchi, *al-Ta'rikh al-Siyasi lil-Turkman al-Iraq* (The political history of the Turkman of Iraq) (London, 1999).

Iraq Before the British Mandate

This book does not deal with Iraq's ancient or Islamic history, but two classical works can be suggested for these periods: Georges Roux, *Ancient Iraq* (New York, 1964), and Marshall G. S. Hodgson, *The Venture of Islam* (Chicago, 1974), vols. 1–2. The Ottoman period has been neglected by scholars and there is no good general history. The two standard works are Stephen Longrigg, *Four Centuries of Modern Iraq,* first published in 1925 by Oxford University Press, and Abbas al-Azzawi, *Ta'rikh al-Iraq bain Ihtilalain* (The history of Iraq between two occupations), 8 vols. (Baghdad, 1956), but both are little more than chronologies. Two more recent studies focus on economic and social life in the nineteenth century: Hala Fattah, *The Politics of Regional Trade in Iraq, Arabia and the Gulf, 1745–1900* (New York, 1997), and Sarah Shields, *Mosul before Iraq: Like Bees Making Five Sided Cells* (New York, 2000). The classic study on the social aspects of Iraq in this period is to be found in Ali al-Wardi, *Lamahat Ijtima'iyya min Ta'rikh al-Iraq al-Hadith* (Social aspects of the modern history of Iraq) (Baghdad, 1969–1972), 6 vols. but especially vols. 1–4. The *shi'a* in this period are well covered in Pierre-Jean Luizard, *La Formations de l'Irak Contemporain* (Paris, 1991), and a shorter work, Abd al-Hadi Hairi, *Shi'ism and Constitutionalism* (Leiden, The Netherlands: 1977). The section on Iraq in *The Economic History of the Middle East, 1800–1914,* edited by Charles Issawi (Chicago, 1966), has excellent excerpts dealing with economic changes in Iraq in the last century of Ottoman rule. A colorful picture of life at the end of the Ottoman era is contained in several memoirs of Iraqi politicians, chief among them Sulaiman Faidi, *Fi Ghamrat al-Nidal* (In the heat of the struggle) (Baghdad, 1952), and Abd al-Aziz Qassab, *Min Dhikrayati* (From my memories) (Beirut, 1966).

The British Occupation, the Mandate, and the Struggle for Independence

This subject has been dealt with extensively and only the most important works can be mentioned here. The most essential is Abd al-Razzaq al-Hasani, *Ta'rikh al-Wizarat al-Iraqiyya* (The history of Iraqi cabinets), 10 vols. (Sidon, Lebanon,

1953–1967); although weak on analysis, it is exhaustive in facts, documents, and statements from participants. In English the classic study is now Hanna Batatu, *The Old Social Classes and the Revolutionary Movements of Iraq* (Princeton, 1978), mainly a social history but containing a wealth of political data. Two standard older works, still useful, are Stephen Longrigg, *Iraq, 1900 to 1950* (London, 1953), and Philip Ireland, *Iraq: A Study in Political Development* (New York, 1938). The view of the India School can be found in A. T. Wilson, *Loyalties: Mesopotamia, 1914–1917,* and *Mesopotamia, 1917–1920: A Clash of Loyalties* (London, 1930). For the opposing view, see Elizabeth Burgoyne, *Gertrude Bell: From Her Personal Papers, 1914–1926* (London, 1961). Two more recent works on British policy in the region are Aaron S. Klieman, *Foundations of British Policy in the Arab World: The Cairo Conference of 1921* (Baltimore, 1970), and David Fromkin, *A Peace to End All Peace* (London, 1989), as well as Peter Sluglett, *Britain in Iraq, 1914–1932* (London, 1976). Official British accounts can be found in records in the India Office and Colonial Office and in the Foreign Office in London. Good published accounts include Great Britain, India Office, *Review of the Civil Administration of Mesopotamia* (London, 1920), and Great Britain, Colonial Office, *Special Report on the Progress of Iraq During the Period 1920–1931* (London, 1931).

The material on the struggle for independence is scarcer, but studies on the 1920 revolt are numerous. In Arabic the most important are Abd al-Razzaq al-Hasani, *al-Thaura-l-Iraqiyya-l-Kubra* (The great Iraqi revolt) (Sidon, Lebanon, 1952); Muhammad Mahdi al-Basir, *Ta'rikh al-Qadiyya-l-Iraqiyya* (The history of the Iraqi question), 2nd ed. (London, 1990); and Abd Allah al-Nafisi, *Daur al-Shi'a fi Tatawwur al-Iraq al-Siyasi al-Hadith* (The role of the *shi'a* in the development of the modern political history of Iraq) (Beirut, 1973); and a good study in English is Ghassan Atiyyah, *Iraq, 1908–1921: A Political Study* (Beirut, 1973). Several memoirs deal with the mandate period; most important are Sati'-l-Husri, *Mudhakkirati fi-l-Iraq* (My memoirs in Iraq), 2 vols. (Beirut, 1967); Muhammad Mahdi al-Jawahiri, *Dkhirayati* (My memories), 2. vols. (Damascus, 1988); and Ali Jaudat, *Dhikrayati* (My memories) (Beirut, 1968).

Erosion of the British Legacy, 1932–1945

The best accounts covering this period are found in Majid Khadduri, *Independent Iraq, 1932–1958* (London, 1960); Batatu, *The Old Social Classes*; and a good general history by Charles Tripp, *A History of Iraq* (Cambridge, 2000), which emphasizes alternative narratives in Iraqi history. The Assyrian affair is dealt with by R. S. Stafford, a British officer who served in Mosul at the time, in *The Tragedy of the Assyrians* (London, 1935). A more nationalist view is found in Khaldun S. Husry, "The Assyrian Affair of 1933," I and II, *IJMES* 5:2 and 3 (1974). Two good studies on army politics in this period are Mohammad Tarbush, *The Role of the Military in Politics: A Case Study of Iraq to 1941* (London, 1982), and Reeva Simon, *Iraq Between the Two World*

Wars: The Creation and Implementation of a Nationalist Ideology (New York, 1986), which deals, among other things, with education and textbooks in this period. On the Rashid Ali movement there is no dearth of material. German involvement is meticulously presented by the Polish scholar Lukasz Hirszowitz in *The Third Reich and the Arab East* (Toronto, 1966). The German point of view is put forth by Fritz Grobba, the German representative in Baghdad who played an important role in the prelude to the coup, in *Irak* (Berlin, 1941). Iraqi accounts of the movement, mainly from a nationalist point of view are found in Abd al-Razzaq al-Hasani, *al-Asrar al-Khafiyya* (The hidden secrets) (Sidon, Lebanon, 1958), and Mahmud al-Durra, *al-Harb al-Iraqiyya-l-Baritaniyya, 1941* (The Iraqi-British war of 1941) (Beirut, 1969). A thorough academic study of the movement is Ahmad Yaghi, *Harakat Rashid Ali al-Kailani* (The Rashid Ali al-Kailani movement) (Beirut, 1974), and a biography of Yunis al-Sab'awi by Khairi-l-Umari, *Yunis al-Sab'awi: Sirat Siyasi 'Isami* (Yunis al-Sab'awi: Biography of a self-made politician) (Baghdad, 1980). Among the memoirs by major participants are those of Salah al-Din al-Sabbagh, *Mudhakkirati* (My memoirs) (Damascus, 1956); Uthman Haddad, *Harakat Rashid Ali al-Kailani* (The Rashid Ali al-Kailani movement) (Sidon, Lebanon, n.d.); Naji Shaukat, *Sira wa Dhikrayat Thamanin Amman, 1894–1974* (Biography and memoirs through eighty years, 1894–1974) (Beirut, n.d.); Taha-l-Hashimi, *Mudhakkirati, 1919–1943* (My memoirs, 1919–1943) (Beirut, 1967); and Ali Mahmud al-Shaikh Ali, *Muhaka-matuna-l-Wajahiyya* (Our face-to-face trials) (Sidon, Lebanon, n.d.). A different view is found in the memoirs of Taufiq al-Suwaidi, *Mudhakkirati* (My memoirs) (Beirut, 1969). A British perspective from a participant in the aftermath is found in Freya Stark, *Baghdad Sketches* (London: 1946).

The End of the Old Regime, 1946–1958

The best overall view of the period is found in Batatu, *The Old Social Classes;* Khadduri, *Independent Iraq:* and Tripp, *A History of Iraq;* a critique and review of Batatu's work with several decades of hindsight is found in a collection of essays in Robert Fernea and William Louis, eds., *The Iraqi Revolution of 1958: The Old Social Classes Revisited* (London, 1991). Elie Kedourie, "The Kingdom of Iraq: A Retrospect," in *The Chatham House Version and Other Essays* (New York, 1970), has a critical but incisive analysis of the monarchy and its politicians. The main wealth of material for these years, however, is to be found in the memoirs published by leading Iraqi politicians since 1958. Their usefulness varies. Most significant are those of Taha-l-Hashimi, *Mudhakkirati* [Memoirs]; Taufiq al-Suwaidi, *Mudhakkirati* [My memoirs]; Ali Jaudat, *Dhikrayat Ali Jaudat;* Khalil Kanna, *al-Iraq, Amsuhui wa Ghaduhu* (Iraq: Its past and its future) (Beirut, 1966), and Abd al-Karim al Uzri, *Ta'rikh fi Dhikrayat al-Iraq, 1930–1958* (History in memories of Iraq). (Beirut, 1982). A number of works, both memoirs and studies, depict the opposition to the Old

Regime. On the left, these include the memoirs of Kamil al-Chadirchi, *Mudhakki-rati* (My memoirs) (Beirut: 1970); *Min Awraq Kamil al-Chadirchi* (From the papers of Kamil al-Chadirchi) (Beirut, 1971); Fadil Husain, *Ta'rikh al-Hizb al-Watani al-Dimuqrati* (the history of the National Democratic Party) (Baghdad, 1963); and Ibrahim Abd al-Fattah, *Mutala'a fi-l-Sha'biyya* (A study in populism) (Baghdad, 1935). On the nationalist side, there is Muhammad Mahdi Kubba, *Mudhakkirati* (My memoirs) (Beirut, 1965); Abd al-Amir al-Akam, *Ta'rikh Hizb al-Istiqlal al-Iraqi, 1946–1958* (The history of the Iraqi Independence Party, 1946–1958) (Baghdad, 1980); and Talib Mushtaq, *Awraq Ayyami* (Papers from my days) (Beirut, 1968). For a Communist version of events, see Abd al-Karim Hassun al-Jar Allah, *Tasaddu'-l-Bashariyya* (The crackup of humanity) (Beirut, n.d.).

The economic and social conditions that contributed to the overthrow of the regime have received considerable attention. Batatu, *The Old Social Classes,* remains the key study. A short but excellent summary of social conditions has been written by David Pool, "From Elite to Class: The Transformation of Iraqi Political Leadership," in *The Integration of Modern Iraq,* edited by Abbas Kelidar (New York, 1979). A number of studies have focused on peasant conditions and the need for reform, including Muhammad Ali al-Suri, *al-Iqta' fi-l-Liwa' al-Kut* (Feudalism in the Kut Liwa) (Baghdad, 1959), and Abd al Razzaq al-Zahir, *Fi-l-Islah al-Zira'i wa-l-Siyasi* (Toward agrarian and political reform) (Baghdad, 1959); and on land policy, including Ernest Dowson, *An Inquiry into Land Tenure and Related Questions* (Letchworth, England, 1932), the examination of the landholding system that led to the misguided policy followed by the government; Doreen Warriner, *Land Reform and Development in the Middle East* (London, 1957); and Robert Fernea, *Shaikh and Effendi* (Cambridge, Mass., 1970). On the overall economy and the development of oil, the best and most incisive study is Edith Penrose and E. F. Penrose, *Iraq: International Relations and National Development* (Boulder, Colo., 1978). A review of the development program as seen by one of its architects is found in Abd al-Rahman al-Jalili, *al-I'mar fi-l-Iraq* (Development in Iraq) (Beirut, 1968). This should be counterbalanced by James Salter, *The Development of Iraq* (Baghdad, 1955), which criticizes aspects of development policy and which helped set new directions in development policy. More detailed monographs include Khair al-din Haseeb, *The National Income of Iraq, 1953–1961* (London, 1964); Ferhang Jalal, *The Role of Government in the Industrialization of Iraq, 1950–1965* (London, 1972); Kathleen Langley, *The Industrialization of Iraq* (Cambridge, Mass., 1961); and Abbas al-Nasrawi, *Financing Economic Development in Iraq: The Role of Oil in a Middle Eastern Economy* (New York, 1967). A work that puts this development into theoretical context is Samira Haj, *The Making of Iraq, 1900–1963* (Albany, 1997). Fairly accurate statistical data are available in statistical abstracts published by the Ministry of Economics in this period.

Revolutionary Regimes of the Military Era

The causes of the 1958 revolt and the Free Officers' movement are well set forth in several histories of this period: Majid Khadduri, *Republican Iraq* (London, 1969); Batatu, *The Old Social Classes*; Penrose and Penrose, *Iraq*; and Marion Farouk-Sluglett and Peter Sluglett, *Iraq Since 1958: From Revolution to Dictatorship* (London, 1987); as well as in an account by an unidentified Englishman, Caractacus (a pseudonym) in *Revolution in Iraq: An Essay in Comparative Public Opinion* (London, 1959). The Free Officers' movement is dealt with in several works, including that of an insider, Sabih Ali Ghalib, *Qissat Thawrat 14 Tammuz wa-l- Dubbat al-Ahrar* (The story of the revolution of 14 July and the Free Officers) (Beirut, 1968), and a good historical account by Laith Abd al-Hasan al-Zubaidi, *Thaura 14 Tammuz 1958 fi-l-Iraq* (The revolution of 14 July 1958 in Iraq) (Baghdad, 1981). The best account of the end of the royal family is found in Falih Hanzal (a member of the Royal Guard), *Asrar Maqtal al-A'ila-l-Malika fi-l-Iraq 14 Tammuz 1958* (Secrets of the murder of the royal family in Iraq, 14 July 1958), 2nd ed. (n.pl., 1992). Although it has to be dealt with carefully, the trial of Abd al-Salam is recorded in Iraq, Ministry of Defense, *Muhakamat* (Trials), vol. 5 (Baghdad, 1958–1962); this volume has fascinating material on the Free Officers' movement as well as the later split between Arif and Qasim. On the Qasim era itself, Uriel Dann, *Iraq Under Qassem* (New York, 1969), presents a straightforward account drawn mainly from newspaper sources. On the role of the Communist Party under Qasim, Batatu's work is the definitive source, using a wealth of data, including the Iraqi government's secret data. Rony Gabbay, *Communism and Agrarian Reform in Iraq* (London, 1978), is more limited in scope. Ibrahim Kubba, *Hadha Huwa Tariq 14 Tammuz* (This is the way of July 14) (Beirut, 1969), the defense of Ibrahim Kubba before the Revolutionary Court, represents the left-wing view in this period, whereas Jasim Mukhlis, *Mudhakkirat al-Tabaqchali wa Dhikrayat Jasim Mukhlis, al-Muhami* (Memoirs of al-Tabaqchali and memories of Jasim Mukhlis the lawyer) (Sidon, Lebanon, 1969), expresses the nationalist opposition to Qasim. The 14 Ramadan coup and the short-lived Ba'th regime of 1963 need to be put in the perspective of Ba'th politics. Several good books in English do this, among which are Kemal Abu Jaber, *The Arab Ba'th Socialist Party* (Syracuse, 1966); John Devlin, *The Ba'th Party: A History from Its Origins to 1966* (Stanford, 1976); and Malcolm Kerr, *The Arab Cold War* (London, 1971). Ba'thists themselves have written voluminously on their party and its ideology. On the latter, the classic is still Michel Aflaq, *Fi Sabil al-Ba'th al-Arabi* (In the cause of the Arab rennaissance), 2nd ed. (Beirut, 1963). The Ba'th Party National Command has published a multivolume work, *Nidal al-Ba'th* (The Ba'th struggle) (Beirut, 1964); volume 4 includes the important proceedings of the sixth Ba'th congress in 1963, which contributed to the downfall of the Ba'th regime in Iraq in that year. Also useful in shedding light on this experience is Munif al-Razzaz, *al-Tajriba-l-Murra* (The bitter experience) (Beirut, 1967), and from a Ba'thist who later defected, Fu'ad al-Rikabi, *al-Hall al-Awhad* (The sole solution) (Cairo, 1963). Among the most penetrating criticisms of the 1963 Ba'th regime is that of one of its main participants, Hani al-Fukaiki, *al-Aukar al-Hazima Tajrubati fi Hizb al-Ba'thi al-Iraqi* (Dens of defeat: My experience in the Iraqi Ba'th Party) (Beirut, 1993). Another semimemoir comes from Talib Shabib, written down just before his death and edited with careful footnotes by Ali Karim Sa'id: *Iraq 8 Shabat 1963. Min Hawar al-Maghahim ila Hawar al-Dam. Maraja'at Dhakirat Talib Shabib* (Iraq of 8 February 1963: From the dialogue of conceptions to the dialogue of blood, reviews in Talib Shabib's memory) (Beirut, 1999). On the Arif regime, little has yet been published. Of the standard works mentioned above, Khadduri's *Republican Iraq* deals most extensively with the regime. Arif's own views, as told to Ali Munir, are represented in "Mudhakkirat Abd al-Salam Arif" (The memoirs of Abd al-Salam Arif) *Ruz al-Yusuf,* 30 May 1966, but these must be used with caution. Also interesting are a series of articles by Abd al-Rahim Mu'adh, a participant in events who was close to Arif, in "Dhikrayati wa Intaba'at" (My memoirs and impressions), in *al-Ittihad* (Amman), 9 October 1989–May 8, 1990. On the struggle over oil in the Qasim and Arif periods, Penrose and Penrose, *Iraq,* is the best source, with a wealth of detail and firsthand accounts. For an analysis of changes in the structure of political elites in this period, see Phebe Marr, "Iraq's Leadership Dilemma: A Study in Leadership Trends, 1948–1968," *Middle East Journal (MEJ)* 24 (1970), and "The Political Elite in Iraq," in George Lenczowski, ed., *Political Elites in the Middle East* (Washington, 1975).

The Ba'th Regime to 1990

The Ba'th regime has generated a plethora of journalistic accounts but few good, indepth studies. Both Batatu and Penrose and Penrose cover the onset of the regime but stop in the mid–1970s; Tripp's book, *A History,* however, does bring the regime up to the end of the century. Among the best analyses of the political structure of the regime are Falih Abd al-Jabbar, *al-Dawla; al-Mujtama' wa al-Tahawwal al-Dimuqrati fi-l-Iraq* (State, society, and the democratic transition in Iraq) (Cairo, 1995), and Faleh A. Jabbar, "The State, Society, Clan, Party and Army in Iraq," in Faleh A. Jabbar, Ahmad Shikara, and Keiko Sakai, eds. *From Storm to Thunder* (Tokyo, 1998). Keiko Sakai has an excellent article on "Tribalization as a Tool of State Control in Iraq," in Jabar and Dawod, *Tribes and Power.* Amatzia Baram has analyzed the ethnic and social background of the elite in "The Ruling Political Elite in Ba'thi Iraq, 1968–1986," *IJMES* 21 (1989), and in "La 'Maison' de Saddam Husayn," in Pierre Bonte, Edouard Conte, and Paul Dresch, eds., *Emirs et Presidents* (Paris, 2001). Trenchant but accurate critiques of the regime are to be found in Samir al-Khalil (Kanan Makiya), *Republic of Fear* (Berkeley, 1989), and Hasan al-Alawi, *al-Iraq: Daulat al-Munadhima-l-Sirriyya* (Iraq: A state of secret organization) (London, 1990).The opposition group, the Campaign Against Repression and for

Democratic Rights in Iraq (CARDRI) has assembled some good essays by scholars of the regime in *Saddam's Iraq: Revolution and Reaction* (London, 1986). A collection of works on the regime can be found in Tim Niblock, ed., *Iraq: The Contemporary State* (New York, 1982), and Abbas Kelidar, ed., *The Integration of Modern Iraq* (New York, 1979). An interesting analysis of political dynamics in the regime is to be found in Abbas Kelidar, "Iraq: The Search for Stability" (London, 1975). The ideological factor has been dealt with by Amatzia Baram in "Qawmiyya and Wataniyya in Iraq," *Middle East Studies* 19 (1983), and in *Culture, History and Ideology in the Formation of Ba'thist Iraq, 1968–1989* (New York: 1990), and by Ofra Bengio, *Saddam's Word: Political Discourse in Iraq* (New York, 2002). Two works that reflect the regime's own view are Christine Moss Helms, *Iraq: Eastern Flank of the Arab World* (Washington, 1984), and Majid Khadduri, *Socialist Iraq* (Washington, 1978). There are four biographies of Saddam Husain that also deal with the politics of Iraq. Two are semiofficial but nonetheless have important facts and reflect Saddam's thinking in the late 1970s: Amir Iskandar, *Saddam Husain: Munadilan, Mufakkiran wa Insanan* (Saddam Husain: The fighter, the thinker and the man) (Paris, 1980), and Fuad Matar, *Saddam Hussein: The Man, the Cause and the Future* (London, n.d.; 1st ed., in Arabic, 1981). Efriam Karsh and Inari Rautsi, *Saddam Hussein: A Political Biography* (New York, 1991), is an excellent analytical study. Said Aburish, *Saddam Hussein: The Politics of Revenge* (London, 2000), reflects an Arab perspective and has some interesting insights. For the Ba'th's own perspective, there are party reports, most important of which is the report of the eighth party congress, published as *Revolutionary Iraq, 1968–1973* (Baghdad, 1974), reflecting the policy it was to take thenceforth. Saddam's writings and speeches have been published as pamphlets but also collected in *al-Mu'allafat al-Kamila* (The complete works) (Baghdad, 1987–1990). Iraq's foreign policy has been analyzed in several works. Eberhard Kienle looks at the conflict with Syria in *Ba'th vs. Ba'th: The Conflict Between Syria and Iraq, 1968–1989* (New York, 1990). Soviet relations have been dealt with in Oles Smolansky with Bettie Smolansky, *The USSR and Iraq: The Soviet Quest for Influence* (Durham, 1991), and Haim Shemesh, *Soviet-Iraqi Relations, 1968–1988* (Boulder, Colo., 1992). Two good analytical chapters on Iraq's foreign policy by Charles Tripp are to be found in "Iraq," in Yezid Sayigh and Avi Shlaim, eds., *The Cold War and the Middle East* (Oxford, 1997), and "The Foreign Policy of Iraq," in Raymond Hinnebusch and Enoushiravan Ehteshami, eds., *The Foreign Policies of Middle East States* (Boulder, Colo., 2002). For a general overview of Iraq's foreign policy see Phebe Marr, "Iraq: Balancing Foreign and Domestic Realities," in L. Carl Brown, ed., *Diplomacy in the Middle East* (New York, 2003).

The Iran-Iraq war has been well covered in a number of works. A valuable insider view of the war is to be found in Wafiq al-Samarra'i, *Hitam al-Bawaba-l-Sharqiyya* (Shattering the eastern gates) (Kuwait, 1997). Samarra'i was in charge of the Iraqi Military Intelligence division responsible for Iran during the war and has since defected. The causes of the war are dealt with in several works, including Ralph King, *The Iran-Iraq War: The Political Implications* (London, 1987); Efriam Karsh, "Geopolitical Determinism—The Iran-Iraq War," *MEJ* 44 (1990); Majid Khadduri, *The Gulf War: Origins and Implications* (New York: 1988); and Tareq Ismael, *Iraq and Iran: Roots of Conflict* (Syracuse, 1982), which has a useful appendix of documents relating to the crisis. The latter two works present the Iraqi case. A blow-by-blow account of the war is given in Dilip Hiro, *The Longest War* (New York, 1991). The military side is examined in Anthony Cordesman and Abraham Wagner, *The Lessons of Modern War, vol. II: The Iran-Iraq War* (Boulder, Colo., 1990). The way the war affected domestic political dynamics is dealt with in Charles Tripp and Shahram Chubin, *Iran and Iraq at War* (Boulder, Colo., 1988). The consequences are examined in Efraim Karsh, ed., *The Iran-Iraq War: Impact and Implications* (New York, 1989), and Christopher Joyner, ed., *The Persian Gulf War* (New York, 1990).

The Gulf War and Its Aftermath

The Gulf War and the events leading up to it have generated an enormous amount of material, much of it uneven. On the Iraqi side are three good accounts: Sa'd al-Bazzaz, *Harb Tulid Ukhra* (One war gives birth to another) (Amman, 1992), and *al-Janaralat Akhar min Ya'lim* (The generals are the last to know) (London, 1996); and Wafiq al-Samarra'i, *Hitam al-Bawaba-l-Sharqiyya* (Shattering the eastern gates). Bazzaz was among the outer circle of the Ba'th during the crisis and recreates the thinking and atmosphere in Baghdad; his second book updates the first. Samarra'i was a responsible for military intelligence during the crisis and later defected. Other good accounts are found in Gregory Gause, "Iraq's Decision to Go to War, 1980 and 1990," *MEJ* 56:1 (winter 2002), and Amatzia Baram and Barry Rubin, eds. *Iraq's Road to War* (London, 1993) (especially the chapter by Baram on decisionmaking in Baghdad). Also recommended are Roland Dannreuther, *The Gulf Conflict: The Political and Strategic Analysis* (London: 1991–1992); Charles Tripp, "Symbol and Strategy: Iraq and the War for Kuwait," in Wolfgang F. Danspeckgruber with Charles Tripp, ed., *The Iraqi Aggression Against Kuwait* (Boulder, Colo., 1996), and Ofra Bengio, "Iraq," *Middle East Contemporary Survey* (1990). Two accounts from an Arab perspective are Majid Khadduri and Edmond Ghareeb, *War in the Gulf: The Iraq-Kuwait Conflict and Its Implications* (New York: 1997), and Mohamed Heikal, *Illusions of Triumph: An Arab View of the Gulf War* (London, 1993). On the American decision, the two best sources are George Bush and Brent Scowcroft, *A World Transformed* (New York, 1998), chapters 13–19, and Bob Woodward, *The Commanders* (New York, 1991). On the war itself, two works stand out: Lawrence Freedman and Efraim Karsh, *The Gulf Conflict, 1990–1991* (Princeton, 1993), the most objective and detailed thus far, and Michael Gordon and Bernard Trainor, *The General's War* (Boston, 1995). On the background to the tangled Iraq-Kuwait border dispute, the best historical study is Richard Schofield,

Kuwait and Iraq: Historical Claims and Territorial Disputes (London, 1991). Two worthwhile pieces on the impact of the war on Iraq are John Heidenrich, "The Gulf War: How Many Iraqis Died?" in *Foreign Policy* 90 (spring 1993), and Nuha al-Radi, *Baghdad Diaries* (London, 1998).

The *intifada* has been more difficult to research because of its nature and the difficulty of getting accurate information. A number of participants have written accounts and a few studies have been attempted, but most should be treated with some caution. Among the best is a series of five articles written by Fa'iq al-Shaikh Ali, "al-Intifada-l-Iraqiyya fi Dhikraha al-Khamisa" (The Iraqi uprising in its fifth anniversary), *al-Hayat* (London), 22–26 March 1996. Also important are Majid al-Majid, *Intifadat al-Sha'b al-Iraqi* (Beirut, 1991), which traces its background and how it unfolded in different places; Ibrahim Nawwar, *al-Ma'arida-l-Iraqiyya wal-Sira'a-l-Isqat Saddam* (The Iraqi opposition and the struggle to remove Saddam) (London, 1993), which deals with the outside opposition and has lengthy interviews with opposition leaders; Najib al-Salihi, *al-Zalzal* (The earthquake) (London, 1998), the story of the uprising by a retreating officer, with considerable detail on the north and the south; Faleh Abd al-Jabbar, "Why the Uprisings Failed," *Middle East Report* 22 (May–June 1992); Pierre Martin, "Les Chiites d'Irak de Retour sur la Scene Politique," *Monde Arabe Maghreb Machrek*, 132 (April–June 1991); and Kanan Makiya, *Cruelty and Silence* (New York, 1993).

On the last decade of the regime, especially the sanctions regime and the conflict over inspections, there is much good material in English. The best record of the dispute is the United Nations volume, *The United Nations and the Iraq-Kuwait Conflict, 1990–1996* (New York, 1996), containing a good narrative summary by Boutros Boutros-Ghali of UN involvement, together with all relevant documents and reports. On the military background to Iraq's conventional and unconventional weapons, the best work is Anthony Cordesman, *Iran and Iraq: The Threat from the Northern Gulf* (Boulder, Colo., 1994), and on the conflict, Iraq's response, and its military posture in the aftermath, Anthony Cordesman and Ahmad Hashim, *Iraq: Sanctions and Beyond* (Boulder, Colo., 1997). On the impact of sanctions and the politics involved, Sarah Graham-Brown, *Sanctioning Saddam: The Politics of Intervention in Iraq* (London, 1999), gives a detailed account, largely from the NGO viewpoint. The topic is also well covered in a special issue of *Middle East Report*, "Intervention and Responsibility: The Iraq Sanctions Dilemma," vol. 22, no. 193 (May–June 1992). The economic impact of sanctions on Iraq has been controversial but can be traced in voluminous reports from the UN secretary general, Food and Agricultural Organization (FAO), World Food Program (WFP), UNICEF, UN Human Rights Commission, and various NGO organizations, mainly on their Web sites. A good corrective to some of these reports, many of which rely on Iraqi government statistics, is to be found in Amatzia Baram, "The Effect of Iraqi Sanctions: Statistical Pitfalls and Responsibility," *MEJ* 54 (Spring 2000). On the complex technical issue of arms control and inspections, several sources can be recommended to help the general reader understand the fundamentals. The main sources are the UN reports of the IAEA and UNSCOM, but a basic primer on what Iraqis developed and the weapons' locations is Robert Chandler, *Tomorrow's War, Today's Decisions* (McLean, Va., 1996). Other good sources include, Phebe Marr, "Iraq and the Nuclear Non-Proliferation Treaty: The Case of a Nuclear Cheater," in Thomas Wander, Eric Arnet, and Paul Bracken, eds., *The Diffusion of Advances in Weaponry Technologies: Regional Implications and Responses* (Washington, D.C., 1994); David Albright and Mark Hibbs, "Iraq and the Bomb: Were They Even Close?" *Bulletin of the Atomic Scientists* (March 1991), and "Iraq's Nuclear Hide-and-Seek," *Bulletin of the Atomic Scientists* (September 1991); Kathleen Bailey, *The UN Inspections in Iraq: Lessons for On-Site Verification* (Boulder, Colo., 1995), and International Institute for Strategic Studies (IISS), *Iraq's Weapons of Mass Destruction: A Net Assessment* (London, 2002). Also recommended are Scott Ritter, *Endgame: Solving the Iraq Problem Once and for All* (New York, 1999), which details his confrontation with Iraqis as an inspector, and Seymour Hersh, "Saddam's Best Friend," which discloses CIA involvement in the *New Yorker*, 5 April 1999.

The restructuring of Iraq and its political system after the Gulf War and the *intifada* has been more difficult to document. Among the most reliable works on this subject are Amatzia Baram, *Building Toward Crisis: Saddam Husayn's Strategy for Survival* (Washington, 1998); Saddam's Power Structure: The Tikritis Before, During, and After the War," in Toby Dodge and Steven Simon, eds., *Iraq at the Crossroads: State and Society in the Shadow of Regime Change* (London, 2003); and "Neo-Tribalism in Iraq: Saddam Hussein's Tribal Policies, 1991–1996," *IJMES* 29 (1997); and Faleh Abdul Jabar, "Sheikhs and Ideologues," in Jabar and Dawod, eds., *Tribes and Power,* and "The State, Society and Clan." A good journalistic account is Andrew and Patrick Cockburn, *Out of the Ashes: The Resurrection of Saddam Hussein* (New York, 1999). Two collections of essays by scholars have varied content: D. Hopwood, H. Ishaw, and T. Koszinowski, eds., *Iraq: Power and Society* (Reading, 1993), tends to be favorably disposed to Iraq; Fran Hazelton, ed. (for CARDRI), *Iraq Since the Gulf War: Prospects for Democracy* (London, 1994), tends to be virulently opposed to the regime. A balanced but critical view of Iraq's human rights record is dealt with in Judith Yaphe, "Iraq: Human Rights in the Public Fear," Paul Magneson, ed., *Human Rights and Governance in the Middle East* (London, 1998). An excellent article by Isam al-Khafaji, "The Myth of Iraqi Exceptionalism," *Middle East Policy* 7:4 (October 2000), compares Iraq's development—unfavorably—over two decades with other Middle Eastern countries. Good analyses of the reorganization of the military and the security systems can be found in Cordesman and Hashim, *Iraq: Sanctions and Beyond*; Michael Eisenstadt, *Like a Phoenix from the Ashes* (Washington, 1993); and Sean Boyne, "Inside Iraq's Security Network," part 2, *Jane's Intelligence Review* (August 1997). The regime's own view can be found in

Saddam Husain's collected works and in Arab Ba'th Socialist Party, *al-Bayan al-Siyasi ['an]an al-Mu'tamar al-Qutri al-Ashir* (Political report of the tenth regional congress) (Baghdad, 1991); and for those who like unorthodox source material, there is the novel said to be authored by Saddam Husain himself and reflective of his views toward the end of his regime, *Zabiba wal-Malik* (Zabiba and the king) (Baghdad, n.d.). A collection of high-quality journalistic articles from a variety of Western, Iraqi, and Middle Eastern sources on Iraq in the period is contained in *al-Malaf al-Iraqiyya* (The Iraqi file), published monthly by Ghassan Atiyya in London. On the outside opposition, a very good, if brief, summary is Rend Rahim Francke's, "The Opposition," in Hazelton, ed., *Iraq Since the Gulf War*; this book, published by CARDRI is itself representative of opposition views. A good survey in Arabic is Ibrahim Nawwar, *al-Mu'arida-l-Iraqiyya*. For future scholars, an unparalleled source on the detailed workings of the government awaits mining in documents removed from northern Iraq after the rebellion in 1991. Most of this material is now available to the public and housed in the Iraq Research and Documentation Project at Harvard University; details are available on the IRDP Web site.

On economics and oil since 1958, the Penroses' book, *Iraq,* has the most depth, although it stops in the mid–1970s. Land reform measures have been analyzed in Doreen Warriner, *Land Reform in Principle and Practice* (Oxford, 1969), and John Simmons, "Agricultural Development in Iraq: Planning and Management Failure," *MEJ* 19:2 (1965). The views of longtime Ba'thist minister Sa'dun Hammadi are reflected in *Nahwa Islah Zira'i Ishtiraki* (Toward a socialist agrarian reform) (Beirut, 1954). Two excellent overall assessments of economic change in Iraq in the 1960s and 1970s are found in Yusif Sayigh, *The Economics of the Arab World: Development Since 1945* (New York, 1978), and in chapter 7 of the Sluglett's book, *Iraq Since 1958. Peuples Mediterraneen* has a special issue, *L'Irak, Le Petrole et la Guerre*, vol. 4 (July–September 1987), with very good articles by Springborg, the Slugletts, and Eftekhari on oil during the Iran-Iraq war. Abbas al-Nasrawi deals with the impact of the war on Iraq in "The Economic Consequences of the Iran-Iraq War," *Third World Quarterly* 8 (July 1986), and Robert Springborg has written on privatization in "Iraqi Infitah: Agrarian Transformation and the Growth of the Private Sector," *MEJ* 40:1 (winter 1986). On Iraq's economy after the Gulf War and imposition of sanctions, the best overall studies are Abbas al-Nasrawi, *The Iraqi Economy: Oil Development, War, Destruction and Prospects* (Westport, Conn., 1994), and Kamran Mofid, *The Economic Consequences of the Gulf War* (London, 1990). Also recommended is a group of papers published by the Iraqi Economics Forum, *Studies on the Iraqi Economy* (London, 2002), and J. Dreze and H. Gazdar, "Hunger and Poverty in Iraq," in *World Development* 20:7, pp. 921–945. A perceptive analysis of the economy of post-Gulf War Iraq is to be found in Kiren Chaudhry, "On the Way to Market," *Middle East Research and Information Project (MERIP)* 170 (May–June 1991). Two studies deal with "state capitalism" in Iraq: Isam al-Khafaji, *Ra'smaliyyat al-Dawla-l-Wataniyya* (National state capitalism) (Beirut, 1979), and *al-Dawla wal Tatawwur al-Ra'smali fil-Iraq, 1968–1978* (The state and the development of capitalism in Iraq, 1968–1978) (Tokyo and Cairo, 1983). Studies on social change in the 1980s and 1990s are scarce. One broad-ranging collection provides an interesting snapshot of the social and intellectual diversity in Iraq: Pierre-Jean Luizard, "Memoires d'Irakiens: a la Decouverte d'une Society Vancue," in a special issue of *Monde Arab Maghreb-Machrek* 163 (January–March 1999). The Iraqi Economists Association, in conjunction with the UN Development Program, presents one of the few sources of data and analysis on urbanization, education, and economic development in the 1990s in *The Human Development Report, 1995* (Baghdad, 1995), but the data must be viewed with some skepticism since they were put out under the auspices of the Baghdad government. Since the sanctions regime, the UN and NGO organizations have issued a huge volume of reports, often the subject of criticisms because of the inability to conduct independent research or acquire statistics other than those blessed by the Iraqi government. These have been cited previously. For more up-to-date material on the economy, the best sources are the *Middle East Economic Digest (MEED)* (London), the *Middle East Economic Survery (MEES)* (Nicosia: Middle East Research and Publishing Center), and the *Quarterly Economic Review, Iraq,* published by the *Economist* (London). The Iraqi government published statistical abstracts each year, *Annual Abstract of Statistics (AAS),* but in the decade of the 1990s these were difficult to obtain, and since the early 1980s their statistics have been increasingly sparse and viewed as suspect.

The *Shi'a*

In the past two decades more attention has been given to the *shi'a* of Iraq and to the emergence of their Islamic movements. On the historical background of the *shi'a,* there are a number of new studies, including Meir Litvak, *Shi'i Scholars of Nineteenth-Century Iraq: The "Ulama" of Najaf and Karbala* (Cambridge, 1998); Nakkash, *The Shi'is of Iraq;* al-Nafisi, *Daur al-Shi'a fi Tatawur al-Iraq;* and a number of chapters in Abdul-Jabar, *Ayatallahs, Sufis and Ideologues.* Also useful is Fadil al-Jamali, "The Theological Colleges of Najaf," *Moslem World* 50:1 (January 1960). On relations between *shi'a* and *sunni* in Iraq, from the *shi'i* point of view, two books stand out: Abd al-Karim al-Uzri (a former minister), *Mushkilat al-Hukm fi-l-Iraq* (The problem of governance in Iraq) (London, 1991), and Hasan al-Alawi (a former Ba'th party member), *al-Shi'a wal-Daula-l-Qaumiyya fil-Iraq* (The shi'a and the nationalist state in Iraq) (France, 1989). On Baqir al-Sadr and the rise of the *shi'i* Islamic movements, the most definitive study is Faleh Abdul-Jabar, *The Shi'a Movement of Iraq* (London, 2003). On Sadr himself, there are numerous studies, among the best being Shaikh Muhammad Rida al-Na'mani, *al-Shahid al-Sadr: Sanawat al-Mihna wal-Ayyam al-Hisar* (The martyr Sadr: Years of tribulation, days of blockade) (n.pl., 1997); Ali al-Mu'min, *Sanawat al-Jumar: Musirat al-Harakat al-Islamiyya fi-l-Iraq, 1958–1986*

(Years of embers: The journey of the Islamic movement in Iraq, 1958–1986) (London: 1993); T. M. Aziz, "The role of Muhammad Baqir al-Sadr," *IJMES* 25 (1993); and Chibli Mallat, "Religious Militancy in Contemporary Iraq: Muhammad Baqer as-Sadr and the *Sunni/Shia* Paradigm," in *Third world Quarterly* 10:2 (April 1988). The best example of Sadr's own work is to be found in *Falsafatuna* (Our philosophy) (1959) and *Iqtisaduna* (Our economics) (1960). On the death of Muhammad Sadiq al-Sadr and interesting material on the politics of the *hauza,* see Fa'iq al-Shaikh Ali, *Aghsal Sha'b* (The assassination of a people) (London, 2000).

The Kurds

The Iraqi Kurds have received considerable attention in a number of recent works. The best general history of the Kurds is David McDowall, *The Modern History of the Kurds* (London, 1997). On the early phases of the Kurdish nationalist movement, there are numerous good studies, some scholarly, some journalistic, drawing on interviews with the main participants. These include Chris Kutschera, *le Mouvement national Kurde* (Paris, 1979); Sa'ad Jawad, *Iraq and the Kurdish Question, 1958–1970* (London, 1981); and Edmond Ghareeb, *The Kurdish Question in Iraq* (Syracuse, 1981). The Kurdish point of view is well represented by Ismet Cheriff Vanley, *le Kurdistan Irakien Entite Nationale* (Boudry-Neuchatel, Switzerland, 1970), and "Le Kurdistan d'Irak" in Gerard Challiand, ed., *Les Kurdes et le Kurdistan* (Paris, 1978). There are also works by some of the main participants. These include Jalal al-Talabani, *Kurdistan wal-Haraka-l-Qaumiyya-l-Kurdiyya* (Beirut, 1971); and works by Mustafa Amin Nushirwan (originally a member of the Komala, now in the PUK): *Al-Akrad wal-Barliman* (The Kurds and Parliament) (Arbil, 1993); *Hukumat Kurdistan: Kurd la Gama Soviet da* (The government of Kurdistan: The Kurds in the Soviet Game) (Utrecht, 1993), *Fingers That Crush Each Other: Iraqi Kurdistan from 1979 to 1983* (in Kurdish) (Sulaimaniyya, 1998); and *Going Around in Circles: Events in Kurdistan, 1984–1988* (in Kurdish) (Berlin, 1999). The parties have published records: KDP, *Kurdistan Democratic Party Congresses, 1946–1993 (*Arbil, 1993); and PUK, *Revolution in Kurdistan: The Essential Documents of the Patriotic Union of Kurdistan* (New York, 1977). A number of good studies have dealt with the Kurdish uprising of 1991 and subsequent events in Iraqi Kurdistan. The best scholarly study is Gareth Stansfield, *Iraqi Kurdistan.* For a strategic view, see Robert Olson, *The Kurdish Nationalist Movement in the 1990s: Its Impact on Turkey and the Middle East* (Lexington, 1996). On the civil strife between the parties, see Michael Gunter, "The KDP-PUK Conflict in Northern Iraq," *MEJ* 50:2 (spring 1996), and two "white papers" put out by both parties: the KDP, "What Happened in Iraqi Kurdistan in May 1994" (June 1994), and PUK, "Iraqi Kurdistan: A Situation Report on Recent Events" (February 1995). Jonathan Randall gives a sympathetic but thorough journalistic account of these years in *After Such Knowledge, What Forgiveness? My Encounters with Kurdistan* (New York,

1997). An important critical view of the Kurdish government in the north, but one with much valuable detail on the Kurdish government and its workings, is found in Amnesty International, *Iraq: Human Rights Abuses in Iraqi Kurdistan Since 1991* (London, 1995). The Anfal campaign against the Kurds is best dealt with in Middle East Watch, *Genocide in Iraq: The Anfal Campaign Against the Kurds* (New York, 1993).

INDEX